Revolutions in Music Education

Revolutions in Music Education

Historical and Social Explorations

Edited by
Andrew Sutherland,
Jane Southcott, and Leon de Bruin

LEXINGTON BOOKS
Lanham • Boulder • New York • London

Published by Lexington Books
An imprint of The Rowman & Littlefield Publishing Group, Inc.
4501 Forbes Boulevard, Suite 200, Lanham, Maryland 20706
www.rowman.com

86-90 Paul Street, London EC2A 4NE

Copyright © 2022 by The Rowman & Littlefield Publishing Group, Inc.

All rights reserved. No part of this book may be reproduced in any form or by any electronic or mechanical means, including information storage and retrieval systems, without written permission from the publisher, except by a reviewer who may quote passages in a review.

British Library Cataloguing in Publication Information Available

Library of Congress Cataloging-in-Publication Data

Names: Sutherland, Andrew (Musician) editor. | Southcott, Jane, editor. | De Bruin, Leon R., editor.
Title: Revolutions in music education : historical and social explorations / edited by Andrew Sutherland, Jane Southcott and Leon de Bruin.
Description: Lanham : Lexington Books, 2022. | Includes bibliographical references and index. | Summary: "This volume explores music education locally and globally, and critically investigates where music education has come from, where it is, and where it may be going in the future, as well as what this means to us in the twenty-first century"—Provided by publisher.
Identifiers: LCCN 2022015412 (print) | LCCN 2022015413 (ebook) | ISBN 9781666907056 (cloth) | ISBN 9781666907070 (paperback) | ISBN 9781666907063 (epub)
Subjects: LCSH: Music—Instruction and study. | Music—Instruction and study—History. | Music—Instruction and study—Technological innovations. | Music—Instruction and study—Social aspects. | Educational change.
Classification: LCC MT1 .R513 2022 (print) | LCC MT1 (ebook) | DDC 780.71—dc23/eng/20220408
LC record available at https://lccn.loc.gov/2022015412
LC ebook record available at https://lccn.loc.gov/2022015413

*For the revolutionary R. Murray Schafer
(1933–1921), a truly revolutionary and
conspicuous rhinoceros in music education.*

Contents

Foreword   ix
Howard Goodall CBE

Introduction   1

PART 1: THE GREAT LEAP FORWARD—EARLY TRADITIONS: CULTURAL, ENVIRONMENTAL, AND DEVELOPING METHODS   13

1. Movable "Do," Sol-Fa, and Vertical Ladders: Guido to Glover to Curwen to Kodály   15
   Jane Southcott

2. The Role of the Cantor in the Performance of Liturgy: Council of Laodicea in the Mid-Fourth Century to Guido of Arezzo (*c.* 990–1040)   31
   Carol Williams

3. Orff's *Schulwerk*: Gestation, Interruption, Revival, and Dissemination   49
   Jane Southcott and Andrew Sutherland

4. Shinichi Suzuki and Talent Education: From Beginnings in Japan to the United States and the World   65
   Jane Southcott

5. Émile Jaques-Dalcroze and the Movement of Music   79
   Karin Greenhead

PART 2: INFLUENCES OF CULTURAL SHIFTS IN SOCIETY ON TEACHING AND LEARNING — 97

6 Jazz Education: Revolution or Devolution? — 101
   Leon de Bruin

7 A Global Revolution in Music for Social Change: El Sistema from Chile to Venezuela and the World — 121
   Alexandra Carlson and Andrew Sutherland

8 Televised Music Instruction — 139
   Paul Louth

9 Subverting the Hegemony: The Popular Music Revolution — 155
   Geoffrey M. Lowe

10 Progressing Multicultural Music Education from Colonialism, Othering, and Tokenism — 179
    Andrew Sutherland

PART 3: ADVANCING PEDAGOGY WITH TECHNOLOGY AND CREATIVE REVOLUTIONS — 195

11 Class Piano—Democratizing a Nineteenth-Century Status Symbol — 199
    Timothy J. Groulx

12 R. Murray Schafer—Celebrating a 1960s Visionary — 217
    Ros McMillan

13 The Evolution of Music Notation Software — 233
    Patrick Horton

14 Musical Futures: Developing an Informal Learning Model for Mainstream Music Education since 2003 — 253
    Hilary McQueen

15 New Interfaces for Musical Expression: Instrument Making as Music Learning — 271
    Andrew Brown

16 The Intimate Relationship between Technology and Music and Its Revolutionary Impact on Music Education — 287
    Renée Crawford

Conclusion — 315

Index — 319

About the Contributors — 329

Foreword
Howard Goodall CBE

A historical sweep through the major breakthroughs and interventions in music education around the world, spanning a millennium, is long overdue. Perhaps its earliest precedent in the post-antiquity era is Boethius's *De institutione musica, c.* 510 CE, which was still well-known enough to merit being one of the first musical works to be printed in Venice's cutting-edge presses in the early 1490s. To find a new, wider readership, a thousand years after authorship, is something most modern writers would find inconceivable: never mind imagining the technology available on such a time frame, it is a stretch to imagine human civilization making it that far, the way things are going. Like *Revolutions in Music Education*, Boethius himself was looking back at previous sources, philosophies, and innovations in the field of music theory and practice. Nicomachus's *Manual of Harmonics* was one such source, 400 or so years old by the time Boethius discovered it, and Nicomachus was itself indebted to Pythagoras's theories (from 500 years earlier) and to those of Aristoxenus (from 400 years earlier). The point about the necessity of these periodic summaries is that each "Big Bang" in the field is likely to trigger further innovations that spring from knowledge of previous successes. One notable example of this virtuous process is the river of learning that runs from Sarah Anna Glover's development of a method of sol-fa in the 1820s (the source of which we would trace back to Guido of Arezzo 800 years previously); its dissemination in the published *Scheme for Rendering Psalmody Congregational* (1835); Curwen's *Grammar of Vocal Music* (1843), which wrapped in advances from Galin, Paris, and Chevé; followed by his *Standard Course of Lessons on the Tonic Sol-fa Method of Teaching to Sing* (1858), *Musical Theory* (1879), *Tonic Sol-fa Primer* (1878) and *The Teachers' Manual* (1875), all of which fed into Kodàly's Method in the 1930s. Word of mouth and local best practice would simply never have made those leaps possible, certainly not on that scale or at that speed, without these published books, primers, and methods.

What unites so many of the significant advances in this book are the powerful impetus behind most, if not all, of them: the desire to open the benefits and wonders of music to as many "ordinary" people, especially children, as possible and to reach beyond what, until the nineteenth century at any rate, was a tiny community of musical families and professionals scattered hither and thither, with what seemed like magical, impenetrable knowledge of the mysteries of music. I hasten to add that then, as now, some musicians rather liked this shamen-like superiority over their awestruck peers and guarded it jealously. Not the community of music educators. Their mission has always been to open the gates wide and invite participation, enjoyment, and emotional reward. During the transmission of one of my TV series, *How Music Works*, I watched open-mouthed as a well-regarded opera singer, on an arts magazine program reviewing my efforts, bemoaned the very fact that I was "revealing" music's secrets, thereby spoiling its mystery and enchantment. People would enjoy their music better, he argued, if they knew less about it. I have never met a member of the public who agreed with this approach. YouTube is awash—in a good way—with "ordinary" folk explaining things to each other, whether it is the harmony of a Led Zeppelin song or the inner workings of a vacuum cleaner. In my experience, people actively seek knowledge to further enhance their experience of stuff they like or that intrigues them. Boethius acknowledged the universality of the love of music, even if he could not possibly have imagined the spread, scale, and diversity of the music of our time: "Music is so naturally united with us that we cannot be free from it even if we so desired."

There is another reason why this book is timely, and it is a less heartwarming but arguably more urgent one. Reading about the great campaigns and advocacy for music education of former times, whether it was Glover and Curwen, Kodály, Orff, or Suzuki, it was taken for granted by society at large, by parents and teachers, and broadly speaking by governments (even those of despotic, oppressive regimes) that these programs were a good thing and that children would benefit and thrive by exposure to and immersion in musical activity and appreciation. When I made the case for a national singing program to reinvigorate group singing in primary schools in England and Wales, in the early 2000s, I made my plea to UK government minister for schools Andrew Adonis and two secretaries of state for education Ed Balls and Alan Johnson, who welcomed the proposal enthusiastically. There was never a debate about the need for it or its huge benefits; there was—as you would expect—a discussion merely about practicalities. That conversation and its outcome are more or less unthinkable now, at least in England, with the sustained downgrading of music as a classroom subject (and, by extension, as an extracurricular activity, since without classroom music teachers these rarely exist on a school campus), a process that has been a decade in the making. While I appreciate that this is a parochial problem connected with one party of government, in one country, and this book is rightly worldwide in its scope, conversations with colleagues in school music in many countries suggest that music education as a given in every child's development is being questioned or undermined in many places at this time. Seeing it in its historical perspective, as this collection of essays allows, lends some perspective to these concerns: music education has always been a stop-start affair, as public attitudes and governmental support ebb and flow. Being inspired by so many examples of progress and fruitful outcomes gives one hope that in time the tide may turn even in places where it currently struggles. We can't all be Finland, all of the time, after all.

In 1999, I filmed a TV series called *Big Bangs*, presenting five musical turning points, or revolutions, through history—musical notation, opera, equal temperament, the piano, and recorded sound. At the end of the first film, which started with Guido of Arezzo, I briefly discussed what was then a relatively new phenomenon—the arrival of music notation software available to everybody with a computer, even those who hitherto could not read music themselves, since even then versions of Sibelius and Finale software could transcribe played-in scores from a keyboard, in real time. I posed a question as to whether music notation for those who did not read music might become the norm and the ability to read and write notation might render itself a redundant skill. Musical Instrument Digital Interface had been around for general use for twenty years by then, and the technologies of sequencing and notation have leapt ahead prolifically since then. I worried then that participation in music might turn into a two-tier system of those that could understand and originate music purely from their individual learning, imagination, and aptitude and those that could only do so via the medium of a computer. Two decades on, that suggestion is our reality. Millions more people now make music with the indispensable aid of machines, vastly democratizing the process of musical invention. The technology available is more intuitive, more apparently human, and significantly more adaptive as we approach an era where artificial intelligence is ever more deeply embedded in our world. The challenge for music educators, as it has been throughout history, is to ensure that as many people are masters and mistresses of their music-making as possible; that they can derive creative autonomy, gratification, and achievement from *their* active participation; and that their learning is focused on them as people, not merely as passive consumers of others' fecundity. All around us, music as a commodity is being manipulated, exploited, and anonymized:

music education, in all its forms, is our best possible tool for resisting and reshaping that trend. As Boethius might remind us, "It is because you don't know the end and purpose of things that you think the wicked and criminal possess power and happiness."

Introduction

Of all art forms, music has always been unequivocally and distinctly separate in its development across millennia. In the West, the Christian transformations of music into first conceptual and then written forms have propelled its development and evolution. Music and musicians have always had the ability to adapt and metamorphize in relation to social, religious, industrial, mechanistic, and technological change. This has meant that music and music education have evolved through unprecedented and decisive turns throughout history. It is these momentous moments in history that continue to shape the way Western art music is played, viewed, and learned.

To imagine a world without music is to imagine a world without a sonic, notated, or literary wealth of information that traces, captures, accompanies, and fosters humans' development. Innovation and creativity have forefronted this development. From a Western art music perspective, ever since monkish scribes cast their creations to vellum and parchment, the evolution of civilizations has developed hand in hand with the learning and teaching of music. Amid a largely illiterate European population with sophisticated Byzantine and Islamic empires to the East and South, the Judaist and Roman remnants of memorized and aurally transmitted bodies of music such as Gregorian Chant were transformed to the page in written form and then so too its means of being communicated and preserved beyond the confines of immediate time and space.

In Western traditions, the ancient Egyptians and Greeks were among the first to cultivate musical theories that could codify practice and advance musical styles and forms. The concept of music notation and the fact that musical ideas could be faithfully transferred from one to another represent the first fundamental revolution in music education. Although this occurred in many ancient traditions, the codification of Western liturgical song and the subsequent and pressing priority of a commonality of interpretation and more than a millennium later was to accelerate invention in music so too the simple red line found in manuscripts of the Monastery of Fonte Avellana and the adaptation by Guido d'Arezzo changed music forever. It was not just notation that changed music but, through choir schools, the pedagogical applications and approaches to teaching that also changed, heralding a harbinger of evolutionary change ever since.

Written notation facilitated not only replication but also, in the voices of practitioners, the ability to cultivate musical instinct—what began the evolution of musical qualities in which the musician could audiate, interpret, embellish, elaborate, extemporise, create, and compose with limitless possibility. Human inquisitiveness drove investigation of all elements of music melody, harmony, instrumentation, timbre, tempo, and dynamic. Polyphonic writing for both choir and instruments inspired curiosity concerning these elements. Musical structures evolved hand-in-hand with the innovations by musical instrument makers.

Of course, such music revolutions did not come about within an idealistic musical vacuum. Music ideas and concepts borrowed from mathematics and architecture then, as they do now, continue to both impose order and constraint, simultaneously provoking humans with new materials at our disposal to perpetually challenge for change. Acknowledged, other arts reflect similar ancient roots, influenced by available technologies and more recently by digitization. But the portability and spontaneity of music places it at the vanguard of creativity, innovation, and change in its making and its methods of passing on to others. Renaissance Northern Italy provided further reason for this justification. While artists were still grappling with the innovation or perspective in art, musicians and composers investigated their intrigue in the notion that perspective and depth could be represented on music harmonically, tonally, dynamically, and orchestrally. Just as the Florentine Camerata, Da Vinci, and Galileo were pushing the boundaries of science, so too were composers exploring various soundscapes, forms, structures, and systems organization of sounds. Inspired by mathematics, aesthetic for a "purely organized" form, the musical landscape of Western Europe was similarly transformed irreversibly by a groundbreaking evolutionary development. Equal temperament made possible much of the beauteous music we hold dear today, as without it such music would not be possible.

It is evident that from cave to concert hall, our relationship with music is very much connected with our understanding of nature and with the sciences. In the Middle Ages, music was one of the four subjects of the trivium (with arithmetic, geometry, and astronomy) foundational to the study of philosophy and theology. Moving from pure theory, tampering with temperament has allowed us to align richer and more homogenous sonorities, played on instruments that took full opportunity of evolving technologies. Just as we have manipulated our understanding of time via the clock and the calendar, restructuring the nature of things resonant, harmonic, and melodic has increased our capacity for creative acts and vision. A revolution that started with the ancient Greeks as they tried to assemble a series of notes within a ladder or scale, this initial Pythagorean vision and idea continues to influence most musical cultures of the world. Whether through sheer determination or exasperation at the need for twelve keyboards in a room, in 1722, J. S. Bach's well-tempered klavier established another revolution that established the capacity for unfettered exploration of all keys and possibilities. The secondary part of this revolution is that it set in stone the learning and study of music and thus initiated a critical turning point in the evolution of European music and music education.

History shows that technical evolution traversed hand in hand with musical revolution, and the industrial revolution provided the economic basis on which the piano, the accordion, and all other musical instruments could be made and exported to the masses worldwide. The now seemingly innocuous hammer system developed in Cristofori's pianoforte changed forever the expressive capacity and thus the requirement for the keyboard instruments that has followed since. The development of the piano enabled the ability to tell a more complete story of human expression. Though the machine itself was startling, so too were the number of pedagogues: Bach, Beethoven, Czerny, Liszt, Chopin, Lichetivsky, Debussy, and Bartok to name but a few, who developed their approach to piano teaching and performance. Here the second impact of its double-barreled revolutionary impact, this time on music education worldwide, can also be felt to this day. The popularity of the piano across the world and its occurrence in a rich diversity of ensemble settings also substantiates its popularity and influence in music education. While much is said of the piano's influence on the music world, the accordion made its way to many more societies, connecting their folk and communities in ways that the piano could not. Its affordability and unerring "accord" to well temperament forced other ethnically arranged and tuned instruments to conform, providing a realignment of ages-old scales and tuning systems. Other instruments similarly received ongoing pedagogical evolutions, such as those for the violin (Tartini, Mozart, Kreutzer, Spohr, Joachim and Moser, Flesch, and Suzuki) and for the flute (Hotteterre, Quantz, Altes, and de Lorenzo).

The history and development of Western music is also reflected in our need and desire to preserve, first via notation, and since the nineteenth century humans have striven to develop the capacity to preserve the aural artifact. The revolution of recording music was to change music forever. The impact of recorded music allowed music to take flight across the world, changing social perceptions, expectations, and behaviors toward music as a society. Edison's phonograph cylinder changed forever how we share and experience music. Little did he know that the wax cylinder would give way to the record, the cassette, the compact disc, and now the MP3 file. What could be transported in a car and played in the open air can now be transferred and sent several times around the world in a matter of seconds. There are major implications of increasing portability and access to music for music education, affording the use of recorded music as an artifact for musical appreciation and knowledge transfer. In the mid-twentieth century, the eerie and ephemeral *musique concrète* experimentations of Pierre Schaeffer led to the electronic music of Berio and Stockhausen. *Musique concrète* eventually appeared in school music about two decades later. For many Western countries, general music education utilized creative and inquiry-based learning, manipulating the magnetized sonic imprints on recorder tape. In the 1970s, experimentation and accessibility further facilitated the capacity for midi-interfaced manipulation of sound in a digital format. Of great irony in the march to innovation inherent in this revolution is that the innovative hammer mechanism of the "modern" piano had now become for some musicians obsolete, the expressive capacities now centered on the adjustment and manipulation of first electronic sine waves and then spatial frequency of a digitized sample. With this transformation of manipulability, there also came an economic rationalization and ubiquitous access to such creative sound manipulation devices. Today, across the world, more students engaging in music education in schools make their own digitally created sounds than play a conventional instrument. This set of developments in turn has placed other sets of cause and effect upon music-making and the increasing role technology plays in our decision-making as music educators. Low-cost digital "encoders" allow ease and function with the now ubiquitous laptop, a one-stop recorder, manipulator, and dissemination machine that can allow music to be uploaded in full view of the world in seconds.

The role of radio, television, and now online social media platforms have transported music and musical ideas and revolutionized the concepts that underpin our approaches to music education. By the mid-twentieth century, we had reached the age of access to music belonging to everyone (though identity and belonging to certain musics still remain a greatly socioculturally mediated phenomenon). While recorded music helped capture the classical canon and all it stood for, recorded music did also allow the capture and dissemination of local popular musicmaking and its distribution, usage, and synthesis into newer and developing forms of music. Recorded music helped cement social identity and belonging, emphasizing a global resistance against homogenizing universal influences. Here music education played a significant part in maintaining individualist and regional difference against a large and incessant tide of conformity.

The advent of free-to-air music on radio, television, and the Internet have undoubtably changed the value, style, and purposes we use music for, perhaps more so than any other development on history. The twentieth century has, through this super-freeway–like access to diverse music, allowed styles to blend, collide, and synthesize with each other. Gershwin's *Rhapsody in Blue* was acclaimed as the first blending of classical and jazz genres, when music of the people, jazz, was on the rise and classical music deemed to be waning. Recordings of jazz greats such as Armstrong, Parker, Monk, Powell, and Davis contributed to a recorded history that continues to serve as an aural encyclopedia of jazz knowledge and culture. Jazz was and continues to be a music of various manifestations, a genre that espouses improvisation over the printed page, enacting collective democracy over ordered leadership, and that allows freedom of expression instead of conformity and stasis and that splintered into multitudinous shards of subgenres. Music education was to be altered forever as jazz first became a viable option to classical study. This instatement of jazz as a valuable pursuit and its organization from an informal and aural transmission to a formal and theorized one transformed the way many participants would experience learning jazz. Jazz and popular musics have become a staple in school music education which in turn can challenge its spontaneity.

The revolution of pop and rock eras of the 1960s and 1970s changed and were themselves changed by various styles. This music and its undeniable presence in the households and minds of a new generation of music enthusiasts brought the guitar and amplification of instruments to the fore. Bands such as the Beatles—another revolution—changed the sound, form, ambition, and language of popular music and how music education might adapt (or not) to this seismic change. Their music challenged melodic pop structures, while at the same time experimentation with recording, looping, and overdubbing changed pop music forever and again pointed the direction in which music education could glean creative and educative substance with which to develop young minds.

The plight of mass refugee and migrant movements and mixing of various nationalities and societies reflected the movement and collision of ethnic musics around the world. While one might be able to hear classical music, traditional jazz, bebop, and avant-garde on the same night in many cities, so too could one now experience South African highlife, Puerto Rican salsa, North Pakistani tala, and Indonesian Gamelan just as easily. This social and musical revolution, in some countries called "multiculturalism," spawned incredibly diverse blends of multiethnic strands of music. Such is the power of music and musicians to adapt, change, and create, that this perpetual evolution continues today. This impact on music education, the revolution of what may be dubiously dubbed the phenomenon of "world music," continues to be a powerful mode of bringing to life the culture and musical experience of other cultures into the music classroom.

What is evident in music, and in particular music education, is that regardless of nationality, class, racial stereotype, or stylistic label, ways to perform, to learn, and to educate will innovatively break out of convention. In this era of disruption and the creative economy, if there is one thing to be sure of, it is that music will continue to change and so too will the ways in which we teach it.

These developments, particularly those deriving from the twentieth century, culminate in what is today a profound moment in music education, potentially foreboding an existential crisis of what music education is and how it might be taught in schools. We now enter the third decade of the twenty-first century knowing that technological innovation and societal accessibility to digital platforms will challenge the notion that Guido's "five lines" are the most potent of compositional tools. The ownership of music has moved with the status of music, the societal climates music reflects, and the capacity for ownership and distribution that can now be imbued upon anyone who chooses. Where once music belonged to certain people, it now has greater aspects of access and equity to those who make it, although equity to the rewards of music as a product seem challenged now more so than ever. Unrelenting changes have seen the power and ownership of the composer eroded, challenged as well as championed. Until the late twentieth century, the bastion of the composer remained unchallenged. The scope of the composer's oeuvre had now expanded to include symphonic works that not only threaded nationalist, multicultural, and ethnic materials but also now include film, radio, and a plethora of online audiences for both commercial and recreational applications. That being said, adventuresome, inventive seventeen-year-olds are making hit records and soundtracks to blockbuster films in their bedrooms. Technology and digitization have not only made the world smaller but also made access to music making, storage, retrieval, sharing, and performing within the realms of many.

Society has changed music, and consequently music has changed society. We can also remark at how the first millennium of humans' creation of and with music has been an intriguing and creative journey. In many ways music education has kept up and in others has for various reasons or another languished. The regard and value for music as central and core values held by the ancient Greeks and medieval scholars has long gone. Or has it? Despite the rush of time and innovation, organized schooling for the masses, crowded curricula, Common Core biases, STEM priorities, and device-laden youth open to distraction, music continues to adapt, endure, and touch younger and older learners. Music education of some sort is perhaps in the most freely accessible state that it has ever been in. Where innovation has occurred, music and importantly music education have found a way of reaching the masses, affecting the lives of generations of school children.

Intentionally a provocation, our intention with this book is to explore important moments in the development of music education. We also seek the instigators of these moments, where possible exploring who they were, what they did, and the immediate and ongoing impact of their revolutions. Most, but not all, of the revolutions we have identified have manifested in the primary or secondary music classroom. In all cases, the important changes to our pedagogy have had lasting impact on teaching and learning. We have chosen ideas that have had international impact, rather than localized practices with limited transferability. We acknowledge that we have been selective—there are many more revolutions that we could have chronicled. We have chosen those ideas that seem most impactful to us.

When were these pivotal moments that changed our teaching practice? In each chapter, the author focuses on a particular event/person in the process from which there was no turning back. We explore the progression from concept to international adoption. Often, the critical point was not at the beginning of this process but when it was possible for the benefits to be seen by music practitioners as useful. To be included, the revolution must still be influencing current thinking and practice. Like all revolutions, we seek those moments, events, and people that cannot be ignored. Once a revolution happens, its impact is undeniable.

In discussing Miles Davis's *Kind of Blue* album (1959), the late Chick Corea (1941–2021) remarked, "It's one thing to just play a tune, or play a program of music, but it's another thing to practically create a new language of music." The revolutions in music education selected for discussion in this book reflect Davis's creation of a new language. They are changes that have been so impactful to music education that they represent "big bang" moments. Many other developments have provided opportunities to experiment with new technologies, try innovative pedagogies, or incorporate alternative methods but have either not made a significant global impact or been absorbed into the panoply of temporally fashionable concepts.

Part 1, entitled "The Great Leap Forward—Early Traditions: Cultural, Environmental, and Developing Methods," begins with introduction of "movable do" into the process of teaching pitch through solfège. Jane Southcott outlines the shift from Guido's fixed "do" approach to the adoption of "movable do" into the work of Sarah Glover (1786–1867), John Curwen (1860–1880), and then Zoltan Kodály (1882–1967). Solfège remains a mainstay for choral directors and classroom teachers around the world.

Guido is also discussed by Carol Williams, who outlines the importance of Council of Laodicea in establishing the Schola Cantorum. The establishment of choir schools throughout Europe in the Middle Ages became essential in the delivery of quality devotional music, and the lasting impact can still be seen in many high-profile choir schools today. Singing forms such an integral part of music-making in schools that it begins our exploration of music education revolutions.

In the following chapter, Karin Greenhead looks at the creation and development of Émile Dalcroze's (1865–1950) approach. The rigorous and immersive training involved in becoming a certified practitioner with a Certificate, License, or *Diplôme Supérieur* has limited the popularity of Dalcroze's method. The innovative application of Eurythmics and unique approach to kinesthetic musical learning have allowed the ideas to spread globally, and its appeal to classroom music teachers has ensured its longevity on the music education landscape.

The subsequent chapter continues the exploration of teaching methods with a detailed discussion of the work of Carl Orff (1895–1982). Jane Southcott and Andrew Sutherland discuss this revolution in music education in terms of its initiation in the Orff's collaborative work with Dorothea Gunther, post–World War II renewal, and its transformation into a global phenomenon which saw the majority of music classrooms around the world with at least one Orff instrument lurking in the music cupboard. Orff's work is explored with special focus on the indispensable women without whom *Schulwerk* may never have revolutionized the world's school music programs.

The next revolution began when Japanese music educator Shinichi Suzuki (1898–1998) traveled to Germany, gathering ideas for his new method of instrumental teaching. Jane Southcott points out that until his ideas made their way to the United States, they remained a localized concept. Since American educators saw the value of Suzuki's methods, they were quickly adopted around the world and remain an important component of our studio teaching pedagogy.

Part 2, "Influences of Cultural Shifts in Society on Teaching and Learning," includes discussions on the merging of, creation of, and consumption of music and how that manifested in the classroom.

Leon de Bruin examines the explosion of Jazz into music curricula and school ensembles. With the institutionalization of jazz education and the codification of jazz language, there is much debate concerning issues of the didactic over the creative experiential, the formulaic individualist imitative approach to production over personal voice, creative concepts and collective creativity, jazz education has much work to do. The implementation of a musical style that is inherently the national music of the United States, and its usage in school music programs worldwide, has been an observable phenomenon.

El Sistema is largely understood to have been introduced into Venezuela by musician and politician José Antonio Abreu (1939–2018). Alexandra Carlson and Andrew Sutherland discuss the origins of the "music for social change" movement from the earlier work of Chilean musician and agitator Jorge Peña Hen (1928–1973). Although 1975 marks the year that Abreu's ideas began taking shape, following a concert organized by three of Hen's colleagues, the turning point for El Sistema was 2009. This was the year that protégé Gustav Dudamel, a product of the Venezuelan system, was appointed conductor of the Los Angeles Philharmonic, with a pledge to introduce El Sistema to the United States. In the same year, Abreu was awarded the Crystal Award of the World Economic Forum and the TED prize. The world was listening, and the global juggernaut became a must-have, branded commodity for developing and developed countries alike.

Paul Louth explores the phenomenon of televised Music Lessons. With the early efforts from the BBC to Leonard Bernstein's groundbreaking Young People's Concerts with the New York Philharmonic, entire generations of children were introduced to the wonder of classical music. There is now a plethora of audiovisual material to help educate audiences about the gamut of musical genres, the mechanics of music, and other explorations of musical concepts.

The inclusion of popular music in school curricula did not immediately follow the explosion of Rock 'n' Roll in the mid-1950s. Geoff Lowe notes the importance of early advocates in the United Kingdom and their contribution to the scholarly debate and the influence of the Tanglewood Symposium on music curricula in the United States. Contemporary or popular music now exists in many secondary music curricula internationally, providing an antidote to the perception that Western art music is the only worthwhile musical context for students to study.

The emergence of djembes, gamelan orchestras, tablas, and other instruments in music classrooms has created a significant shift in our approach to teaching music. Although the term "world music" is problematic, the renewed enthusiasm for exploring music from different cultures has provided further revision of the Western art music cannon being uniquely superior. Andrew Sutherland traces some of the earliest academic observations of world music in music classrooms shifting from a rare fascination to a quintessential component, noting the problems of authenticity along the way.

Part 3, "Advancing Pedagogy with Technology and Creative Revolutions," provides an exploration of innovations that impact creativity in the music classroom.

Timothy Groulx explores the introduction of electronic keyboards into music classrooms. Once an expensive novelty for pioneering music educators, the keyboard has become a ubiquitous piece of equipment. By providing comparatively inexpensive access to a piano keyboard, the fast-changing technology saw the keyboard laboratory being introduced into classrooms around the world. With the addition of headphones, music teachers now found a blissful quiet while students were practicing. When Musical Instrument Digital Interface (MIDI) provided fresh opportunities for creative practice, the traditional keyboard laboratory morphed into a "music technology" classroom, allowing students to compose using a variety of emerging software.

Celebrated Canadian composer and music educator, R. Murray Schafer, contributed enormously to the discussion surrounding music composition activities. Ros McMillan provides an insight to the importance on Schafer's background with graphic scores in reimagining a more creative approach to writing music. He espoused the replacement of didactic, theory-driven composition exercises with imaginative responses to technology and alternative scoring methods. By allowing greater access to the creative process for students, Schafer opened up musical composition for teachers and students, spreading the message with his frequent travels.

The development of music notation software, as explored by Patrick Horton, is presented distinct from the final chapter on music technology not just because it forms such an important leap forward in pedagogical practice but also because the specific nature of the software spawned an entire industry of its own. For those of us who learned to compose with pencil paper, the rapid development of notation software in its varied forms has been an unmitigated game-changer. Horton highlights some of the most important developments and the ways in which music students currently benefit from this development.

Recognized in 2017 as one of the most innovative education projects across the globe, Musical Futures was established as a way to revolutionize classroom practice. Hilary McQueen explores the formation of this pioneering project and the ways it has impacted pedagogy in the classroom and wider musical community. Musical Futures is based on pedagogy that is reflective of the musical culture of the learners, providing a real-world view of music learning that promotes inclusion and diversity. There is a focus on student-focused, informal learning which acknowledges the globalization of music and culture.

The penultimate chapter presents a historical view of the electronic instrument culture in music classrooms. Andrew Brown discusses the making of music instruments and early music technology such as *musique concrète* and the evolution into experimental technology such as the maker culture. With the shift from traditional approaches to music technology, which focused on audio engineering and studio recording techniques, to newer topics, including microcontrollers, interaction, and programming, music students can now discover skills that are more applicable to careers in the modern music industry.

Renée Crawford provides the final chapter, exploring the impact of music technology on classroom pedagogy more broadly. Our understanding of the term "technology" often reflects our own usage, but Crawford traces our interaction with it from Gray's Musical Telegraph in 1874 to the interactive platforms used in classrooms today. With the prevailing view that technology enhances learning, it seems as though its use in the music classroom is likely to be an ongoing fixture.

All of the revolutions, especially those discussed in Part 1, demonstrate the importance of a child-centered approach to the delivery of musical experiences. Music education does not live in a vacuum. The chapters that constitute Part 2 provide a discourse in which changes in society are absorbed into classroom practice in an effort to maintain relevance for students. Similarly, Part 3 demonstrates that changes in technology, and the involvement of industry, can quickly and directly alter classroom music practice.

As we emerge from the first phases of a Covid-19 pandemic, we can reflect and adapt our principles, beliefs and approaches to teaching and music education. From this experience, we can identify how new opportunities arose for teaching online that has led to a proliferation of new ideas for successful delivery of music experiences. As a human endeavor, music education will remain adaptable and continue to exist albeit with the eternal possibility of reinvention and chimeric change. As globalization continues to change the way we experience the world and emerging technologies maintain a frantic pace of progress, it is not difficult to imagine the next major revolution in music education transpiring soon.

Part 1

THE GREAT LEAP FORWARD— EARLY TRADITIONS

CULTURAL, ENVIRONMENTAL, AND DEVELOPING METHODS

Revolutions are often violent affairs. National revolutions such as the infamous eighteenth-century blood-letting in France, the murderous revolt which ended the Russian Tsarist dynasties in the early part of the twentieth century, and the protracted revolution in China, which eventually saw communism firmly established in 1949, are three notable examples. Revolutions bring seismic change, and change is often greeted with a mixture of distrust, antipathy, and skepticism which takes time to revolve. The idea for change must be worthy enough to convince large swathes of the population to support it, and it must be supported with passionate advocacy and a firm conviction of its potential for good. These qualities are present in the four revolutions presented in this chapter.

This text is arranged with a broadly chronological approach and focuses on the creation of new ways of learning. For each of the chapters in Part 1, the pioneers that forged systematic approaches to music education based on improving foundational musical skills, there are many shared elements. These elements developed largely as responses to particular, localized deficiencies in developing internalized musicianship but gained traction throughout the world as classroom practitioners began to understand the power of each method. In this chapter, the development of each revolution is explored in terms of its development from an idea to a globalized network of practitioners.

In the chapter "The Role of the Cantor in the Performance of Liturgy: Council of Laodicea in the Mid-Fourth Century to Guido of Arezzo (*c.* 990–1040)," Carol Williams discusses the foundations of what was arguably the greatest of all revolutions to change music education. Williams establishes the importance of the meeting of the Council of Laodicea in the fourth century in establishing the basis for functioning choirs in churches. In addition, the role of Guido d'Arezzo in developing the practice of regular singing by introducing theoretical pedagogy which finally allowed the singing of chant to move forward from being an exclusively aural tradition. This revolution is evident in any school music program in which group singing takes place.

Jane Southcott explores the transformative effects of the world's most groundbreaking instrumental pedagogy in "Shinichi Suzuki and Talent Education: From Beginnings in Japan to the United States and the World." Her focus underscores the need for a revolution such as Suzuki's to not remain the hidden secret of localized practice but be disseminated effectively and to a global market. The gradual evaporation of some of Suzuki's foundational philosophical principals, in particular, the more creative components, suggest a review of the method may be timely for many practitioners.

Carl Orff's alleged relationship with the Nazi Party during World War II has obfuscated the work he undertook in educating adult amateur musicians and, then later, children. Like Suzuki, some of the elements of Orff's *Schulwerk* have been unevenly preserved in modern practice. In chapter 3, Southcott and Sutherland follow the creative process of gestation, interruption, revival, and dissemination that Orff explored, inspired by his experiences at the Güntherschule. Orff's work is almost unique in the way that his approach is intimately intertwined with the creation of a set of instruments. These can be found in music classrooms worldwide; however, due to the time demands of becoming a fully qualified practitioner, all too few fully understand their purpose. As with other revolutions, the dissemination of the *Schulwerk* was vital in progressing the ideas from a parochial concept to an international movement. From conception through to dissemination, it was because of several important women that Orff's techniques garnered such traction internationally.

In Karin Greenhead's chapter, "Émile Jaques-Dalcroze and the Movement of Music," the ability of Dalcroze's method to be applied to areas beyond music education is discussed, marking this revolution as truly remarkable. The formative influences of Dalcroze's transformative work which developed as the world was mired in the Great War are revealed, and Greenhead explores the challenges for a more comprehensive, global dissemination of his processes. Dalcroze's ideas are as potent a force in music education as ever but remain the purview of relatively few educators given the rigor needed to fully embrace them.

Chapter 1

Movable "Do," Sol-Fa, and Vertical Ladders

Guido to Glover to Curwen to Kodály

Jane Southcott

This chapter captures two revolutions that occurred about a thousand years apart. The effects of these inventions continue to impact how we envision and transmit relational pitch in music teaching. The initial revolution is that of Guido d'Arezzo (*c*. 995–1040) who is credited with the revolutionary invention of the sol-fa syllables (*ut, re, mi, fa, sol, la*) as a mnemonic device for teaching musical pitch to singers. As western music became increasingly complex over the centuries, music theoreticians suggested alternatives and additional complexities in how relational pitch might be taught. The most significant was changing the first syllable from *ut* to the more sonorous *do*. In the early nineteenth century, in response to calls for reform of congregational singing and class instruction, Sarah Anna Glover (1786–1865)[1] developed a revolutionary approach to music teaching and learning based on the relative (or movable) *do* (*doh*) system presented as a vertical ladder. In this, the rise and fall of pitch and the relative spaces between notes could easily be seen. To make her system accessible and easily affordable, Glover represented each note by one letter only, necessitating the change in the seventh note *Si* to *Te*, making the Anglicized notes *doh, ray, me, fah, soh, lah*, and *te*. Glover positioned vertical ladders so that doh in the central column aligned with soh to the left and fah to the right, making it visually clear and aurally easy to modulate from one key to its dominant and subdominant. This revolutionary idea was a cornerstone of her method, quickly appropriated by John Curwen (1816–1880) in the Tonic Sol-fa System and then, decades later, adapted by Zoltan Kodály (1882–1967) to underpin his music pedagogical approach. These important advances continue to be applied by important music educators and underpin much music education practice.

THE BEGINNINGS OF SOLMIZATION

In the *Epistola ad Michahelem*, Guido initially used the six syllables *ut, re, mi, fa, sol, la* as an aid to singing, the syllables having been taken from the first notes of each phrase of the Hymn to Saint John, *Ut queant laxis*.[2] In which each phrase begins one note higher in the natural hexachord. These sol-fa syllables are relative to each other, not defined by a fixed pitch. By the late middle ages, Guido's syllables were the only ones used in vocal education to represent relative note position. In England, notes were at that time named by their alphabetical pitch and their sol-fa name or names, for example, C-*fa-ut*, G-*sol-re-ut*. The note added below A to complete the first hexachord was the lowest theoretical pitch recognized. To indicate this, the note, a G, was always given its Greek alphabetical equivalent—Gamma or Γ. This note was called *gamma-ut* which leads to the whole system being referred to as the "Gamut."

"Solmization," meaning singing by sol-fa syllables, became the standard method of learning to sing.[3] Guido may not have intended this particular set of syllables to become the sole pattern,[4] but, by the late Middle Ages, they were understood as the only set used for three distinct purposes:

1. As names for the scale position of sounds apart from any particular pitch;
2. As pitch names (in some European countries but in England the letters C, D, E, F, &c. were used); and
3. As voice training aids.[5]

    The first natural hexachord of six tones encompassed the majority of melodies employed; however, when a greater compass was required, the sequences of the six syllables could be overlayed to cover the three octaves necessary for vocal music. Frequently, the Gamut was represented as a chart of ascending notes and hexachords, and this system was, as described in the first edition of Grove's *Dictionary of Music and Musicians* (1879–1889), "immeasurably superior to any that preceded it; and, so long as the Modes continued in general use, it fulfilled its purpose perfectly"[6] (table 1.1).

This Guidonian hexachordal system represented a fixed succession of tones and semitones and comprised smaller tetrachords of various shapes. It was considered to be "a welcome advance upon the tetrachordal system, and marked an emancipation from a narrower view of tonal relations."[7] This complex system remained the cornerstone of western musical theory until the seventeenth century.

By the sixteenth century, this system was also referred to as the "sol-fa" system, but there is no clear indication of where this term came from.[8] As

Table 1.1 Guido's Overlapping Hexachords

Region	Note							
Super-Acute	e*							la
	D						la	sol
	C						sol	fa
	B nat.							mi
	B b						fa	
	A					la	mi	re
	G					sol	re	ut
Acute	F					fa	ut	
	E				la	mi		
	D				la	sol	re	
	C				sol	fa	ut	
	B nat.				mi			
	B b				fa			
	A			la	mi	re		
Grave Octave	G			sol	re	ut		
	F			fa	ut			
	E		La	mi				
	D		Sol	re				
	C		Fa	ut				
	B	Mi						
	A	Re						
	Γ	Ut						

Source: McNaught, "The History and uses," 3.

music became more chromatically complex, the system was increasingly found wanting, although there were continued representations of the notes and intervals in the form of a ladder or several parallel ladders. There were many suggestions by music theoreticians to increase the syllables or change them. At the end of the sixteenth century, the seventh syllable, *Si*, was added. It is suggested that the syllable was formed from the initials of the last two words of the hymn Guido used, *Sancte Iohannes*, thus giving the two letters S and I. Several musicians were credited for this innovation. In the earliest surviving treatises on musical instruction diagrams of the Gamut or "Scale of Music" appeared.[9] In 1899 Venables[10] mentions "Thomas Morley's 'Introduction to Music' (published in 1597), C. Simpson's 'Compendium of Practical Music' (1667),[11] [and] W. Tansur's 'New Musical Grammar' (1746)"[12] in confirmation.[13] For example, in 1597, Thomas Morley published *A Plain and Easy Introduction to Practical Music*, in which Guido's overlapping hexachords are represented as a chart of ascending notes and intervals.[14]

There was another proposal that the whole scale could be Sol-faed by the syllables *fa*, *sol*, *la*, and *mi*. In the eighteenth century, music historian Charles Burney described the English use of only four of the six syllables of the hexachord. He cited *Principles of Musick* by Charles Butler (1559–1647) who discussed the omission of *ut* (or *do*) and *re*. Burney pointed out that, although hexachords had governed solmisation in most parts of Europe, from the time of their first arrangement till the latter end of the last century, the English musicians, differing from all others, exploded the two last syllables, *ut, re,* and only used in their solmisation the remaining four, *mi, fa, sol, la;* which was reducing the scale to *tetrachords* like the ancient Greeks.[15]

Despite Morley's important work, by 1650 in England, the general practice continued to be to use *mi, fa, sol,* and *la* exclusively.[16] There were many calls for reform of a system that was seen to be obscure and unnecessarily complex. In 1686, the anonymous author of *A New and Easie Method to Learn to Sing by Book* captured these concerns announcing them as:

> (1) a long bead-roll of hard and useless Names, to be conn'd backwards and forward in the *Gam-ut* . . . (2) When this Drudgery is over, follows a worse, to learn the differing Names of the Notes, according to the several places of *Mi* which in each Cliff [clef] hath several Stations . . . (4) the many Cliffs, with no less than seven ways change the places of the notes upon the Lines and Spaces.[17]

Once this was learned, it did not help with how to sing in tune or how to tune an instrument, nor did the system relate consistently to the five lines and four spaces of the musical stave. Finally, chromatic notes were not easily represented.[18] The overlapping hexachords and tetrachords of the gamut had no relation to the traditional western stave—there is no difference, visually, in the representation of tones and semitones. At this time, there were many new sets of syllables suggested, but only one proposal seems to have stuck. Although unsubstantiated, the story is offered that *Ut* was replaced by the more sonorous *Do* in honor of Giovanni Battista Doni (*c.* 1593–1647), an Italian musicologist.[19] The problems of representing increasing musical complexity in outmoded systems had been recognized for several centuries; there were increasingly strident calls for reform and for the creation of an easy and accessible way to teach basic pitch relationships to beginners. From the middle of the eighteenth century, these calls concerning the improvement of congregational singing in churches (also known as psalmody) were particularly loud.

THE INNOVATIONS OF SARAH ANNA GLOVER (1786–1867): NORWICH SOLFA

In England, in the eighteenth century, the complete series *Do-Si,* movable and fixed, was being used side by side with the movable limited series (*fa, sol, la, mi*), and numerous other often idiosyncratic plans, mostly movable in principle, were advocated and practiced. This complex system was in existence when Sarah Anna Glover (1786–1867) began her experiments to develop an effective method of class music instruction. She was responding to calls for reform in ways that would profoundly affect classroom music teaching to this day. Glover began her work in 1812 but only published the first edition of her teaching text, *Scheme for Rendering Psalmody Congregational*, in 1835. Glover was concerned about the poor state of congregational church singing which she thought had fallen into disrepute. Further, there was no effective method of class music instruction available for the many small, fledgling schools springing into existence in England at that time. Glover's experiments led her to devise a new notation that could be combined with traditional notation and could be printed using only conventional printers' type. This obviated the need for expensive music engraving which made classroom and congregational materials affordable. Glover wanted to use the sol-fa syllables so that children could practice hymn tunes without using the sacred words and thus debase their meaning. Glover had four basic objections to traditional music notation:

1. The scale was inadequately shown on the musical stave with no differences being apparent between tones and semitones;
2. The use of non-accidental sharps and flats makes music theory and music reading more confusing than necessary;
3. The same note could be shown very differently using different clefs;
4. The needless variations on how a note could be shown, depending on its octave.[20]

In her system, Glover made a number of changes. She divorced the syllables from their alphabetical pitch names—no longer would there be C-*fa-ut* or G-*sol-re-ut*. As she wanted to just use the initials for the sol-fa syllables, Glover replaced *Si* with *Te* (otherwise two syllables began with an "S"), and she added new syllables for the chromatic notes needed to show the melodic minor scale. Glover also Anglicized the syllables to make accurate pronunciation easier—thus, *La* became *Lah*, *Re* became *Ray*, and so forth, as shown in table 1.2.

An inveterate inventor, Glover began her experiments by creating a "little paste-board ladder . . . with a sliding major-scale on one side, and a sliding minor-scale on the other,"[21] which helped her teach intervals to beginners. But the device did not work very well, and after further experimentation she created a ladder of three parallel scales that she called the Norwich Sol-fa Ladder (figure 1.1).

In the ladder, the three columns make it possible to move easily from one key to its dominant (to the right) or subdominant (to the left), these being the most common modulations in the more simple music that was used for

Table 1.2 Glover's Solmization Syllables

	Major	Minor
	Doh	
	Te	
(b 7th) Cole		
	Lah	Lah
(b 6th) Gah		Ne
	Sole	
(# 4th) Tu		Bah
	Fah	
	Me	Me
	Ray	
	Doh	

Source: McNaught, "The History and uses," 50.

Figure 1.1 Norwich Solfa Ladder. *Source*: John Curwen, *The Teacher's Manual of the Tonic Sol-fa Method* (London: J. Curwen and Sons, 1875), frontispiece.

congregational singing and for songs deemed suitable for children. The ladder also made it easy to see the relationship between the natural minor scale and the major scale. Glover extended the Norwich Sol-fa Ladder to create the Sevenfold Ladder that encompassed all the keys with "twelve columns of scale-notes, arranged in the order of the keys in Kollman's 'Circle of Modulation.'"[22, 23] We would recognize this as following the "Circle of Fifths" as shown in the top line of table 1.3.

Glover also developed a complete "Table of Tune" which included all keys, also organized according to the circle of fifths. This chart was included as an appendix in the *Scheme for Rendering Psalmody Congregational*. Thus, Glover had developed a visual ladder demonstrating clearly the intervallic distances between the notes and created charts that facilitated modulation from one key to related keys with clarity and logic. In addition, all the didactic materials for classroom use did not require expensive music engraving.

THE DEVELOPMENTS OF JOHN CURWEN (1816–1880)

In 1841, John Curwen became aware of Glover's method and, with minor alterations, appropriated it almost in its entirety. He renamed the trifold and

Table 1.3 Glover's Sevenfold Ladder with the Seven Tonics Illustrated by the White Keys of the Piano-Forte

F	C	G	D	A	E	B
t	m	l	R	S	d	f
		ng		b		
l	r	s	D	F		
ng			T	m	l	r
s	d	f			ng	
b	t	m	L	r	s	d
f			ng		b	t
m	l	r	S	d	f	
			b	t	m	l
r	s	d	F			ng
		t	M	l	r	s
d	f			ng		b
t	m	l	R	s	d	f
		ng		b	t	m
l	r	s	D	f		
ng			T	m	l	r
s	d	f			ng	
b	t	m	L	r	s	d
f			ng			t
m	l	r	S	d	f	

Source: Sarah Anna Glover, *Rules for Sol-fa-ing the Established Notation* (unpublished manuscript), 3.

sevenfold ladders, calling them "modulators." Curwen publicly acknowledged his debt to Glover but did not heed her criticisms of his modifications to her system. Curwen saw himself as a "methodizer," and he greatly expanded the reach of what he now termed the Tonic Sol-fa System. Curwen gave primacy to Doh, although Glover long held to her preference for seeing the patterns of tetrachords. Admittedly, Glover's fascination with musical theory did make her system less "user-friendly"; however, her system was more in alignment with correct western musical theory. Curwen dismissed Glover's objections and even ascribed the ascendancy of the tonic to Guido, who, Curwen stated, "introduced the Tonic principle of teaching and of naming the notes by syllables in the eleventh century."[24] Curwen's adaptations were highly systematized and soon regimented into levels with certificates and examinations. Curwen's Tonic Sol-fa Method spread across the English-speaking world, becoming the standard in many British colonial educational systems in the late nineteenth and early twentieth centuries. Curwen modified the Glover's syllables a little, making the naming of the sharps and flats more consistent (table 1.4).

Venables ascribed the coining of the term "modulator" to Curwen in 1842 but realized that only the name was new. Venables did not make the direct link to the scale ladder of Glover but acknowledged that "from the introduction of the sol-fa syllables, diagrams of the scale both on the staff and by means of the syllables have been used in the education of singers."[25] A comparison of Curwen and Glover's modulators makes Curwen's indebtedness to Glover clear (figure 1.2).

Curwen saw the use of the modulator and the tonic sol-fa notes as "a set of symbolic signs bearing constant reference to a picture which has been

Table 1.4 Curwen's Tonic Sol-Fa Syllables

Flats Add "a" (pronounced au) to initial				Sharps. Add "e" to initial
		Doh¹		
		Te		
	Ta		Le	
		Lah		
	La		Se	
		Soh		
			Fe	
			Ba*	
		Fah		
		Me		
	Ma		Re	
		Ray		
	Ra		De	
		Doh		

Note: * Ba is fah# and only used in the minor scale.
Source: McNaught, "The History and uses," 59.

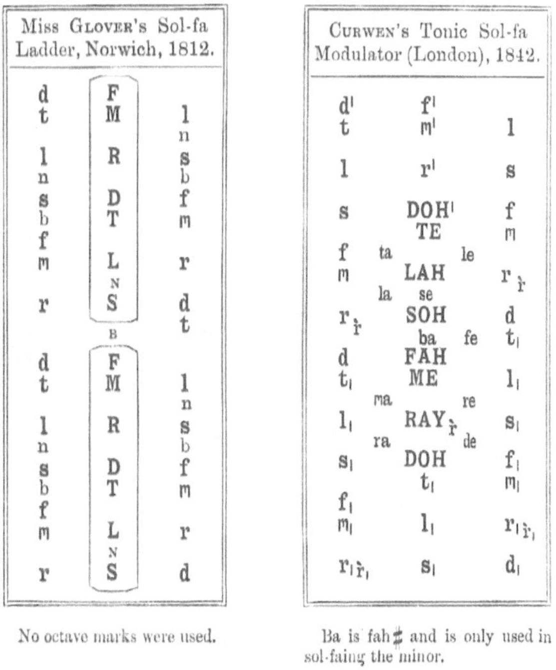

Movable "Do," Sol-Fa, and Vertical Ladders

Miss Glover's Sol-fa Ladder, Norwich, 1812.			Curwen's Tonic Sol-fa Modulator (London), 1842.		
d t	F M	l n	d¹ t	f¹ m¹	l
l n	R	s b	l	r¹	s
s b f m	D T	f m	s	DOH¹ TE	f m
	L ɴ S	r	f m	ta le LAH	r r̩
r		d t		la se	
	B		r r̩	SOH ba fe	d t₁
d t	F M	l n	d t₁	FAH ME	l₁
l n	R	s b		ma re	
s b f m	D T	f m	l₁	RAY r̩ ra de	s₁
	L ɴ S	r	s₁	DOH t₁	f₁ m₁
r		d	f₁ m₁	l₁	r₁ r̩₁
			r₁ r̩₁	s₁	d₁

No octave marks were used.   Ba is fah♯ and is only used in sol-faing the minor.

Figure 1.2 Modulators by Glover (Left) and Curwen (Right). *Source*: Venables, "Modulators," 156.

previously imprinted on the mind's eye."[26] Venables explained that from "this simple, but scientifically accurate diagram grew the extended modulator in which is to be found a column for each of the fifteen major keys requiring not more than seven sharps or flats . . . and their relative minors."[27] The extended modulator was included in many versions of the Tonic Sol-fa method (figure 1.3).

This systematic chart offered a clear visual representation of the relationships between sol-fa notes in all the scales and in their relative minors. The smaller threefold modulator was a common sight in school music classrooms in England, her colonies and dominions, and in other English-speaking countries. For example, their presence was a staple in Australian government primary schools up until the 1950s and 1960s.[28] Occasionally, the much larger sevenfold modulator would be hung in classrooms and Sunday schools, but these were rarer. Gradually, the term "modulator" has come to signify any diagram containing a single scale or even part of a scale. Often, the modulator also showed the sol-fa hand signs devised by Curwen to represent the different degrees and adopted with only small modification by Kodály. These hand signs are often shown as a ladder, mirroring the scale ladder or modulator.

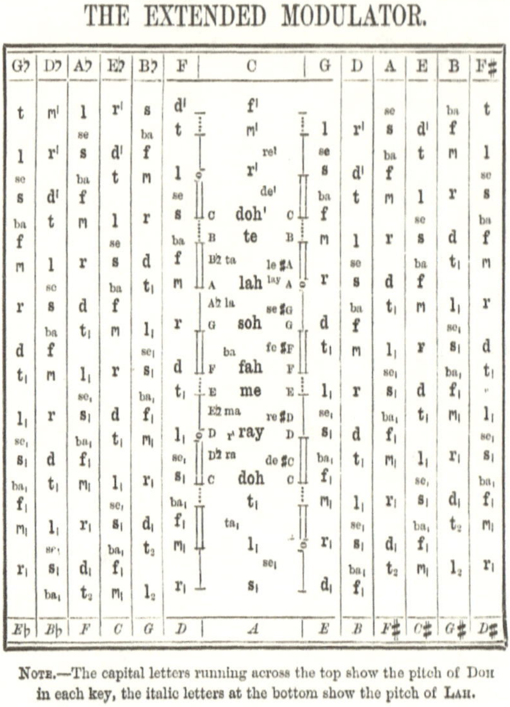

THE EXTENDED MODULATOR.

[Figure: The Extended Modulator table with columns headed G♭, D♭, A♭, E♭, B♭, F, C, G, D, A, E, B, F♯ across the top, and E♭, B♭, F, C, G, D, A, E, B, F♯, C♯, G♯, D♯ across the bottom]

NOTE.—The capital letters running across the top show the pitch of DOH in each key, the italic letters at the bottom show the pitch of LAH.

Figure 1.3 The Extended Modulator. *Source*: John Curwen, *The Standard Course of Lessons and Exercises in the Sonic Sol-fa Method of Teaching Music* (London: J. Curwen & Sons, 1901), viii.

THE ADAPTATIONS OF ZOLTÁN KODÁLY (1882–1967)

In the late 1920s, Kodály was introduced to the English Tonic Sol-fa method.[29] Erzsébet Szőnyi[30] listed a number of sources that influenced Kodály and his coworkers as they developed their method of music education. Bernarr Rainbow unpacked these, pointing out a number of perceived inaccuracies and hoping for a reappraisal of source texts.[31] Within a year Cecilia Vajda responded, strongly refuting and correcting Rainbow's assertions.[32] She pointed out that Kodály acknowledged his debt to what he had learnt from the English approach.[33] Despite the debate, Kodály's debt to English music education is not in question. János Breuer confirmed that it was "well known that the Hungarian master drew upon English musical practice. In his music pedagogy he applied John Curwen's Tonic Sol-Fa method. In choral culture he regarded the practice in England as a direct example."[34] In a letter to Percy M. Young, Kodály stated that for him, the "high level of English choral-singing was . . . a stimulating example."[35] Kodály had also been impressed by well-established, English choral culture that facilitated "difficult works being performed by workers' choirs as Handel's oratorios and Bach's great Mass."[36] Kodály may have had direct experience of this at the renowned Three Choir Festival in Gloucestershire where his work *Psalmus Hungaricus* was performed in 1928.[37] The author has seen inscribed copies of Tonic Sol-fa texts from this time in the archives of the Kodály Institute in Kecskemét, Hungary.

Szőnyi pointed out that

> Kodály first referred to the results of musical education in England, in particular to the tonic sol-fa (movable doh) and the results achieved by its use. . . . Tonality expressed through this medium gives meaning to notation, and musical form can be better understood.[38]

Kodály modified concepts from the Tonic Sol-fa method, for example, using the term "pillar tones" to refer to the foundational importance of the pentatonic scale (*d-r-m-s-l*).[39] One of the elements adopted by Kodály and his coworkers was the use of the modulator but usually only a single column, better described in Glover's term as a ladder. Bridges (1984) acknowledges that "Kodály modified and extended the hand signs to make them more logical and freed 'tonic sol-fa' from the nineteenth century concept that *Doh* was always the tonic."[40] Thus, Kodály was returning to Glover's original position—that *Doh* was not necessarily the tonic. It had been Curwen who asserted this. It should be noted that the hand signs were the contribution of Curwen, chosen to accord with his assertion of the primacy of the major scale and the "mental effects" of the tones heard individually in key. He divided the seven tones into three steps. The First Step *Doh*, *Me*, and *Soh* were the "bold, strong, pillar tones of the scale";[41] thus, the hand signs for these tones were solid and horizontal. The Second Step were the tones *Te* and *Ray*, both understood as "rising" tones; thus, the hand signs both point upward. The Third Step were the tones *Lah* and *Fah*, both understood as "falling" tones; thus, the hand signs both point downward. Once divorced from Curwen's notion of mental effects, the hand signs lose their symbolic and gestural meaning, making less sense to those singing music based on modes and other tonal systems.

The Kodály approach did not reach England until the 1960s. Until that time, tonic sol-fa continued to be the mainstay of many school music programs across the globe. In 1959, the official English text, *Primary Education*, stated that the "pitch names can be practised . . . on the solfa ladder. This, incidentally, should not invariably rise from lower to upper doh with one or two steps by way of extension at either end. Probably as many major tunes lie between the dominants (*soh* and *soh*) as between the tonics (*doh* and *doh*). Nor should modal scales (*lah* to *lah*, *ray* to *ray*, etc.) be neglected."[42] As had been asserted more than half a century earlier, the modulator offered a perfect pictorial representation of the scale and its related keys and readied the learner for the transition to reading music from traditional western notation. Venables encouraged earnest teachers to avail themselves of all the educational appliances within their grasp such as modulators (printed or written on blackboards) but not to allow their use to become mechanical.[43] Gradually the term "modulator" was applied to just a single column of tones. The Kodály system reinvigorated classroom music education, as it spread from Hungary in the 1960s. As a part of this approach, there were scale ladders, sometimes as a column, sometimes as a set of steps. This pervasive and long-employed pictorial representation of a pillar of tones facilitates teaching and learning.

It can be argued that the Kodály system with its use of abbreviated notation and vertical pillars of tones was comparatively easily accommodated in music education practices in countries already steeped in Tonic Sol-fa. For example, in Australia, in the early 1960s each state had its own rather similar music curriculum that relied on the Tonic Sol-fa method. For example, in the 1963 Music Curriculum for Primary Schools in New South Wales, the use of the modulator was standard in teaching pitch.[44] In South Australia the same year, the modulator was introduced in Grade III and used in all subsequent grades.[45] The accompanying *Method in the Teaching of Music in Schools* included a prefatory history of the use of sol-fa syllables that began with Guido d'Arezzo (quoting the Hymn to St. John) and mentioned the contributions of Sarah Glover and John Curwen. The text then introduced the sol-fa syllables, the hand signs, and the modulator, stating that "The idea of height and depth, as applied to pitch, is indicated to the eye by a diagram . . . which is called a MODULATOR."[46] Thus, when Geoffrey D'Ombrain first described the Kodaly approach in the pages of the *Australian Journal of Music Education* in 1968 as a brilliant revolutionary approach,[47] there were elements that teachers could recognize (sol-fa syllables, abbreviated notation, hand signs, and vertical columns of pitch) that made this final revolution not quite so unfamiliar.

IMPACT OF SOLMIZATION AND MOVABLE DOH

The use of sol-fa syllables and pictorial representations of ascending columns of musical tones have been with us in Western music and music education since the days of Guido. This revolutionary idea has become embedded in our practice. Over centuries the increasing complexities of music and the calls for reform to support music in schools and church congregations resulted in the revolutionary ideas of Sarah Glover—to show syllables by one letter and to show those letters in vertical columns arranged to demonstrate intervallic distances and create an effortless way to modulate between keys. Her revolutions fuelled the juggernaut that was Curwen's Tonic Sol-fa Method that spread with the British Empire across the globe in the nineteenth century. Tonic Sol-fa became the mainstay of music curricula in educational systems in colonies, dominions, and other English-speaking countries. Eventually, the "modulator" contracted to a single column, but that and the use of sol-fa syllables abbreviated to single letters survived in class music approaches of Kodály. This chapter has encompassed a series of evolving revolutions by Guido, Glover, Curwen, and Kodály (and no doubt others)—one leading to another and profoundly influencing contemporary music education.

NOTES

1. Jane Southcott, *Sarah Anna Glover: Nineteenth Century Music Education Pioneer* (Lanham, MD: Lexington Books 2020).

2. John Hawkins, *A General History of the Science and Practice of Music*, 5 volumes (London: T. Payne and Sons, 1776, facsimile reprint 2005), book IV, Chapter 8, 445.

3. Bernarr Rainbow, *Music in Educational Thought and Practice* (Aberystwyth: Boethius Press, 1989), 160.

4. Stefano Mengozzi, "Virtual Segments: The Hexachordal System in the Late Middle Ages," *The Journal of Musicology* 23, no. 3 (2006), 426–467.

5. William Gray McNaught, "The History and uses of the So-fa syllables," *The School Music Review* 3, no. 25 (1894), 2.

6. George Groves, *Dictionary of Music and Musicians*, 4 vols. (London: Macmillan, 1879–1889), Vol. 1, 735.

7. McNaught, "The History and uses," 2–3.

8. McNaught, "The History and uses," 22.

9. McNaught, "The History and uses," 22.

10. Leonard Charles Venables, "Modulators," *The School Music Review* 7, no. 81 (1899), 154.

11. Christopher Simpson, *A Compendium of Practical Music in Five Parts: Teaching, by a New and Easie Method, 1. The Rudiments of Song. 2. The Principles of Composition. 3. The Use of Discords. 4. The Form of Figurate Descant. 5. The Contrivance of Canon* (London: W. Godbid for H. Brome, M.DC.LXVII, 1667).

12. William Tans'ur, *A New Musical Grammar* (Leicester: The Author, 1746).

13. Leonard Charles Venables, "Modulators," *The School Music Review* 7, no. 81 (1899), 154.

14. Morley, Thomas, *A Plain and Easy Introduction to Practical Music* (London: William Randall, [1579, reprinted 1771]).

15. Charles Burney, *A General History of Music* vol. 1, edited by Frank Mercer (1935), reprinted (New York, 1957), 463 & 477.

16. McNaught, "History and uses," 22.

17. *A New and Easie Method to Learn to Sing by Book* (London: William Rogers, 1686), Preface.

18. John Stainer, "On the Musical Introductions Found in Certain Metrical Psalters," *Proceedings of the Musical Association* (1900–1901), 27–30.

19. Albert Ernest Wier, *The Macmillan Encyclopedia of Music and Musicians in One Volume* (London: Macmillan, 1938), 474.

20. Sarah Anna Glover, *Scheme for Rendering Psalmody Congregational* (Norwich: Jarrold & Sons, 1835).

21. Sarah Anna Glover, *A History of the Norwich Sol-fa System for Teaching Music in Schools* (Norwich: Jarrold & Sons, 1845), 1.

22. Sarah Anna Glover, *A History of the Norwich Sol-fa System for Teaching Music in Schools*, 1845), 1.

23. August Friedrich Christoph Kollmann, *A New Theory of Musical Harmony* (London: W. Bulmer & Co., 1806), 14.

24. John Curwen, *The Teacher's Manual of the Tonic Sol-fa Method* (London: J. Curwen and Sons, 1875), 2.

25. Venables, "Modulators," 154.

26. Curwen, *The Teacher's Manual of the Tonic Sol-fa Method*, 17.

27. Venables, "Modulators," 155.

28. Robin Stevens, and Jane Southcott. "Australia: Recurring problems and unresolved issues," in *The Origins and Foundations of Music Education*, eds. Graham Cox and Robin Stevens, (London: Bloomsbury, 2010), 178–179.

29. Bernarr Rainbow, *Music in Educational Thought and Practice* (Aberystwyth: Boethius Press, 1989).

30. Erzsébet Szönyi, "Sol-fa Teaching in Music Education," in *Music Education in Hungary*, ed. Frigyes Sándor (London: Boosey & Hawkes, 1975), 28–94: 30.

31. Bernarr Rainbow, "The Kodály Concept and its Pedigree." *British Journal of Music Education* 7, no. 3 (1990): 197–203.

32. Cecilia Vajda, "A reply to the article by Bernarr Ranbow, 'The Kodály Concept and its Pedigree.'" *British Journal of Music Education* 8, no. 1 (1991): 7376.

33. Vajda, "A reply to the article," 73.

34. Breuer, János, "Kodály in England—A Documentary Study (I: 1913–28)." *Tempo*, no. 143 (1982): 2.

35. Percy M. Young, *Zoltan Kodaly, a Hungarian Musician* (Ernest Benn, London 1964). Foreword: "A letter to the author from Zoltan Kodaly," viii.

36. Zoltan Kodály. ed., "The National Importance of the Workers' Choruses" (1947), in *The Selected Writings of Zoltan Kodály* (Boosey & Hawkes: London, 1974), 157.

37. Young, Barbara, *In Our Dreaming and Singing. The Story of the Three Choirs Festival Chorus* (Little Logaston Wooton Almely, Hereford: Logaston Press, 2000), 97.

38. Szönyi, Erzsébet, *Kodály's Principles in Practice* (London: Boosey & Hawkes, 1973), 14.

39. Zoltan Kodály, "Let us sing correctly!" (1952). *The Selected Writings of Zoltan Kodály* (Boosey & Hawkes: London, 1974), 216.

40. Doreen Bridges, "Eclecticism in Early Music Education," *International Journal of Music Education* 3, no. 1 (1984): 35–37.
41. John Curwen, *The Standard Course of Lessons and Exercises in the Sonic Sol-fa Method of Teaching Music* (London: Tonic Sol-fa Agency, 1859), 4.
42. *Primary Education* (London: Her Majesty's Stationery Office, 1959), 271.
43. Venables, "Modulators," 155.
44. *Curriculum for Primary Schools Music* (Sydney: New South Wales Department of Education, 1963), 64–66.
45. *Course of Instruction for Primary Schools Music* (Adelaide: Education Department of South Australia, 1963), passim.
46. Alva I. Penrose, *Method in the Teaching of Music in Schools* (Adelaide: Education Department of South Australia, 1957), 24.
47. Geoffrey D'Ombrain, "Kodaly and Music Education," *Australian Journal of Music Education*, no. 3 (1968): 33.

BIBLIOGRAPHY

A New and Easie Method to Learn to Sing by Book. London: William Rogers, 1686.
Breuer, János. "Kodály in England—A Documentary Study (I: 1913–28)." *Tempo*, no. 143 (1982): 2–9. doi:10.1017/S0040298200032733.
Bridges, Doreen. "Eclecticism in Early Music Education". *International Journal of Music Education* 3, no. 1 (1984): 35–37.
Burney, Charles. *A General History of Music*. London: For the author, 1776, 1782, 1789.
Course of Instruction for Primary Schools Music. Adelaide: Education Department of South Australia, 1963.
Curriculum for Primary Schools Music. Sydney: New South Wales Department of Education, 1963.
Curwen, John. *The Standard Course*. London: J. Curwen & Sons, 1859.
Curwen, John. *The Standard Course of Lessons and Exercises in the Sonic Sol-fa Method of Teaching Music*. London: J. Curwen & Sons, 1901.
Curwen, John. *The Teacher's Manual of the Tonic Sol-fa Method*. London: J. Curwen and Sons, 1875.
D'Ombrain, Geoffrey. "Kodaly and Music Education." *Australian Journal of Music Education*, no. 3 (1968): 33–35.
Glover, Sarah Anna. *Scheme for Rendering Psalmody Congregational*. Norwich: Jarrold and Sons; London: Hamilton and Co., 1835.
Glover, Sarah Anna. *A History of the Norwich Sol-fa System, for Teaching Music in Schools*. Norwich: Jarrold and Sons, 1845.
Groves, Sir George. *Dictionary of Music and Musicians*. London: Macmillan, 1879–1889.
Hawkins, John. *A General History of the Science and Practice of Music*. London: T. Payne and Sons, 1776.

Kodály, Zoltan. "Let us sing correctly!" (1952). In *The Selected Writings of Zoltan Kodály,* 216–219. London: Boosey & Hawkes, 1974.

Kodály, Zoltan. "The National Importance of the Workers' Choruses." In *The Selected Writings of Zoltan Kodály,* 156–159. London: Boosey & Hawkes, 1974.

Kollmann, August Friedrich Christoph. *A New Theory of Musical Harmony.* London: W. Bulmer & Co., 1806.

Mengozzi, Stefano. "Virtual Segments: The Hexachordal System in the Late Middle Ages." *The Journal of Musicology* 23, no. 3 (2006): 426–467. doi: 10.1525/jm.2006.23.3.426

McNaught, William Gray. "The History and uses of the So-fa syllables." *The School Music Review* 3, no. 25 (1894): 2–4; 3, no. 26 (1894): 22–23; 3, no. 27 (1894): 41–42&50; 3, no. 28 (1894): 58–59.

Penrose, Alva I. *Method in the Teaching of Music in Schools.* Adelaide: Education Department of South Australia, 1957.

Primary Education. London: Her Majesty's Stationery Office, 1959.

Rainbow, Bernarr. *Music in Educational Thought and Practice.* Aberystwyth: Boethius Press, 1989.

Rainbow, Bernarr. "The Kodály Concept and its Pedigree." *British Journal of Music Education* 7, no. 3 (1990): 197–203. doi: 10.1017/S0265051700007786

Simpson, Christopher. *A Compendium of Practical Music in Five Parts: Teaching, by a New and Easie Method, 1. The Rudiments of Song. 2. The Principles of Composition. 3. The Use of Discords. 4. The Form of Figurate Descant. 5. The Contrivance of Canon.* London: W. Godbid for H. Brome, M.DC.LXVII, 1667.

Southcott, Jane. *Sarah Anna Glover: Nineteenth Century Music Education Pioneer.* Lanham, MD: Lexington Books, 2020.

Stainer, John. "On the Musical Introductions Found in Certain Metrical Psalters," *Proceedings of the Musical Association* (1900–1901), 27–30.

Stevens, Robin and Jane Southcott "Australia: Recurring problems and unresolved issues." In *The Origins and Foundations of Music Education,* edited by Gordon Cox and Robin Stevens, 223–239. London: Bloomsbury, 2017.

Szönyi, Erzsébet. *Kodály's Principles in Practice.* London: Boosey & Hawkes, 1973.

Szönyi, Erzsébet. "Sol-fa Teaching in Music Education." In *Music Education in Hungary,* edited by Frigyes Sándor, 28–94. London: Boosey & Hawkes, 1975.

Tans'ur, William. *A New Musical Grammar.* Leicester: The Author, 1746.

Vajda, Cecilia. "A reply to the article by Bernarr Rainbow, 'The Kodály Concept and its Pedigree.'" *British Journal of Music Education* 8, no. 1 (1991): 73–76. doi:10.1017/S0265051700008081

Venables, Leonard Charles. "Modulators," *The School Music Review* 7, no. 81 (1899), 154–156.

Wier, Albert Ernest. *The Macmillan Encyclopedia of Music and Musicians in One Volume.* London: Macmillan, 1938.

Young, Barbara. *In Our Dreaming and Singing. The Story of the Three Choirs Festival Chorus.* Little Logaston Wooton Almely, Hereford: Logaston Press, 2000.

Young, Percy M. *Zoltan Kodaly, a Hungarian Musician.* London: Ernest Benn, 1964.

Chapter 2

The Role of the Cantor in the Performance of Liturgy

Council of Laodicea in the Mid-Fourth Century to Guido of Arezzo (c. 990–1040)

Carol Williams

When the Council of Laodicea met in the mid-fourth century and became the first to regulate music in the liturgy, it was confirming an already well-established custom of the functioning of music in worship in the Christian religion.[1] Evidence from the New Testament Epistle to the Colossians attests to the use of "psalms and hymns and spiritual songs" in worship, and the same musical elements are found in the Epistle to the Ephesians.[2] While the nature and sound of these elements can only be speculated about now, what is certain, is that the music of early Christian worship was sung by all the community in attendance.[3] It was perhaps the sense of solidarity that community singing cultivates that was essential for this fledgling and often proscribed religious cult in the earliest years. By the fourth century, through a process of ecclesiastical upheaval and expansion, much had changed. It was the optimistic age of Constantine and the Edict of Milan (313) which brought newly won legality to Christianity. At this time, a considerable amount of information concerning the musical practices of Christians begins to appear in the writings of the Western fathers from the generations that emerged approximately between 350 and 425, particularly Augustine, Hilary, Jerome, and Ambrose.[4] The Council of Laodicea in its canons presented a range of reactions to contemporary circumstances.

THE CANONS OF THE COUNCIL OF LAODICEA

Though the Council of Laodicea is perhaps best known for establishing the canon of the accepted books of the Old and New Testament (canon 60), it is of particular importance to the history of music since it introduces the cantor as a performer in three different canons:

i) "No other shall sing in the assembly except the canonical singers, who ascend to the platform and read from a parchment" (canon 15).[5]
ii) "The readers and singers have no right to wear the *orarium*,[6] and to read or sing thus" (canon 23).[7]
iii) "No one of the clergy, from presbyters to deacons, and so on in ecclesiastical rank from subdeacons, readers, singers, exorcists, doorkeepers or any of the order of ascetics, ought to enter a tavern" (canon 24).[8]

It also provided detail on the relationship between singing and reading in canon 17 which required that psalms should not be performed one after another but always interspersed with a reading after each psalm. "It is not proper for psalms to be woven together but after each psalm there should be a space interjected for a reading."[9] It appears that psalmody was no longer regarded as a form of reading and that there was a growing distinction between the singer and the reader. Taking these canons as a group, we can deduce that the singers were to be recruited from literate men who had passed through some form of induction. Exactly what the nature of that induction was is not discoverable now, but it probably involved some form of music pedagogy. The two essentials of this pedagogy must have been the teaching of the ability to improvise a simple melody to a given text and the ability to learn, memorize, and pass on specific melodies using rote methods of oral transmission.

THE BEGINNINGS OF MUSIC NOTATION

While the canon of texts accepted into the performed liturgy was expanding and being collected together and ordered, there can be no assumption that the same is true of the accompanying melodies. The cantor may well have rehearsed the allotted text and marked it up with punctuation marks as would an orator to remind him when the voice was to be raised or lowered and when pauses should be made so that the articulation of clauses and sentences would help to clarify the sense of the text for listeners.[10] Instructions for doing this had been handed down through the treatises of ancient grammarians and would have been available to the literate elite from which these early cantors were drawn. These punctuation elements are the tools of the orator or rhetorician and, along with the use of dynamics and pitch contrast, form a simple guide to melodic improvisation on a given text. If the performing cantor was pleased with his performance, attempts might be made to remember it either for repetition purposes or to serve as a model which could be adapted to suit other texts. This lies at the root of the oral transmission process where remembered performance serves as the conduit between the performer's and auditor's memories.[11] While this is still speculative, it seems that melodies appear not to have been written down in musical notation before the ninth century, and Isidore of Seville (c. 559–636) stated that "unless sounds are remembered by man, they perish, for they cannot be written down."[12]

This statement by Isidore reminds us that at least in seventh-century Visigothic Spain, there was no music notation and emphasizes the essential nature of memory in the transmission of the chant. Implicit in this is that there is a need to remember the chant. It seems there are at least two possible explanations for this: first, the dying away of the practice of improvising a melody to the canonic text and, second, that a canon of chant where specific melodies are associated with specific texts was being developed. However, it seems that each major city or region developed its own local repertory of texts and melodies, and it was a number of centuries before we can speak of a universal canon of Christian chant. In the Latin-speaking West, the great cities and monasteries of North West Africa, Italy, Dalmatia, Gaul, Ireland, and Spain were all home to flourishing local chant traditions.[13] The best documented of these regional chant traditions was that of Rome, where the papal resources were focused on the expansion of the church's influence. A string of early popes made decisions about the musical performance of liturgy that were to have an impact on the future of music history. In the fourth century, St. Damasus (366–384) prescribed the chanting of psalms day and night in all the churches, a practice that was to be refined by St. Celestin (422–432) who required that the 150 psalms be sung daily before the sacrifice. St. Sixtus (432–440) founded a monastery at the Catacombs with the express purpose of singing the chant, and St. Leo the Great (440–461) is understood to have organized the chant for each day of the liturgical year. In order to make this a permanent commitment, he established a monastic community in the vicinity of St. Peter's Basilica which was charged with the observance of the canonical hours according to a temporal and sanctoral cycle. St. Hilary (461–468) followed up this lead by founding two monasteries for the care of the chant.[14] But by far the most important pope in this early period was St. Gregory the Great (590–604).

ST. GREGORY THE GREAT

Medieval depictions of Pope Gregory I show him listening to the Holy Spirit who appeared to him in the form of a dove. As the dove sang the chants, Gregory dictated them to a scribe. This is significant because it directs our attention perhaps for the first time to the wordless melody of the chant. Up to this point, references to the chant reflect the significance of the text since it is this which decides its function in the liturgy. From the depiction, we can imagine that the receiving amanuensis is somehow notating the melody he hears from Gregory's singing onto the texts that he has before him. But what did this notation look like, and how accurate could it have been at recording the melody given that there is no evidence that music notation was in use before the Carolingian era?

There were two main motivations behind the use of music notation being adopted: first, the need for a memory aid and, second, the need to communicate it accurately. As a memory aid, it could assist in realizing chant that was known but not remembered perfectly, and later, it became the means of reading music at sight. The earliest surviving neumatic notations dating from the ninth century represent the rise and fall of the melodic line graphically.[15] While the neumes in application to the liturgical text captured nuances of phrasing and approximate melodic shape, they were mnemonic in that they could only remind the reader of a melody already known. The further development of positioning the neumes around an imaginary and then dry point line supported more accurate recall of a known melody while falling short of a pitch accurate system. The need for a notation which could capture accurately the melody of the chant is closely bound to the growth toward the universal canon of chant known later as Gregorian chant.

Gregory has been identified as the single most important figure in the development of Roman liturgy and chant. Though the view that he single-handedly codified, organized, and transmitted a canon of chant that was to be known as Gregorian chant has been questioned, it is nonetheless true that sometime in the seventh century, a canon of Roman chant was taking shape that was projected as the benchmark for all chant.[16] This canon or *ordo psallendi* denoted a schedule of sung interventions at Mass or Office. The meaning of *ordo psallendi* was expanded between 450 and 650 from a schedule of psalms and canticles assigned for monastic offices to encompass a fixed schedule of texts to be sung and eventually of fixed melodies against a background which shows the concern for the broader understanding of uniformity. The key factor in the emergence of such a repertory is the existence of a *schola cantorum* or at least a foundation of singers supported in the difficult task of developing and learning such a repertory. The greatest of these is the *Schola Cantorum* at Rome, reputedly founded sometime in the second half of the seventh century by Pope Gregory I.

THE *SCHOLA CANTORUM* AT ROME

The biography of Gregory the Great completed by John the Deacon between 875 and 882 in Rome provides the earliest support for the connection between Gregory and the *schola cantorum*.[17]

In the House of the Lord, in the manner of the most wise Solomon, and because of the spur to devotion that the sweetness of music affords, he assembled an extremely useful antiphoner for cantors in a most studious manner; he also created the *schola cantorum* which sings in the Holy Roman Church to this day on the same bases; he also used the revenue of certain estates to construct two small dwellings, that is to say one at the bottom of the stairs of the basilica of Saint Peter the Apostle, the other below the residential buildings of the Lateran palace, where, to this day, the bed in which he used to compose while reclining is kept together with his rod, with fitting veneration, the one he used to chastise the boys, and the authentic antiphoner. With a *praeceptum*, on pain of anathema, he decided the daily grace of divine service between these places.[18]

Provided we remember that John the Deacon was writing the biography of Gregory more than two and a half centuries after his death, there is much we can gather from this excerpt. John believed that Gregory founded a *schola* which, until his own time, centuries later, sang according to the rules laid down by Gregory. We also learn that Gregory built two dwellings to house the chanters, one at the foot of the steps of St. Peter's and the other near the Lateran *patriarchium*. These houses were located on either side of the city so that their inmates could fulfill their daily duties in accordance with a series of obligatory statutes. Both houses were built with the one purpose of guaranteeing a daily round of services at the two principal churches on either side of the city. John paints Gregory as someone devoted to music and the compiler and perhaps composer of an antiphoner, a book which remained preserved in Gregory's chamber until John's day. Along with the book was also preserved a rod which Gregory used to chastise the boys, presumably as they were in the process of learning the chant from the antiphoner. It seems the rod was an essential tool of medieval music pedagogy.

MEDIEVAL MUSIC PEDAGOGY

Though we know little for certain about medieval music pedagogy, it is clear that the learning of music was a long and arduous journey made almost intolerable by the ample application of the rod. Many hours of liturgical song, *cantus*, had to be learnt entirely by rote and committed to memory. The first stage of training filled the years between seven and fourteen, when the memory was fresh. The second stage, from fourteen to young manhood, bolstered memory by providing the theoretical framework within which the *cantus* operated. The process was reliant on a steady supply of very young children who were given into the care of the monasteries as an act of oblation. Child oblation or consecration was a religious act with the child being offered to God as a living sacrifice and was a practice that was generally accepted and widely practiced in the early Medieval West.[19] The children played a fundamental role in the daily life of the monastery, especially in its time-consuming liturgy, spending most of their daily waking hours singing eight offices, from Matins in the dark hours before dawn to the final office of Compline in the evening before the monks retired to sleep. In addition to these were also processions and other ceremonies associated with Sundays and important feast days in the church calendar.[20] In some places, oblates formed more than one-fifth of the monastic population.[21] This caused some special problems, particularly not only in student/staff ratios but also in the practical business of pedagogy, specifically music pedagogy, which was reliant on the staff and the time-intensive process of rote learning.

Learning to sing and read, a lengthy process that constituted most if not all of a monk's formal education, occupied every free moment of the day. The oblates learned chant by listening and then repeating after their teacher, the traditional method of instruction specifically mentioned in the Cluniac customary of Ulrich: "The boys sit in the chapter house and learn the chant from someone singing it before them."[22] They also learned to read by rote by reciting the psalter. Even monks who, joining as adults, never learned to read, eventually memorized the psalter by rote since the entire psalter of 150 psalms was to be sung every week.[23] In 830, Agobard of Lyon described the demands made on monastic singers, "Most of them have spent all the days of their life from earliest youth to grey age in the preparation and development of their singing."[24] The advantage that the oblates had over monks that found their vocation later in life was that they had greater time to commit to memorize all the chant required, and they were also able to dedicate themselves to the task since they were not required to labor.

Much was written about the importance of memory. Aurelian of Réôme wrote that the singer "cannot be perfect unless he has implanted by memory in the sheath of his heart the melody of all the lines of text through all the modes and the difference both of the modes and of the lines of text of the antiphons, introits and the responses."[25] That there were rewards for this is hinted at by Odo of Arezzo:

> He who wants to hold the highest position in the teaching of chant in the church must endeavour to study with the greatest attention the formulas which I have organised in writing for you to be sung, how every singer of the church ought to maintain the tone of the antiphons, introits, or communions, or whatever kind of chant he is able to approach. I admonish also, all singers, in particular those who appear to be in charge in the church, that they provide those under them every day with these examples in a very exact manner so that when they begin the antiphons in church they will not create uncertainty in the beginning of the psalm and begin to wander in various directions.[26]

The exactitude which Odo of Arezzo demanded in the delivery and transmission of the chant must have been difficult to achieve given that it was entirely reliant on memory and that the repertory of chant was continually growing.

THE ROMANIZATION OF AN EXPANDING LITURGY

When a psalm was performed in the Office, it was framed by an antiphon of which there existed 3,000 or more by the end of the Middle Ages. For the Mass, there were also about 560 chants, so if we add the Ordinary and Proper material, the result is between seventy-five and eighty hours of memorized matter, which as Levy explains would correspond to the selection of Beethoven's instrumental works plus the full Wagnerian canon.[27] Added to this, significant parts of the body of chant were expanding from within with the development of the trope. This term is given, from the ninth century onward, to a number of closely related genres consisting essentially of additions to preexisting chants. Three types of addition are found: (1) that of a musical phrase, a melisma without text; (2) that of a text to a preexisting melisma; (3) that of a new verse or verses consisting of text and music. As well as this growth from within, there was also the exponential growth in the creation of new chants for the feasts of the ever-expanding number of saints on the sanctoral calendar. This growth in the celebration of the saints was the result of the need of local communities to particularize their liturgical use specific to their region. There was no universal canon of chant.

In the eighth century, these flourishing local traditions began to lose ground to the more prestigious liturgy and chant associated with the city of Rome.[28] In the Lombardic South of Italy, Roman chant was superseding the so-called "Ambrosian" chant usually associated with Milan. With respect to Gallican chant, Pippin III (714–768), Charlemagne's father, had asked Pope Stephen III (752–757) for clerics to teach the chant in Carolingian lands, and the successor Pope Paul I (757–767) sent Roman chant books to the same area to "increase unity through Pippin's domain by imposing the Roman rite."[29] Charlemagne argued in front of Frankish cantors that his father had already tried to Romanize the liturgy of the Empire, and he confirmed his own wishes in writing:

> To all clergy. That they fully learn Roman chant and correctly celebrate the night and day offices, as our father of blessed memory, King Pippin, decreed when he abandoned the Gallican [chant] for the sake of unity with the Apostolic chair and pacific concord within the holy church of God.[30]

To facilitate the acquisition of this corpus of chant a regulated oral transmission process was set up by borrowing Symeon, one of the directors of the

Roman *Schola cantorum*, so that he might teach the chant to a selection of Frankish cantors. The detail of this process is preserved in a letter written by Pope Paul I to Pippin:

> We have assigned your brother's aforesaid monks to Symeon [at Rome] and installed them properly and ordered that they be taught the music of psalmody, with frequent exercise, until they are perfectly instructed. For the ample delectation of Your Excellency and the noble enjoyment of your brother, we will have the ecclesiastical chants maintained with rigorous care.[31]

Through the synod of Frankfurt (794), the Carolingian reform became official, and the cantores had to abandon the familiar Gallican rite and along with it that particular regional identity. The same Romanization drive was happening throughout Europe.

The Roman consolidation of liturgical practices continued through the ninth and tenth centuries with the musical sources, such as the antiphoners, cantatoria, sequentiaries, and missals, beginning to appear around 900.[32] The neumatic notation capturing the melody of the chant in these books, however, remained mnemonic, that is, it served to remind the cantor of a chant already known. As a consequence, the process of oral transmission was essential to maintain the unity of the chant canon. Indeed, there was an element of resistance to reliance on the written record of chant, for it was understood to take from the ear and give to the eye. From the end of the ninth century, we have very clear confirmation that the manner of performance was regarded as integral to the chant melodies and was encoded in the oldest notations but lost in the simpler but cruder more recent ones. Hucbald (c. 850–930), one of the foremost expositors of music theory in the Carolingian era, was critical of the neumatic notation of his day and analyzed an example of the notation saying:

> The first note seems to be higher. You can sing it wherever you like. The second you can see is lower, but when you try to join it to the first you are at a loss as to how you should do so, whether by one tone, or two or three. Unless you hear another sing it you cannot tell what was intended by the composer.[33]

But, though Hucbald had developed an accurate pitch notation system using a system of alphabet letters developed by Boethius, he was aware of its shortcomings. The new system was incapable of indicating the slowing down or quickening of pace of the chant, how and where to use the ornamental trembling of the voice, how the tones are to be joined or separated, and the peculiarities of the pronunciation of certain letters.[34] He continued: "Therefore if these little letters which we accept as a musical notation are placed above the customary notes, sound by sound, there will clearly be on view a full and flawless record of the truth, the one set of signs." Hucbald's decision to use both systems in two parallel streams, one of letters and the other of neumes, carefully positioned above the syllables of the text, exposed the competitive demands for certainty of pitch against the fluid expressiveness of the mnemonic neumes. Certainty of pitch was to win the day with the innovations of Guido of Arezzo.

GUIDO OF AREZZO AND THE REVOLUTION OF MUSIC PEDAGOGY

Guido's fame as a pedagogue was legendary in the Middle Ages, and his four surviving works were copied and transmitted more than the works of any other music theorist of the period.[35] The most popular was the *Micrologus*, a handbook of practical theory directed to the older boys.[36] This was an early work of Guido and made no mention of any of the innovations for which he was later revered. The *Prologus in Antiphonarium*[37] and the versified *Regule rhythmice*[38] were designed as introductions to the now lost antiphoner which provided the full demonstration of his system of precise pitch notation using staff lines. The final work, the *Epistola ad Michahelem*[39] explains the hexachordal system of solmization. Perhaps the most significant of the pedagogic innovations of Guido of Arezzo (c. 990–1040) was a system of precise pitch notation, where four staff lines represented notes a third apart, the intermediate notes being placed on the spaces between. The pitch of the lines is indicated by letter clefs, letters of the traditional alphabet being set at the start of the line. In the eleventh and twelfth centuries, the lines were normally scored into the parchment (dry point lines), but those representing the upper note of a semitone step could be distinguished by colored ink: red for the F line, yellow for the C line. One can only speculate on the kind of impact this would have had on the use of memory in the process of music learning. While it is commonly believed that once something can be written down, there is no need to memorize it, and in the case of music, musicians can read and sing directly from notation without recourse to memory, the historical record suggests that notation does not replace memory but assists it.[40] It is likely that the smaller boys would have continued to learn chant by rote, whereas at the most advanced monasteries, the older boys would probably have been taught staff notation and been able to confirm their memorized chant from it and also of course to learn to sing the song unknown.

More interesting from a pedagogic point of view is the solmization system which relies on the use of syllables in association with pitches as a mnemonic device for indicating melodic intervals. These serve as aids in the oral transmission of music and may be used either for direct teaching or as a means of memorizing what has been heard. This is actually not a notation system since it is a method of aural rather than visual recognition. The solmization system as Guido developed it was always meant to be a mnemonic system and was designed around a hymn to St. John, *Ut queant laxis*. The salient feature of this hymn is that the first syllables of the opening six lines of the hymn are *ut, re, mi, fa, sol,* and *la* which coincide with the stepwise pitch rise from C to A. The association between the syllables and the pitch series soon gained hold, and the system acquired its chief pedagogic principle, that *mi-fa* is always a rising semitone. The placing of the whole syllable series on the pitch set from G to E (with B natural) and from F to D (with B flat) encompassed a fully transposable system. As well as a method of learning to sing unknown chants, the system enabled teachers and singers to distinguish between different species of interval: the minor third D–F (*re-fa*) is different in its interval structure from E–G (*mi-sol*). In the *Epistola*, where the method is described, Guido requires the student to first commit the hymn *Ut queant laxis* to memory and then to practice the use of the derived syllables and also memorize the didactic interval exercise *Alme rector*. With both these mnemonic melodies in memory store, the singer would have ready access to the most common intervals both in abstract terms and in relationship to a given tone.

Another pedagogic innovation associated with Guido and carrying his name is the Guidonian hand. Though there is no description of the hand in any of Guido's writings, theorists very shortly after his death also attributed this innovation to him perhaps because it is so closely dependent on his system of solmization. The solmization system is illustrated by means of the hand on which the syllables are united with the alphabetic series of pitch letters (A–G) and allocated to a finger joint or tip. These three pedagogic methods, pitch notation on staff lines, solmization, and the union of pitch name and solmized syllable on the one hand, were absorbed into the theory canon very quickly as evidence from John Cotton (*c.* 1100) confirms. In his work *De musica*, he assumes knowledge of the system and effortlessly connects staff notation with the solmized syllables as well as making reference to the hand. For Guido, however, it was not just about the notes, and he wanted his singers to take that extra step beyond memory to devotion:

> Finally, know that if you now wish to make progress with these notes it is necessary that you learn by heart a considerable number of chants so that, by individual neumes you may perceive from memory which or of which kind all intervals or sounds are. Because it is very different to know something by heart than to sing it from memory, since only the wise may do the former but fools often do the latter.[41]

CONCLUSION

When the Council of Laodicea recognized the role of the cantor, it at once established a ministry of music and, by elevating one voice to sing and read on behalf of all the worshippers, threatened the participatory model of worship that had characterized the early Christian rite. In the first instance, the cantor would deliver the often scriptural and fixed text in a cantillation style borrowed from the synagogue with rhetorical ornamentation derived from classical oratory; it was almost certainly improvised. With practice and increasing skill more musical elements were drawn in to serve the word, and as increasingly virtuosic melody emerged the improvisatory element declined as the singer relied more on memory. From the very start, oral transmission smoothed the passage from singer's voice to listener's ear, and there was little reliance on any written markings to record the melody. This was to remain the case for at least half a millennium more as there was no understanding that melody could be captured in notation. Nonetheless, the canon of fixed texts began to gather up specific melodies and chant families emerged particularized to the regions or towns which had nurtured them. The largest and strongest body of chant, Roman chant, developed under the influence of a string of strong popes, among them Pope Gregory I (590–604). As a means of maintaining and preserving this expanding body of song, schools of singers were established as performance academies supporting the cantors who were to lead the services of the *Opus Dei* and Mass. The greatest of these was the Roman *Schola Cantorum*, but the model was to be followed by cathedral schools and monasteries across Europe. In the eighth century, the directives of a number of church councils reflected the desire for the unification of liturgy so that all Christians would worship following the Roman model. The Carolingian education reforms were to help in accelerating this drive for Romanization, and prized singers were sent from the Roman *Schola Cantorum* to the furthest reaches of civilization to teach the local cantors. This process of teaching was a long and arduous one, involving hours of repetitive rote learning as oral transmission reliant on expansive memories was the main pedagogic tool. By about 900, the regional chant families had mostly disappeared, and the canon of chant across all Europe was Roman, newly named for Gregory as Gregorian chant.

Music notation was relatively slow to develop, and the earliest surviving neumatic notation date from the ninth century representing the rise and fall of the melodic line graphically. While the neumes in application to the liturgical text captured nuances of phrasing and approximate melodic shape, they were strictly mnemonic in that they could only remind the reader of a melody already known. Of course, the revolution in music pedagogy which the invention of accurate pitch notation on staff lines represents took decades to evolve. It was not entirely the work of one mind, but it was Guido of Arezzo who had the necessary zeal and intellectual clarity to gather the threads of development together into one simple system. Perhaps more revolutionary than staff notation, however, is the solmization method which does seem to be Guido's own idea. This amazing system enabled confident sight singing and, in combination with the staff notation, equipped anyone to sing a chant unknown and unheard. From the first mention of the cantor in the canons of the Council of Laodicea to the end of the eleventh century, this must surely be the greatest revolution in the teaching and learning of music.

NOTES

1. See Philip Schaff and Henry Wace, eds. *A Select Library of Nicene and Post-Nicene Fathers of the Christian Church. Second Series. Translated into English with Prolegomena and Explanatory Notes, under the Editorial Supervision of Philip Schaff and Henry Wace* Vol. XIV (New York: The Christian Literature Company, 1900), 123–44.

2. *Colossians* 3:16. "Let the word of Christ dwell in you richly in all wisdom; teaching and admonishing one another in psalms and hymns and spiritual songs, singing with grace in your hearts to the Lord." See also Ephesians 5:19. "Speaking to one another in psalms and hymns and spiritual songs, singing and making melody in your heart to the Lord, . . ."

3. Ulrich Huttner. *Early Christianity in the Lycus Valley* (Boston: Brill, 2013), 312.

4. Christopher Page, *The Christian West and Its Singers: The First Thousand Years* (New Haven: Yale University Press, 2010), 133.

5. "Non oportere praeter canonicos cantores, qui suggestum ascendunt, et ex membrana legunt, aliquos alios canere in ecclesia." Giovanni Domenico Mansi, and Philippe Labbe. *Sacrorum conciliorum, nova et amplissima collectio* (Graz: Akademische Druck- und Verlagsanstalt, 1960), 2: 568.

6. Or *orarion* which was a long stole which was clearly a desired object, at least by the cantors. This is evidence that the liturgy was acquiring its own sumptuary laws.

7. "Quod non oportet lectores vel cantores ferre orarium, et sic legere vel canere." Mansi, "Sacrorum conciliorum," 568.

8. "Quod non oportet sacratos, a presbyteris ad diaconos, et deinceps quemlibet ecclesiastici ordinis usque ad ministros, vel lectores, vel cantores, vel exercitatorum ordinis, in cauponam ingredi." Mansi, "Sacrorum conciliorum," 568.

9. Mansi, "Sacrorum conciliorum," 568.

10. Leo Treitler, "Reading and Singing: On the Genesis of Occidental Music-Writing," *Early Music History* 4 (1984): 139.

11. Leo Treitler, "The Early History of Music Writing in the West," *Journal of the American Musicological Society* 35, no. 2 (1982): 237–79.

12. Isidore of Seville, "De Musica," in *Isidori Hispalensis episcopi Etymologiarum sive originum libri XX*, ed. Wallace Martin Lindsay (Oxford: Clarendon, 1911), iii,

15. "Nisi enim ab homine memoria teneantur soni, pereunt, quia scribi non possunt."

13. Peter Jeffery, *Re-Envisioning Past Musical Cultures: Ethnomusicology in the Study of Gregorian Chant* (Chicago: The University of Chicago Press, 1992), 7.

14. Robert F. Hayburn, *Papal Legislation on Sacred Music, 95 A.D. To 1977 A.D.* (Collegeville, MN: The Liturgical Press, 1979), 2–4.

15. Ian D. Bent, David W. Hughes, Robert C. Provine, Richard Rastall, Anne Kilmer, David Hiley, Janka Szendrei, *et al.* "Notation," in *Grove Music Online* (Oxford University Press, 2001).

16. James W McKinnon, "Gregory the Great," in *Grove Music Online* (Oxford University Press, 2001).

17. Stephen J. P. van Dijk, "Gregory the Great, Founder of the Urban Schola Cantorum." *Ephemerides liturgicae* 77 (1963): 335–56.

18. "In domo domini more sapientissimi Salomonis propter musicae compunctionem dulcedinis antiphonarium centonem cantorum studiossissimus nimis utiliter compilavit. Scolam quoque cantorum quae hactenus eiusdem institutionibus in sancta Romana ecclesia modulatur, constituit; eique cum nonnullis praediis duo habitacula, scilicet alterum, sub gradibus basilicae beati Petri apostoli, alterum vero sub lateranensis patriarchii domibus, fabricavit ubi usque hodie lectus eius, in quo recumbens modulabatur, et flagellum ipsius, quo pueris minabatur, veneration congrua cum authentico antiphonario reservatur. Quae videlicet loca per praecepti seriem sub interposition anathematis ob ministerii quotidiani utrobique gratiam subdivisit." Quoted in Dijk, "Gregory the Great," 341.

19. Mayke de Jong, "Samuel's Image: Child Oblation in the Early Medieval West," (in English) in *Brill's Studies in Intellectual History*. Ed. Arie. J. Vanderjagt (Leiden: Brill, 1996), 1.

20. Susan Boynton, and Isabelle Cochelin, "The Sociomusical Role of Child Oblates at the Abbey of Cluny in the Eleventh Century," in *Musical Childhoods and the Cultures of Youth*, ed. Susan Boynton and Roe-Min Kok (Middletown, CT: Wesleyan University Press, 2006), 3–24: 3.

21. Boynton, and Cochelin, "The Sociomusical Role," 10.

22. "Pueri sedent in capitulo, et per aliquem praecinentem cantum addiscunt." Ulrich of Zelle, "Consuetudines cluniacenses," *Patrologia Latina*, ed. Jacques-Paul Migne, vol 149, col. 687.

23. Anna Maria Busse Berger, *Medieval Music and the Art of Memory* (Berkeley: University of California Press, 2005), 48.

24. Berger, "Medieval Music," 48.

25. "Porro autem et si opinio me non fefellit, liceat quispiam cantoris censeatur vocabulo, minime tamen perfectus esse poterit nisi modulationem omnium versuum per omnes tonos discretion[m] que tam tonorum quamque versuum antiphonarum seu introitum necne responsorium in teca cordis memoriter insitum habuerit." Aurelianus

Reomensis, "Musica Disciplina," in *Aureliani Reomensis Musica disciplina*, ed. Lawrence Gushee (Rome: American Institute of Musicology, 1975), 118.

26. "Formulas, quas vobis ad cantandum scribere procurari, qualiter omnis cantor ecclesiae tenere debeat tonum antiphonarum, officiorum seu communiorum, vel qualemcumque cantum adire poterit, cummo cum studio legere studeat qui arcem magisterii in ecclesia tenere voluerit in cantu. Admoneo autem omnes cantores, praecipue tamen eos, qui in ecclesia maiores praeesse videntur, ut quotidie subditis suis haec exempla subtilius subministrent, ne quando antiphonae in ecclesia inceperint, scrupulum generent in incipientia psalmi, et per diversa incipiant evagari." Odo of Arezzo(?), "Tonarium," in *Scriptores ecclesiastici de musica sacra potissimum*, ed. Martin Gerbert (St. Blaise /R Hildesheim: Typis San-Blasianis /R Olms, 1784 / R1963), I. 248.

27. Kenneth Levy, *Gregorian Chant and the Carolingians* (Princeton, NJ: Princeton University Press, 1998), 175.

28. Peter Jeffery, "Re-Envisioning Past Musical Cultures: Ethnomusicology in the Study of Gregorian Chant," in *Chicago Studies in Ethnomusicology*. Eds. Philip V. Bohlman and Bruno Nettl (Chicago: The University of Chicago Press, 1992), 7.

29. Kenneth Levy, "Toledo, Rome and the Legacy of Gaul," *Early Music History* 4 (1984): 49.

30. Omni clero. Ut cantum Romanum plenitier discant, et ordinabiliter per nocturnale vel gradale officium peragatur, secundum quod beatae memoriae genitor noster Pippinus rex decertavit ut fieret, quando Gallicanum tulit ob unanimitatem apostolicae sedis et sanctae Dei eclesiae pacificam concordiam. *Admonitio generalis*, 23 March 789. Boretius, A., ed. *Capitularia Regum Francorum* Vol. 1, Monumenta Germaniae Historica. Berlin, 1883, p. 61.

31. In eis [litteris vestris] siquidem conperimus exaratum, quod presentes Deo amabilis Remedii germani vestri monachos Symeoni scole cantorum priori contradere deberemus ad instruendum eos psalmodii modulationem, quam ab eo adprehendere tempore, quo illic in vestris regiminibus extitit, nequiverunt; pro quo valde ipsum vestrum asseritis germanum tristem effectum, in eo quod non eius perfecte instruisset monachos. Et quidem, benignissime rex, satisfacimus christianitatem tuam, quod, nisi Georgius, qui eidem scolae praefuit, de hac migrasset luce, nequaquam eundem Simeonem a vestri germani servitio abstolere niteremur . . . Sed defuncto praelato Georgio et in eius isdem Symeon, utpote sequens illius, accedens locum, ideo pro doctrina scolae eum ad nos accersivimus. Nam absit a nobis, ut quippiam, quod vobis vestrisque fidelibus onerosum existit, pergamus quoquomodo; potius autem, ut praelatum est, in vestrae caritatis dilectione firmi permanentes, libentissimae, in quantum virtus subpetit, voluntati vestrae obtemperandum decertamus. Propter quod et praefatos vestri germani monachos saepe dicto contradimus Simeoni eosque obtine collocantes sollerti industria eandem psalmodii modulationem instrui praecepimus et crebro in eadem, donec perfectae eruditi efficiantur, pro amplissima vestrae excellentiae atque nobilissima germani vestri delectione, ecclesisticae doctrinae cantilena disposuimus efficaci cura permanendum. Merowingici et Karolini aevi I, "Epistolarum tomus III, section VIII," in *Codex Carolinus*, ed. W. Gundlach (Monumenta Germaniae Historica, Berlin, Berolini, 1892), 553–54.

32. Page, "The Christian West," 207.

33. "Primam enim notulam cum aspexeris, quae esse videtur elatior, proferre eam quocumque vocis casu facile poteris. Secundam vero, quam pressiorem attendis, cum primae copulare quaesieris, quonam modo id facias, utrum videlicet uno vel duobus aut certe tribus ab ea elongari debeat punctis, nisi auditu ab alio percipias, nullatenus sic a compositore statutam esse pernoscere potes." Hucbald, "De Harmonica Institutione," in *Scriptores ecclesiastici de musica sacra potissimum*, ed. Martin Gerbert (St. Blaise/Repr. Hildesheim: Typis San-Blasianis /Repr. Olms, 1784/Repr. 1963), I–117.

34. "Hae autem consuetudinariae notae non omnino habentur non necessariae; quippe cum et tarditatem cantilenae, et ubi tremulam sonus contineat vocem, vel qualiter ipsi soni iungantur in unum, vel distinguantur ab invicem, ubi quoque claudantur inferius vel superius pro ratione quarumdam litterarum, quorum nihil omnino hae artificiales notae valent ostendere, admodum censentur proficuae." Hucbald. "De Harmonica Institutione" I: 118.

35. Claude V. Palisca,, and Dolores Pesce, "Guido of Arezzo," in *Grove Music Online* (Oxford University Press, 2001).

36. Guido Aretinus. *Micrologus*, ed. Joseph Smits van Waesberghe (Rome: American Institute of Musicology, 1955).

37. Guido d'Arezzo. "Prologus in Antiphonarium," In *Guido d'Arezzo's Regule rithmice, Prologus in Antiphonarium and Epistola ad Michahelem: A Critical Text and Translation*, ed. Dolores Pesce (Ottawa: The Institute of Mediaeval Music, 1999), 406–34 (even).

38. Guido d'Arezzo, "Regule rhithmice," in *Guido d'Arezzo's Regule rithmice, Prologus in Antiphonarium and Epistola ad Michahelem: A Critical Text and Translation*. ed. Dolores Pesce (Ottawa: The Institute of Mediaeval Music, 1999), 328–402.

39. Guido d'Arezzo, "Epistola ad Michahelem," in *Guido d'Arezzo's Regule rithmice, Prologus in Antiphonarium and Epistola ad Michahelem: A Critical Text and Translation*, ed. Dolores Pesce (Ottawa: The Institute of Mediaeval Music, 1999), 438–530.

40. Anna Maria Busse Berger, "Medieval Music," 45.

41. "Illud tandem cognosce, quia si vis in his notis proficere, necesse est ut aliquantos cantus ita memoriter discas, ut per singulas neumas modos vel sonos omnes, qui vel quales sint, memoriter sentias. Quoniam quidem longe aliud est memoriter sapere quam memoriter canere, cum illue soli habeant sapientes, hoc vero sepe faciant inprudentes." d'Arezzo, "Prologus in Antiphonarium," 432–34.

BIBLIOGRAPHY

Bede. *A History of the English Church and People*. Translated by Leo Sherley-Price. London: The Folio Society, 2010.

Bede, *Historia ecclesiastica gentis Anglorum*. Edited by J. P. Migne. *Patrologia Latina*, vol 95, Paris, 1855. Repr. Turnhout: Brepols, 1976. Cols 23–289.

Bent, Ian D., David W. Hughes, Robert C. Provine, Richard Rastall, Anne Kilmer, David Hiley, Janka Szendrei, *et al.* "Notation." In *Grove Music Online,* Oxford University Press, 2001.

Berger, Anna Maria Busse. *Medieval Music and the Art of Memory.* Berkeley: University of California Press, 2005.

Boddens Hosang, F. J. E. *Establishing Boundaries: Christian-Jewish Relations in Early Council Texts and the Writings of Church Fathers.* Leiden, Boston: Brill, 2010.

Boretius, A., ed. *Capitularia Regum Francorum* Vol. 1, Monumenta Germaniae Historica. Berlin, 1883.

Boynton, Susan, and Isabelle Cochelin. "The Sociomusical Role of Child Oblates at the Abbey of Cluny in the Eleventh Century." In *Musical Childhoods and the Cultures of Youth,* edited by Susan Boynton and Roe-Min Kok, 3–24. Middletown, CT: Wesleyan University Press, 2006.

de Jong, Mayke. *In Samuel's Image: Child Oblation in the Early Medieval West.* [in English] Brill's Studies in Intellectual History. Edited by A. J. Vanderjagt. Leiden: Brill, 1996.

Dijk, S. J. P. van. "Gregory the Great, Founder of the Urban Schola Cantorum." *Ephemerides liturgicae* 77 (1963): 335–56.

Gelineau, J. "Music and Singing in the Liturgy." In *The Study of Liturgy,* edited by Geoffrey Wainwright, Cheslyn Johnes, and Edward Yarnold, SJ, 440–54. London: William Clowest and Sons Limited, 1978.

Guido d'Arezzo. "Epistola ad Michahelem." *Guido d'Arezzo's Regule rithmice, Prologus in Antiphonarium and Epistola ad Michahelem: A Critical Text and Translation.* Edited by Dolores Pesce, Ottawa: The Institute of Mediaeval Music, 1999. 438–530 (even)

Guido Aretinus. *Micrologus.* Edited by Joseph Smits van Waesberghe. Rome: American Institute of Musicology, 1955.

Guido d'Arezzo. "Prologus in Antiphonarium." *Guido d'Arezzo's Regule rithmice, Prologus in Antiphonarium and Epistola ad Michahelem: A Critical Text and Translation.* Edited by Dolores Pesce. Ottawa: The Institute of Mediaeval Music, 1999, 406–34 (even).

Guido d'Arezzo. "Regule rhithmice." *Guido d'Arezzo's Regule rithmice, Prologus in Antiphonarium and Epistola ad Michahelem: A Critical Text and Translation.* Edited by Dolores Pesce. Ottawa: The Institute of Mediaeval Music, 1999, 328–402 (even)

Hayburn, Robert F. *Papal Legislation on Sacred Music, 95 A.D. To 1977 A.D.* Collegeville, Minnesota: The Liturgical Press, 1979.

Hucbald. "De Harmonica Institutione." In *Scriptores ecclesiastici de musica sacra potissimum,* edited by Martin Gerbert, St. Blaise/Repr. Hildesheim: Typis San-Blasianis/Repr. Olms, 1784/Repr. 1963, I:103–25.

Huttner, Ulrich. *Early Christianity in the Lycus Valley.* Boston: Brill, 2013.

Jeffery, Peter. *Re-Envisioning Past Musical Cultures: Ethnomusicology in the Study of Gregorian Chant.* Chicago Studies in Ethnomusicology. Edited by Philip V. Bohlman and Bruno Nettl. Chicago: The University of Chicago Press, 1992.

Johannes Affligemensis. "De Musica Cum Tonario." In *Johannes Affligemensis, De musica cum tonario*, edited by J. Smits van Waesberghe, 43–200. Rome: American Institute of Musicology, 1950.

Levy, Kenneth. "Toledo, Rome and the Legacy of Gaul." *Early Music History* 4 (1984): 49–99.

Levy, Kenneth. *Gregorian Chant and the Carolingians*. Princeton, NJ: Princeton University Press, 1998.

Mansi, Giovanni Domenico, and Philippe Labbe. *Sacrorum Conciliorum, Nova Et Amplissima Collectio*. 53 vols. Graz: Akademische Druck- und Verlagsanstalt, 1960.

McKinnon, James W. "Gregory the Great." In *Grove Music Online*, Oxford University Press, 2001.

Odo (of Arezzo?). "Tonarium." In *Scriptores ecclesiastici de musica sacra potissimum*, edited by Martin Gerbert, I:247–50. St. Blaise/Repr. Hildesheim: Typis San-Blasianis /Repr. Olms, 1784 /Repr. 1963.

Page, Christopher. *The Christian West and Its Singers: The First Thousand Years*. New Haven: Yale University Press, 2010.

Palisca, Claude V., and Dolores Pesce. "Guido of Arezzo." In *Grove Music Online*. Oxford University Press, 2001.

Reomensis, Aurelianus. "Musica Disciplina." In *Aureliani Reomensis Musica disciplina*, edited by Lawrence Gushee, 53–135. Rome: American Institute of Musicology, 1975.

Schaff, Philip and Henry Wace, eds. *A Select Library of Nicene and Post-Nicene Fathers of the Christian Church. Second Series. Translated into English with Prolegomena and Explanatory Notes, under the Editorial Supervision of Philip Schaff and Henry Wace* Vol. XIV. New York: The Christian literature company, 1900.

Seville, Isidore of. "De Musica." In *Isidori Hispalensis episcopi Etymologiarum sive originum libri XX*, edited by W. M. Lindsay. Oxford: Clarendon, 1911.

Treitler, Leo. "Reading and Singing: On the Genesis of Occidental Music-Writing." *Early Music History* 4 (1984): 135–208.

Udalricus Cluniacensis monachus. *Antiquiores consuetudines Cluniacensis monasterii*. Edited by J. P. Migne. Patrologia Latina 149. Paris, 1855. Repr. Turnhour: Brepols, 1976. Cols 643–779.

Chapter 3

Orff's *Schulwerk*

Gestation, Interruption, Revival, and Dissemination

Jane Southcott and Andrew Sutherland

Reflecting on the origins of Orff-Schulwerk, in 1963 German composer and music educator Carl Orff (1895–1982) described the Schulwerk as a "wildflower" that grew "from ideas that were rife at the time and that found favourable conditions in my work. The Schulwerk did not develop from any preconsidered plan . . . but came from a need."[1] Since its gestation, interruption, revival, and ultimate global dissemination, Orff-Schulwerk offered a revolution in how we approach music making with children. Most visible are the now pervasive signature musical instruments that exploded class music making possibilities. Less visible but of equal or greater importance was the emphasis on creativity and musical improvisation. It should be noted that Orff was not alone in the development and spread of the Schulwerk. Without the crucial work of German musician and educator Gunild Keetman (1904–1990), Canadian music educator Doreen Hall (*b.* 1921) and English music educator Margaret Murray (1921–2015), the approach would not be as we know it today. In this revolution, there were a number of revolutionaries who took the advanced guard in furthering the work. It is also important to note that the Schulwerk is not a method *per se*. Essentially, it is a set of materials and practices that can be molded to fit space, place, and context. Generally referred to as an approach, Benedict observes that "it is only the subsequent ritualisation, systematisation and codification of these approaches that have rendered them methods."[2]

ORIGINS, INNOVATION, AND GESTATION

Nothing occurs in a vacuum without influences and experiences. Raised in a musically rich home, Orff received piano, organ, and cello lessons from the age of five, but his preferred pastime was improvisation. His first compositions were published in 1911. His growing interest in music caused a growing disinterest in school, and he left early to prepare for the entrance examination for the Munich Academy of Music. Once there he found the teaching conservative and old fashioned.[3] As early as 1914, Orff recounted experiences with dance. At that time Germany was dominated by the influences of "Émile Jaques-Dalcroze, Bess Mensendieck, Rudolf van Laban, and Mary Wigman."[4] Orff was very influenced by Wigman's modern dance practices which he encountered in the early 1920s. He stated: "She could make music with her body and transform music into corporeality. I felt that her dancing was elemental. I, too, was searching for the elemental, for elemental music."[5] Orff was fascinated by Wigman's use of "exotic percussion instruments and flutes . . . coming from Far Eastern of African Cultures."[6] The rich foment of artistic and educational ideas in Germany resulted in the foundation of many gymnastic and dance schools. In 1923, Dorothee Günther arrived in Munich and soon met Orff who found he had an "immediate rapport with her."[7] In 1924, they together founded the Günther-Schule, a School of Dance with the aim "to unify the disciplines of dancing and gymnastics."[8] There Orff found an "ideal field for educational and artistic research, from which developed, up to 1930, the first great idea of the *Schulwerk*."[9] Orff recognized the "possibility of working out a new kind of rhythmical education, and of realizing my ideas about a reciprocal interpenetration of movement and music education."[10] While still in the planning stage, Orff visited Curt Sachs in Berlin. Sachs was the director of the prestigious Staatlichen Musikinstrumenten-Sammlung (State Collection of Musical Instruments). Showing Orff the collection, Sachs referred to his current work on a world history of dance[11] and made incidental remark that "In the beginning was the drum."[12]

In his development of elemental music with the students at the Günther-Schule, Orff asserted the primacy of the drum: it "induces dance [which] has the closest relationship to music. My idea and the task that I had set myself was a regeneration of music through movement, through dance."[13] He deemed rhythm to be the "unifying power of language, music and movement."[14] In his teaching and experimentation with his students, Orff used body percussion (hand clapping, finger clicking, and stamping), rattles, diverse drums, cymbals, and so forth. Recounting his early decisions, in 1963, Orff explained that he was seeking something new and very different. He wanted to transfer the musical center of gravity from the harmonic to the rhythmic which "led quite naturally to the favoring of rhythmic instruments."[15] Orff sought instruments that students could play themselves, particularly while moving, so he turned to the "indigenous and exotic."[16] Untuned percussion instruments such as hand drums, tambours, rattles, jingles, and so forth, were plentiful, but tuned or melodic instruments were more problematic. A meeting with two Swedish sisters who were puppeteers led to Orff receiving "a large African xylophone, a marimba such as those [he] had seen in collections, but had never had the opportunity to play."[17] Orff experimented with the instrument and found that this was what he needed for his educational ideas as it could supply resonances, ostinato, and melodies. Sachs advised Orff not to try to replicate the instrument, but suggested Orff incorporate the newly revived recorders into his educational practice. Orff continued to think of the marimba but ordered a full set of recorders. While waiting for them to arrive, Orff's students and colleagues continued to find exotic instruments for him, including a simple xylophone from the Cameroons which had strung bars suspended over a resonance box. Orff turned to the skilled piano and harpsichord maker Carl Maendler who agreed to make an alto xylophone, then a soprano xylophone; both were made in D to match the awaited recorders.[18] With the arrival of the recorders, what is now recognized as Orff percussion instruments was in its embryonic form. Gradually, the familiar set of melodic instruments in various sizes and forms, and the familiar xylophones, metallophones, and glockenspiels, came into being. Capable of melody, some were new, and some also took inspiration from Indonesian gamelan instruments. The ranges were extended to include soprano, alto, tenor, and bass versions of both wood and metal timbres, and the addition of resonance boxes and mallets of varying materials provided a broader range of sonic possibilities.[19]

Much experimentation continued as the Schulwerk evolved. Instrumental in this work was a young student of Orff's, Gunild Keetman who had arrived at the Günther-Schule in 1926. Recalling the early work, Keetman stated that she and her colleagues were quite unaccustomed to the revolutionary music that Orff introduced to them.[20] Keetman explained that

> often the sounds [Orff] made were strange to us and our ears had to slowly get accustomed to them. . . . It was often a vigorous, attractive music in fifths and fourths, seconds were also prevalent, in which there were no cadences, seldom simple triads, but long free lines of melody that mostly eluded all the rules of symmetry and proportion, creating their own new, wide spaces.[21]

Keetman recounted the enthusiasm and wonder of the early years of experimentation. When she completed the course, Orff invited her to become his colleague. Keetman "agreed joyfully, not foreseeing that out of this a lifelong co-operation would ensue, not foreseeing the outcome and the way these experiments, begun in our restricted circle, would later spread."[22] Orff freely admitted his debt to Keetman, who developed the playing techniques for the new tuned percussion and created the first pieces for them and much of the subsequent work that comprises the Schulwerk. Orff said, "I am not exaggerating when I say that without Keetman's decisive contrition through her double talent [dancer and musician], 'Schulwerk' could never have come into being."[23]

In 1930, Orff began discussions with two publisher friends, brothers Ludwig and Will Strecker. With the assistance of others, including Hans Bergese and Dr. Wilhelm Twittenhoff, between 1931 and 1934, fourteen Schulwerk books were published[24] by Schott, Mainz under the title *Elementare Musikübung* (Elemental Music exercises).[25] Authorship was by Orff (one volume), Bergese (five volumes), and Keetman (eight volumes). The music selected for teaching was termed "elementary" or "elemental" in style. Orff linked the term to its Latin root *elementarius* which meant "pertaining to the elements, primeval, rudimentary, treating of first principles" which when applied to participatory musicking was inextricably linked with movement, dance, and speech.[26] Nick Wild offers a pragmatic definition, "Elemental music is pattern-based music built on natural speech and body rhythms, familiar melodic patterns, and simple forms that can be learned, created, understood, and performed without extensive technical or theoretical musical training."[27] This revolutionary approach required careful training for musicians and teachers who were presented with a very unfamiliar, child-centered, participatory, and improvisatory practice using new-to-the-classroom instruments and musical examples. The first iteration of the Schulwerk "placed too great demands on music teachers and also stood in opposition to the educational ideology of the Nazi state; for this reason, the publication was not continued."[28] The Günther-Schule continued to flourish, moving to new premises in 1936. There has been discussion of Orff's position under the Nazi regime,[29,30,31] but it is beyond the scope of this chapter to pursue this further. Orff himself stated that

> the political wave swept away all the ideas developed in Schulwerk as undesirable . . . the Günther-Schule in Munich as completely destroyed and burnt out, which meant the loss of most of the instruments. . . . I turned away completely from educational work and was waiting, quite unconsciously, for a new call.[32]

REDISCOVERY AND REVIVAL

The catalyst for a revival of Orff's method came in 1948 when he received a call from the Bavarian radio. An official at the station, Dr. Erwin Panofsky, had discovered an out-of-print recording of *Einzug und Reigen der Kinder und Mädchen* from the Festival of the Ninth Olympic Games in Berlin in 1936 in an antique shop.[33] Panofsky played the recording for the director of school programming who asked whether Orff could write music like this that children could play themselves as they were planning a series of broadcasts.[34]

Orff faced a pivotal moment which was "yet another opportunity for experiment."[35] He faced a number of problems, the instruments had perished in the fire, raw materials to reconstruct them were virtually unobtainable, and his method was designed with adults, rather than children. Orff saw the possibilities of applying his ideas to preadolescent children and quickly understood that the missing element that of text and the singing voice was needed. It was at this point that the fundamental idea of children's rhymes as the foundation for composition and improvisation was applied, and the revolutionary technique began its final phase.

Orff collaborated with Keetman and an experienced teacher Rudolf Kirmeyer to develop the initial radio broadcasts. They worked with children aged between eight and twelve to cultivate the series which became Schulwerk. They used the falling minor third as the foundation, which gradually broadened to include the pentatonic scale devoid of semitones. The literary material consisted of the simplest of concepts and rhymes for maximum child-friendly accessibility, intended to draw upon the innate musicality which Orff believed was present in each child.[36] The broadcasts in which children made music with and for children began in autumn 1948 using the few remaining instruments from the Günther-Schule. Maendler no longer wished to make the instruments. A young colleague of his, Klaus Becker, answered the call, making xylophones from whatever materials were at hand. Orff described that the "first xylophones were made from the shelves of a built-in cupboard in a flat that had been bombed."[37] Within a year, Becker opened his own workshop called Studio 49, not only improving on previous versions but also creating a new string instrument, the "Bordun."[38] That same year Orff wrote the text and Keetman the music for a Christmas play for children, *Die Weihnachtsgeschichte* (The Christmas Story) which remains popular.[39] In October 1963, the new building of the Orff-Institut was ready for occupation. Dr Hermann Regner was appointed as the director of the Institut, and Orff spoke at the occasion, "With all the joy in a new home . . . I think of the task that now lies before me . . . I hope to drive the development forward [so] that I can hand the work over to my successors and young teachers."[40]

Orff was appointed professor of composition at the Hochschule für Musik in Munich in 1950, a post he held for ten years. During his time there, he disseminated his techniques, conducting numerous workshops and master classes in which students were able to "find themselves."[41] In 1955, he returned to the Amersee region where he had spent his youth and immersed himself in composition, surrounded by the idyllic, natural setting in Diessen-St Georgen. It was in his final decade, until his death in 1982, that he compiled his eight-volume *Dokumentation*, a record of his creative output with the help of Hannelore Gassner and other friends.[42]

Dissemination

The dissemination of Orff's Schulwerk began in earnest after the Bavarian Radio broadcasts. In 1951, Keetman began classes for children at the Mozarteum in Salzburg. The early publications were withdrawn and reworked. The now-familiar five volumes of *Musik für Kinder* (Music for Children) were published between 1950 and 1954 "under the editorship of Carl Orff and Gunild Keetman."[43] Subsequently, Keetman published the prefatory *Elementaria. First Acquaintance with Orff-Schulwerk.*[44] Now established at the Mozarteum Academy, the Schulwerk began to become more widely known. The first occasion was in 1953 when Keetman gave demonstration lessons at an international conference for music school directors. In attendance was Dr. Arnold Walter, Director of the Royal Conservatory of Music in Toronto, Canada.[45] Walter had fled Germany, narrowly escaping deportation to a Nazi concentration camp, journeying to Paris, then Spain, England, and finally Canada, where he settled from 1937.[46] Walter felt that every young Canadian should have "the opportunity to benefit by such a system."

After extensive correspondence with Orff, Walter arranged for Doreen Hall, an experienced music teacher from New Brunswick, Canada, traveled to Salzburg, Austria, to study under Carl Orff. Hall recounted her experiences, returning in 1955, teaching the Orff approach at the Royal Conservatory of Music. At that time in Toronto, a generation of teachers had been introduced to the "High Road of Song" series of books by Ontarian G. Roy Fenwick who sought to provide resources that were more comprehensive in terms of pedagogical instruction that had previously been available. Despite many differences, these books shared some philosophical components with Orff's approach. Hall set about developing materials that had some authentic connection to both the lives of children and their musical world, disregarding much of Fenwick's material and turning instead to the folk traditions of Canada. Hall began to offer courses to teachers in 1955 and began publishing the Canadian edition of Orff-Schulwerk between 1955 and 1960. Teachers had become disillusioned with Fenwick's song method and anything related to it and were therefore willing to explore the new ideas found in Schulwerk. Hall was supported by Administrator Keith Bissell and Academic Arnold Walter from the University of Toronto, and the three promoted Orff's techniques at a time when it was yet to be officially recognized by provincial departments of education. By the first half of the 1960s, Orff's Schulwerk became established in many elementary schools in the Toronto area.[47]

There was increasing interest in Canada, North America, and further afield; for example, Hall took a group of children to the Eastern Division

Convention of the Music Educators National Conference in Buffalo in 1959. Hall described that the

> approach was new, the instruments unusual and the allotted space was totally filled with spectators. . . . The audience stood on chairs and tables . . . and still there was not enough room. . . . And so Orff-Schulwerk was well and truly launched in the U.S.A. by the best of all missionaries—children.[48]

Multiple presentations and demonstrations continued while Hall was preparing English-language versions for the *Schulwerk*. In 1960, Hall also published a small *Teacher's Manual* in response to enquiries from "a countless number of educators, music teachers and parents."[49] This concise text did much to introduce and unfold for teachers the basic elements and practices. Hall continued her work, disseminating the approach, preparing materials, presenting widely both nationally and internationally, and hosting visits by other exponents, notably Carl Orff, Gunild Keetman, and others in 1962. The revolutionary approach had found fertile ground in Canada and beyond.

Concurrently, there was considerable interest from many other countries. For example, Professor Naohiro Fukui, director of the Musashino Music Academy in Tokyo, began working independently with the Schulwerk texts. In 1962 on a study tour to Japan, Orff and Keetman found great enthusiasm from children and teachers.[50] With growing interest in his Schulwerk method, Orff was invited to visit Portugal in 1963 and Egypt and Senegal in 1966.[51] Orff wrote of its rapid propagation to other countries, Switzerland, Belgium, Holland, England, Portugal, Yugoslavia, Latin America, Turkey, Israel, Greece, and Japan, necessitating translations and the adaption of local folksongs and nursery rhymes. Many other foreign editions have been prepared[52] including "Canada (1956), Sweden (1957), . . . Argentina (1961), Portugal (1961), Japan (1963), Spain (1965) and 1969), France (1967), Wales (1968), Czechoslovakia (1969), Taiwan (1972), [and] Denmark (1977)."[53] After studying at the Orff-Institut, many former students often had to become pioneers in their own countries. As Haselbach explained, they "had to find work and realistic opportunities for propagating their new ideas, and informing their colleagues and other interested people . . . as the circle of interested people grew, national associations were formed."[54]

Also instrumental in bringing the Orff Schulwerk to English-speaking countries was English musician, educator, and gifted translator Margaret Murray who met Keetman and Orff in 1956 when Orff wanted to make recordings of the first two volumes of the *Schulwerk* with EMI. Shortly after the German recordings were complete, there was a decision to produce an English version and Murray was asked to find appropriate English children's rhymes and texts. This was the inception of the English-language *Music for Children*, published in 1958 in five volumes and several supplements.[55] Murray worked closely with Orff and Keetman and presented Orff Courses in the UK and internationally. She began the English-speaking Summer Courses at the Orff-Institute in Salzburg and is recognized as a gifted teacher and an exceptionally skilled translator of Orff-related German language documents.[56] For example, it was Murray who translated Keetman's *Elementaria*. In the decades that followed her first meeting with Orff and Keetman, Murray was tireless in her work disseminating the Orff approach. She traveled widely beyond the United Kingdom to give presentations and work with teachers, for example, to South Africa in 1975, Australia in 1977, and the United States in 1983.[57] We offer two examples of how the Orff approach became established in different countries.

United States

Although the International Society for Music Education had included sessions on *Schulwerk* at the conferences held in Europe in 1953 and 1955, the American Music Educators National Conference (now the National Association for Music Education) were slower to initiate a national introduction to Orff's work. Hindered by language barriers and geographical distance, the first MENC national conference to introduce Schulwerk to American music teachers labeled an ISME sponsored session, rather than a session for elementary teachers, a political misstep from Vanett Lawler, the executive secretary of the MENC and the inaugural secretary of ISME. Since the 1956 St. Louis MENC conference, when Schulwerk was first formally presented in the United States, until 1966, the philosophy maintained a consistent presence in workshops that included the use of children to demonstrate the approach. Hall's presentation in Buffalo in 1959 has already been mentioned. The American Orff-Schulwerk Association (AOSA) was established in 1968 due in great part to the work of Canadian Arnold Walter and Lawler in exposing American music educators to the benefits of Schulwerk.[58] AOSA was founded by ten "music educator who had heard about the Orff-Schulwerk either by engaging directly with it abroad or by participating in a workshop in the United States."[59] In 2019, there were ninety-six local chapters across the United States.

Emily Spitz explored the introduction of *Schulwerk* to America. Initially, Murray's faithful adaptation of *Music for Children* was the basic teaching resource. The American edition was published in the late 1970s and represented "a considerable departure from the previous English-language editions."[60] One major difference is that, contrary to Keetman's insistence that it would be absurd to divide the materials by age level, the American edition did just that. This was possibly in response to the drive toward national educational standards in all domains. Contradicting Orff's envisaging of the Schulwerk as a "wildflower," the materials and practices that ensued acquired "an unshakably corporate feel."[61] Mary Shamrock noted the difference between the original materials written by Orff and Keetman and the more structured pedagogical approaches developed by others to suit different educational contexts and climates. Jane Frazee described the early resistance to "this immigrant pedagogical approach" Orff-Schulwerk by the U.S. music education establishment.[62] This coolness began to thaw in the 1980s, and by the 1990s the Orff approach was an established part of the eclectic curriculum offered to trainee music educators and to students in schools. Frazee sums up the adaptations and acceptances of the Orff approach in American schools, "transform Orff's wild plant into a cultivar with gratifying pedagogical outcomes. A half-century of careful, caring work has been devoted to the application of the original Schulwerk material and international folk resources to the American school curriculum."[63] Transplantation requires modifications and hybridizations to allow the old/new plant to flourish in foreign soil. This involved many "gardeners"—in discussing the American edition published between 1977 and 1982 and comprising 650 pages, Hermann Regner described the collaborations that shaped the adaptations: "During several years of working together, 33 authors from all regions of the USA have composed, commented and tried out material. Experiences from more than 20 years of practical and theoretical work with Schulwerk ideas have poured into this publication."[64] It is little wonder that the result differed considerably from the initial revolutionary materials.

Australia

A different example of the process of assimilation occurred in Australia. For decades, the use of untuned percussion instruments in elementary school music teaching in Australia in the form of the Percussion Band (Rhythm Band) was well established in Australia. This meant that the Orff instruments slipped easily into the repertoire of teaching, but the Orff approach itself took longer.[65] In the early to mid-1960s, a number of Australian music educators chose to study in Salzburg and then introduced Orff Schulwerk in their respective Australian locations. The introduction of Orff-Schulwerk into Australian schools is widely believed to have started with Queensland educator Keith Smith who founded the first state Orff Association in Australia in Queensland in the late 1960s.[66] He was one of the first Australian educators to study in Salzburg and returned home to offer workshops and Summer Schools in Armidale in New South Wales.[67] John Morris promoted the approach in Victoria and, later, Tasmania.[68] Possibly predating these endeavors, South Australian music educator Patricia L. Holmes was well informed about the

Orff approach by 1959. In 1961, as part of a Carnegie Scholarship, Holmes attended the ISME Seminar in Vienna and the Orff Institut in Salzburg. She also spent time at the University of Toronto with Doreen Hall.[69] Regardless of who was first, all these music educators became enthusiastic exponents of the Orff approach and disseminated it among their students and other teachers.

Summing up progress to date in 1970, William Geen noted widespread interest, the formation of Orff-Schulwerk Associations in different states, and quoted a 1969 letter from Orff, "I should be happy if in other places my ideas were understood and presented in such a way."[70] The approach was encouraged by state education departments; for example, the Queensland government subsidized the purchase of Orff instruments for elementary schools.[71] A decade later Orff instruments featured in the new Victorian elementary school music curriculum with improvisatory activities employing speech, ostinato, melody, and rhythm, and five Orff-related texts were listed in the select bibliography.[72] The Australian experience had been smooth, although there were the same elements of adaptation to fit educational standards as seen elsewhere.

CONCLUSION

Criticisms have been leveled at *Schulwerk* that it frequently requires time, money, and human resources in order to adequately train a teacher to become competent with the necessary skills.[73] This perception has sparked an ongoing debate in which Orff devotees defend the level of skill needed to teach the approach.[74] Orff indicates that his resources need not be followed sequentially nor be limited to pentatonicism for any prescribed time period, stating, "Those who look for a method or a ready-made system are rather uncomfortable with the Schulwerk; people with artistic temperament and a flair for improvisation are fascinated by it."[75] He further stated,

> Anyone wishing to advance on his own needs a thorough professional training and, in addition, an intimate knowledge of the style of the Schulwerk, a grasp of its aim and potential. Unfortunately it has been misinterpreted, exploited, and falsified to the point of caricature.[76]

Orff's techniques draw upon the creativity of the teacher in order to stimulate the interests of the children through the physical embodiment of composition, improvisation, and performance, in a process that is never finished and constantly developing.

Orff's philosophy of teaching music to children stemmed from his personal belief that every child has the capability of learning, transforming, reasoning, and expressing creatively. Discussing Orff's compositional works Werner Thomas said that Orff might have said, "'I do not seek I find.' He found the right compositional subjects, when the *Kairos* was there, and the right books to help him . . . he found the right friends, collaborators and interpreters."[77] The same could be said for the inception, development, and dissemination of his educational ideas. Orff was the initiator of elemental music with its links to speech and movement, but without the contribution of collaborators, experimenters, composers, editors, translators, advocates, and skilled exponents, the revolution that was Orff-Schulwerk would not have made the lasting impact that it has. It is hard to imagine a music classroom that is not populated by Orff-instruments (xylophones, metallophones, glockenspiels, and myriad untuned percussion), hopefully employed to foster creativity through improvisatory musicking. Orff ended his 1963 recounting of the evolution of the approach by stating,

> The structure of the Schulwerk, however, is such that the existing material can be development in many ways. In all modesty, but with emphasis, I would like to conclude with Shiller: *Ich habe das Meinige gethan* [I have done my part].[78]

This is a narrative of revolutionary ideas and experimentation that involved Orff and significant others. Orff himself suggested that the revolution was not yet over.

NOTES

1. Carl Orff, "Orff-Schulwerk: Past & Future," in *Texts on Theory and Practice of Orff - Schulwerk: Basic Texts from the Years 1932–2010*, ed. Barbara Haselbach, trans. Margaret Murray, 134–157 (Mainz: Schott Music GmbH & Co. 1963): 134.

2. Cathy Benedict, "Processes of alienation: Marx, Orff and Kodaly," *British Journal of Music Education* 26, no. 2 (2009): 213–224.

3. Werner Thomas, *Carl Orff* (London: Schott, 1985), 4.

4. David B. Pruett, "Orff before Orff: The Güntherschule (1924–1945)," *Journal of Historical Research in Music Education* 24, no. 2 (2003): 178.

5. Carl Orff, *The Schulwerk*. Volume 3 of Carl Orff Documentation of his life and works (New York: Schott Music Corp., 1976): 8–9.

6. Orff, *The Schulwerk*, 9.

7. Orff, *The Schulwerk*, 10.

8. Andreas Liess, *Carl Orff* (London: Caldor and Boyars, 1966): 17.

9. Liess, *Carl Orff*, 17.

10. Carl Orff, "Orff-Schulwerk: Past & Future," in *Texts on Theory and Practice of Orff - Schulwerk: Basic Texts from the Years 1932–2010*, ed. Barbara Haselbach, trans. Margaret Murray, 134–157 (Mainz: Schott Music GmbH & Co. 1963): 136.

11. Curt Sachs, *World History of the Dance* (New York: W. W. Norton & Company, 1937).
12. Orff, *The Schulwerk*, 15.
13. Orff, *The Schulwerk*, 17.
14. Orff, *The Schulwerk*, 17.
15. Orff, "Orff-Schulwerk: Past & Future," 136.
16. Orff, "Orff-Schulwerk: Past & Future," 136.
17. Orff, *The Schulwerk*, 88.
18. Orff, *The Schulwerk*, 104.
19. Orff, "The Schulwerk: Its Origin and Aims," 70.
20. Stephanie K. Andrews, "Gunild Keetman: Das Schulwerk, music and movement education, and critical pedagogy." *American Educational History Journal* 38, no. 1/2 (2011): 310.
21. Gunild Keetman, "Memories of the Günthers-Schule," in *Texts on Theory and Practice of Orff - Schulwerk: Basic Texts from the Years 1932–2010*, ed. Barbara Haselbach, trans. Margaret Murray (Mainz: Schott Music GmbH & Co. 1963): 50.
22. Keetman, "Memories," 54.
23. Orff, *The Schulwerk*, 67.
24. Orff stated in *The Schulwerk* that the books were published but later refuted this stating that "these books were never printed" in "Orff-Schulwerk: Past & Future," 142.
25. Orff, *The Schulwerk*, 132.
26. Orff, "Orff-Schulwerk: Past & Future," 144.
27. "Defining Elemental Music," Nick Wild, The New England Orff Chapter, accessed February 20, 2022, http://www.neaosa.org/defining-elemental-music.html.
28. "Carl Orff," Carl-Orff-Stiftung, accessed February 20, 2022, https://www.orff.de/en/orffr-schulwerk/development/
29. David B. Pruett, "Orff before Orff: The Güntherschule (1924–1945)," *Journal of Historical Research in Music Education* 24, no. 2 (2003): 184.
30. Michael H. Kater, *Composers of the Nazi Era: Eight Portraits* (Oxford University Press, 1999).
31. Barbara England, and Richard England. "Kurt Huber and Carl Orff: Two Conflicting Ideologies," Forum on Public Policy: A Journal of the Oxford Round Table (University of Oxford, 2008).
32. Orff, "Orff-Schulwerk: Past & Future," 142.
33. Orff, *The Schulwerk*, 212.
34. Orff, "The Schulwerk: Its Origin and Aims," 72.
35. Orff, "Orff-Schulwerk: Past & Future," 144.
36. Orff, "Orff-Schulwerk: Past & Future," 144–146.
37. Orff, *The Schulwerk*, 218.
38. Orff, *The Schulwerk*, 219.
39. Carl Orff and Gunild Keetman, *The Christmas Story* (New York: Schott Music Corp., 1962.
40. Orff, *The Schulwerk*, 249. The building was extended in 1970.

41. Werner Thomas, "Carl Orff: A Concise Biography," (Berlin: Propyläen Verlag, 1985), 19.
42. Thomas, "A Concise Biography," 20.
43. Liess, *Carl Orff*, 158.
44. Gunild Keetman, *Elementaria. First Acquaintance with Orff-Schulwerk* (London: Schott and Co., 1970).
45. Orff, *The Schulwerk*, 239.
46. Barclay McMillan, Paul McIntyre, and Elaine Keillor. "Arnold Walter." *The Canadian Encyclopedia*. Historica Canada. Article published June 12, 2008; Last Edited February 23, 2015.
47. Raymond Joseph Sanborn, *The Contribution of Doreen Hall to the Development of Orff-Schulwerk in Canada, 1954–1986* (PhD diss., Library and Archives Canada, Bibliothèque et Archives Canada, Ottawa, 2006), 65–94.
48. Doreen Hall, "Foreword," in *Orff-Schulwerk in Canada*, ed. Doreen Hall (Mainz: Schott, 1992): xiii.
49. Doreen Hall, *Teacher's Manual* (Mainz: B. Schott's Söhne, 1960), 5.
50. Orff, *The Schulwerk*, 239.
51. Thomas, "A Concise Biography," 19.
52. Orff, "The Schulwerk: Its Origin and Aims," 73.
53. Mary Shamrock, "Orff-Schulwerk: An Integrated Foundation," *Music Educators Journal*, 72, no. 6 (1986): 52.
54. Barbara Haselbach, "Orff-Schulwerk Origins and Development," in *Reflections on Orff-Schulwerk* ed. Sarah Hennessy (London, Schott Music, 2013): 13.
55. Barbara Haselbach, "An Exceptional Translator," in *Reflections on Orff-Schulwerk* ed. Sarah Hennessy (London, Schott Music, 2013): 19.
56. Sarah Hennessy, "Margaret Murray: A Chronology," in *Reflections on Orff-Schulwerk* ed. Sarah Hennessy (London, Schott Music, 2013): 4.
57. Hennessy, "Margaret Murray: A Chronology," 5.
58. Patricia W. Hughes, "The Evolution of Orff-Schulwerk in North America (1955–1969)," *The Bulletin of Historical Research in Music Education* 14, no. 2 (July, 1993): 73–91.
59. Emily Spitz, "From Idea to Institution: The Development and Dissemination of the Orff-Schulwerk from Germany to the United States," *Current Musicology*, 104 (2019): 29.
60. Spitz, "From Idea to Institution," 26–27.
61. Spitz, "From Idea to Institution," 30.
62. Jane Frazee, "Orff-Schulwerk in the United States: Cultivating the Wildflower," in *Reflections on Orff-Schulwerk* ed. Sarah Hennessy (London, Schott Music, 2013): 48.
63. Frazee, "Orff-Schulwerk in the United States," 54–55.
64. Hermann Regner, "'Musik Für Kinder—Music for Children—Musique pour Enfants.' Comments on the Adoption and Adaptation of Orff-Schulwerk in other Countries," in *Texts on Theory and Practice of Orff - Schulwerk: Basic Texts from the Years 1932–2010*, ed. Barbara Haselbach, trans. Margaret Murray (Mainz: Schott Music GmbH & Co., 1963): 236.

65. Jane Southcott, "The Classroom Percussion Band-Osaurus" (IXth ASME Conference Proceedings, Perth, July, 1993): 202.

66. Noela Hogg. "Orff Schulwerk," in *Currency Companion to Music & Dance in Australia*, ed. John Whiteoak and Aline Scott-Maxwell (Sydney: Currency House, 2003), 485.

67. Susie Gerozisis, "A Tribute to Diana Humphries and Lorna Parker." *Musicworks* 7 (2002): 22.

68. Jane Southcott, and Wei Cosaitis, "'It All Begins with the Beat of a Drum': Early Australian Encounters with Orff Schulwerk," *Australian Journal of Music Education* 2 (2012): 20.

69. Southcott and Cosaitis, "It All Begins with the Beat," 24.

70. William A. Geen, "Orff-Schulwerk," *Australian Journal of Music Education*, no. 6 (April 1970): 25.

71. Geen, "Orff-Schulwerk," 25.

72. Education Department of Victoria, *A Guide to Music in the Primary School* (Victoria: Publications and Information Branch, Education Department of Victoria, 1980: passim.

73. Janice M. Thresher, "The Contributions of Carl Orff to Elementary Music Education," *Music Educators Journal* (January 1964): 47.

74. Ruth Pollock, "Orff Defended," *Music Educators Journal*, 50, no. 5 (April–May, 1964): 90–92.

75. Orff, "The Schulwerk: Its Origin and Aims," 69.

76. Orff, "The Schulwerk: Its Origin and Aims," 72.

77. Thomas, "A Concise Biography," 17.

78. Orff, "Orff-Schulwerk: Past & Future," 156.

BIBLIOGRAPHY

Andrews, Stephanie K. "Gunild Keetman: Das Schulwerk, music and movement education, and critical pedagogy." *American Educational History Journal* 38, no. 1/2 (2011): 305–320.

Benedict, Cathy. "Processes of alienation: Marx, Orff and Kodaly." *British Journal of Music Education* 26, no. 2 (2009): 213–224.

Education Department of Victoria, *A Guide to Music in the Primary School*. Victoria: Education Department of Victoria, 1980.

England, Barbara, and Richard England. "Kurt Huber and Carl Orff: Two Conflicting Ideologies." *Forum on Public Policy: A Journal of the Oxford Round Table*, University of Oxford (2008).

Frazee, Jane, "Orff-Schulwerk in the United States: Cultivating the Wildflower." In *Reflections on Orff-Schulwerk*, edited by Sarah Hennessy, 48–55. London, Schott Music, 2013.

Geen, William A., "Orff-Schulwerk." *Australian Journal of Music Education* 6 (1970): 23–25.

Gerozisis, Susie, "A Tribute to Diana Humphries and Lorna Parker." *Musicworks* 7 (2002): 22–23.

Hall, Doreen, "Foreword." In *Orff-Schulwerk in Canada*. Edited by Doreen Hall, v–xv. Mainz: Schott, 1992.
Hall, Doreen. *Teacher's Manual*. Mainz: B. Schott's Söhne, 1960.
Haselbach, Barbara, "An Exceptional Translator." In *Reflections on Orff-Schulwerk*, edited by Sarah Hennessy, 19–21. London, Schott Music, 2013.
Haselbach, Barbara, "Orff-Schulwerk Origins and Development." In *Reflections on Orff-Schulwer*, edited by Sarah Hennessy, 10–18. London, Schott Music, 2013.
Hennessy, Sarah, "Margaret Murray: A Chronology." In *Reflections on Orff-Schulwerk*, edited by Sarah Hennessy, 4–5. London, Schott Music, 2013.
Hogg, Noela, "Orff Schulwerk." In *Currency Companion to Music & Dance in Australia*, edited by John Whiteoak and Aline Scott-Maxwell, 485. Sydney: Currency House, 2003.
Hughes, Patricia W. "The Evolution of Orff-Schulwerk in North America (1955–1969)," *The Bulletin of Historical Research in Music Education* 14, no. 2 (1993): 73–91.
Kater, Michael H. *Composers of the Nazi era: Eight portraits*. Oxford University Press, Oxford, 1999.
Keetman, Gunild. *Elementaria. First Acquaintance with Orff-Schulwerk* (London: Schott and Co., 1970).
Keetman, Gunild, "Memories of the Günther-Schule." In *Texts on Theory and Practice of Orff - Schulwerk: Basic Texts from the Years 1932–2010*, edited by Barbara Haselbach, translated Margaret Murray, 44–65 (Mainz: Schott Music GmbH & Co., 1963).
Liess, Andreas. *Carl Orff*. London: Calder and Boyars, 1966.
McMillan, Barclay, Paul McIntyre, and Elaine Keillor. "Arnold Walter." *The Canadian Encyclopedia*. Historica Canada. Article published June 12, 2008; Last Edited February 23, 2015.
Orff, Carl. "Orff-Schulwerk: Past & Future." In *Texts on Theory and Practice of Orff - Schulwerk: Basic Texts from the Years 1932–2010*, edited by Barbara Haselbach and translated by Margaret Murray, 134–157. Mainz: Schott Music GmbH & Co. 1963.
Orff, Carl. "The Schulwerk: Its origin and aims." *Music Educators Journal* 49, no. 5 (1963): 69–70, 72, 74.
Pollock, Ruth. "Orff Defended." *Music Educators Journal* 50, no. 5 (1964): 90–92.
Pruett, David B. "Orff before Orff: The Güntherschule (1924–1945)." *Journal of Historical Research in Music Education* 24, no. 2 (2003): 178–196.
Regner, Hermann, "'Musik Für Kinder—Music for Children—Musique pour Enfants'. Comments on the Adoption and Adaptation of Orff-Schulwerk in other Countries." In *Texts on Theory and Practice of Orff—Schulwerk: Basic Texts from the Years 1932–2010*, edited by Barbara Haselbach, translated Margaret Murray, 44–65. Mainz: Schott Music GmbH & Co., 1963.
Sanborn, Raymond Joseph. *The Contribution of Doreen Hall to the Development of Orff-Schulwerk in Canada, 1954–1986*. Ottawa: Library and Archives Canada, Bibliothèque et Archives Canada, 2006.
Shamrock, Mary. "Orff-Schulwerk: An Integrated Foundation." *Music Educators Journal* 72, no. 6 (1986): 51–55.

Southcott, Jane. "The Classroom Percussion Band-Osaurus." *IXth ASME Conference Proceedings, Perth* (1993): 202–204.

Southcott, Jane, and Wei Cosaitis. "'It All Begins with the Beat of a Drum': Early Australian Encounters with Orff Schulwerk." *Australian Journal of Music Education* 2 (2012): 20–32.

Spitz, Emily. "From Idea to Institution: The Development and Dissemination of the Orff-Schulwerk from Germany to the United States." *Current Musicology* 104 (2019): 7–43.

Thomas, Werner. *Carl Orff: A Concise Biography*, originally published in "Die Grossen unserer Epoche," Berlin: Propyläen Verlag (1985).

Thresher, Janice M. "The contributions of Carl Orff to elementary music education." *Music Educators Journal* 50, no. 3 (1964): 43–48.

Werner, Thomas. *Carl Orff*. London: Schott, 1985.

Wild, Nick. "Defining Elemental Music." *The New England Orff Chapter*, http://www.neaosa.org/defining-elemental-music.html

Chapter 4

Shinichi Suzuki and Talent Education

From Beginnings in Japan to the United States and the World

Jane Southcott

Japanese musician and music educator Dr. Shin'ichi Suzuki (1898–1998) was a German educated violinist who returned to his country of birth, Japan, and developed his philosophy and method of Talent Education while seeking a way to help post–World War II Japanese children develop to their full potential. The method, *Talent Education*, is founded on Suzuki's theory of education and based on psycholinguistic development. Suzuki called his method the "mother tongue method." Becoming aware of how naturally children learn their mother tongue Suzuki realized that young children had the potential to learn far more than expected. He argued that young children learn by observation, imitation, repetition, and gradually developing intellectual awareness. He applied this understanding to the learning of the violin. Suzuki taught individual children, beginning with immersive listening to selected classical music repertoire. Children do not begin to play the violin until the age of three, but they already hold in their minds the model of the sound they seek to play. Working through a set repertoire provided in ten books, children progress to high levels of instrumental proficiency before learning to read music. In the late 1950s, Suzuki's work came to the attention of two American string educators, Professor John Kendall (Director of the Conservatory of Music at Muskingum College, New Concord, Ohio) and Professor Clifford Cook (Oberlin College, Ohio). They championed and disseminated the Talent Education approach in the United States, introducing it to string teachers via presentations, demonstrations, and publications. Although never considered a group learning activity by Suzuki, the approach began to include group instruction as part of the adaptations for American markets. Other educators heard about Talent Education from their American counterparts, and it initially spread to Canada and Australia. Today, Suzuki's *Talent Education* approach is found in both studio music teaching and in schools. Despite its early resistors who argued that preschool children were too young to teach violin and that massed group performances seemed "robotic," the approach changed how we think about the inclusion of music in the education of young children. Many music educators have long argued for the importance of "sound before symbol," but it was Suzuki who demonstrated just how effective this approach could be.

DR. SHINICHI SUZUKI AND THE DEVELOPMENT OF HIS APPROACH

Shin'ichi Suzuki was born in 1898 into a family of musical instrument makers in Nagoya City, Japan.[1] His father, Masakichi (1859–1945), owned the Suzuki Violin Factory, the first such in Japan. In his youth, Suzuki learnt about violin design and construction, and after graduation from a commercial college entered the factory as a regular staff member in charge of the export section, packing, and booking. Suzuki was enthralled by a gramophone recording of violinist Mischa Elman playing Schubert's *Ave Maria*.[2] Initially essentially self-taught, he described his initial violin technique as "more a scraping than anything else."[3] He finally managed to play a Haydn minuet which he considered his first "piece." After two years, he became unwell and was sent to convalesce at the seaside where he made an acquaintance who gained him an invitation to take part in a scientific expedition led by Marquis Tokugawa to the northern Chishima Islands.[4] He took his violin on the expedition where he played in the evenings with another passenger, violinist and pianist Miss Kohda Nobu. At the end of the trip, Marquis Tokugawa and Miss Kohda suggested that Suzuki should leave the violin factory and study music. Tokugawa helped persuade his father. Suzuki went to Tokyo to study violin playing with Andoh Koh (younger sister of Miss Kohda), staying in the mansion of Tokugawa and becoming friends with him. Suzuki continued violin, theory, and acoustics lessons with private teachers for over a year. With his father's approval, Suzuki accompanied Tokugawa on a world tour.

Suzuki left Japan in 1920 at the age of twenty-two with the intention of studying violin in Germany. He began studying violin privately with Professor Karl Klingler (1879–1971) in Berlin.[5] While in Berlin, Suzuki married Waltraud Prange. After eight years of study in Germany, Suzuki recorded Franck's *Sonata in A Major* in 1928 at *Deutsche Grammophon Gesellschaft*. He returned to Japan where he was active as a soloist, playing with the *Shin-Koukyohgakudan* (New Symphony Orchestra), and was the leader of the Suzuki Quartet which gave concerts all over Japan and via radio from 1929.

Suzuki taught at the *Kunitachi* Music School (precursor of Kunitachi College of Music) from 1930 to 1931. He then became a professor at the Imperial Music Institute (1931–1943). At this time, he formed the Tokyo String Orchestra, giving concerts in Japan from 1932.[6] Once back in Japan, among his other duties, Suzuki taught violin. He came to realize that teaching young children well would be preferable to correcting the playing of older students.[7] Counter to conventional wisdom that it took three years for a student to produce a good tone, Suzuki believed that children could far exceed this expectation.

THEORY OF TALENT EDUCATION

Suzuki based his educational system, called Talent Education, on the realization that young children learn to speak their mother tongue before the age of three. Echoing Rousseau, Suzuki stated that

> man is born with natural ability. A newborn child adjusts to his environment in order to live, and various abilities are acquired in the process. . . . Many children grow up in an environment that stunts and damages them, and it is assumed that they are born that way, they themselves believe it too. But they are all wrong.[8]

Suzuki believed that language learning required a suitable environment, immersion, and repeated practice.[9] Suzuki argued that young children can learn more than is expected, evidenced by "how easily and naturally children learn that which most adults learn only with great difficulty—their mother tongue. Young children become expert in their own language no matter how difficult and complicated it may be."[10] Transferring this ability to learn to other domains and skills could be accomplished by "observation, imitation, repetition, and gradually developing intellectual awareness."[11] Several of Suzuki's key points included that the human is the product of their environment: "Repetition of experience is important for learning. . . . The earlier the better—not only music, but all learning . . . [and] The human being is the product of his [sic] environment."[12] It was deemed the responsibility of teachers and parents to provide the environment and conditions for learning. Suzuki considered the word "Talent" to mean inherent ability, something that all are endowed with.

THE SUZUKI TALENT EDUCATION METHOD

The method is based on how language communication skills are developed and on the understanding that people are the products of their environment. In this approach, in infancy recorded music becomes part of the child's environment, seeding the aural model firmly in the child's mind. Playing the violin is delayed until the age of three when the child is physically able to manipulate a small (1/10th) violin. Listening is vital, and children continually hear the teacher and more advanced students play. Playing and developing technique precedes music reading, as language-speaking ability precedes reading. Children memorize all music, not learning to read notation until later, thus separating the two activities (playing and reading). All students learn the same music, progressing through music that introduces new technical skills in sequence. In Japan, in its original form, instrumental lessons were given individual, with parents deeply involved, and at least one learning with the child in the initial stages. Students stand to play to develop good posture and allow greater flexibility of movement. All the music to be learnt was also played repeatedly in the home; thus, the child already knew the music before it was played. Suzuki believed firmly in the importance of repetition. Group lessons allow younger students to hear others play. All music learnt remains in the repertoire of the student and is played in the concerts that were a signature of Talent Education.[13]

BEGINNINGS IN JAPAN

In 1942, Suzuki had implemented his revolutionary concept of Talent Education (Saino-Kyoiku) in Matsumoto, Nagano Prefecture, Japan. He first presented his work at the Hibiya Auditorium in Tokyo. More than thirty children (aged between four and nine years old) performed. The audience was "astonished to hear the children play a Concerto by Seitz after only a year of lessons. The audience of more than three thousand recognised that a new idea and method was daunting in this world."[14] In 1948, the Saino Kyoiku Kenyu Kai (Talent Education Research Institute) was founded and, in 1950, incorporated as a nonprofit organization. From this time, Dr. Masaaki Honda joined the board of directors and was convinced of the need to take the method to the United States where he had lived as a boy.[15]

Suzuki developed ten volumes in his sequential method. These volumes include a large amount of "Baroque violin music from Vivaldi, Bach, and Handel, as well as Beethoven, Mozart, Weber and some folk melodies."[16] There were punctuation points in the sequence where students could be granted graduation certificates: at the end of Volume Three, *Loure* by Bach; Volume Five, the First Movement of *Concerto G minor* by Vivaldi; Volume Seven Bach *Concerto in A Minor;* and Volume Ten *Concerto No. 4* by Mozart. All pieces could be performed at concerts.[17] The first graduation concert (196 graduates) occurred in October 1952 in Kyoritsu Hall, Tokyo.

The following year, 369 children graduated at the ceremony held at Aoyama Gakuin Hall, Tokyo. In subsequent years, the ceremony was held in March at the Metropolitan Gymnasium Centre, Tokyo, to accommodate the growing numbers, allowing more than a thousand children to play together. In 1955, the first national concert was held with prominent guests including Mr Ragnar Smedsland, Finnish minister, who published a report of the event in the Hufvudstadbladet Helsinki[18] on April 29, 1955. One of the first international reports, Smedsland, described that the "galleries are full of 10,000 spectators who spellbound are following the spectacle on the arena where 1200 violin playing children of the age of 4 to 15 playing Vivaldi's Concerto in A Minor."[19] The report captured the earnestness and devotion of the children who played with purity of tone, precision within the ensemble, uniform bowing, and rich modulation. At this time, the headquarters of the Talent Organization were in Matsumoto with sixty-five branches across Japan. The national concert and graduation ceremony became an annual event. In 1967, the Talent Education Institute in Matsumoto, Japan, was completed, financed by private donations and the proceeds of Suzuki's workshops and student concerts.[20]

TALENT EDUCATION IN THE UNITED STATES

A young Japanese theology student, Kenji Mochizuki, was studying at Oberlin College (Ohio). He was also a violinist and had attended the first graduation concert (Kyoritsu Hall) in Japan and was keen to spread Talent Education in the United States.[21] Mochizuki played in a college-community string festival organized by Professor Clifford Cook. Mochizuki encountered reluctance in the United States to accept that 500 young children could play a violin concert. Mochizuki asked Honda and Suzuki for a movie with sound. Although difficult to finance, a short film of a large group of Japanese children playing Bach's *Concerto for Two Violins* at the first National concert was made and sent to Mochizuki in 1958. Cook was impressed by the film and invited Mochizuki to show his film and speak at the Ohio String Teachers Association in Oberlin in 1958. The audience that day included sting teacher and director of the Conservatory of Music John Kendall of Muskingum College[22] who traveled to Japan in the summer of 1959 to investigate the Talent Education approach.

Kendall spent forty-six days in Japan observing the method, visiting sixteen cities, hearing about a thousand students, and meeting with parents, teachers, and Suzuki. On his return to the United States, Kendall began enthusiastically sharing Talent Education. He published a short article in the national journal, *Violins and Violinists*,[23] introducing Talent Education to American musicians and music teachers. In this he acknowledged potential skepticism about beginning violin lessons with very young children but asserted that Suzuki had "tried and tested his ideas through private lessons with hundreds of Japanese children, beginning at ages of three years, or even earlier."[24] Kendall returned to Japan in 1962 for further study of the method.[25]

In 1963, Cook also visited Japan to study the method, discussing the possibility of Suzuki and some of his students coming to the United States to demonstrate Talent Education. Opportunely, that same year, the International Society for Music Education held its conference in Tokyo. Honda met with the president of the American Music Educators National Conference (MENC), Alex H. Zimmerman, seeking support for Suzuki and his students to present at their 1964 conference in Philadelphia. Although interested, Zimmerman was not able to offer financial support. Despite a number of invitations from American schools, Suzuki was reluctant to agree to the trip which was not unreasonable given the lack of financial aid and the risks of taking young children overseas. Honda convinced Suzuki, then Cook, and Kendall began to make preparations. Kendall managed the schedule which eventually included nineteen cities in twenty-two days. A small group of children (and some mothers) were chosen because they were "qualified in ability, in health and from homes which could afford to pay the round-trip fare."[26] In all, nineteen people made the tour[27] which left Japan at 9:50 p.m., March 5, 1964. This first tour to the United States can be considered the beginning of the international spread of Suzuki's Talent Education. The tour was grueling.[28] The group arrived in Seattle, Washington, at 2:00 p.m., and the children performed one hour later at the University of Washington without rehearsal. They performed again that evening. In most locations, they were billeted with local families few of whom spoke Japanese. On the second day in Seattle, on a visit to Holy Name Academy, they were met by twenty children playing the signature piece, *Twinkle, Twinkle, Little Star*. Their teacher Sister Marion Schrieber was an early adopter of the method, having heard Kendall's lecture. In what became "routine," the group then flew to another state, performed, sometimes several times and at different locations, including Northwestern University and the University of Southern Illinois, Evanston, Illinois; the New England Conservatory in Boston; the Juilliard School of Music in New York; the United Nations; and the suburbs of New York and Trenton. After that, Philadelphia, which included a performance at the Music Educators National Conference (MENC) convention. Kendall explained the importance of Suzuki's Talent Education, stating that

> Suzuki's ideas have struck fire in America, not because they are exotic, or revolutionary, but because they go directly to the heart of a process universally intriguing: how infant human beings emerge from early shapelessness to the

phenomenal powers of the formative years. In the understanding of this process, as Suzuki points out, lies the future of the human race.[29]

After this presentation (and two more concerts in a different venue), the group flew to Cleveland, proceeding to Oberlin. They stayed for two nights, then continued on their whistle-stop tour,[30] returning to Tokyo via Honolulu on March 26. During their hectic trip, the group had traversed the United States, performing multiple times to large and enthusiastic audiences.

The 1964 tour effectively began a wave of popular enthusiasm for Suzuki's Talent Education. There were demands for return visits, study trips, and advocates lecturing and writing. Michael Mark described the "group's performance and the demonstration of the method [as] a revelation to the American teachers."[31] Immediate comparisons were drawn—Japanese preschool children were playing music at a very high standard, whereas American children of the same age were still several years from beginning to learn the violin. Adjustments had to be made to accommodate cultural differences between Japan and the United States. For example, many American parents both worked, making their attendance at lessons problematic. Further, American preschool institutions were not run in ways that would easily accommodate the intense instruction required by Talent Education.

Responding to a clamor for more, a second tour was undertaken in 1966 with equal success.[32] Suzuki held workshops in the United States initially in West Coast institutions such as Oberlin College and the University of Southern California. The approach was applied and shared with others; for example, by 1965 American concerts were being shown on European television.[33] In 1967, more than fifty American string teachers went to Japan to investigate talent education. After attending the summer school in Matsumoto, a discussion was held in the hall. The main sticking point for the visiting teachers was the individuality of the child—the approach had been dogged by claims of "robotic children." Many instrumental teachers "recognised the sanctity of the printed page since the type of Beethoven, and any pedagogical system placing its emphasis elsewhere was immediately suspect."[34] It was believed that rote playing might hamper the development of young musicians. Suzuki's approach refuted this perception, arguing that in the past two decades more than 10,000 children had graduated from the school, but "not one played absolutely the same though the foundation was the same. . . . The children speak through their violins and so they speak in the same language, the feeling and the expression are all different."[35] In *Suzuki Education in Action*, early convert Professor Clifford Cook not only recounted examples of success but also addressed (and refuted) all initial criticisms of Talent Education. He referred to an unnamed critic who suggested that the main purpose of Talent Education is to sell violins and books—Cook's response was that he suspected that "the wine being served comes from sour grapes!"[36]

Adaptations occurred in different contexts. For example, initially in Japan, lessons were private not in groups, which only occurred at the large concerts and festivals. In the United States, group instruction became prevalent.[37] In 1973, Diana Tillson explained the superiority of Suzuki class teaching to traditional string class methods based on seven years' experience in New York State, "I can state equivocally that I would never return to traditional string class teaching."[38] Suzuki did not develop his system as a class instruction method, but American school music practices were predicated on instrumental class instruction. Modifying Suzuki's approach to class teaching accelerated its adoption in U.S. schools, community music centers, and teachers' studios across the globe. Numerous advocates introduced the method to other music educators and simultaneously addressed possible criticisms. For example, in an article entitled "Suzuki Training: Musical Growth or Hindrance?" Augustus Brathwaite attended to the question of "What happens after Suzuki?" arguing that the approach gives the young player a strong foundation for the development of future musical maturity.[39]

In the late 1970s, renowned music education historian Michael Mark captured the then understanding of the Suzuki approach. He described the familiar concerts, where sometimes thousands of children performed;

> Usually the most advanced play first. When they have completed their high-level music, a slightly less advance group joined them, and the two combined groups play the next lower level of music. When the next group arrives, it joins the others and they all play together the music of the least advanced students. In this way, the number of performers continually increases as the level of difficulty of music decreases. When the younger students join in, the entire assembly plays the beginners' literature, including "Twinkle, Twinkle Little Star."[40]

These events afford opportunities for teachers to demonstrate the efficacy of the approach and the abilities of the students. The mass concerts are also effective opportunities for public advocacy. Writing for American teachers, Mark explained that it was proven that young children could perform challenging, authentic string repertoire, that they learnt by rote rather than reading music was not problematic, and that "Despite the criticisms, talent education is most successful in terms of its own purposes, and the movement continues to grow."[41]

INTERNATIONAL UPTAKE

It was not long before Suzuki Talent Education spread further. It is not possible to chronicle just how and when this occurred in each region, but the following examples capture some of this movement. In 1969 an article on the Suzuki approach appeared in the *Australian Journal of Music Education*. It was a reprint of an article by Alfred Garson from the *Canadian Music Educator*. Garson quoted a speech by Kenji Mochizuki, given at the Music Educators National Conference in Atlanta City, New Jersey, in 1960. Garson mentioned that the first Canadian Suzuki school was established by Mr. Jean Cousineau in Montreal in 1965, but it may be that Thomas Rolston began teaching according to the method in Canada in 1964.[42] Garson recounted exchanges between Canadian and Japanese teachers and himself invited Suzuki to visit Canada. Within a few years, there were nearly a thousand violin students in Canada learning via the approach. He anticipated that other countries would soon enthusiastically adopt the method.[43] It was not long before this occurred. For example, in 1970, Australian violist Peter Komlos received a Churchill Fellowship to study the Suzuki approach in Japan and, on return, started what was probably the first Suzuki program in Australia in Tasmania.[44] The Suzuki Association of the Americas (founded in 1972) offers a timeline that chronicles the spread of the approach across the Americas. For example, programs were established in Cordoba, Argentina, in 1967, Brazil in 1973, Costa Rica and Columbia in 1975, and Ecuador in 1992. Further, the European Suzuki Association was formed in 1980.[45] State and regional organizations were established from the 1970s, and gradually the method included other instruments such as cello, viola, piano, flute, and guitar.[46] Although exact dates and names of specific teachers may be questioned, it is undoubtable that the Suzuki Talent Education Method had spread well beyond the bounds of its Japanese origins. Margaret Mehl offers a nuanced interpretation of the different uptakes of the approach in the United States and in Europe, referring to the former as "explosive," whereas the latter is "much slower."[47]

THE PRESENT

Despite the occasional hyperbole, Suzuki's philosophical assertions, the claims of Suzuki and his adherents, and sometimes trenchant criticism, there is no question of the continuing impact of his method on music education internationally. Across the globe, there are multitudes of students and teachers following this approach. There are associations for teachers in numerous countries and regions, and since 1983, a coalition of international Suzuki Associations organizations, The International Suzuki Association has been an umbrella organization, coordinating efforts, maintaining standards, and protecting the name of Suzuki *per se* (see International Suzuki Association website). Different sources make claims about the numbers of teachers of the method, estimated to be in the thousands (or tens of thousands), with students, estimated in the hundreds of thousands.

The approach continues to be a subject of debate. For example, Taichi Akutsu cites M. Kojima's discussion of recent changes in Suzuki teaching in Japan and notes "a lack of investigation pertaining to contemporary uses and changes in pedagogy after Suzuki's death."[48] Hendricks notes an increasing emphasis on pedagogical matters in the *American Suzuki Journal* and decreasing discussion of Suzuki's philosophy. She argues that "it is Suzuki's philosophy of love and the potential for every child to learn that sets Suzuki teaching apart from other music education approaches."[49] Greater attention appears to have been given to the practical applications of the approach, with less discussion of the overall philosophy that drove Suzuki and his ideas for education. Pedagogical matters such as the acquisition and development of instrumental technique seem to have been increasingly codified. Akutsu confirms that

> the actual lessons also have become more rigid with less communication among learners, caregivers, and teachers . . . there are clear benefits, especially in technical aspects of violin learning, [but] the family atmosphere and playful stance, which were unique to the Suzuki Method, have diminished in the past 40 years.[50]

One of the interesting aspects of Suzuki's music teaching approach is that it accords with German violin instruction, rather than Japanese traditional instrumental teaching. Margaret Mehl points out that the Suzuki method should be judged "on its pedagogical merits rather than on its Japanese provenance."[51] The latter may be more connected to the philosophical tenets and styles of teaching and learning. Many years ago, a Japanese colleague pointed out to me that, musically, the Suzuki method was not her mother tongue, but it is more complicated than that. There has been a long history of the adaptation of Western music in Japan, in society and particularly in school music.[52] This does not negate the revolutionary effect of this approach; it just emphasizes that this is a fascinating contribution to music teaching and learning, one that, once it occurred, could not be ignored. George Coleman, the reviewer of Suzuki's *Nurtured by Love* in the *Australian Journal of Music Education*, captured it well writing that "this is not exactly a book on how to play the violin. It is rather a great teacher's ideas on the child's total human development, and applicable not only to violin playing, but to all fields of learning."[53] Over years of pedagogical application and adaptation for different educational and social contexts, the philosophical underpinning of Suzuki's work seems to have been less well maintained. It is time for a reappraisal of how the method is employed by its adherents, possibly with a return to the playfulness that was the signature of Suzuki's teaching.

NOTES

1. Biographical data based on material in Shin'ichi Suzuki, *Nurtured by Love. A New Approach to Education* (New York: Exposition Press, 1969); Masaaki Honda, *Talent Education. A Program for Early Development* (Tokyo, Japan: Early Development Association, 1970); Masaaki Honda, *The Vehicle of Music. Reflections on a Life with Shinichi Suzuki and the Talent Education Movement* (Miami, FL: Summy-Birchard, 2002).

2. Taichi Akutsu, "Changes after Suzuki: A Retrospective Analysis and Review of Contemporary Issues Regarding the Suzuki Method in Japan," *International Journal of Music Education* 38, no. 1 (2020): 18–35.

3. Suzuki, *Nurtured by Love*, 79.

4. Marquis Tokugawa was the fifth son of Lord Matsudaira of Echizen Province and had been adopted by Owari Tokugawa. Marquis Tokugawa later became honorary president of the Talent Education Institute. Honda, *Talent Education*, 102.

5. German composer, violinist, teacher and writer. Albert E. Weir, ed. *The Macmillan Encyclopedia of Music and Musicians in One Volume* (London: Macmillan and Co., 1938), 956.

6. Norman Lebrecht, "Just in: Suzuki Empire Strikes Back at Fraud Allegations," Slipped Disc, Last modified November 1, 2014, https://slippedisc.com/2014/11/just-in-suzuki-empires-strikes-back-at-fraud-allegations/

7. Akutsu, "Changes after Suzuki," 18–35.

8. Suzuki, *Nurtured by Love*, 7.

9. Hondo, *Talent Education*, 35.

10. Michael L. Mark. *Contemporary Music Education* (New York: Schirmer Books, 1978), 136.

11. Mark, *Contemporary Music Education*, 136.

12. Hondo, *Talent Education*, 11.

13. Hondo, *Talent Education*, passim.

14. Hondo, *Talent Education*, 2.

15. Honda, *The Vehicle of Music*, 87.

16. Honda, *Talent Education*, 6.

17. Alfred Garson, "Learning with Suzuki: Seven Questions Answered." *Music Educators Journal* 56, no. 6 (1970): 64–154.

18. Based in Helsinki, *Hufvudstadsbladet* is the highest-circulation Swedish-language newspaper in Finland.

19. Honda, *Talent Education*, 34.

20. Garson, "Learning with Suzuki," 153.

21. Honda, *The Vehicle of Music*, 103; Clifford A. Cook, *Suzuki Education in Action: A Story of Talent Training from Japan* (New York: Exposition Press, 1970).

22. In 2009, Muskingum College became Muskingum University.

23. John Kendall, "A Report on Japan's Phenomenal Young Violinists," *Violins and Violinists*, 20, no. 6 (November-December, 1959), 241–244, 249.

24. Kendall, "Japan's Phenomenal Young Violinists," 241.

25. Honda, *The Vehicle of Music*, 107.

26. Honda, *The Vehicle of Music*, 38.

27. The group comprised Dr and Mrs Shinichi Suzuki, Dr Masaaki Honda, Mr Hachiro Hirose (Instructor), Mrs Schizuko Suzuki (Accompanist), Mitomi Kasuya (six) with mother, Isako Fukazawa (six) with mother, Chiharu Tamura (six), Keiko Fukuda (six), Yasuko Ohtani (seven) with mother, Asako Hata (seven), Ryugo Hayano (ten), Fumiyo Kaneko (twelve) Yoshibumi Kawana (8) with mother.

28. Honda, 2002, gives an account of the itinerary and repeated performances and lectures.

29. Honda, *The Vehicle of Music*, 41.

30. They performed at Wayne State University, Detroit, Wichita University, Kansas, the University of Arizona, Tucson, Arizona, San Fernando State College, near Los Angeles, for the California String Teachers' Association, San Mateo and on the way home trip stopped in Honolulu, performing with the Honolulu Youth Symphony (Honda, *Talent Education*, 42).

31. Mark, *Contemporary Music Education*, 140.

32. Honda, *The Vehicle of Music*, 43.

33. Suzuki, *Nurtured by Love*, 116.

34. James A. Keene, *A History of Music Education in the United States* (Hanover and London: University Press of New England, 1982), 352.

35. Honda, *Talent Education*, 28.

36. Clifford A. Cook, *Suzuki Education in Action: A Story of Talent Training from Japan* (New York: Exposition Press, 1970), 101.

37. Mark, *Contemporary Music Education*, 1978.

38. Diana Tillson, "Teaching Suzuki in a Public School System," in *The Suzuki Concept: An Introduction to a Successful Method for Early Music Education*, eds. Elizabeth Mills and St. Therese Cecile Murphy (Berkeley and San Francisco: Diabolo Press, 1973), 131–137.

39. Augustus Brathwaite, "Suzuki Training: Musical Growth or Hindrance?," *Music Educators Journal* 75, no. 2 (1988): 45.

40. Mark, *Contemporary Music Education*, 139.

41. Mark, *Contemporary Music Education*, 140.

42. Suzuki Association of the Americas, "Timeline," accessed December 29, 2021 https://suzukiassociation.org/about/timeline/

43. Alfred Garson, "The Suzuki Teaching Method," *Australian Journal of Music Education*, 4 (1969): 9–14.

44. Komlos's work was continued by his wife, Maxine and his daughter Alina in Adelaide, South Australia. Professor Max Cooke was an early supporter in Australia. Max Cooke, *Japanese Music Teaching Methods in Australia* (Sydney, NSW: The Australia/Japan Foundation, 1981).

45. Suzuki Association of the Americas, "Timeline."

46. Suzanne Leslie Blaker, "A Survey of Suzuki Violin Programs in Community Music Schools in the United States" (PhD diss., The Ohio State University, 1995), 4.
47. Margaret Mehl, "Cultural Translation in Two Directions: The Suzuki Method in Japan and Germany," *Research & Issues in Music Education*, 7, no. 1 (2009): n1.
48. Akutsu, "Changes after Suzuki," 21.
49. Karin S. Hendricks, "The Philosophy of Shinichi Suzuki: 'Music Education as Love Education.'" *Philosophy of Music Education Review* 19, no. 2 (2011): 136–154.
50. Akutsu, "Changes after Suzuki," 34.
51. Mehl, "Cultural Translation in Two Directions."
52. Sondra Wieland Howe, Mei-Ling Lai, and Lin-Yu Liou, "Isawa Shuji, Nineteenth-Century Administrator and Music Educator in Japan and Taiwan," *Australian Journal of Music Education*, no. 2 (2014), 93–105.
53. George Coleman, "Nurtured by Love—A New Approach to Education by Shinichi Suzuki," *Australian Journal of Music Education*, no. 16 (April 1975), 63.

BIBLIOGRAPHY

Akutsu, Taichi. "Changes after Suzuki: A retrospective analysis and review of contemporary issues regarding the Suzuki Method in Japan." *International Journal of Music Education* 38, no. 1 (2020): 18–35.

Brathwaite, Augustus. "Suzuki Training: Musical Growth or Hindrance?" *Music Educators Journal* 75, no. 2 (1988): 42–45.

Coleman, Georgie. "Nurtured By Love-a New Approach to Education [Book Review]." *Australian Journal of Music Education* 16 (1975): 63.

Cook, Clifford A. *Suzuki education in action: A story of talent training from Japan.* New York: Exposition Press, 1975 (2nd ed.).

Cooke, Maxwell. *Japanese music teaching methods in Australia.* Wilke & Company for the Australia/Japan Foundation, 1981.

Garson, Alfred. "The Suzuki teaching method." *Australian Journal of Music Education* 4 (1969): 9–14.

Garson, Alfred. "Learning with Suzuki: seven questions answered." *Music Educators Journal* 56, no. 6 (1970): 64–66, 153–154.

Hendricks, Karin S. "The philosophy of shinichi suzuki: "Music education as love education"." *Philosophy of Music Education Review* 19, no. 2 (2011): 136–154. https://doi.org/10.2979/philmusieducrevi.19.2.136

Honda, Masaaki. *Talent Education. A Program for Early Development.* Tokyo, Japan: Early Development Association, 1970.

Honda, Masaaki. *The Vehicle of Music: Reflections on a Life with Shinichi Suzuki and the Talent Education Movement.* New York: Alfred Music, 2002.

Howe, Sondra Wieland, Mei-Ling Lai, and Lin-Yu Liou. "Isawa Shuji, nineteenth-century administrator and music educator in Japan and Taiwan." *Australian Journal of Music Education* 2 (2014): 93–105.

Keene, James A. *A history of music education in the United States.* Glenbridge Publishing Ltd., 2009.Kendall, John. "A Report On Japan's Phenomenal Young

Violinists." *Violins and Violinists* 20, no. 6 (November–December, 1959): 241–244, 249.

Mark, Michael L. (1978). *Contemporary music education.* New York: Schirmer Books.

Mehl, Margaret. "Cultural Translation in Two Directions: The Suzuki Method in Japan and Germany." *Research and Issues in Music Education* 7, no. 1 (2009): n1. http://www.stthomas.edu/rimeonline/vol7/mehl.htm

Suzuki, Shin'ichi. "Nurtured by Love: A New Approach to Education. Translation by Waltraud Suzuki." New York: Exposition Press, 1969.

Suzuki, Shinichi. "Outline of Talent Education Method." *Violin and Violinists* 21, no. 2 (March–April, 1960), 59–62.

Chapter 5

Émile Jaques-Dalcroze and the Movement of Music

Karin Greenhead

Sometimes, an insight, idea, or event leads to the creation of work that goes beyond anything its creator first imagined.[1] Such was the case with the Swiss composer, performer, and animateur Émile Jaques-Dalcroze (1865–1950, henceforth Dalcroze) who, following his appointment as professor of harmony (1892) and solfège[2] (1893) at the Conservatoire de Genève, embarked on what became his lifework. In response to the deficits he identified in his students' musicianship and musical performance, Dalcroze introduced improvisation and modulation to the curriculum and experimented with using gesture and rhythmic movement to improve musical understanding and interpretation. In 1902, the Committee of the Conservatoire de Genève granted him permission to open a special class to trial a new method of rhythmic education, but, despite the growing interest and the evident success of his performances and public demonstrations, his experiments, frequent absences, and cavalier attitude irritated his superiors. In 1910 he resigned, moving to Germany and the garden-city of Hellerau, a suburb of Dresden, where his supporters were building a theater and training center for the development of his work. From 1911, until the outbreak of World War I in 1914, the general public and leading writers, directors, architects, artists, pedagogues, and psychologists from across the world came to study with him and his team of teachers or to attend performances of groundbreaking productions such as the Appia-Dalcroze *Orpheus and Eurydice* in Hellerau's *Festspielhaus*.[3,4]

From the turn of the twentieth century, Dalcroze's ideas influenced developments in Modern American Dance, German *Ausdruckstanz*, modern theater, somatic practices, and music-movement therapy.[5] His own work focused on his teaching, mounting productions and festivals, giving demonstrations, writing, and composition, but many of those who studied and worked with him took what they had learnt and developed their own artistic and therapeutic practices. The turbulent upheavals and migrations of the twentieth century dispersed students and teachers all over the world, and training in DE developed separately in different countries, while Dalcroze's ideas, with or without his name, took root in music and music education, piano pedagogy, dance, theater, physical education, somatic practices, therapy, and other fields.[6]

One hundred and twenty years later, Dalcroze Eurhythmics (DE), as it came to be called, has emerged from a period during which it was known chiefly as a music education method for children, its many other applications in all the arts and in personal and social development and therapeutic contexts, temporarily forgotten. More recently, his methods have attracted international attention across diverse disciplines, including medicine, therapy, and education. The application of DE in performance contexts has been rediscovered and further developed,[7] while greater understanding of its potential has led to new, experimental, and groundbreaking work with seniors and patients with Parkinson's.[8] These developments are informed by neuroscientific discoveries that support DE's teaching and learning processes. A sudden increase in research and publication has raised awareness of the significance of Dalcroze's ideas, revealing DE once more as a form of music education with applications in other arts disciplines, elite performance, and mental and physical health and well-being.[9]

In this chapter, I look at the nature and practice of DE in an attempt to uncover the sources of its extraordinary range of applications and seemingly insuppressible perennity. I consider the many formative influences that led Dalcroze to develop his method, its content and techniques—a method that emphasizes process and requires flexibility and creativity of its teachers but has proven hard to describe, even for its practitioners. The dance historian Selma Odom concluded that it was "essentially a way of teaching and learning,"[10] while the composer and Dalcroze student, Frank Martin, noted its diverse applications,

> It is above all a pedagogical method ... originally for teaching music but also a way of working and researching ... founded on the principle of never working the brain, the intellect, the psyche, intelligence, emotions and feelings without connecting them closely to the body, or asking for a gesture or movement, however simple or complex, without attaching it to feeling or mental effort. ... At every moment during the rhythmics lesson students must respond to a musical phrase with feeling while grasping its elements mentally if they are to realise it in natural bodily movement or, depending on the situation, by using the conventions of rhythmics technique.[11]

DE is a living method that, going beyond the purview of music education, reveals a capacity for renewal and responsiveness to the artistic, health-related, personal, and social needs of people and the times and places in which they live.[12] The chapter concludes with a consideration of the future of DE and the difficulties in disseminating this practice since, despite its demonstrated efficacy and usefulness, it is taught in few educational institutions worldwide and the number of fully qualified teachers remains small.

ÉMILE JAQUES-DALCROZE IN CONTEXT

Dalcroze[13,14] was born in 1865 in Vienna, at that time a city in ferment with new ideas in politics, psychology, education, and the arts. His father was descended from three generations of pastors which may be the origin of his reforming zeal. From an early age, he and Hélène, his sister, were encouraged to sing and play by their mother, who was influenced by Pestalozzi's ideas, and Émile composed and performed songs, pantomimes, and musical plays. When he was ten years old, the family returned to Switzerland and had a very different life.

In Geneva, Dalcroze attended the Collège Jean Calvin, where he had some excellent teachers and generally did well but was not happy. He ascribed his interest in teaching and its reform to bad memories of his schooldays,

> Most of the teachers imposed tasks on us without ever explaining the reason for them. . . . They showed no interest in our hearts or even our minds, their only concerns being the obedience of their little servants and the filling up of our memories.[15]

As for the music lessons, "there was nothing about sonority, melody, harmony, emphasis . . . no emotion or style, no examples of beautiful compositions; in a word, no music!" Furthermore, "the teachers of gymnastics did not know how to teach the close relationship between mind and body."[16] The Collège also celebrated no *fêtes*, the traditional Swiss festivals in which the entire community sang, told stories, and danced together and which were for him the most joyous and miraculous initiation into social life.

Dalcroze left Geneva to study in Paris and Vienna. In Paris, he studied music with Gabriel Fauré, while training in theater arts with Talbot of the Comédie-Française, and encountered Delsarte's system of bodily expression of emotion which influenced his early teaching. While studying contemporary music and performing in cabaret, he pursued various ways of integrating music, text, and gesture and hesitated between a career in music and one in the theater.[17] Among the influences on Dalcroze's development were two particularly revered teachers, Adolf Prosnitz, who had his students improvise commentaries in their own style on the repertoire they played, and the theoretician Mathis Lussy who taught him the importance of anacrusis in music and gesture[18] and the study of agogic nuance,[19] both of which were key to understanding the interrelationships of body, mind, and musical feeling.

In 1886, Dalcroze accepted a post for one season as conductor of a theater orchestra in Algiers. There he encountered Arabic music and dance and was inspired by the performers' freedom of movement, their mastery of complex rhythms, and the drama of their performances. He considered the theater orchestra incapable of playing in time, so he used gestures to help them and later stated that the origins of his method lay in the experiences he had in Algeria. These experiences and those he had with his teachers all came together when he became accompanist to the great Belgian violinist Eugène Ysaÿe in 1891. Ysaÿe, a warm and generous man, was very demanding regarding musical interpretation, and Dalcroze was inspired by his ideas as they toured through Germany together.[20] He had ingenious ways of practicing on the train including following the cadence and accents of the wheels while rehearsing his bow strokes in imagination. He practiced his rubato by placing the first beat of the bar on the arrival of each passing telegraph pole and told Dalcroze that he wanted to rely on him maintaining a steady pulse and leave him free to use rubato and return to tempo as he wished.[21] He also used movement when working on his repertoire.

One day, Dalcroze heard strange, grunting noises coming from Ysaÿe's room, and tentatively opening the door he saw Ysaÿe running and jumping, punching the air with his fists in an attempt, he said to get the *Polonaise* of Vieuxtemps into his body: "The sound vibrations must penetrate us entirely right down to our viscera, and rhythmic movement must enliven all our muscular system, without resistance or exaggeration."[22] There is a striking similarity between his words and Dalcroze's later writing. They were firm friends until Ysaÿe's death in 1931, and he remained a central point of reference in Dalcroze's teaching.[23]

Dalcroze developed his method experimentally and looked to a number of people for support, among them the psychologist Claparède who confirmed the validity of his methods and the theater reformer Adolphe Appia from whom he learnt about rhythmic space and how to use it expressively. He was the eye to Dalcroze's ear and probably the first to see the full potential of Dalcroze's work which, he thought, would in time change the brains of people. Today, neuroscientific research confirms Appia's prophetic intuition in showing that the brain develops deep connections between music and movement that are affected when they are brought together both actively and in imagination. A full account of the research in this area is beyond the limits of this chapter, but three articles in English can be found in the *Actes du congrés de l'Institut Jaques-Dalcroze*, 2015.[24]

Dalcroze felt that his conservatoire pupils' innate musicality had been crushed by the education they had received.[25] In a 1925 essay addressed "To Mothers" worried about their children's reluctance to practice, Dalcroze underlined the importance of developing a number of essential faculties before taking piano lessons. These include a love for music, a desire to make music oneself, a sense of beauty, well-developed aural skills, rhythmical feeling, and singing. He thought that teaching only required awakening and freeing what was natural to human nature and the appropriate education of the individual as a social being. His method was intended to foster "the blossoming of personality,"[26] emotional engagement, and the development of the imagination. In his view, piano practice "undertaken without a certain aural culture, utterly oppresses the individuality and does away with the spirit of enquiry. The duty of a pedagogue is to teach children to become—and to remain—themselves."[27] These expressions and ideas are central to Dalcroze's thinking and pervade his writing.

DALCROZE EURHYTHMICS—THREE-IN-ONE

This account of the method draws on the guiding document for training professional Dalcroze teachers,[28] *The Dalcroze Identity*, and on my practice as explored in my doctoral thesis, *Dynamic Rehearsal and Dalcroze Eurhythmics*.[29]

DE consists of three interrelated branches: rhythmics, a movement class in which all the elements of music are studied in and through movement; solfège;[30] and improvisation. These three are applied in a fourth, *Plastique Animée*—generally the realization of a piece of music in movement. Figure 5.1 shows this structure underpinned by theory, philosophy, practice, and principles, all of which derive from DE, which, as noted earlier, was developed not according to any theory or model but experimentally in response to a perceived need.

While professional training will include all of these elements, an application of DE to a specific field or situation may emphasize certain aspects or practices more than others or even exclude them. In either case, the principle of developing the work creatively on the ground in response to a current need while using its ways and means of teaching and learning and remaining true to its principles is an identifying feature of the method. This remains the modus operandi of DE today both during lessons and in the development of the method generally.

The core of the method is the rhythmics class. During these lessons, students learn to use and share space and to match their bodily movement (locomotor or gestural) to musical sound, mostly that of the teacher's instrumental

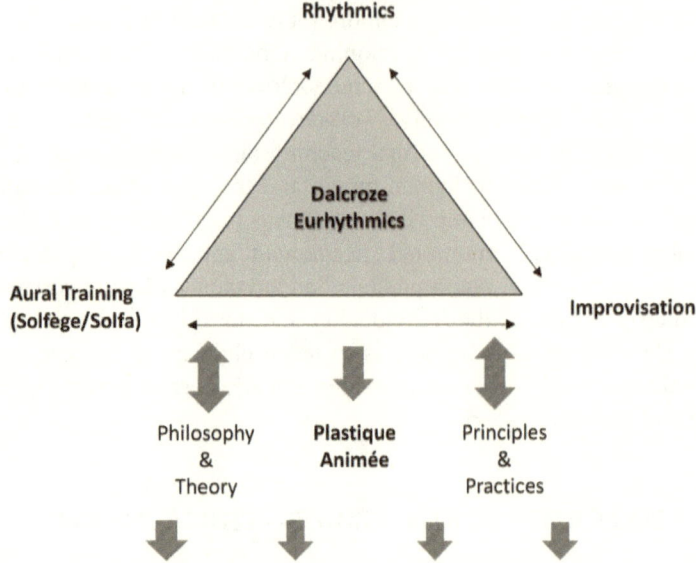

Figure 5.1 Dalcroze Eurhythmics: Three-in-One. Author.

improvisation, although repertoire in various styles is also used. The main instrument used in teaching is the piano for the wide range of pitch and dynamics it offers together with the possibility of playing in two or more parts and creating harmonic color. The teacher's improvisation should incite a response in movement in students and often replaces verbal instruction as the main means of teaching them. In matching their movement response to the music they hear, students "latch on"[31] to the music and follow it so that, by means of music, ear and body are tuned together.

In most of the first lessons, students will use natural movements such as walking, running, skipping, jumping, and swaying and learn to identify these motional qualities in music. Through games and exercises, they use and share space with others and learn to start, stop, and change direction and speed with ease, gaining control of balance and developing focus and adaptability. They are invited to match their steps to the pulse and rhythm patterns and to experience and understand differences of duration and meter through bodily experience before naming them or looking at notational symbols. Their studies include discovering and expressing dynamic changes and differences in metrical feeling and musical style while working collaboratively in pairs and groups, using materials such as balls, scarves, sticks, hoops, ropes, and tambours and a gestural system of analyzing meter using full arm beats. These lessons also contain typical Dalcroze exercises in quick response, inner hearing and feeling, canon, and memorization, most of which are guided by the teacher's improvisation. As the students gain skill and confidence, lessons will become more complex, incorporating solfège content, *Plastique Animée*, working with text and visual images, their own musical improvisation, and the study of repertoire in diverse styles.

While rhythmics is a kind of aural training in movement, there is a separate solfège class using singing, rhythm, improvisation, space, gesture, and whole-body movement in the development of aural perception and a sense of pitch, pitch relations, and harmony and their notation in diatonic and nondiatonic music. These lessons include solo and part-singing, sight-singing, the study of repertoire, and choral conducting.

Improvisation, the third principal branch of DE, is a means of teaching and learning in rhythmics and solfège lessons. Instrumental and vocal improvisation is also studied separately using the tools of rhythmics and solfège. In improvisation lessons, students study different kinds of musical vocabulary such as intervals, scales, chords, and diverse musical styles in order to use them when creating their own music. They improvise in pairs and groups and learn to play to incite or accompany movement. Students also study harmony and composition either separately or within the improvisation course and create their own, often multidisciplinary works that bring together every aspect of their studies. In professional training the core subjects with *Plastique Animée* are supported by additional lessons in Dalcroze pedagogy, principles and practices, the Dalcroze Subjects,[32] and related studies in piano, harmony, composition, movement technique, ensemble singing, voice production, and some kind of body awareness method such as Eutony or Feldenkrais.

THE PROCESS

Many rhythmics exercises take the form of "follow the music," in which the teacher plays and the students move according to what is happening in the music or what it suggests. They may also counterpoint the music, play with its elements or alternate between going against it and following it. Trying to show what the music is *not* is a good way of finding out what it *is*. There are many different kinds of "follow" exercises.[33]

The students' first response to the teacher's improvisation is pre-reflective. They latch on to the music and literally "go with the flow." When the teacher notices that students are becoming increasingly aware of the musical content and how it affects them, she invites them to experiment with different responses and to analyze what they are hearing using movement and gesture. For example, the ability to follow, maintain, and produce a steady, slow tempo is established by measuring the time between beats, not only by counting but also by using gestural or circular claps or smooth, continuous steps that move through space from one beat to the next providing a global sensation of duration and tempo. In the circle described between the meeting of hands on one beat to their meeting again on the following one, nerves and muscles experience the sensation of time passing, while the eyes observe the movement. At some point, any supporting music is removed and the students, having to rely on themselves, hold the tempo by maintaining the movement. Following a signal to stop, they pause, remembering the sensation of the movement just suspended and reproduce it when asked to start again. In this way students acquire a reliable sense of duration and tempo. This process of internalizing bodily experience engrains knowledge in memory through repetition with variation (such as playing with the direction of movement, dynamic changes, contrasting or combining it with other durations, speeds and patterns, creating movement canons) and can be recalled and reproduced at will. This process of working from a response in pre-reflective, improvised body movement to a response that is considered and planned suggests that the primary movement response to music is actual as DeNora implies and challenges current scholar's assertions that movement in response to music is metaphorical in nature.[34]

The same process applies to the study of all the musical elements. Through experience in movement guided by music, the student's body learns what forte, leggiero, legato, 6/8 time, two-against-three, sforzato, diminuendo, musical articulations and emphases, and harmonic changes of all kinds *feel* like. This bodily acquired knowledge is inseparably linked to emotion and other kinds of feeling (such as the feeling of being together or being right) and informs cognitive understandings. As all this takes place within a social context, students learn how to relate and tune in to others in a variety of ways, such as being in perfect unison; being different but together in canon or counterpoint; separating and coming together; deciding, showing clearly and knowing that they are seen; leading and following and adjusting the energy put into bouncing a ball on the first beat of a bar so that another can receive it easily. This social learning and coconstruction of knowledge in which students experience themselves developing personal skills together with others not only improves ensemble skills, projection, and communication, but it also enormously enhances both musical and teaching and learning experience and is a key ingredient in the therapeutic effect of lessons reported by participants. The process can also be applied to the study of phrase and cadence and to whole pieces of music, simple or complex, and is probably what Appia meant when he said that Dalcroze's work would change people's brains. In short, through music and movement in DE, the body corrals the sensory-kinaesthetic system and emotions to feed the brain with impressions and sensations so that it can learn, understand, and develop cognitive and executive abilities.

By means of improvised music, the teacher proposes musical questions and puzzles inciting the students to use space and move. Seeing their movement response, the teacher replies by modifying her improvisation (faster, slower, denser, more spacious, and accented) or changing it completely (a different meter, a different rhythm pattern), and the students adapt. In this way, what my teacher, Elizabeth Vanderspar, called "a kind of conversation" is built up between the teacher and the students. In this dialogue, the teacher also creates surprises in the form of quick response or "Hipp-Hopp" exercises. These generally include the use of agreed signals following which the students perform an agreed action. For example, the teacher plays crotchets, and the students walk. When she calls a number, say "two," the students subdivide the next beat into two by stepping quavers and returning to walking. Gradually numbers between two and six are called with increasing frequency. This exercise requires and develops quick verbal processing, quick movement reactions, and good use of space and control of acceleration and of the pause on the next long note so as not to fall over. The exercise is then adapted so that the signal is played instead of called, so when a triplet is played the students subdivide the next beat into three (see figure 5.2). If a triplet is followed immediately by a duplet, the students are tricked into performing two-against-three since they step the evenly spaced triplet while hearing the duplet. In the hands of a skillful teacher, this often produces smiles as the students begin to realize what is going on.[35]

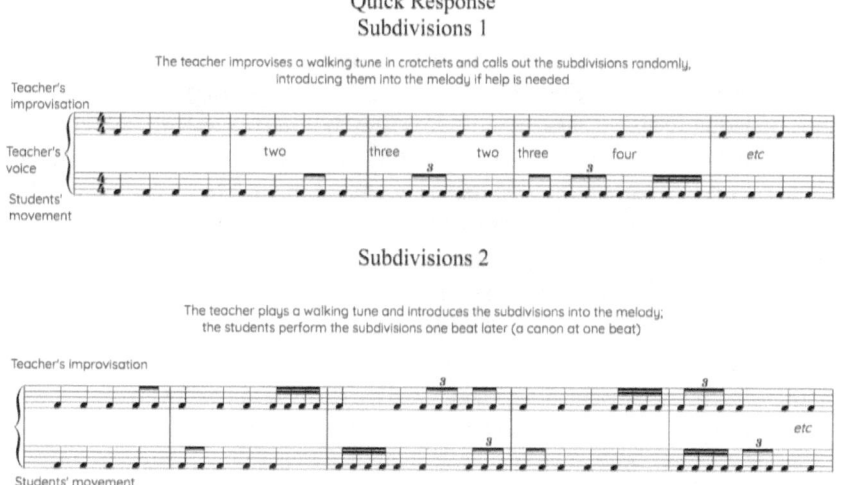

Figure 5.2   **Quick Response: Subdivisions.** Author.

Any discussion of the method must include the use of materials mentioned earlier. These balls, sticks, scarves, beanbags, and other materials are not "props": they are educational tools or instruments and should be of good quality, enjoyable to use, and attractive to the eye and the sense of touch which they awaken. They provide stimulus to the imagination and operate as extensions of the body into space and a means of communicating intentions to others. Each material provides the student with opportunities for learning different sensations and qualities of movement and different skills. The Rhythmics Gymnastic (RG) ball is an important tool for learning the sense of rebound and an elasticity in movement essential to good tone production. Its weight and size encourage movement of the whole body in relation to space and gravity compared with the tennis ball which requires more manual dexterity. Materials are also useful in teaching those with poor coordination, loss of hearing or vision, or impaired locomotion. Beginning in 2020 and during lockdown under Covid-19, my students took their lessons online in their own rooms, and materials (sometimes objects to hand such as kitchen utensils or empty water bottles) were extremely useful tools for building sensory perception and in creative work.

Most of the exercises used in lessons are polyvalent and multimodal. They are engaging, fun to do, and also challenging. Students wrestle with their polyrhythms or the effort to sustain a long, smooth phrase line through to its cadence. Some of the practices in Dalcroze's early lessons were abandoned as outmoded such as the lessons in breathing or, in some instances, the full arm beats that allow the student to feel the different quality of each beat in a meter rather than just mark time.[36] Today, the benefits of these early techniques are being rediscovered as practitioners begin to understand what they offer.

Students frequently report epiphanic, transformational, or life-changing experiences in lessons. For the first time, suddenly or perhaps after many lessons of growing awareness or skill, they find themselves able to hear the bass line, perform a cross-rhythm with ease, or sustain a phrase and so experience success in doing something that had long eluded them. They also say that DE provides them with a "creative toolbox" for solving performance problems and teaching.[37] DE reveals human nature and addresses and works with it.

Dalcroze explained the aims and benefits of his method as follows:

> The creation in the body of a rapid and light system of communication between all the agents of movement and thought gives free and untrammeled action to the personality; it strengthens and vivifies this personality in the most amazing way. It also gives the individual the self-confidence necessary for well-balanced vital functions, since it enables him easily to give effect to each of his conceptions.[38]

His work had a double goal: the preparation of the artist and, concomitantly, the liberation of the natural person from unnatural constraints. The training of this free person in musicianship and self-mastery through music would bring the ability to express oneself, freedom and joy. "I like joy, for it is life. I preach joy, for it alone gives the power of creating useful and lasting work,"[39] and in the rhythmics class, the child will "conceive a profound joy of an elevated character, a new factor in ethical progress, a new stimulus to will power."[40]

The preceding account of DE gives some indication of why it is popular with so many students and why they return for Summer Schools and other events and teach, even in very insecure situations. Unlike most methods, it can be taught effectively to students of any age or stage from infants, preschool, primary and secondary school, and university. It benefits students in conservatoires of music, dance, and drama; adult amateurs; and professional performers and is effective in therapeutic situations for those with Specific Learning Differences (SpLDs), those recovering from trauma, Parkinson's patients, and seniors.

However, Dalcroze himself was not without his critics including the conductor Ernest Ansermet, an admirer who nevertheless felt he was overly concerned with metrics, rhythmic detail, and complexity at the expense of cadence.[41] The early period of Dalcroze's work was characterized by daring and creative imagination, but he became increasingly conservative in response to the heavy criticism he received in Paris. Today, teachers under pressure to produce a measurable result may tend to focus on elements that are easier to teach, such as beat and musical literacy, and neglect expressive elements requiring more exploration, especially when time and space are short. Researchers, too, have generally preferred to study those elements that are easily measurable and containable, all of which give a distorted impression of DE and its potential and affect both the understanding and dissemination of it.

DISSEMINATION

The practice of DE has traditionally been passed on from teacher to student as an oral tradition or apprenticeship with teachers choosing the areas in which they want to apply their training. While difficult to describe, it is easily understood in lessons as students discover it for themselves through experience and show their knowledge in their actions. This knowledge, acquired nonverbally, touches and moves every aspect of the person, the body, all its senses, mind, and spirit; intellect, emotion, and intuition; and memory, imagination, and creativity. It is difficult to explain its range, depth, and complexity in a few words as almost anything one might say would be simultaneously correct and misleading. This situation is not helped by the fact that very little of Dalcroze's writing has been translated. In short, DE is difficult to market. In response to the need for instructional literature, the new Translation and Publication Committee of the Collège of the Institut Jaques-Dalcroze, Geneva, has launched a project to understand what texts are used and needed in the training centers worldwide and to plan for translation of the more essential of Dalcroze's writings, all of which are in French with only two books translated into few languages.

In the UK, most Dalcroze teachers work in schools where music is not part of the core curriculum, the teacher has few hours, and the focus is on rhythmics or rhythmic-solfège for younger children. Those who teach in specialist music or dance schools or conservatoires are usually engaged to teach only rhythmics classes because other teachers teach the rest of the musicianship course (often via the Kodály method), and any improvisation classes tend to focus on jazz styles. Only seeing rhythmics classes, sometimes with some solfège, creates a false impression of DE and compromises any understanding of how the whole process works over time.

It is interesting to compare Dalcroze's reforms in music education at the Conservatoire and the reasons for them with the situation in tertiary music education today. There are few, if any, classes devoted to musical rhythm, although vocal and instrumental teachers complain about their students' poor mastery of it. Aural training seems unconnected to musical feeling and interpretation and may be perfunctory. Students benefit from a coherent training, but for reasons related to policy, funding, and institutional structure, most courses in tertiary institutions now consist of short modules bolted on without apparent consideration of how they might relate to one another. Education has become subject to a market in which money seems to be the only value: lessons are "delivered," students are "instructed," and outcomes are tested. In schools, music education is not a valued core subject and may be taught by nonspecialists since teachers can be required to teach subjects in which they have very little training. Short teacher training courses tend to focus on policy and class management rather than music pedagogy and the acquisition of practical skills such as the ability to lead students to make discoveries for themselves through their own bodily experience. The very aspects of music-making and music education that give music its unique, educational, social, and artistic value are consistently undermined by the way it and the education of its teachers are treated. Assuredly "Movement moves the mind and engraves knowledge in memory"[42] which in turn develops agency and a sense of self in learners. Both music itself and the rich gifts offered by DE are needed now more than ever in situations where people, communities, and whole nations are fractured. As a response to

Table 5.1 Glossary

British English Dalcroze and music terminology	American English Dalcroze and music terminology
Dalcroze Eurhythmics	Sometimes Jaques-Dalcroze Eurhythmics
rhythmics	eurhythmics
crotchet	quarter-note
quaver	eighth note
bar	measure

demonstrable need, DE could be considered the most cost-effective of courses since it delivers so much on so many levels in a single lesson.

Although many schools and music centers actively seek teachers with a training in DE, there are few places where such teachers can be trained except on private training courses after they have graduated and at their own expense. Such courses often take place during evenings, weekends and holiday periods because the students work during the day. The numbers of teachers are growing, but the knowledge and skill required to teach DE in its fullness or apply it in a particular field cannot be acquired quickly or purely online as presence with other students and a teacher in an adequate space is essential.

At its best, DE is a transformative, even delicious experience that catches body and soul and is a joy to teach. It has more in common with the slow food movement than instant coffee and could align itself with slow food's way of thinking: attentive, grounded, and dwelling in the moment; tasting, exploring, experimenting, making connections, and creating; and mindful and tuned in to the subject of attention for the benefit of self and others (table 5.1).

NOTES

1. The teacher is referred to as she in this chapter to avoid confusion between a non-gendered singular "they" and "they" the students. All translations by Karin Greenhead unless otherwise attributed.

2. The French term *solfège* will be used to refer to aural training, ear training and solfa throughout this chapter for simplicity and convenience.

3. Alfred Berchthold, *Émile Jaques-Dalcroze et Son Temps* (Republished in Lausanne: Éditions L'Age d'Homme, 2005, original work, 1965).

4. Wolf Dohrn, *Der Rythmus, ein Jahrbuch herausgeg. Von der Bildungsanstalt Jaques-Dalcroze Dresden-Hellerau*, 1 Band (Jena: Eugen Diederichs, 1911). Lessons began in 1910 in Dresden and included professional training, personal and professional development classes, and classes for local children. The teachers in Dresden-Hellerau included colleagues and students such as Nina Gorter, Paul Boepple, Suzanne Perrottet, Placido de Montoliu, Myriam Ramberg (Marie Rambert), Marie

Adama van Scheltema, Albert Jeanneret, Annie Beck, Elfriede Feudel, Valeria Kratina, Vera Griner (née Alvang) (see also Berchtold).

5. Karin Greenhead and John Habron, "The Touch of Sound: Dalcroze Eurhythmics as a Somatic Practice," *Journal of Dance and Somatic Practices* 7, no. 1 (2015): 93–112. doi: 10.1386/jdsp.7.1.3_2.

6. Karin Greenhead, *Dynamic Rehearsal and Dalcroze Eurhythmics: a phenomenological investigation into participants' experiences and their implications for the practice, teaching and learning of music and musical performance* (PhD thesis, Royal Northern College of Music and Manchester Metropolitan University, 2019).

7. Karin Greenhead (London and Manchester, UK) whose Dynamic Rehearsal uses silent, actual, and imagined movement away from the instrument to improve performers' musical interpretation and performance and Diane Daly (Irish Chamber Orchestra and Limerick University, ROI) who uses movement while playing in ensemble performances with gifted young musicians. Conductor Kristin Bowtell (Australia) applied his Dalcroze knowledge to preparing his scores; Piano accompanist Chris van de Kuilen (Tilberg, Netherlands) to rehearsing his ensembles and teaching; and Sarah Mayo (Manchester, UK) to teaching young string players. These and other applications have been the subject of research and publication.

8. Research into the use of DE in working with seniors was initiated by gerontologist Dr. Reto Kressig and Dalcroze Diplômée Ruth Gianadda, who has become a specialist in this work. Its success in fall prevention and with dementia sufferers has led to the establishment of several centers in Switzerland where seniors receive regular lessons. The newer application to Parkinson's patients is proving very effective with results awaiting publication.

9. From 2013 the biennial International Conference of Dalcroze Studies (ICDS) has contributed to the research and publication in DE.

10. Selma Odom, "Delsartean Traces in Dalcroze Eurhythmics," *Mime Journal* 23, Article 9 (April, 2005): 137–151. doi: 10.5642/mimejournal.20052301,09.

11. Frank Martin, *Écrits sur la Rythmique et pour les Rythmiciens, les Pédagogues, les Musiciens* (Genève : Éditions Papillon, 1995), 21–22. Composer, Dalcroze student and then colleague, Martin taught improvisation and rhythmic theory at the Institut Jaques-Dalcroze, Geneva from 1928–1937.

12. These include non-Western cultures such as Japan, China, South Korea, ASEAN cultures, South Africa, and South America. Most teachers train in Western countries and use Western musical ideas and notation. They apply Dalcroze principles when working with every kind of music including non-Western styles.

13. This section draws heavily on Greenhead, "Dynamic Rehearsal," 2019.

14. At this stage he was Émile Jaques. He added "Dalcroze" to his name at his publisher's request to avoid confusion with another composer with the same name.

15. Émile Jaques-Dalcroze, *Notes Bariolées* (Genève: Édition Jeheber, 1948), 195. Dalcroze's accounts of his student life reveal him as an expert learner able to learn from both good and bad experiences.

16. Berchtold, "Émile Jaques-Dalcroze," 23–24.

17. Odom, "Delsartean Traces," 139–140.

18. In DE, anacrusis refers to every kind of preparation, gestural, sensory or musical, for an action, event, arrival or emphasis and is one of the most important subjects of study in DE. It goes beyond the notion of 'upbeat' which is one example of it.

19. Berchtold, "Émile Jaques-Dalcroze," 41–42. Nuance in music refers to expressive shading such as crescendo, diminuendo, staccato, legato, heavy, light... Agogic nuance is a nuance of time such as accelerando and ritenuto.

20. Greenhead, "Dynamic Rehearsal," 39–41.

21. Émile Jaques-Dalcroze, *Souvenirs, notes et critiques* (Neuchâtel: Éditions Victor Attinger, 1942), 43.

22. Jaques-Dalcroze, *Souvenirs*, 44.

23. Greenhead, "Dynamic Rehearsal," 39–41.

24. Silvia del Bianco, Sylvie Morgenegg & Hélène Nicolet (Eds.), *Pédagogie, Art et Science: L'Apprentissage par et pour la musique selon la méthode Jaques-Dalcroze: Actes du Congrés de l'Institut Jaques-Dalcroze, 2015* (Genève: Droz/ Haute École de Musique de Genève, 2017), Chapters 7, 8, 9. Also in research by gerontologist Reto Kressig, Eckart Altenmüller and many neuroscientists with interests in this area such as Robert J. Zatorre, Joyce L. Chen and Virginia P. Penhune, "When the Brain plays Music: Auditory-Motor Interactions in Music Perception and Production," *Nature Reviews Neuroscience* 8 (August 2007): 547–558.

25. Émile Jaques-Dalcroze, "An essay in the reform of music teaching in schools" (1905), in *Rhythm, Music and Education*, trans. Harold F. Rubinstein (Woking, Surrey: The Dalcroze Society, 1967, original work published 1921), 6–35.

26. Émile Jaques-Dalcroze, "L'education par le rythme et pour le rythme," *Le Rythme* 2, no.3 (1910): 22.

27. Émile Jaques-Dalcroze, The Piano and Musicianship (1925), in *Eurhythmics, Art and Education*, trans. Frederick Rothwell, ed. Cynthia Cox (London: Chatto & Windus, 1930), 129.

28. This section draws on Le Collège de l'Insitut Jaques-Dalcroze (CIJD), *The Dalcroze Identity: theory and Practice of Dalcroze Eurhythmics*, 2nd edition, eds. Karin Greenhead and Louise Mathieu (Geneva: Institut Jaques-Dalcroze, 2019), www.dalcroze.ch – le Collège; Greenhead, *Dynamic Rehearsal*, 2019; and Greenhead and Habron, *The Touch of Sound*, 2015.

29. Greenhead, "Dynamic Rehearsal," 2019.

30. See note 1

31. Tia DeNora, *Music in Everyday Life* (Cambridge, UK: Cambridge University Press, 2000).

32. The Dalcroze Subjects are the fundamental elements of experience and expression in nature, the world of human experience, and across the arts and form both the subject-matter of lessons and the ways of teaching and learning. See CIJD, *The Dalcroze Identity*, 2019.

33. Examples of "follow" exercises and a discussion of the role of improvisation in DE can be found in Karin Greenhead, "Adventures in Music and Movement – the essential means of teaching and learning in Dalcroze Pedagogy" filmed July 31, 2017, at the International Conference of Dalcroze Studies (ICDS3), Université Laval, Québec City, Québec, Canada. https://dalcroze-studies.com/View the ICDS gallery/

View all videos on YouTube/ICDS International Conference of Dalcroze Studies/ Videos/Keynote: Karin Greenhead (ICDS3) https://www.youtube.com/results?search_query=ICDS3%3AK.Greenhead.

34. Greenhead, "Dynamic Rehearsal," 61–65.
35. Greenhead, "Dynamic Rehearsal," 2019; and Greenhead and Habron, *The Touch of Sound*, 2015.
36. In recent years, the Institut Jaques-Dalcroze, Geneva, has brought the international professional Dalcroze training centers together to improve communication and mutual understanding in the worldwide Dalcroze community, offer support and introduce greater standardization in professional training.
37. Greenhead, "Dynamic Rehearsal," 2019, Chapters 5–9. "BiS" or Breakthroughs in Skilfulness featured strongly in students' self-reports on experiences in lessons and contribute to the joy experienced by both students and teachers in lessons.
38. Jaques-Dalcroze, "Eurhythmics, Art and Education," 55.
39. Émile Jaques-Dalcroze, From the lectures of Émile Jaques-Dalcroze (Address to Students, Vol 1, p. 41 et seq.), in *The Eurhythmics of Jaques-Dalcroze* (illustrated edition) (London: Constable and Company, 1915 reprinted by Dodo Press), 15.
40. Jaques-Dalcroze, "Rhythm, Music and Education," 98.
41. Ernest Ansermet, "Les Structures du Rythme, " in *Deuxième Congrés International du Rythme et de la Rythmique, Genève, 9-14 août 1965* (Genève: Institut Jaques-Dalcroze), 156–166.
42. Greenhead, "Dynamic Rehearsal," 275.

BIBLIOGRAPHY

Ansermet, Ernest. "Les Structures du Rythme." *Deuxième Congrés International du Rythme et de la Rythmique, Genève, 9-14 août 1965*, 156–166. Genève: Institut Jaques-Dalcroze, 1965.

Berchthold, Alfred. *Émile Jaques-Dalcroze et Son Temps*. Republished in Lausanne: Éditions L'Age d'Homme (original work 1965), 2005.

CIJD, see Le Collège de l'Institut Jaques-Dalcroze, 2019.

Del Bianco, Silvia, Sylvie Morgenegg, and Hélène Nicolet, eds. *Pédagogie, Art et Science : L'Apprentissage par et pour la musique selon la méthode Jaques-Dalcroze: Actes du Congrés de l'Institut Jaques-Dalcroze, 2015*. Genève: Droz/ Haute École de Musique de Genève, 2017.

DeNora, Tia. *Music in Everyday Life*. Cambridge, UK: Cambridge University Press, 2000.

Dohrn, Wolf. *Der Rythmus, ein Jahrbuch herausgeg. Von der Bildungsanstalt Jaques-Dalcroze Dresden-Hellerau*, 1 Band. Jena: Eugen Diederichs, 1911.

Greenhead, Karin. "Adventures in Music and Movement—the Essential Mean of teaching and Learning in Dalcroze Pedagogy. Filmed July 31, 2017 at the International Conference of Dalcroze Studies (ICDS3), Université Laval, Québec City, Québec, Canada. https://dalcroze-studies.com/View the ICDS gallery/View all videos on YouTube/ICDS International Conference of Dalcroze Studies/ Videos/Keynote: Karin Greenhead (ICDS3)

Greenhead, Karin. *Dynamic Rehearsal and Dalcroze Eurhythmics: A Phenomenological Investigation into Participants' Experiences and Their Implications for the Practice, Teaching and Learning of Music and Musical Performance.* PhD thesis, Royal Northern College of Music and Manchester Metropolitan University, 2019. British Library, EThOS, 2020.

Greenhead, Karin and John Habron. "The Touch of Sound: Dalcroze Eurhythmics as a Somatic Practice." *Journal of Dance and Somatic Practices* 7, no. 1 (2015): 93–112, 2015. doi: 10.1386/jdsp.7.1.3_2

Jaques-Dalcroze, Émile. "L'education par le rythme et pour le rythme." *Le Rythme* 2, no.3 (1910).

Jaques-Dalcroze, Émile. "From the lectures of Émile Jaques-Dalcroze (Address to Students, Vol 1, 41 et seq. *The Eurhythmics of Jaques-Dalcroze* (illustrated edition). London: Constable and Company, 1915 (reprinted by Dodo Press), 12–16.

Jaques-Dalcroze, Émile. "The Piano and Musicianship (1925)." *Eurhythmics, Art and Education.* Translated by Frederick Rothwell, ed. Cynthia Cox, 118–144. London: Chatto & Windus, 1930.

Jaques-Dalcroze, Émile. "An essay in the reform of music teaching in schools (1905). "*Rhythm, music and education.*" Translated by Harold F. Rubinstein, 6–35. Woking, Surrey: The Dalcroze Society, 1967 (original work published 1921).

Jaques-Dalcroze, Émile. *Souvenirs, notes et critiques.* Neuchâtel: Éditions Victor Attinger, 1942.

Jaques-Dalcroze, Émile. *Notes Bariolées.* Genève: Édition Jeheber, 1948.

Le Collège de l'Insitut Jaques-Dalcroze (CIJD), *The Dalcroze Identity: theory and Practice of Dalcroze Eurhythmics,* 2nd edition, edited by Karin Greenhead and Louise Mathieu. Geneva: Institut Jaques-Dalcroze, 2019. www.dalcroze.ch – Informations pratiques—organisation—le Collège—informations.

Martin, Frank. *Écrits sur la Rythmique et pour les Rythmiciens, les Pédagogues, les Musiciens.* Genève: Éditions Papillon, 1995.

Odom, Selma. "Delsartean Traces in Dalcroze Eurhythmics." *Mime Journal* 23, Article 9 (April, 2005): 137–151. doi: 10.5642/mimejournal.20052301,09

Zatorre, Robert J., Joyce L. Chen, and Virginia P. Penhune. "When the Brain plays Music: Auditory-Motor Interactions in Music Perception and Production." *Nature Reviews Neuroscience* 8 (August 2007): 547–558.

Part 2

INFLUENCES OF CULTURAL SHIFTS IN SOCIETY ON TEACHING AND LEARNING

Throughout the twentieth century, music has maintained an at times intimate and symbiotic relationship with science and technologies that have shaped thinking and invention within the artform and how it is taught. The recording, storing, transferring, transporting, and manipulating music mark the ways in which music education has adapted to utilize music and technology in evolving ways. From a social sciences perspective, the way we come together, commune, perform and learn, has evolved in step with the changing attitudes to collaboration and development as musicians and thinkers in and on music.

In chapter 6, Leon de Bruin responds to the development of jazz education and the changing ways we engage with the subject matter and the act of learning. Surveying Jazz music's educational impress from band-stand to educational institution, de Bruin describes first the barriers to its inclusion, its gradual acceptance as a legitimate academic and artistic pursuit, and its diaspora and adaptation worldwide. Here de Bruin challenges fundamentalist attitudes and prescriptive approaches to jazz education. The juxtaposition of seminal pedagogic thinkers whose aim of creative thinking and personalized approaches stand in stark contrast to the formulaic educational approaches that dominate secondary and tertiary music education. Examined through the lenses of vocabulary, pedagogy, and learning environment, de Bruin argues for a reappraisal of imitative over creative. He addresses the embodied dualisms and polarities of power within education settings and how jazz education can clearly perform a number of roles, from the critical to subversive, creative to political. He lastly challenges the way jazz educators approach and evolve pedagogy with capacity to embed itself in the realities of diverse social and cultural elements of jazz.

Mass migrations and the intersections of various nationalities and societies are reflected in the global movement and collision of ethnic musics. What is evident in music, and in particular music education, is that regardless of nationality, class, racial stereotype, or stylistic label, ways to learn, perform, and educate will find new dimensions in which to engage learners with musics' rich history. In chapter 7, Alexandra Carlson and Andrew Sutherland explore this notion by investigating the phenomenon that is El Sistema. They uncover the beginnings of this movement in Venezuela and its expansion not only across the Americas but also as a system of education that can be utilized to promote localized and indigenous music making and learning possibilities.

The development and use of the TV was a technological development that became ubiquitous across most first-world nations. Paul Louth in chapter 8 overviews the early and developing applications of the television as an educational device as live transmitter of programs, as well as applications for recorded programs. Louth discusses the use of this technology across predominantly English-language nations, touching on its reach, inclusivity, but general lack of effectiveness as an educational medium. Despite limitations, televised music allowed the world to become a smaller, more connected place, that in a music education sense over time unbridled the firm boundaries between so-called direct teaching and the pedagogy of mass media, and the latter developments of multi diversity in screen use that was to become a defining mark in education across the world. Louth argues an enduring theme in music education and perhaps education generally; that no matter what device and what IT application teachers may use, it is the discrete and refined pedagogical approaches that teachers use that can enhance television and recorded visual information to most effectively engage students in music learning.

Aspects of technology impacted the way music could be recorded and enjoyed, both educationally and for enjoyment. This became prevalent in the 1950s postwar boom that saw the fast-paced travel of contemporary musics, such as rock'n'roll, rhythm, and blues, as well as music diasporas such as reggae, ska, and jazz. Popular forms of music were powerful forms of community building as well as promoting senses of belonging and identity within social structures. The 1950s arguably mark a time of great disparity between how music was used as a societal engagement and how it was taught in schools—a continuing schism today.

In chapter 9, Lowe explores how the inclusion of Popular Music in school curricula did not immediately follow the explosion of rock'n'roll in the mid-1950s. Lowe reviews the developmental history of popular music in education across the United Kingdom, United States, and Australia. He argues that American critique of popular music in school music education has focused upon issues of legitimacy and quality, whereas elsewhere in English-speaking nations discourse has focused on utility and agency, with greater emphasis on the quality of learning and pedagogies used. Lowe lastly synthesizes the social context discourse surrounding concepts of worthiness, relevance, and motivational value before examining pedagogical implications and the impact of technology impacting popular music education.

Multicultural music education rightly represents a multiplicity of global music systems. Ongoing limitations and challenges for music education highlight not only the struggle for expertise, but also countering the prevailing perception and approach that "West is best" when it comes to music education. Large-scale population movements across the globe, particularly over the past fifty years, have allowed the distribution of diverse musics and music practices, with globalization facilitating concepts of "world music" as well as the promotion and discovery of nonlocal cultures that have found their way into music classrooms, particularly as nations and societies reconceptualize and realign their thinking as multicultural societies.

Acknowledging the myriad and complex ways multiethnic musics ebb and flow within societies and nations, this chapter provides a focused overview of music education and its traditions across much of the English-language diaspora. A common theme is the adherence to ethnic folk songs, their reinterpretation within a local and decontextualized setting, and engagement through singing. Despite major immigrant influx in these countries, it was not until the 1980s that curriculum began to incorporate notions of engagement in multicultural musics with thought to multidisciplinary contexts, authentic engagement, and the notion of culture bearers acting as the "voice" or conduit for immersion in music making. The chapter illuminates the tokenism, trivialization, and in some cases blatant ignorance of both the necessity and compulsion to represent diverse cultures the students present with in the music classroom, with what is valued and studied there. The work of music teacher organizations such as ISME and MENC advance policy and curriculum that establishes rights and cultures of musical explorations. No matter where we are in the world, music education, and music teachers can enrich personal and societal perspectives, redistributing knowledge and its cultural wealth across borders.

Chapter 6

Jazz Education
Revolution or Devolution?
Leon de Bruin

Jazz has long sat as a troubling concept within academia. Jazz is a dynamic and fluidly evolving set of substyles that relies on the core technique of improvisation that is all too infrequently found within the western art music curriculum. Jazz, as a predominantly improvised music, began its academic life with a fundamentally different identity within the academy that continues to put itself at odds with academic musical culture. Jazz was, and continues to be, an evolving genre that chooses improvisation over the printed page, collective democracy over ordered leadership, and freedom of expression instead of conformity and stasis. Music education was to be altered forever as jazz first became a viable option and then a defining "classical study" in its own right.

In comparing the creative process of jazz and improvisation to the process of human development, Sawyer[1] finds parallels in the ways both are emergent, involve change and adaptability over time in response to interactions with conditions, events, people, and environment. Such assertions suggest promising directions for jazz and music improvisation research which may inform teaching practices and support a diversity of creative and interdisciplinary understandings of musical activity.

The beginnings of jazz are copiously researched; the synthesis of African musical culture and western harmony percolated in New Orleans, where it then traveled up the Mississippi across the United States, and then the Atlantic. By the mid-1920s, exponents such as Louis Armstrong and Sidney Bechet had "turned jazz into a soloists', and therefore an improviser's art form."[2] Jazz as a verb (as in "jazz" the music) had become interchangeable with the descriptive noun and definition of improvisation.[3] In their own and wider creative communities, jazz musicians were described as improvisers, and improvisers were labeled as jazz musicians.[4] Despite this, reading notated music at a high level was desirable and seen as advantageous. Many pioneering jazz musicians learned, played, and developed skills in reading bands. Kinzer[5] suggests that whatever formal methods existed at the time for learning theory or jazz performance were of European origin. Print culture imported from Europe allowed transcription that could equip the masses with a new textual practice. Printed books covering an array of ragtime piano methods had been available, and Louis Armstrong's *50 Choruses for Cornet* appeared in 1927, heralding the arrival of instrument-specific manuals. Jazz "fakebooks" containing hundreds of standard songs became an essential text for the developing improviser.

Contrary to this approach were practicing jazz musicians who initiated formalized classes for musicians wishing to learn. Diverse approaches to the teaching of improvisation encapsulated varying perspectives about the role of the educator and what was deemed essential to the needs of the student. Noted practitioners such as Lennie Tristano, George Russell, Warne Marsh and Bill Evans adopted a personalized approach to inculcating improvisational processes and skill. Evans recalls his thoughts on teaching at The Lenox School of Jazz in the early 1950s and the tempering of pedagogical approaches with his own experiences in jazz and evolving creative processes and discovering

> different ways an idea can be treated: expand it, contract it, add notes to it, subtract notes, play it on different levels, play it in sequence, play it upside down, play it backwards, play a contrasting idea; I listed almost all the devices that one can treat an idea by. I didn't want to get hung up teaching style. . . . I wanted to give some principles to the people that they could carry with them, make exercises out of them, and they could apply to any style.[6]

The move of jazz from "informal" classes to formalized university classes faced significant criticism, in which the elements of culture, sophistication, and identity within society were attacked as a form of deviant music that was labeled "a crying evil,"[7] ugly and of deliberate vulgarity.[8] Culturally, jazz was perceived as "a music evolved by black men and in general best played by black men, which white men can play and sometimes play excellently."[9] In this sense, jazz was associated with what was deemed undesirable cultural attitudes and behaviors that veered toward the pathological and criminal. Writing in 1921, Anne Shaw Faulkner wrote about jazz as a clear and present danger to the more accepted forms of musical styles of the day:

> Jazz originally was the accompaniment of the voodoo dancer, stimulating the half-crazed barbarian to the vilest deeds. The weird chant, accompanied by the syncopated rhythm of the voodoo invokers, has also been employed by other

barbaric people to stimulate brutality and sensuality. That it has a demoralizing effect upon the human brain has been demonstrated by many scientists.[10]

From an academic viewpoint, jazz was perceived as distinctly separated from the established traditions of musical culture. European traditions were believed to be of higher artistic quality than new-world or vernacular traditions (i.e., African-American traditions); the argument assumed that composed music was superior to jazz and improvised music. Yet, such was the impetus of jazz as a popular form that institutions were compelled to begin establishing courses that somehow "taught" jazz.

HISTORY AND DEVELOPMENT OF JAZZ EDUCATION IN THE UNITED STATES

In the United States, jazz began to acquire serious educational and critical scholarship. The University of North Texas "began the first jazz/dance Band course in 1947."[11] While the wholesale growth of the field occurred after the development of improvisational methods and the creation of "jazz theory" in the 1950s and 1960s,[12] institutions such as Berklee School of Music and Alabama State University, Tennessee State University increased participation in jazz studies, leading to formal instruction. For the first time, musical academia interpreted jazz practice, performance, and soloing not only as a musical art form but also as a "musical art form in which traditional music notation and transcription would only partly represent the intent and meaning of improvisation."[13]

Jazz education in the United States "was slow to develop throughout the 1950s."[14] However, the development of instrumental music programs in American high schools, the returning of World War II war veterans, and the popularization of jazz were major catalysts in advancing the development of improvisation education.[15,16,17] By the 1960s, "jazz had become a more permanent component of the music curriculum"[18] in American high schools as school bands "became increasingly dominant in instrumental music education."[19] In this era, high school concert bands/wind ensembles began to achieve a new status comparable with that of the school orchestra. From this platform, an industry of new works by dedicated wind band composers facilitated the transition of more students learning and playing wind instruments in organized school ensembles including jazz combos.[20]

Concurrently, major jazz ensembles and big bands of the era were de-mythologizing aspects of jazz and improvisation. Improvised music brought a rethinking of social, cultural, and philosophical relations; a "symbiotic and recursive relationship between musician and audience [that] integrated patterns of movement, sound, mood, and attitude."[21] Major ensembles such as the Count Basie, Duke Ellington, and Stan Kenton bands notably involved themselves in breaking down education and color barriers through mixed bands and antidiscrimination clauses with organizers, other bandleaders and the wider entertainment industry.[22,23,24] Several bands actively participated in early education programs. Bandleaders such as "Don Ellis, Maynard Ferguson, Woody Herman, Thad Jones with Mel Lewis, and Stan Kenton [took] their entire bands to various schools to give clinics and concerts."[25] One important moment in this massive growth was the Stan Kenton Band Clinic at Indiana University in 1959 that started a popular trend—the summer jazz camp—that was and continues to be replicated across the United States.

Many young instrumentalists wanted to play music that featured improvisation and were now being encouraged to do so in their high school jazz ensemble.[26] The institutionalization of jazz in the United States propagated a demand for pedagogical methods that could deliver a common, accessible, and assessable stream of information, teachers, and experiences. Introducing improvisation into university music programs established a jazz pedagogy removed from the active, dynamic environments that facilitated the development of pertinent skills, knowledge, and refinement of performance in the first generations of jazz performers. Many educators were perplexed as to how to effectively instil methods that develop improvisatory musical practice traditionally acquired through processes of imitation, trial and error, facilitating students' absorption of experiences gleaned from powerful informal learning environments like "jam sessions."

The publication of Russell's *Lydian Chromatic Concept of Tonal Organisation*[27] offered an underlying theoretical framework with which educators could communicate improvisational techniques. Russell's connecting of vertical harmonic structures with horizontal melody was a major breakthrough "for the burgeoning field of jazz education."[28] Jazz musicians like Jerry Coker[29] established a sequential framework that identified significant practices improvisers employ, such as scale choices, harmonic progression, voice leading, and rhythmic essentials such as swing.

A further influence upon the learning of jazz was the advent and development of "fake" books. Often containing hundreds of jazz songs and standards, these generic transcriptions of mostly hand-written and copied songs became a means of common connection between musicians in practice and at gigs. Ideally a way of getting to know songs, for many learners this way of learning circumvented the more aurally absorbed way of learning. A third contribution to the jazz education literature was from Jamey Aebersold.[30] Understanding that skill development relied on playing with other musicians, Aebersold's "play-a-long" method situated the student engaging with a prerecorded rhythm section in lieu of a real one. Ever popular to this day via record, CD or App via a range of audio technologies, these kinds of tools allow many musicians the opportunity to practice improvisation in a faux-group setting, achieving continued universal acceptance.

Emphasizing the widening dichotomy of institutionalized constructs of "jazz ed" and the authentic lived experience of its masters, early scholarship such as Gunther Schuller's essays examining the music, life, and concepts of various notable jazz musicians were first published. Investigative studies such as "Sonny Rollins and the Challenge of Thematic Improvisation" in *Jazz Review*[31] (1958) and "Ornette Coleman"[32] (1961) explored improvising musicians' perspectives of their life and work, revealing that improvisation is personal and meaningful. Scholarly work revealed that hearing improvised music is not only an act of creation, in that we hear the music with special receptivity and personal voice that is dynamic, creative, but also steeped in traditions that are not just learned but acquired through rich acculturational experiences. How jazz educators responded to this was to set a course for jazz education over the ensuing fifty years.

FORMAL JAZZ EDUCATION GOES INTERNATIONAL

Expatriate musicians from the United States have found warm and enthusiastic welcome across Europe since the 1940s. This led to formal institutional organization of jazz learning, as well as the development of local communities that asserted global reimaginings of jazz that sought difference from its North American roots. Whyton[33] claims that in contrast to what is described as the American approach, the European approach to jazz was, and continues to be, characterized as more eclectic, reflecting both the multinational perspectives of different jazz communities and a lesser fixation with the idea of one "authentic" canon. From 1964 to 1967, jazz courses were developed across Europe, such as the Hochschule für Musik in Cologne, the Béla Bartók Konzervatórium in Budapest and the Leeds Music Centre in England.[34] By the mid-1980s, jazz was becoming an organic part of the general music education in Sweden and the Federal Republic of Germany, with progress in Italy as well. In Holland and England, many kinds of private schools and courses covered teaching jazz, though not yet becoming part of the state music education system.[35] Yet what was clear was that the place of jazz education in these countries varied according to local cultures. Among countries outside Europe, particularly Japan and Australia, jazz found a foothold in the secondary education co-curriculum. Jazz education across Africa and South America remains unsupported and rarely present, largely dependent on a significant performer/educator driving jazz education within a particular school or district.[36]

Despite more adventurous forms of experimentation such as free jazz becoming a stand-alone genre in many countries, jazz educators found their voice and power more fully represented in the emulation of the conventional paradigm. Sarath notes that "it was only natural that the big band, which was most like conventional school bands and orchestras, would emerge as the centerpiece."[37] This situation remains largely unchanged.

BIG BAND ORIENTATIONS—THE ERODING OF IMPROVISATION

In secondary schools worldwide, the Big Band proliferated as the vehicle through which jazz culture and knowledge were transmitted. This problematized the development and sophistication of some of the most significant characteristics inherent in jazz. While establishing a well-engineered template that involves twenty or so musicians, the big band ran contrary to a great deal of the contextual history of community in music making which was primarily small-group based. Second, the methods of instruction were established on European models that fore-fronted ensemble activity, notational adherence, and the creative act of improvisation relegated to a subjugated and minor role in jazz education. Practitioners and educators of jazz met head-on with the task of confronting musical and institutional traditions in which improvisation was largely unknown or regarded with hostility. Improvisation in academic musical studies has long been the exception rather than the rule, generally confined to performance of early music and rarely extending beyond the classical period. Improvisation's downward trajectory and regard as a valuable skill (in jazz or otherwise) have clearly diminished. As Christopher Small notes:

> In the western classical tradition, the art of improvisation is today to all intents and purposes dead, and resists all efforts to revive it. The resistance, surprisingly, comes largely from performers themselves, who mostly have little idea of what improvisation is or what it entails . . . both performers and listeners in the classical tradition have learnt to think of music as a collection of sound objects bequeathed to us from the past . . . this idea is negated in improvisation.[38]

From the perspective of young high school musicians who are inquisitive about jazz, many often strike pedagogical frustrations.[39] McPherson found that many students cut short their instrumental musical studies due to "frustration with traditional pedagogical methods."[40] Many improvisation methods and teaching manuals deliver to the student exactly the same kind of stylistic and aesthetic cul-de-sacs that they were trying to escape. This legitimizing, codification, and accreditation has transformed much improvisatory practice and pedagogy from a creative to a re-creative practice. Many existing formal jazz education methods have been reduced to a set of musical patterns, developmental models, and theory sets that have been described as creatively and pedagogically stultifying[41,42] and that are overwhelmingly performance-based rather than process-oriented.

The argument within secondary education is that big band rehearsal leaves little room for either individual or group improvisation, where most high school charts contain written out improvised solos. The huge growth of high school jazz education from the early 1970s onward also led to the production of a multitude of improvisation method books spanning theory and history, as well as a big band writing industry that now rivals school concert/symphonic wind band repertoire in quantity of production. This informs us that even big band writers and arrangers for high school ensembles are aware of the pedagogical deficiencies and unsatisfactory time allocations existing in many schools.

Of further significance is that many professional musicians who played in Big Bands likely did not receive their primary musical training there. The legitimization of jazz education in schools in terms of participation levels and its official sanctioning by education and even music organizations runs counter to the experientially diverse ways the development of musical skills and attitudes cultivated in the real world of jazz. While published texts and pedagogical aids have been blamed for moving jazz to a "written tradition,"[43] they also "relinquished the fundamentally oral identity"[44] to a solely written form of understanding and engagement in the high school big band class.

The institutionalization of jazz in high school and higher education brought with it the creation of formal pedagogies and curricula for jazz improvisation that constructed relatively stable definitions of improvisation delivered in a linear, prescribed, and sequenced course of predetermined musical canon and historical perspectives. The development of the Aebersold play-along publications offers a case in point, providing a very systematic and stylistically determined approach to jazz improvisation.

The repertoire selection within the now-established jazz ensemble idiom is now limited and constrained, emphasizing a few select jazz styles and canonical players as the basis for a pedagogical system. Ake[45] suggests that such methods tend to be based on a relatively narrow view of jazz's improvisational tradition, in particular the emphasis upon those styles and musicians whose playing reinforces an easily classified and teachable improvisational tradition. Mantie is more damning suggesting that "current practices in jazz education at the secondary level largely ignore improvisation in favour of polishing the notes on the printed page,"[46] Nicholson addresses what he sees as a narrow focus of oft-used bebop-based stylistic conventions as a pedagogical basis:

The problem with basing the educational curriculum on a bebop-styled repertoire is that solos in this style—and it is a style that focuses almost entirely on solos—were becoming so circumscribed stylistically and technically it was increasingly difficult for musicians to say anything original in this idiom.[47]

Within secondary education settings, such historical pedagogical narratives and traditions exerted considerable influence over methods used to structure musical learning, determining what and who is appropriate for formal study. As a consequence, if students and teachers of jazz ensemble—or jazz improvisation can find the time within the curriculum for immersion—they continue to face competing institutional, cultural, and historical forces of the jazz canon. Even then, they must negotiate between cultivating individual processes and conceptions of creativity and the impetus of these constraining pedagogical systems.

The "Big Band competition" has been a recent development that has entered the calendars of thousands of secondary schools in many countries. The Netherlands, Austria, New Zealand, and Australia each have their own regional dialect, with the Marsalis' fronted Essentially Ellington competition expanding beyond the United States in becoming a multinational proposition. While not doubting the merits of students discovering Ellington's compositional and creative flair, one might question whether students are exposed educationally to the experimental and explorative personal and collaborative musical investigations that were a cornerstone of the Ellington band's ethos. Today, eager secondary school musicians interested in improvisation may meticulously be copying Bubber Miley, Harry Carney, and Joe "Tricky" Nanton solos, ninety years after they were first played. Jazz education remains a puzzling paradox between creative and re-creative urges, made all the more predictable when it vociferously champions imitation.

WHAT WE MIGHT LEARN FROM PAST AND CURRENT PRACTICES

Jazz is a dynamic aspect of secondary music departments worldwide and part of critical educational discourse in many school instrumental music programs in the twenty-first century. The argument no longer exists in its presence, but jazz education remains a fertile land for tillage and further sophistication. Jazz educators may wish to adopt a more critical stance toward jazz education for lifelong learners, the schools they come from, and the cultures they wish to instil in their charges. First, current jazz education practices are less effective in addressing aspects of jazz that are in accord with its creative, cultural, and sociological roots. There are many arguments proffered that the teaching of jazz improvisation in higher education is perceived as taught and performed with a lack of creativity and originality.[48] If students are progressing through several years of high school and equipping themselves with these very re-creative limiting views to musical exploration and improvisation, their habits have been formatively embedded, making creative change all the more difficult. In fact, those rewarded by acceptance into tertiary study are perpetuating the prevailing constraining classroom climates, abetted by the audition jurists who can work with compliant and like-minded student tastes.[49]

Prouty asserts that power, in the narrative of jazz performance, is often seen to rest with the individual performer, whose self-learning of the language of the music stands sharply at odds with institutional study.[50] Critics of jazz education from within the jazz community argue that formal study of improvisation strips performers of this individualism and personal voice. Both Prouty[51] and Giroux[52] adopt a critical pedagogical stance on how the western canon, the jazz tradition, and the academy itself have each impacted jazz education and its historical and social relationality that is core to jazz as a democratic, collaborative, and collective art form.

The education movement to Common Core[53] standards in the United States is in many ways similar to that of the Australian Curriculum[54] and emphasizes the imperative to develop creative and critical thinking in students, sharing alignments in music/educational performance standards. The ability to demonstrate a fluency, fluidity, adaptability, and criticality of thought and process is central to this push that highlights the efficacy of jazz education as a focal point for effective individual and group immersion and development in secondary education. The argument had progressed beyond ideological semantics as to whether school jazz musicians exhibit good ensemble skills but poor improvisational skills. Mantie[55] points out that music education is under no obligation to the jazz tradition, and current practices should meet the arbitrated policy directives outlined in national standards. However, educational standards have developed, evolved, and responded to changing social needs. While these may be contested, they do need to *attempt* to achieve the stated national goals and aims.

School practices may not adequately reflect the jazz tradition and fail to deliver on educational guidelines. This raises questions regarding how effectively teachers are able to impart knowledge to students, how school administrations direct teachers to meet standards, and how policy-makers may fail to provide oversight and accountability for the educational visions they instigate. This all contributes to a systemic failure to adapt and innovate to meet the needs of todays' students.

Improvisation offers a way to coalesce individual specialization with group interaction. Improvisers should potentially be knowledgeable, creative, collaboratively mindful, expressively able, and capable of innovative thoughts, processes, and products. Improvisation should be not only at the forefront of musical accomplishment but also utilized as a formative educational skill base that facilitates mastery of critical and creative thinking and transformative capabilities in and through *creative* (not re-creative) music making.

What does education stand for? What understandings do students derive, and what meanings do students cultivate in their own minds from a high school Big Band model that devalues improvisation in content and in pedagogy? As Mantie[56] asserts,

> What message is communicated when improvisation is largely or completely neglected in favour of "polishing" the sound of orchestrated passages? What sort of societal values arise from such a music education system? Viewed from the perspective of situated learning, it appears current practices in jazz education help to produce individuals who do not see themselves as part of an in-the-world community. In addition, those who are exposed to these practices experience a society that has no reason to value, or means to negotiate, improvisational practices.

At a time when creative and critical thinking are bywords for what education demands from a school experience, we are at a crucial point in asking why this should matter.

CONCLUSION

The American, or canonical, approach to jazz education has asserted advantages to legitimizing jazz as a serious artform, within a set of standards and definable history. As jazz has gained an increased degree of legitimacy in both the academy and the secondary schools that feed it, the ability to classify and objectify the music and its history provides a defined and expedient knowledge base that can justify funding education initiatives and scholarly discourse. A distinct lineage supports the construct of a rich, definable, cultural, African-American history and how it can reside within the broader framework of American history.

This overview of jazz education history both domestically in the United States and on selected sites throughout the world shows how from a sociological perspective it is clear how education reflects a form of social reproduction. Whether from an immersive sociocultural perspective[57] argued by Rogoff or sociocritical *habitus and field* espoused by Bourdieu and Passeron,[58] high school education acts as a powerful influence on the breadth and scope of learning and teaching, as well as the wider forces or presses toward stasis and change. Bourdieu places musicians as "epistemic individuals within a field of differentiation."[59] Within this field, musicians interact in social environments inhabited by groups in which spheres of play are dynamic, negotiated areas and in which systems of hierarchy are challenged and evolving innovative concepts are placed in contestation with enduring traditional ways and methods.

Reflecting on the development of jazz education and its nestling within secondary education, how might this dynamic, exciting art form that is steeped in tradition yet perpetually evolving continue to adapt and reflect this genesis and evolution within educational settings. The answer to this question may lay in contemplating what kinds of people we may wish to cultivate through the experience of jazz education. Jazz education that relies on the written note rather than the improvised experience, recreation rather than creativity, and product over process will forge people from the experiences that will shape our societies to come and the values they will hold dear.

Learning jazz and improvisation avails the opportunity to learn through improvisation how and why relationships are constructed between musicians. As a provocation, this chapter argues for a more inclusive, comparative, and interdisciplinary approach to jazz studies, where the canon is subject to continual appraisal and discursive methodologies. By exposing the embodied dualisms and polarities of power within education settings, jazz education can clearly perform a number of roles, from the critical to subversive, creative to political. In this sense, the way jazz educators approach and evolve pedagogy has the potential to embed itself in the realities of diverse social and cultural elements of jazz, while challenging, problematizing, and confounding the ideologies that support the romanticized conception of jazz culture.

Within jazz education, teachers, school administrations, and district, state, and national jurisdictions are all influenced by power mechanisms that promote the "what" and "how" of jazz teaching and performance. Power has defined the struggle from acceptance of jazz in the twentieth century, its place as a significant footprint upon African-American and North American culture that has traveled the world, influencing other cultures as it traveled. Democracy and power play their part in shaping learners values and beliefs, the evolution of jazz reflecting innovation through technologies of the self.[60]

The jazz education context implicates teachers as agents who exercise positional power when they judge students' performances. Teachers in the western canon might make assessments based on their roles in interpreting how students should play a score,[61] teachers of jazz improvisation make assessments based on the appropriateness of harmony and melody, whether students have mastered patterns, clichéd licks, or are interpreting a recording correctly. Jazz educators proffer the tunes to learn, the styles to listen to, patterns to practice, and the people to listen to. Teachers translate and implant the notions of a tradition for students.

Institutionalized pedagogy has the propensity to disrupt tradition and take power away from the performer, limiting the ability to interpret and apply historical narratives and musical language for themselves. A century ago, jazz moved from significance of the group to that of the individualist soloist. Now jazz, from a learning perspective, has moved from inspiration to reiteration. Iteration itself is not anathema to acquiring knowledge and skill. Jazz performer and mentor Clark Terry repeatedly advocated learning through an "imitate, assimilate, innovate" process.[62,63]

Improvisation in music education per se should involve innovation and the ongoing development of creative processes. The delivery of improvisation education becomes problematic when assimilationist and imitative processes overbear the innovative processes of novel thought, practice, and strategy. As a means of alleviating this imbalance, secondary education should encompass the learning that inculcates not stored artifacts but more deeply knowledge that is constructed as capability-in-action, placing learning, knowledge, and teaching as situated and distributed; as something shared, negotiated, coauthored and of value, shaping a field and habitus within communities of practice.[64]

Improvisational expression understood and beyond the canon can be challenged or balanced with more creatively inspired processes, thought, and action. If creative impulses are being dulled by reductionist concepts, copying, and rote learning, then as Levinas asserts, "it is of the highest importance to know whether we are not duped" by convention.[65] In practice, this is not always the case. Innovation can be seen by many educators as a challenge to impart due to institutional and organizational constraints, limited pedagogy, and de-personalized approaches. Innovative educational measures in improvisation education could deliver more meaningful, forward-thinking direction, orientation, and identity-building.

The challenge for twenty-first-century jazz educators and musicians is to question and reconstruct the thinking that creates interesting artful music. Jazz/improvisation pedagogy continues to retain binaries of perception: technicist/liberal, school/real world, tradition/avant-garde, canonization/deconstruction, and process/product. Embracing and exploring the tensions that exist in the learning of improvisation, its environments and communities can enhance the vibrant kaleidoscope of improvisatory styles and expression possible in the genre. Deeper pedagogical exploration of these elements can give justification to questioning our creative musical determination by responding to an emerging sensitivity to issues of aesthetic quality, meaning, value judgment, and innovation. The challenge remains for music educators to counteract the tendency to reproduce a society largely ignorant of or uninterested in change and seek the wellspring of creativity and balance to meld the flashes of inspiration with solid information streams acquired through formal education.

NOTES

1. Keith R. Sawyer, *Group Creativity: Music, Theatre, Collaboration* (Erlbaum, 2003).
2. James L. Collier, *The Making of Jazz* (Dell publishing, 1978), 141.
3. John A. Whiteoak, *Playing Ad Lib: Improvisatory Music in Australia, 1836-1970* (Currency Press, 1999), 168.
4. John Corbett, ed., "Ephemera Underscored: Writing Around Free Improvisation," in *Jazz among the Discourses* (Durham, NC: Duke University Press, 1995), 217–240.
5. Charles, E. Kinzer, "The Tios of New Orleans and Their Pedagogical Influence on the Early Jazz Clarinet Style," *Black Music Research Journal* (1996): 279–302.
6. Evans cited in: Henry Martin and Robert Wason. "Constructing a Post-Modern- Jazz Pedagogy," *Jazzforschung/Jazz Research*, 3 (2005): 163–177: 163.
7. Percy Stickney Grant. Quoted in New York Times, January 30 (1922), also quoted in "Talk about a bad press, would hysteria be closer?" New York Times, January 6 (2001).
8. Eric Hobsbawm (Francis Newton), *The Jazz Scene* (Orig. London: MacGibbon and Kee 1959. This edn. London: Penguin, 1961).
9. Martin Williams, *The Jazz Tradition* (New York, NY: Grove Press, 1959): 8.
10. Anne Shaw Faulkner, "Does Jazz Put the Sin in Syncopation?" *The Ladies' Home Journal* 38, no. 8 (1921): 16–34.
11. Bryce Luty, "Jazz Ensembles' Era of Accelerated Growth, Part II," *Music Educators Journal*, 69, no.4 (1982): 49–64, 37.
12. Kenneth E. Prouty, "Toward Jazz's "Official" History: The Debates and Discourses of Jazz History Textbooks," *Journal of Music History Pedagogy*, 1, no. 1 (2010): 19–43.
13. James Lincoln Collier. *The Making of Jazz* (Dell publishing, 1978): 451.
14. McDaniel, William. T. "The Status of Jazz Education in the 1990s: A Historical Commentary," *International Jazz Archives Journal* 1, no. 1 (1993): 119–132.
15. Austin B. Caswell and Christopher Smith, "Into the ivory tower: Vernacular music and the American academy," *Contemporary Music Review*, *19*, no.1 (2000): 89–111.
16. Randy Lee Snyder, "*College Jazz Education During the 1960s: Its Development and Acceptance*" (PhD diss., University of Houston, 1999).
17. Jack Wheaton, "Jazz in Higher Education," *NAJE Jazz Educators Journal*, 2 (1970): 9–10.
18. Richard Colwell, and Michael Hewitt. *Teaching of Instrumental Music* (Abingdon, UK: Routledge, 2015): 397.
19. Jere Humphreys, "Instrumental Music in American Education: In Service of Many Masters," *Journal of Band Research*, 30, no. 2 (1995): 39–52.
20. Victor Bordo, "Wonderful Band Transcriptions Should Be Played and Enjoyed," *The Instrumentalist 55*, no. 10 (2001): 42–48.
21. Albert Mosley, "The Moral Significance of the Music of the Black Atlantic," *Philosophy East and West*, 57, no. 3 (2007): 345–356.

22. Gene Lees, *Cats of Any Color: Jazz Black and White* (Boston, MA: Da Capo Press, 2009).

23. Ingrid Monson, *Freedom Sounds: Civil Rights Call Out to Jazz and Africa* (Oxford: Oxford University Press, 2010).

24. Basilio Serrano, *Juan Tizol-His Caravan Through American Life and Culture* (Indiana: Bloomington, Xlibris Corporation, 2012).

25. Bryce Luty, "Jazz Ensembles' Era of Accelerated Growth, Part II," *Music Educators Journal*, 69, no. 4 (1982): 49–64.

26. Luty, "Jazz Ensembles' Era," 50.

27. George Russell, *The Lydian Chromatic Concept of Tonal Organization for Improvisation* (New York, NY: Concept Publishing, 1959).

28. Kenneth E. Prouty. *Knowing Jazz: Community, Pedagogy and Canon in the Information Age* (Jackson: University Press of Mississippi, 2012), 55.

29. Jerry Coker. *Improvising Jazz* (Cammeray: Simon and Schuster, 1987) [1964].

30. Jamey Aebersold. *How to Play Jazz and Improvise* (Jamey Aebersold Jazz, 1974): 122–145.

31. Gunther Schuller. "Sonny Rollins and the Challenge of Thematic Improvisation," *Jazz Review*, 1, no. 1 (1958): 6–11.

32. Gunther Schuller, *A Collection of the Compositions of Ornette Coleman* (New York: *MJQ Music*, 1961).

33. Tony Whyton, "Birth of the School: Discursive Methodologies in Jazz Education," *Music Education Research*, 8 (2006): 65–81.

34. Rolf Sudmann, ed., "Popmusik in Studiengängen deutscher Hochschulen," in *Handbuch Jugend und Musik* (Wiesbaden: VS Verlag für Sozialwissenschaften, 1997) 457–476.

35. Janos Gonda, "Jazz Education: Improvisation and Creativity," *International Journal of Music Education*, no. 1 (1983): 19–22.

36. Nhlanhla Thusi. "Jazz Education for Post-Apartheid South Africa" (Masters diss., University of Natal, 2001).

37. Ed Sarath, "Creativity, Tradition and Change: Exploring the Process-Structure Interplay in Musical Study," *Jazz Research Papers*, (1996): 123–129.

38. Christopher Small, *Music of the Common Tongue: Survival and Celebration in African American Music* (Hanover: University Press of New England, 1987): 283.

39. Kevin E. Watson, "The Effect of Aural Versus Notated Instructional Materials on Achievement and Self-Efficacy in Jazz Improvisation," *Dissertation Abstracts International*, 69, no. 3 (2010).

40. Gary E. McPherson, "Improvisation: Past, Present and Future," in *Musical connections: Tradition and change*. Proceedings of the 21st ISME World Conference in Tampa, FL, Heath Lees ed. (Auckland: University of Auckland, 1994):154–162.

41. Kenneth E. Prouty. *"From Storyville to State University:* The Intersection of Academic and Non-Academic Learning Cultures in Post-Secondary Jazz Education*"* (PhD diss., University of Pittsburgh, 2002).

42. David Ake. *Jazz Cultures* (California: University of California Press, 2002).

43. Robert Georges Hores, "A Comparative Study of Visual and Aural Oriented Approaches to Jazz Improvisation with Implications for Instruction" (PhD diss., Indiana University, 1977).

44. Kenneth E. Prouty. *From Storyville to State University: The Intersection of Academic and Non-Academic Learning Cultures in Post-Secondary Jazz Education* (PhD diss., University of Pittsburgh, 2002): Galper quoted in Prouty, 81–84.

45. David Ake, "Jazz Cultures."

46. Roger Allan Mantie, "Schooling the Future: Perceptions of Selected Experts on Jazz Education," *Critical Studies in Improvisation/Études critiques en improvisation*, 3, no. 2 (2007): 1–11: 1.

47. Stuart Nicholson, *Is Jazz Dead? (or Has It Moved to a New Address)* (Oxfordshire: Routledge, 2005): 107.

48. See Kenneth E. Prouty. "The History of Jazz Education: A Critical Reassessment," *Journal of Historical Research in Music Education 26*, no. 2 (2005): 79–100, also Joseph Paul Louth, "An Approach to Improvisation Pedagogy in Post-secondary Jazz Programmes based on Negative Dialectics," *Music Education Research*, 14, no. 1 (2012): 9–24, and Eddie Prévost. "The Discourse of the Dysfunctional Drummer," in *The Other Side of Nowhere: Jazz, Improvisation, and Communities in Dialogue*, eds., Daniel Fischlin and Ajay. Heble (Middletown: Wesleyan University Press, 2004), 354–357.

49. Henry Kingsbury. *Music, Talent and Performance: A Conservatory Cultural System* (Philadelphia: Temple UP, 1988), 77–78.

50. Prouty, "The History of Jazz Education," 79–100.

51. Prouty, "The History of Jazz Education," 79–100.

52. Henry Giroux and Roger Simon, "Popular Culture and Critical Pedagogy: Everyday Life as a Basis for Curriculum Knowledge," in *Critical Pedagogy, the State and Cultural Struggle*, eds. Henry Giroux and Peter McLaren (Albany: SUNY Press, 1989), 236–252.

53. "Common Core State Standards Initiative. Common Core State Standards for English language arts & literacy in history/social studies, science, and technical subjects," last modified June 2, 2010). http://www.corestandards.org/assets/CCSSI_ELA%20Standards.pdf

54. "Music," Australian Curriculum, Assessment and Reporting Authority (ACARA), last modified 2016. https://australiancurriculum.edu.au/f-10-curriculum/the-arts/music/(2016).

Creating: Imagine; Plan and Make; Evaluate and Refine, and Present.
Performing: Select; Analyze; Interpret.
Rehearse, Evaluate, and Refine; and Present.
Responding: Select; Analyze; Interpret; and Evaluate.

55. Mantie, "Schooling the Future," 1–11.

56. Mantie, "Schooling the Future," 7.

57. Barbara Rogoff, "Cognition as a Collaborative Process," in *Cognition, Perception, and Language: Vol. 2. Handbook of child psychology* (5th ed.), eds., Deanna Kuhn, Robert S. Siegler, and William Damon (New York, NY: Wiley, 1998), 679–744.

58. Pierre Bourdieu, and Jean-Claude Passeron, *Reproduction in Education, Society and Culture* (Thousand Oaks, CA : Sage, 1977).
59. Pierre Bourdieu, "Understanding," *Theory, Culture & Society*, 13, no. 2 (1996): 17–37.
60. Michel Foucault, "Technologies of the Self," in *Technologies of the Self: A Seminar with Michel Foucault*, eds., Luther H Martin, Huck Gutman, and Patrick Hutton (Amherst: University of Massachusetts Press, 1988), 16–49.
61. Henry Kingsbury. *Music, Talent and Performance: A Conservatory Cultural System* (Philadelphia: Temple UP, 1988).
62. Marc Sabatella, *A Whole Approach to Jazz Improvisation* (Sydney: ADG Productions, 1996).
63. Clark Terry, July 1, 1992, Personal communication to the author, Manhattan School of Music.
64. Jean Lave, and Etienne Wenger, "Learning and Pedagogy in Communities of Practice," *Learners and Pedagogy* (1999): 21–33.
65. Emmanuel Levinas. *Totality and Infinity: An Essay on Exteriority*. Trans. Alphonso Lingis (Pittsburgh: Duquesne University Press, 1969): 21.

BIBLIOGRAPHY

Aebersold, Jamie. *How to Play Jazz and Improvise*. New Albany, IN: Jamey Aebersold Jazz, 1974.
Ake, David. *Jazz Cultures*. Berkely, CA: University of California Press, 2002.
Australian Curriculum, Assessment and Reporting Authority (ACARA). "Music." Retrieved from https://australiancurriculum.edu.au/f-10-curriculum/the-arts/music/ (2016).
Bordo, Victor. "Wonderful Band Transcriptions Should Be Played and Enjoyed." *The Instrumentalist* 55, no. 10 (2001): 42–48.
Bourdieu, Pierre. *Understanding. Theory, Culture & Society* 13, no. 2 (1996): 17–37.
Bourdieu, Pierre, Jean-Claude Passeron, and R. Nice. *Reproduction in Education, Society and Culture*, Sage, 1977.
Caswell, Austin B., and Christopher Smith. "Into the Ivory Tower: Vernacular Music and the American Academy." *Contemporary Music Review* 19, no. 1 (2000): 89–111.
Coker, Jerry. *Improvising Jazz*. New York: Simon and Schuster, 1987. [1964].
Collier, James L. *The making of jazz*. New York: Dell publishing, 1978.
"Common Core State Standards Initiative." Common Core State Standards for English language arts & literacy in history/social studies, science, and technical subjects. (2010) Retrieved http://www.corestandards.org/assets/CCSSI_ELA%20Standards.pdf
Colwell, Richard, and Michael Hewitt. *Teaching of Instrumental Music*. Oxfordshire: Routledge, 2015.
Corbett, Tohn. "Ephemera Underscored: Writing Around Free Improvisation." *Jazz Among the Discourses*, (1995): 217–240.

Fejes, Andreas and Magnus Dahlstedt. "Choosing One's Future? Narratives on Educational and Occupational Choice Among Folk High School Participants in Sweden". *International Journal for Educational and Vocational Guidance* 20, no.1 (2020): 31–47.

Giroux, Henry, and Roger Simon. "Popular Culture and Critical Pedagogy: Everyday Life as a Basis for Curriculum Knowledge." *Critical Pedagogy, the State and Cultural Struggle*. Edited by Henry Giroux and Peter McLaren, 236–252. Albany: SUNY Press, 1989.

Gonda, Janos. "Jazz Education: Improvisation and Creativity." *International Journal of Music Education* 1 (1983): 19–22.

Hores, Robert G. "A Comparative Study of Visual and Aural Oriented Approaches to Jazz Improvisation with Implications for Instruction." Diss. Indiana University, 1977.

Humphreys, J. T. "Instrumental Music in American Education: In Service of Many Masters." *Journal of Band Research* 30, no.2 (1995): 39–52.

Kingsbury, Henry. *Music, Talent and Performance: A Conservatory Cultural System*. Philadelphia: Temple UP, 1988.

Kinzer, Charles E. "The Tios of New Orleans and Their Pedagogical Influence on the Early Jazz Clarinet Style." *Black Music Research Journal*, (1996): 279–302.

Lees, Gene. *Cats of Any Color: Jazz Black and White*. Boston, MA: Da Capo Press: (2009).

Levinas, Emmanuel. *Totality and Infinity: An Essay on Exteriority*. Translated by Alphonso Lingis. Pittsburgh: Duquesne University Press, 1969.

Louth, Joseph Paul. "An Approach to Improvisation Pedagogy in Post-secondary Jazz Programmes based on Negative Dialectics." *Music Education Research* 14 no. 1 (2012): 9–24.

Luty, Bryce. "Jazz Ensembles' Era of Accelerated Growth, Part II." *Music Educators Journal*, 69 no. 4 (1982): 49–64.

Mantie, Roger Allan. "Schooling the Future: Perceptions of Selected Experts on Jazz Education." *Critical Studies in Improvisation/Études critiques en improvisation*, 3, no. 2 (2007): 1–11.

Martin, Henry and Robert Wason. "Constructing a Post-Modern- Jazz Pedagogy." *Jazzforschung/Jazz Research,* 37 (2005), Graz, Austria: Akademische Druck-u. Verlagsanstalt, (2005): 163–177.

McDaniel, William T. "The Status of Jazz Education in the 1990s: A Historical Commentary." *International Jazz Archives Journal* 1, no. 1 (1993): 119–132.

McPherson, Gary E. Improvisation: Past, present and future. In H. Lees (Ed.), *Musical Connections: Tradition and Change*. Proceedings of the 21st ISME World Conference in Tampa, FL, 154–162. Auckland, New Zealand: University of Auckland, 1994.

Monson, Ingrid. *Freedom sounds: Civil Rights Call Out to Jazz and Africa*. Oxford University Press, 2010.

Mosley, Albert G. "The Moral Significance of the Music of the Black Atlantic." *Philosophy East and West* 57 no. 3 (2007): 345–356.

Nicholson, Stuart. *Is Jazz Dead? (or Has It Moved to a New Address)*. Oxfordshire: Routledge, 2005.

Prévost, Eddie. "The discourse of the dysfunctional drummer." In *The Other Side of Nowhere: Jazz, Improvisation, and Communities in Dialogue*. Edited by Daniel Fischlin, Ajay Heble, and Ingrid Monson, 354–357. Middletown, CT: Wesleyan University Press, 2004.

Prouty. Kenneth. E. *From Storyville to State University: The Intersection of Academic and Non-Academic Learning Cultures in Post-Secondary Jazz Education*. Diss. University of Pittsburgh, 2002.

Prouty, Kenneth. E. "The History of Jazz Education: A Critical Reassessment." *Journal of Historical Research in Music Education* 26, no. 2 (2005): 79–100.

Prouty, Kenneth. E. "Toward Jazz's "Official" History: The Debates and Discourses of Jazz History Textbooks." *Journal of Music History Pedagogy* 1, no. 1 (2010): 19–43.

Prouty, Kenneth. E. *Knowing Jazz: Community, Pedagogy and Canon in the Information Age*, Jackson, MS: University Press of Mississippi, 2012.

Rogoff, Barbara. "Cognition as a Collaborative Process." In *Cognition, Perception, and Language: Vol. 2. Handbook of Child Psychology*, 5th ed., edited by Deanna Kuhn, Robert S. Siegler, and William Damon, 679–744. New York: J. Wiley, 1998.

Russell, George. *The Lydian Chromatic Concept of Tonal Organization for Improvisation*. New York, NY: Concept Publishing, 1959.

Sabatella, M. *A whole approach to jazz improvisation*. ADG Productions. (1996).

Sarath, Ed. "Creativity, Tradition and Change: Exploring the Process-Structure Interplay in Musical Study". *Jazz Research Papers*, IAJE Publications, (1996): 123–129.

Sawyer, Keith R. *Group Creativity: Music, Theatre, Collaboration*. Erlbaum, 2003.

Schuller, Gunther. "Sonny Rollins and the Challenge of Thematic Improvisation." *Jazz Review* 1 no. 1 (1958): 6–11.

Schuller, Gunther. *A Collection of the Compositions of Ornette Coleman*. New York: MJQ Music, 1961.

Serrano, Basilio. *Juan Tizol-His Caravan Through American Life and Culture*. Bloomington, IN: Xlibris Corporation, 2012.

Small, Christopher. *Music of the Common Tongue: Survival and Celebration in African American Music*. Hanover, NH: University Press of New England, 1987.

Snyder, Randy Lee. "College Jazz Education During the 1960s: Its Development and Acceptance." Doctoral diss., University of Houston, 1999.

Sudmann, Rolf, ed. "Popmusik in Studiengängen deutscher Hochschulen." In *Handbuch Jugend und Musik*, 457–476. Wiesbaden: VS Verlag für Sozialwissenschaften, 1997.

Tackley, Catherine, and Peter J. Martin. "Historical Overview of the development of jazz in Britain," in *Rhythm Changes: Historical Overview of Five Partner Countries*, edited by Tony Whyton and Christa Bruckner-Haring. Institute for Jazz Research/University of Music and Performing Arts Graz, 2013: 3–27.

Thusi, Nhlanhla B. "Jazz Education for Post-Apartheid South Africa." Masters diss., University of Natal, 2001.

Walser, Robert. *Keeping Time*. New York: Oxford University Press, 1999.

Watson, Kevin E. "The Effect of Aural Versus Notated Instructional Materials on Achievement and Self-efficacy in Jazz Improvisation." *Dissertation Abstracts International* 69, no. 3 (UMI No. 3305685) (2010): 240–259.

Wheaton, Jack. "Jazz in Higher Education." *NAJE Jazz Educators Journal* 2 (1970): 9–10.

Whiteoak, John A. *Playing ad lib: Improvisatory music in Australia, 1836–1970.* Melbourne: Currency Press, 1999.

Whyton, Tony. "Birth of the School: Discursive Methodologies in Jazz Education." *Music Education Research* 8 (2006): 65–81.

Chapter 7

A Global Revolution in Music for Social Change

El Sistema from Chile to Venezuela and the World

Alexandra Carlson and Andrew Sutherland

Since 2009, the youth and children's orchestra program well-known for its origins in Venezuela and commonly referred to as "El Sistema" has proliferated across the globe.[1] As key tenets of the program are replicated, understanding its origin story in Venezuela and its antecedents in an earlier program in Chile is increasingly important. This chapter begins by illuminating the history of the beginning of the El Sistema program in a project under the leadership of Jorge Peña in Chile, whose ideals of democratizing access to Western art music and reforming music education as a whole have endured in international El Sistema programs. It then traces the arrival of these ideals to Venezuela, where colleagues of Peña fled in 1974 to found that country's first children's orchestra in the city of Carora. Meanwhile, José Antonio Abreu created a youth orchestra project in Caracas and the two projects frequently collaborated in their early years, influencing positive outcomes for the creation of youth orchestras throughout the country and continent. In the pivotal year of 2009, Gustavo Dudamel, a product of the Venezuelan program, introduced it to the United States. From there, it became a global movement.

JORGE PEÑA AND DEMOCRATIZING ACCESS TO MUSIC IN CHILE

Born in Santiago, Chile, in 1928, but spending his youth in the smaller cities of Coquimbo and La Serena, Jorge Washington Peña Hen (referred to as Jorge Peña throughout) began music lessons at an early age and returned to

Santiago to study composition at the Conservatorio Nacional. At that time, there were few musical opportunities for students and musicians outside of Santiago. In an interview, Lautaro Rojas, a former colleague of Peña and violinist, noted that "in the 1940s in the provinces there was no serious musical development beyond high school music teachers who organized choirs. There were also a few private academies that had theater. But nothing more. Musical activity was circumscribed to Santiago."[2] Music education was centered in the hands of the elite, with little access for all students. Vanett Lawler, the Executive Secretary of MENC, noted during a visit to Santiago that Latin America had an "acute need for serious emphasis on music education as part of general education for all students in all schools."[3] In the Revista Musical Chilena, Cora Bindhoff de Sigren noted that "Our music education does not comply with its goal of forming musicality in a child; it does not even cultivate his voice to sing or ear to listen, nor stimulate creative musical conditions in any sense."[4]

Peña's drive to increase access to Western art music across geographical boundaries and social classes was core to his life's work, first focusing on professional musicians and later on children. While a student at the Conservatorio Nacional, he became president of the student center and actively organized student concerts and tours to bring Western art music to the broader community; "We the students of the Conservatory think that the Institute can more intensely radiate its musical efforts towards the pueblo. . . . It is indispensable that we focus ourselves on the people, infusing in them a sense of love of music and culture."[5] Jose Weinstein, Minister of Culture under President Ricardo Lagos, reflected in 2003 that "Jorge Peña had the intuition that it was possible to redefine boundaries, to tear down the barrier that had determined Western art music should be reserved for the cultured elite of our country."[6]

In 1950, Peña organized a Bach Society that gave performances all over Chile's north, reaching over 100,000 audience members in its first ten years and "inundating the city of La Serena with music."[7] In 1956, he founded the first musical conservatory outside of the capital city, the Conservatorio Regional, where "The beginning of activities of the first school created by the Universidad in a province [outside Santiago] has special importance because it is an establishment that provides free music education, fulfilling an important educational and cultural need," according to the newspaper *El Dia*.[8]

The year 1964 was a pivotal year for Peña, where he refocused his efforts on the education of children and created the continent's first children's orchestra, *La Orquesta de Niños*.[9] That year, he received a grant from the U.S. State Department to observe music education programs. Alongside his wife, Nella Camarda, they attended the Music Educators National Conference in Philadelphia, where they met the newly famous Japanese pedagogue Shinichi

Suzuki who was touring with an orchestra of small children to demonstrate his innovative educational techniques.[10] While in the United States, Peña attended many rehearsals and performances of youth orchestras. According to a former student and director of the *Orquesta de Niños*, Hugo Dominguez, "He took advantage of all the opportunities given to him to observe youth orchestras there [in the United States], and immediately saw the possibility and implications that this would have in copying, no, *adapting it* to the Chilean reality."[11]

Peña returned to La Serena and proposed the *Plan de Extensión Docente*, a plan that reformed music education for children across the region;

> I do not think there was any fixed moment when Peña decided to give up all his other musical activity to dedicate himself to education. I think it was motivated by his generosity, his social restlessness that "hy is it just that I can enjoy music, where the poor people of the pueblos and the provincias have never been able to?" This social restlessness began to win him over, always more so. And it became the greatest passion of his life, to teach.[12]

In May 1964, 100 fourth-grade children were selected based on their basic musical interest from 5 different primary schools in La Serena to receive a free musical education. Thirty percent of the student participants came from low-income households.[13] They were provided with orchestral instruments, and on December 20, 1964, after only six months of studies and rehearsals, the Orquesta de Niños performed its first concert in La Serena under Peña's baton. The performance was so extraordinary because "it was also considered that the music student in Santiago could only begin orchestral playing after many years of study. It happened here Jorge Peña demonstrated that children with less than one year of study could play an adequate repertoire, and play it with spirit, and get joy from the music."[14] Peña's wife Nella Carmada reflected on the concert; "In December of the same year he gave his first concert of the first children's orchestra of Latin America with unprecedented success. The Liceo de Niños de La Serena theater was filled with workers, parents of small musicians, all familiar with Bach, Schubert, Beethoven, and Mozart."[15]

In May 1965, Peña's project was institutionalized in the founding of the Escuela Experimental de Música de La Serena, a school where students received general educational classes in the morning and music instruction in the afternoons. The school was tuition-free, and in contrast to traditional conservatories, students were not required to purchase their own instruments.[16] This can be considered Latin America's first *núcleo*, or community orchestra center, later replicated throughout the world. From 1967 to 1972, Peña's ideas began to spread throughout the country, with the founding of experimental schools from the southern city of Osorno to the northern city of Antofagasta. Peña took his Orquesta de Niños on tour, around Chile and to Peru and Argentina and later to Cuba and Puerto Rico.

By 1970, Chilean society became increasingly polarized with the election of socialist president Salvador Allende. Although colleagues of Peña's affirm that "his only political candidate was J.S. Bach,"[17] his visions of democratizing access to music education became equated with socialism, quelling his work in 1972 and ending his life in 1973. He was executed on October 16, 1973, by members of the military dictatorship that took power in September 1973. It was not until twenty-five years later, in 1998, that he would be given a funeral as part of a public homage to his life and works. His gravestone, unveiled that day, reads "He lived for music. He died for his ideals." The gravestone has a music stave on which Peña's final composition, written during his final days in jail, is printed.

CHILDREN'S ORCHESTRAS COME TO VENEZUELA

In 1970s Venezuela, the country was experiencing a renaissance of cultural activity due to a combination of recent political stability and revenues from the state-controlled oil industry. By 1975, the capital city of Caracas had a conservatory and music school, national ballet company, professional orchestra, and choirs.[18] That same year, President Carlos Andrés Pérez (president from 1974 to 1979) created the CONAC (Consejo Nacional de la Cultura [National Cultural Advisory Board]) to promote culture and the arts in Venezuela.

Meanwhile, mirroring Peña's work in La Serena in the 1950s and 1960s, the dentist and avid arts advocate Juan Martínez was determined to bring musical opportunities to the people of the small city of Carora, Venezuela. He founded a choir in 1964 and established Carora's Casa de la Cultura in 1969 in order to offer classes and performances for people in the region. His wife Teresa fondly remembered, "He was the craziest man I had ever met,"[19] and guitarist Alirio Díaz said, "To begin this type of adventure in Venezuela one needs great passion, a sense of compassion to face adversity, and generosity of spirit to fight without hope of receiving money or recognition."[20]

When the 1973 Chilean coup ended the life and work of Jorge Peña, Juan Martínez offered to sponsor three of Peña's former colleagues and bring them as teachers to the Casa de la Cultura. Sergio Miranda traveled in December of 1974 to Carora, and Pedro Vargas and Hernán Jérez soon followed.[21] The newspaper *Revista Resumen* described their arrival:

> These three professors, all Chileans, had previously participated in the creation of a children's orchestra in La Serena. Regrettably, after twelve successful

years, this orchestra and the others that had been developed throughout the country were violently silenced due to political events.[22]

Alongside Martínez, the three founded a children's orchestra, the Orquesta Sinfónica Infantil de Carora, in May 1975. In a 1975 interview, Pedro Vargas states, "Our mission in Carora is to create a children's orchestra. I was hired by the Casa de la Cultura, through Sergio Miranda. We have an ambitious project, to create an institute for choir, ballet, theater, and opera."[23] Pedro Vargas, the principal conductor, taught violin and viola, Sergio Miranda, a double-bassist, taught low strings, and Hernán Jérez, an oboist, instructed woodwinds. "At first, we took anyone who played an instrument, including adults. Soon after, it formally became a children's orchestra."[24]

On July 7, 1975, the orchestra performed in Caracas under the baton of Pedro Vargas, receiving its first national newspaper review, which states that 103 children aged 8 to 15 made up the newly created orchestra. From the sixteen who performed in Caracas, "the audience will appreciate the ensemble's future possibilities."[25] A subsequent concert was held in the Teatro Juares of Barquisimeto (the capital of Lara State) in November 1975 and lauded in a review; "the Orquesta Infantil de Carora represents an extraordinary cultural achievement in our country."[26]

FROM HUMBLE BEGINNINGS: CARACAS AND CARORA

Buoyed by burgeoning cultural institutions and governmental support, José Antonio Abreu, well-known in Venezuela as an economist, politician, and musician, began creating music-making opportunities for groups of students in Caracas. Abreu's visit to the United States in 1974 expanded his ideas for the possibilities of music education, and he returned to Caracas to arrange a weekly concert series, known as the "Festival Bach," with local conservatory musicians. Many of these student musicians joined Abreu in establishing the Orquesta Nacional Juvenil Juan José Landaeta," an ensemble that would "promote and stimulate" musical development in the country, encouraging music education for students from preschool through high school.[27] The first rehearsal in February 1975 yielded a paltry eight[28] students, but Abreu's enthusiasm was undiminished, and around eighty musicians took part in the first performance the following April.[29]

It is striking that both Abreu's and Peña's orchestras were influenced by their respective trips to the United States and by the work of Japanese educator Shinichi Suzuki's work with young children. Contrary to a more traditional European conservatory model typically emulated in Latin America, where students would learn "theory, aural skills, and study private lessons for years before being able to play in an orchestra,"[30] both programs emphasized ensemble rehearsals and personal development through teamwork. According to Hugo Dominguez in Chile, "he [Peña] had the philosophy that the musical training of children should occur through ensemble practice, in a group. The larger the group, the better. In other words, a symphonic youth orchestra was the ideal."[31] This group setting allowed children to develop abilities that were applicable outside of a musical environment, such as teamwork and responsibility. The professors in Carora used similar pedagogical practices; "[The students] began with no musical knowledge. Our method is to put the instrument in front of them. Slowly comes the music theory, knowing what it means to be in an orchestra and work in a team."[32]

The educators in Carora shared Peña's ideals "that the students would develop as people through learning music," receiving an integral aesthetic education regardless of future career goals.[33] Guillermo Milla remembers of Peña, "Rehearsals were solemn, serious. He [Peña] taught us discipline, responsibility. . . . This discipline was important whether we went on to be musicians or not, he taught us how to work in a team."[34] José Urquieta, another former member of the Orquesta de Niños, also remembered, "We had to practice a lot, to learn the parts very well . . . and I thank him, because my solid musical training was due to this experience, and today I am very punctual and responsible."[35] In a later interview, José Antonio Abreu echoed, "An orchestra means joy, motivation, teamwork, the aspiration to success. It is a big family dedicated to harmony."[36]

In addition to developing personal responsibility and teamwork, students fondly remembered their time in the rehearsal space. Clarina Ahumada recalled, "For us the school was our ideal and favorite place, we practically lived there. . . . We would finish class at 6:30pm, but the truth is that no one wanted to leave, so we would hide ourselves in the classrooms."[37] The students in Carora shared a similar sentiment: "It was like returning home, everyone came after school every day."[38]

In 1976 and 1977, there is significant evidence of collaboration between the orchestras in Caracas and Carora, including concerts in Caracas, *seminarios* (weekend-long intensive rehearsal sessions), and tours. The partnership between the two orchestras served to buoy both ensembles' future possibilities and national and international recognition.[39]

In their first joint appearance in Caracas in July 1976, the Orquesta Nacional Juvenil and the Orquesta Infantil de Carora received effusive reviews about Venezuela's musical talent. Abreu recognized the work of the teachers in Carora, saying:

> Today . . . we will have the honor during the concert of giving the children of Carora's orchestra the insignia that demonstrates they are accepted members

of the Orquesta Juvenil. . . . Our dignity and decorum compel us to publicly and nationally recognize the successful efforts of Juan Martínez, Pedro Vargas, and Hernán Jérez in having created a project worthy of the support of the whole nation . . . , an archetype dignified of emulation and reflection for the nation.[40]

Juan Martínez went on to say that he believed their project would be reproduced in more children's orchestras throughout the nation, as would go on to happen in the 1970s. He expressed the importance of the collaboration, thanking the "moral support and stimulus of working with the Orquesta Sinfónica Juvenil and Maestro Abreu."[41]

In this same concert, the founders announced that Orquesta Juvenil de Venezuela was selected to participate in the International Youth Orchestra Festival to be held in Aberdeen, Scotland, in 1976. They were joined by many of the members of the orchestra from Carora. The Caroran students also regularly attended Abreu's *seminarios* (weekend-long intensive rehearsal sessions), enjoying the mentorship opportunities from the Orquesta Juvenil's older musicians.[42]

By 1976, the professors' project in Carora was institutionalized in a school, the Instituto Experimental Alirio Díaz (named after the famous guitarist from Carora). Hernán Jérez reflected, "Perhaps our most important achievement to date is that we have been able to consolidate the orchestra project into a conservatory, an idea now being accepted by authorities such as José Antonio Abreu."[43] It is striking that this school, which can be considered an early version of a community-based orchestra núcleo later replicated throughout Venezuela and abroad, shared the name of the earlier institutes in Chile (Escuela Experimental de la Serena, for one). The school followed Peña's model of integrating music education into basic education, with students completing general education classes in the morning and rehearsing during the afternoons. This education would prepare them to enter conservatories and form a new generation of Venezuelan musicians outside the city of Caracas.

In 1977, Abreu founded a national children's orchestra, the Orquesta Nacional Infantil de Venezuela, that performed with the Orquesta Infantil de Carora on a tour to Caracas. The Orquesta de Carora was "the prestigious guest of honor to debut some of the new núcleos that are currently being founded . . . currently, the ties of friendship between the orchestra of Carora and the Orquesta Nacional Juvenil de Venezuela are very strong."[44] In a later recognition of the Chilean teachers, Abreu effused, "We received a significant contribution from Chilean teachers. They pushed us towards a new concept of music education. Because of this, our ties to you [Venezuelans to Chileans] are very deep."[45]

GLOBALIZING EL SISTEMA

The seed had been planted in 1975, and initially, it took time to germinate beyond South America. In Abreu's 2009 TED conference address, he recalled his disappointment with the first rehearsal of his ambitious project when only eight children attended.[46] His work was finally being noticed globally. Eleven years after the inception of El Sistema, the first scholarly publication to discuss the movement appeared in *Departamento de Relaciones Públicas de Lagoven*. In the article, *Historia del movimiento coral y de las orquestas juveniles en Venezuela*, Rugeles, Guinand, and Bottome discussed the status of choral singing in Venezuela and the historical connection with the *Orfeón Lamas*[47] and the nationalist composition school led by Vicente Emilio Sojo (1887–1974), Juan Bautista Plaza (1898–1965), and José Antonio Calcaño (1900–1978).[48]

In 1989, Mexico founded a núcleo inspired by Peña's model. Today, Mexico's El Sistema program has a highly developed network, employing over 40 staff and in excess of 150 music teachers. There are over 180 youth orchestras, 950 choirs, and 100 wind bands affiliated with the *Sistema Nacional de Formento Musical*. It enjoys federal funding, and the organization currently manages the *Iberorquestas* program, which advocates for new projects throughout Latin America.[49] This marked the first step toward an international movement, but it was as yet far from global.

In 1991, Chilean conductor Fernando Rosas traveled to Venezuela. He returned with inspiration to implement a similar system to the one he observed, bringing the work of Peña full circle, and the *Fundación de Orquestas Juveniles* (FOJI) was established in 2001. Awareness of the possibilities of El Sistema continued to spread in Latin America during the 1990s, such as in Columbia (1991) and Brazil (1996). In 1997, Eva Estrada wrote a report for the Inter-American Development Bank (IDB) that presented a mixture of positive and critical responses from current and former members. Estrada discovered that a disproportionately small number of children considered themselves as coming from a "lower-class" background. Nevertheless, the following year, the IDB provided El Sistema loans of $8 million.[50]

The rest of the world remained untouched by the growing momentum until the Simón Bolívar Youth Orchestra, under the baton of rising star Gustavo Dudamel, began touring internationally. Playing to audiences in London, Paris, Berlin, Vienna, Lucerne, and venues across Scandinavia, Russia, and Japan, as well as the Kennedy Center and Carnegie Hall in the United States, Dudamel's concerts dramatically altered the global awareness of El Sistema. One particularly pivotal performance was for the 2007 BBC Proms in London. One encore, a three-minute rendition of *"Mambo!"* from Leonard Bernstein's *West Side Story Suite*, was uploaded onto YouTube and quickly went viral. The orchestra was soon signed to Deutsche Grammophon, and suddenly musical luminaries such as Sir Simon Rattle, Daniel Barenboim, Claudio Abbado, Itzhak Perlman, Martha Argerich, and Placido Domingo journeyed to Venezuela to witness the phenomenon and to work with the ensembles.[51] The El Sistema brand was now trending.

The movement quickly spread beyond Latin America, and, in 2007, the Leading Note Foundation formed in Canada, creating the OrKidstra youth music program. Canada's El Sistema program now involves numerous núcleos, such as Sistema New Brunswick (2009), An Instrument for Every Child (AIFEC, 2010), and Sistema Toronto (2011). The formation of an umbrella organization was mooted, but it was felt that autonomy for each group was fundamentally important to meet the needs of the specific communities.[52]

The following year, Sistema Scotland began their first project in Raploch, Stirling. The year 2008 was important in the growth of El Sistema, when it received a second loan from the IDB, this time to the tune of $150 million. The following year saw three more projects emerge in the UK: Liverpool, Lambeth, and Norwich. Under the name "In Harmony Sistema England" (IHSE), it received funding from the Department for Education and then expanded further in 2012 with additional assistance from Arts Council England to include four new projects. In 2014, a further £1.35 million was provided for the 2015–2018 period.[53]

In 2009, the same year that IHSE expanded its operations, the young and charismatic Venezuelan maestro Gustavo Dudamel accepted the position as the musical director of the Los Angeles Philharmonic starting in the 2009–2010 season and making El Sistema into a global movement.[54] He is likely to be the most famous product of Abreu's project, playing the violin at the age of ten, and, after studying conducting with Abreu, was appointed music director of the *Orquesta Sinfónica Simón Bolívar*, the national youth orchestra of Venezuela. With his appointment with the Los Angeles Philharmonic came a pledge to introduce *El Sistema* to the United States. El Sistema USA was founded the same year.

As El Sistema proliferated across the globe, so did its critics. Even though the program initially served to democratize access to music education and teach extra-musical life skills, the conductor-centered orchestral model is facing criticism both within and outside of the program. The criticism includes the focus on Eurocentric repertoire, archaic models of didactic teaching methods, gender inequality, instances of inappropriate behavior and leadership style from conductors, and high levels of socially advantaged children. In 2011, El Sistema Venezuela introduced the traditional music program called *Alma Llanera*. It allowed the traditional music of Venezuela to be taught, using the same philosophical approach of El Sistema, learning through ensemble music-making. *Alma Llanera* provided a response to at least one of those criticisms by championing the traditional folk music of the region.[55]

The following year, Sistema Japan was founded. In a response to the devastation of the 2011 tsunami and subsequent nuclear power radiation leak, Yatuka Kikugawa felt such a program was much needed to provide a "pedagogy of joy" to the community of Soma. "Many children in Soma lost parents, family members, friends, and homes, and they still live with the fear of radiation from the nuclear power plant."[56] A proud history of music ensembles and music education had already been established in Soma in addition to a rich heritage of traditional folk music. Unlike the rapid growth of Korea's *Orchestra of Dreams* program, founded in 2011, Kikugawa felt that it would be better for this núcleo to grow slowly.

Table 7.1 indicates the various núcleos throughout the world. They are arranged chronologically and with the name of the initial incarnation. Many larger countries have multiple, localized núcleos, and they are often supported in some way by an umbrella organization. Cuba is not listed here, as they have their own version of El Sistema, provided through their free education policy.

The founders of the program that inspired El Sistema in Chile and Venezuela, Jorge Peña, Juan Martínez, and José Antonio Abreu, all shared the conviction that access to music education and performance should become widely accessible to students and adults alike and made it their life's work. All focused on creating opportunities first for performers, often student musicians, and later for children. In the case of Peña and Martínez, this included democratizing access to music education and performance outside of their countries' capital cities. The institutionalization of their efforts in regional conservatories and experimental schools coincided with general governmental interest in and support of the arts in 1960s Chile and 1970s Venezuela. The experimental music schools founded in La Serena and Carora that combined general education in the morning and intensive music education in the afternoon can be considered predecessors of the núcleos that have subsequently proliferated to all corners of Venezuela and around the world. The general pedagogies of each núcleo diverged from the prevalent traditional conservatory training of the time to emphasize group learning, teamwork, and personal development, which make up core values of many El Sistema programs today.

By 2011, El Sistema núcleos were established in Australia and New Zealand, and with them, six out of the seven continents had participant membership of the global movement.[57] Whether a núcleo is ever set up in Antarctica remains to be seen. Abreu was seventy-eight when he died on March 24, 2018. He could surely never have guessed that his efforts in the mid-1970s could have led to the worldwide phenomenon that followed.

Table 7.1 The Chronological Global Spread of El Sistema Núcleos

	Country	Region	Foundation Year	Name of founding organisation
1	Venezuela	Latin America	1975	Fundación del Estado para el Sistema Nacional de las Orquestas Juveniles e Infantiles de Venezuela (FESNOJIV)
2	Mexico	Latin America	1989	El Sistema México
3	Columbia	Latin America	1991	Fundación National Batuta
4	Ecuador	Latin America	1995	Fundación Orquesta Sinfónica Juvenil del Ecuador (FOSJE)
5	Guatemala	Latin America	1996	Sistema de Orquestas y Coros Infantiles y Juveniles de Guatemala (SOG)
6	Uruguay	Latin America	1996	El Sistema de Orquestas y Coros Juveniles e Infantiles del Uruguay
7	Greenland	Europe	1997	Uummannaq Music
8	Greenland	North America	1997	Uummannaq Music
9	Chile	Latin America	2001	Fundación de Orquestas Juveniles
10	Paraguay	Latin America	2002	Sonidos de la Tierra (Sound of the Earth)
11	Bolivia	Latin America	2004	Sistema de coros y orquestas (SICOR)
12	Dominican Republic	Caribbean	2005	Children International El Sistema program
13	Argentina	Latin America	2005	Sistema de Orquestas Infantiles y Juveniles de Argentina (SOIJAR)
14	Turkey	West Asia	2005	Baris Icin Muzik (Music for Peace)
15	Uganda	Africa	2007	Tender Talents Magnet School Supported by Musequality
16	Portugal	Europe	2007	Sistema Portugal Orquestra Geração (Generation Orchestra)
17	Brazil	Latin America	2007	State Center for Youth and Children Orchestras of Bahia (NEOJIBÁ)
18	Costa Rica	Latin America	2007	Sistema Nacional de Educación Musical (SINEM)
19	Canada	North America	2007	Saint James Music Academy
20	Angola	Africa	2008	Kaposoka Music School project
21	England	Europe	2008	In Harmony Sistema England

(Continued)

Table 7.1 (Continued)

	Country	Region	Foundation Year	Name of founding organisation
22	Ireland	Europe	2008	Sing Out with Strings
23	Scotland	Europe	2008	Big Noise - Sistema Scotland
24	India	East Asia	2009	Child's Play India Foundation
25	Austria	Europe	2009	Superar Austria
26	Czech Republic	Europe	2009	Harmonie Foundation (Sistema Europe Network)
27	Norway	Europe	2009	Tøyen Orkester (El Sistema Norge)
28	Philippines	East Asia	2009	Sistemang Pilipino
29	United States of America	North America	2009	El Sistema USA
30	South Africa	Africa	2010	Darling Musiek vir Almal (Darling Music for All, DMA)
31	Puerto Rico	Caribbean	2010	Music 100 x35
32	France	Europe	2010	El Sistema France
33	Italy	Europe	2010	Sisteme Orchestre Giovanile in Italia
34	Sweden	Europe	2010	EL Sistema Sverige
35	Israel	West Asia	2010	Sulamot—Music for Social Change
36	South Korea	East Asia	2011	Orchestra of Dream
37	Jamaica	Caribbean	2011	National Youth Orchestra of Jamaica
38	Trinidad and Tobago	Caribbean	2011	Music Schools in Communities / Kidznotes
39	Holland	Europe	2011	El Sistema Netherlands
40	El Salvador	Latin America	2011	El Sistema, El Salvador
41	Peru	Latin America	2011	Asociación Cultural Arpegio
42	Hawaii	North America	2011	Kalikolehua
43	Australia	Oceania	2011	Sistema Australia
44	New Zealand	Oceania	2011	Sistema Aotearoa
45	Japan	East Asia	2012	Sistema Japan
46	Philippines	East Asia	2012	Sistemang Pilipino
47	Finland	Europe	2012	El Sistema Finland
48	Spain	Europe	2012	Acción Social por la Música
49	Switzerland	Europe	2012	Superar Switzerland
50	Nicaragua	Latin America	2012	Orquesta Sinfónica Juvenil Rubén Darío (OSJRD)
51	Palestine	West Asia	2012	Sounds of Palestine
52	Mozambique	Africa	2013	Xiquitsi project
53	Haiti	Caribbean	2013	The System of Orchestras and Choirs Juvenile and Infantile of Haiti
54	Romania	Europe	2013	Superar Romania
55	Slovakia	Europe	2013	Superar Slovakia

(Continued)

Table 7.1 (Continued)

	Country	Region	Foundation Year	Name of founding organisation
56	Belize	Latin America	2013	National Youth Orchestra and Choir of Belize (NYOCB)
57	Honduras	Latin America	2013	Fundación Artes Educativas Coros Y Orquestas de Honduras. (FARECOH)
58	Armenia	West Asia	2013	Sistema Armenia
59	Kenya	Africa	2014	El Sistema Kenya
60	Hungary	Europe	2014	Symphonia Alapítvány (Symphonia Foundation)
61	Jordan	West Asia	2014	ESKADENIA Chamber of Music
62	Denmark	Europe	2015	MusikSak, El Sistema Denmark
63	Lichtenstein	Europe	2015	Superar Lichtenstein
64	Taiwan	East Asia	2016	El Sistema Taiwan
65	Bosnia and Herzegovina	Europe	2016	Superar Bosnia and Herzegovina
66	Greece	Europe	2016	El Sistema Greece
67	Panama	Latin America	2016	El Sistema de Orquestas y Coros Infantiles y Juveniles de Panama
68	Papua New Guinea	Oceana	2016	Queen of Paradise Project
69	Iran	West Asia	2016	Iran Youth Orchestra
70	Morocco	Africa	2017	El Sistema Maroc
71	Namibia	Africa	2017	Youth Orchestras of Namibia (YONA)
72	Hong Kong	East Asia	2017	El Sistema Hong Kong
73	Germany	Europe	2017	Musaik (Dresden); Consonanza (Munich)
74	Cyprus	Europe	2018	Sistema Cyprus
75	Tunisia	Africa	2019	Elab Project—Tunisia

Equally, Jorge Peña, who was forty-five when he was murdered on October 16, 1973, could have only dreamt that his passionate insistence that ensemble music-making be a part of every child's life would be taken up with equal levels of energy. Despite every criticism that has been leveled at El Sistema, the impact of its global manifestation cannot be disputed, and it is one of the truly important revolutions in music education.

NOTES

1. The Venezuelan program's full name is the State Foundation for the National System of Children and Youth Orchestras of Venezuela (Fundación del Estado para el Sistema Nacional de Orquestas Infantiles y Juveniles de Venezuela, or "FESNOJIV")
2. Lautaro Rojas, interview with Carlson, August 9, 2007.
3. Vanett Lawler, "The Conference in Santiago, Chile," *Music Educators Journal* 50, no. 5 (April–May 1964): 46.
4. Clara Bindhoff de Sigren, "Consideraciones y nuevas experiencias en Educación Musical Escolar," *Revista Musical Chilena* 91 (January–March 1965): 13.
5. "Se celebra el centenario del Conservatorio Nacional," *El Mercurio*, Santiago, Chile. October 27, 1949.
6. Jose Weinstein, qtd Rodriguez Hidalgo, Carmina, "Orquestas Infantiles y Juveniles de Chile: Un viaje por el legado de Jorge Peña Hen" (PhD diss., Universidad de Chile, 2004), 133–134.
7. María Fedora Peña. "Palabras de la hija de Jorge Peña Hen." Transcript, Catedral de la Serena, October 16, 2003.
8. El Día, April 21, 1956. qtd Miguel Castillo Didier, *Jorge Peña Hen (1928–1973): Músico, Maestro y Humanista Mártir* (Santiago, Chile: Gatillo, 2001): 112.
9. Alexandra Carlson, "Inundating the Country with Music: Jorge Peña, Democracy, and Music Education in Chile," *Journal of Historical Research in Music Education* 36, no. 1 (2014), 72.
10. "The 1964 Conference in Philadelphia," *Music Educators Journal* 50, no. 6 (June-July 1964): 34–38. Peña's attendance at the MENC conference is confirmed by a speech that mentions him and his wife, entitled "Breakfast Routine." (Colleen McKnight, email to author, April 22, 2008)
11. Hugo Dominguez, interview with Carlson, August 10, 2007.
12. Miguel Castillo, Peña's biographer, interview with Carlson, August 7, 2007.
13. Samuel Claro, "Actividad Musical Docente en la Serena," *Revista Musical Chilena* 95 (January–March 1966): 3.
14. Lautaro Rojas, interview with Carlson, La Serena, Chile, August 9, 2007.
15. Nella Camarda, personal email to Sutherland, January 29, 2020.
16. Samuel Claro, "Actividad musical docente en La Serena." *Revista Musical Chilena* 95 (January–March 1966): 4.
17. Hugo Dominguez, interview with Carlson, August 10, 2007.
18. Chefi Borzacchini, *Venezuela Sembrada de Orquestas* (Caracas: Banco del Caribe, 2004), 46.
19. Teresa Martínez, interview with Carlson, March 5, 2010.
20. Valentina Tejera, "Un Ejemplo Para América Latina: La Orquesta Infantil de Carora," *Revista Resumen* no. 186 (May 29, 1977): 35.
21. Agustina Jérez, interview with Carlson, March 5, 2010.
22. Tejera, "Ejemplo Para América Latina," 34.
23. José Indave Meléndez, "Por Primera Vez Venezuela Tiene una Orquesta Sinfónica Infantil," *El Diario*, August 8, 1975.
24. Fernando Izcaray, phone interview with Carlson, December 3, 2012.

25. El Nacional, "Orquesta Sinfónica Infantil de Carora Debuta Hoy en el Teatro Nacional," *El Nacional*, July 7, 1975.
26. José Indave Meléndez, "Apoteósico Triunfo de la Sinfónica Infantil," *El Diario*, November 23, 1975.
27. Ana Mercedes Asuaje de Rugeles, María Guinand, and Bolivia Bottome, *Historia del Movimiento Coral y de las Orquestas Juveniles en Venezuela* (Caracas: Departamento de Relaciones Públicas de Lagoven, 1986), 89.
28. Borzacchini (2004) says eight students. In subsequent accounts, Abreu mentions eleven.
29. Chefi Borzacchini. *Venezuela Sembrada de Orquestas* (Caracas: Banco del Caribe, 2004), 38.
30. Fernando Izcaray, phone interview with Carlson, December 3, 2012.
31. Hugo Dominguez, interview with Carlson, August 10, 2007.
32. El Nacional, "El Presente y el Fúturo Musical es de Ellos," *El Nacional*, July 23, 1976.
33. Fernando Briceño, interview with Carlson, March 5, 2010.
34. Guillermo Milla, interview with Carlson, Santiago, Chile, August 17, 2007.
35. Jose Urquieta, interview with Carlson, La Serena, Chile, August 9, 2007.
36. Shirley Apthorp, "Music, Poverty and Self Esteem in Venezuela: Classical escape from life on the mean streets," *Financial Times UK*, August 1, 2005.
37. Clarina Ahumada, interview qtd. Cortes Mendoza, Elizabeth. Jorge W Peña Hen, Vida y Obra (Diss, unpublished. Santiago: Universidad de la Serena, 1994), 124.
38. Fernando Briceño, interview with Carlson, March 5, 2010.
39. Alexandra Carlson, "The Story of Carora: The Origins of El Sistema." *International Journal of Music Education* 34, no. 1 (February 2016), 69.
40. El Nacional, "El Presente y el Fúturo Musical es de Ellos," *El Nacional*, July 23, 1976.
41. El Nacional, "Fúturo Musical."
42. Fernando Izcaray, phone interview with Carlson, December 3, 2012.
43. Ivette Camacho Gonzalez, "Dos Chilenos Pedagogos en Música Dirigen la Sinfónica Infantil de Carora," *El Diario*, September 1, 1976.
44. El Diario, "La Sinfónica Infantil Actuará en el Poleidro de Caracas," *El Diario*, March 11, 1977.
45. Cecilia Valdes Urrutia, "Entrevista con José Antonio Abreu: En la Cruzada Musical," *El Mercurio*, January 15, 1995, sec. E Artes y Letras.
46. Borzacchini (2004) says eight students. In subsequent accounts, Abreu mentions eleven.
47. The Orfeón Lamas was a highly recognized concert choir created by Sojo, Plaza, Calcaño, and others.
48. Maria Guinand, "Renacer de la actividad musical," in Ana Mercedes Asuaje de Rugeles, Maria Guinand, and Bolivia Bottome, Historia del movimiento coral y de las orquestas juveniles en Venezuela (Caracas: Cuadernos Lagoven, 1986) 25–43.
49. Lauren R Silberman, "Globalizing El Sistema: Exploring the growth and development of El Sistema inspired programs around the world" (Master's project, University of Oregon, 2013).

50. Geoffrey Baker and Ana Lucía Frega, "'Producing musicians like sausages': new perspectives on the history and historiography of Venezuela's El Sistema." *Music Education Research* 20, no. 4 (2018): 502–516.

51. Christine Witkowski, *El sistema: Music for social change* (London: Omnibus Press, 2016).

52. Laura Nemoy and David W. Gerry, "Adapting the El Sistema program to Canadian communities." *The Canadian Music Educator* 56, no. 3 (2015): 8.

53. Anna Bull, "El Sistema as a bourgeois social project: Class, gender, and Victorian values." *Action, criticism and theory for music education* 15, no. 1 (2016): 120–153.

54. Erika M. Kitzmiller, "Witnessing the Power of El Sistema in Urban Communities: Sister Cities Girlchoir," *Occasional Paper Series* 2013, no. 30 (2013): 10.

55. Geoffrey Baker, "Citizens or subjects? El Sistema in critical perspective," *Artistic Citizenship: Artistry, Social Responsibility, and Ethical Praxis* (2016): 313–338.

56. Eric Booth and Tricia Tunstall, "Five encounters with "El Sistema" international: A Venezuelan marvel becomes a global movement," *Teaching Artist Journal* 12, no. 2 (2014): 69–81.

57. Geoffrey Baker, Anna Bull, and Mark Taylor, "Who watches the watchmen? Evaluating evaluations of El Sistema," *British Journal of Music Education* (2018): 1–15.

BIBLIOGRAPHY

Apthorp, Shirley. "Music, Poverty and Self Esteem in Venezuela: Classical escape from life on the mean streets." *Financial Times UK*, August 1 2005.

Baker, Geoffrey. "Citizens or subjects? El Sistema in critical perspective." *Artistic Citizenship: Artistry, Social Responsibility, and Ethical Praxis* (2016): 313–338.

Baker, Geoffrey, and Ana Lucía Frega. "'Producing musicians like sausages': new perspectives on the history and historiography of Venezuela's El Sistema." *Music Education Research* 20, no. 4 (2018): 502–516.

Baker, Geoffrey, Anna Bull, and Mark Taylor. "Who watches the watchmen? Evaluating evaluations of El Sistema." *British Journal of Music Education* (2018): 1–15.

Blanco Sanchez, Balbino. "El Ejemplo de Martinez Herrera en Carora." *El Diario* (Carora, Venezuela), May 12, 1975.

Booth, Eric, and Tricia Tunstall. "Five encounters with 'El Sistema' international: A Venezuelan marvel becomes a global movement." *Teaching Artist Journal* 12, no. 2 (2014): 69–81.

Borzacchini, Chefi. *Venezuela Sembrada de Orquestas*. Caracas: Banco del Caribe, 2004.

Bull, Anna. "El Sistema as a bourgeois social project: Class, gender, and Victorian values." *Action, criticism and theory for music education* 15, no. 1 (2016): 120–153.
Camacho Gonzalez, Ivette. "Dos Chilenos Pedagogos en Música Dirigen la Sinfónica Infantil de Carora." *El Diario* (Carora, Venezuela), September 1, 1976.
Carlson, Alexandra. "Inundating the Country with Music: Jorge Peña, Democracy, and Music Education in Chile." *Journal of Historical Research in Music Education* 36, no. 1 (2014): 65–78. http://www.jstor.org/stable/43664221.
Carlson, Alexandra. "The Story of Carora: The Origins of El Sistema." *International Journal of Music Education* 34, no. 1 (February 2016): 64–73. doi: 10.1177/0255761415617926.
Castillo Didier, Miguel. *Jorge Peña Hen (1928–1973): Músico, Maestro y Humanista Mártir*. Santiago, Chile: Gatillo, 2001.
Castillo Didier, Miguel. "Jorge Peña Hen: A 25 Años de su Muerte." *Revista Musical Chilena* no. 189 (June 1998): 90. doi: 10.4067/S0716-27901998019000002.
Claro, Samuel. "Actividad Musical Docente en La Serena." *Revista Musical Chilena* no. 95 (March 1966): 3–5.
Cortes Mendoza, Elizabeth. "Jorge W Peña Hen, Vida y Obra." Unpublished Dissertation, Universidad de La Serena, 1994.
Cullell, Agustin. "Editorial." Las Últimas Noticias. November 25, 1965.
de Rugeles, Asuaje, Ana Mercedes, María Guinand, and Bolivia Bottome. *Historia del Movimiento Coral y de las Orquestas Juveniles en Venezuela*. Caracas: Departamento de Relaciones Públicas de Lagoven, 1986.
"Ejecutivo del Estado Lara, la Secretaría General de Gobierno, Presentan a la Orquesta Sinfónica Infantil de Carora," November 22, 1975.
El Diario. "La Sinfónica Infantil Actuará en el Poleidro de Caracas." *El Diario* (Carora, Venezuela) March 11, 1977.
El Diario. "Triunfa en Caracas el Orfeón de Carora." *El Diario* (Carora, Venezuela), August 31, 1966, sec. Ecos y Glosas.
El Mercurio. "Se Celebra el Centenario del Conservatorio Nacional." El Mercurio. October 27, 1949.
El Nacional. "El Presente y el Fúturo Musical es de Ellos." *El Nacional* (Caracas, Venezuela), July 23, 1976.
El Nacional. "Orquesta Sinfónica Infantil de Carora Debuta Hoy en el Teatro Nacional." *El Nacional* (Caracas, Venezuela), July 7, 1975.
Fedora Peña, María. "Palabras de la Hija de Jorge Peña Hen." Catedral de la Serena, October 16, 2003.
Guinand, Maria, "Renacer de la actividad musical," in Ana Mercedes Asuaje de Rugeles, Maria Guinand, and Bolivia Bottome, *Historia del movimiento coral y de las orquestas juveniles en Venezuela*, 25–43 (Caracas: Cuadernos Lagoven, 1986).
Indave Meléndez, José. "Por Primera Vez Venezuela Tiene una Orquesta Sinfónica Infantil." *El Diario* (Carora, Venezuela), August 8, 1975.
Indave Meléndez, José. "Apoteósico Triunfo de la Sinfónica Infantil." *El Diario* (Carora, Venezuela), November 23, 1975.

Kitzmiller, Erika M. "Witnessing the Power of El Sistema in Urban Communities: Sister Cities Girlchoir." *Occasional Paper Series* 2013, no. 30 (2013): 10.

Maraven. "La Orquesta Sinfónica de Carora: Su Presentación en 'El Carabobo' Fue un Resonante Suceso Artístico." *Maraven*. December 1976, No. 12, Vol. 1 edition.

MENC Editors. "The 1964 Conference in Philadelphia." Music Educators Journal 50, no. 6 (July 1964): 34–38.

Milla Figuroa, Guillermo. "Jorge Peña Hen: Su Música y los Niños." DVD, Documentary. Fondart, 2004.

Molina, Carmen. "Sinfónica Infantil de Carora Triunfó en San Cristóbal." *Vanguardia* (San Cristóbal, Venezuela), May 22, 1977.

Muñoz, María Luisa. "Principios y Orientación de la Educación Musical." Revista Musical Chilena no. 87–88 (July 1964): 28–30.

Nemoy, Laura, and David W. Gerry. "Adapting the El Sistema program to Canadian communities." *The Canadian Music Educator* 56, no. 3 (2015): 8.

Ramón y Rivera, Luis Felipe. *50 Años de Música En Caracas, 1930-1980*. Caracas: Fundación Vicente Emilio Sojo, 1988.

Revista Musical Chilena. "La Sociedad Bach de La Serena." Revista Musical Chilena no. 47 (October, 1954): 50–51.

Revista Musical Chilena. "La Música en Provincia: La Sociedad J.S. Bach de La Serena." Revista Musical Chilena no. 55 (December 1957): 92.

Revista Musical Chilena. "Nace la Segunda Orquesta Infantil en La Serena." Revista Musical Chilena no. 100 (June 1967): 89.

Rodriguez Hidalgo, Carmina. "Orquestas infantiles y juveniles de Chile: Un viaje por el legado de Jorge Peña Hen." Unpublished Dissertation, Universidad de Chile, 2004.

Sanchez, María Luisa. *La Enseñanza Musical en Caracas*. Caracas: Tip. La Torre, 1949.

Silberman, Lauren R. "Globalizing El Sistema: Exploring the growth and development of El Sistema inspired programs around the world." (2013).

Stein, Hans. "Testimonios: Visiones de 30 Años de Música En Chile." Edited by Alejandro Guarello and Carmen Peña. Resonancias no. 12 (May 2003): 5–53.

Tejera, Valentina. "Un Ejemplo para América Latina: La Orquesta Infantil de Carora." *Revista Resumen* no. 186 (May 29, 1977): 34–36.

Valdes Urrutia, Cecilia. "Entrevista Con José Antonio Abreu: En La Cruzada Musical." *El Mercurio* (Santiago, Chile), January 15, 1995, sec. E Artes y Letras.

Villasmil Soules, Pedro Raul. "Un Ejemplo y una Lección para San Cristóbal: La Orquesta Sinfónica Infantil de Carora." *Diario Católico*. May 27, 1977.

Witkowski, Christine. *El sistema: Music for social change*. London: Omnibus Press, 2016.

Chapter 8

Televised Music Instruction
Paul Louth

Almost from its inception, television has been used for instruction as well as commercial entertainment, and music education has been deeply involved in the former. Although it may seem antiquated today to consider television a relevant music education technology, televised music instruction's impact was revolutionary not because of its efficacy or longevity, but because it signaled a cultural shift in conceptions of music teaching and learning. Specifically, it blurred the lines between education and entertainment and marked, or perhaps even facilitated, a reconceptualization of what music teaching could or should look like

The earliest accounts of instructional television use (hereafter ITV) appear to be from English-speaking countries, reflecting the fact that although it has no singular country of invention,[1] television was first mass-marketed in Britain and the United States.[2] Televised instruction can be broken into two main categories: broadcast TV (sending signals of live or videotaped content directly over airwaves) and closed-circuit TV (sending signals through cables to receivers within a closed system).[3] The first regularly televised music instruction was broadcast live in 1948 from commercial television stations in the American cities of Baltimore and Philadelphia to area schools.[4]

Instructional television overlaps with a similar activity: educational television. This is televised content generally intended for use in the home, either as formal or informal distance education or as a preschool or out-of-school supplement to children's education. For simplicity, I will use ITV in a broad sense to incorporate educational as well as instructional television. Children's educational programming is a branch of educational television in which music always seems to have figured prominently. The iconic children's entertainer Fred Rogers (1928–2003), for example, produced the first children's educational program on the first community-owned television station in the

United States in 1954, for which he composed all the music and performed as the organist.[5]

Although Britain was first to market, their experience with ITV began slightly later, in 1957, after a carefully planned, nationally coordinated experimental period. British schools received televised instruction using the state-run British Broadcasting Corporation (BBC) in conjunction with a few independent television companies that were contracted to the government.[6] Within a decade, music was listed in official government reports as one of the subjects regularly taught through ITV both as a supplement to traditional teaching and as a form of "direct instruction."[7] Outside the United States and Britain, ITV generally began a bit later, in the 1960s. For example, Canada began "school telecasts" twice weekly beginning in 1961,[8] the Netherlands made instructional broadcasts, including music courses, available to the general population beginning in 1965,[9] and in Thailand commercial television stations under government control were "experimenting" with broadcasting music lessons directly into Bangkok schools at least as early as 1966.[10]

Suggesting its continuing perceived importance to music education, the Tanglewood Symposium, a 1967 meeting of diverse representatives within American society, convened to debate and propose changes for music education in that country, including televised music instruction in its recommendations.[11] This point through the late 1970s appears to be ITV's "high water mark," at least in the United States, where, by 1968, "large numbers of students" were being taught this way.[12] Thomas Carpenter, who has researched and written more extensively on the subject than most,[13] argued in 1971 that televised music instruction had "improved discernably" from its earliest days when usage was live and highly localized. The advent of delayed and/or repeated videotape broadcasts allowed for lessons to be curated and shared widely among institutions, promoting standardization of resources and, presumably to some extent, expertise.[14]

As for what motivated educators to begin using the technology, some early arguments were based neither on studied effectiveness nor on lack thereof but instead seem to have been driven by a vague sense of technological determinism. Harry Skornia writes in 1955, for example, that because it "seems destined to dwarf all other media of mass communications in its impact, . . . if we fail to understand television and its meaning to education, we do so at our peril."[15] This idea that a technology is "destined" to shape society and educators need to "get ahead of it" to ensure its beneficial use would later be echoed in the rhetoric of arguments for introducing computers into classrooms. But economics figured more prominently when deciding whether to use ITV in the first three decades of its development. It was expensive to equip schools with their own closed-circuit systems and production facilities or to purchase air and studio time; therefore, "the principle reason for nonuse of the medium

... was monetary."[16] For televised music instruction, these overhead costs were often balanced against economic arguments that favored using it in place of traditional instruction.

DIFFERENT APPROACHES TO ITV IN MUSIC

From its inception in 1948 until at least the 1970s and occasionally well beyond, ITV's use in formal music education has been associated with three interrelated but distinct goals. These might be described as supplemental (to enhance face-to-face music instruction), substitutional (to replace such instruction), or convergent (to remove distance barriers to music instruction). Both broadcast and closed-circuit television were used in the 1950s and 1960s to accomplish all three goals. In the United States, although often conceived as supplemental, in reality ITV was commonly substituted for traditional classroom music teaching for primarily economic reasons. Televised lessons were taught by music specialists while being broadcast to students by general classroom teachers with no specialized music training who often lacked effective music teaching skills.[17] For example, Carpenter describes the situation in 1973 in the northern part of the American state of Maryland, where three television music teachers were broadcasting regular lessons to nearly 22,000 students over a 500-square-mile area and visiting the generalist classroom teachers for support only once per year. Had these three individuals suddenly switched modalities to classroom teaching, they would have been able to see each class less than once per month.[18]

This approach obviously saved money by providing specialized music instruction where none existed previously or by augmenting the ability of overstretched music teachers to support general elementary classroom teachers. The practice was widespread in both rural and urban parts of the United States.[19] This was not always intentional. Sometimes telelessons intended to supplement and strengthen classroom music instruction would instead become "the complete means of music instruction" in schools with no music specialist.[20] This outcome was not confined to the United States. A 1966 report on a project to introduce educational television into Columbian schools, for example, noted that some classroom teachers who enjoyed showing music telelessons to first-grade students were, nevertheless, not using the accompanying guides because they could not understand the music notation on them.[21] Presumably offsetting these effects somewhat, ITV was also used to provide additional training for classroom teachers, especially of younger students, in general music pedagogy. Some even considered the in-service training implications the most valuable aspect of the technology.[22] That it was often intended as much for general teachers lacking music pedagogy knowledge as for students is evidenced by the "lengthy and detailed teachers' guides" accompanying many of the programs.[23] This use of ITV was both supplemental and substitutional in the sense that, through supplementing the training of generalist teachers, it became a substitute for some or all of the otherwise needed specialized in-person instruction.

Additionally, broadcasts of music lessons and music-themed educational television served as an early form of distance education.[24] One can apply this term widely to include broadcasts targeted at typical university students unable or unwilling to attend physical institutions, educational content for other adults, and educational TV intended for children outside of school hours. ITV broadcasts targeted at communities (as opposed to schools) were sometimes offered for credit or certification, in which case course registration and/or subscription to accompanying materials such as books or records was required. American students enrolled in the televised music appreciation course at Western Reserve University in 1951, for example, received their course outline, bibliography, and assignment list by mail and mailed their assignments back to the instructor for grading.[25]

Because such lessons were available to whoever was within reception range, inevitably, some passive viewers would simply tune in and watch when a program was on. In the Netherlands, which began offering televised courses including music to the general population in 1965, the public broadcasting service distinguished between course "participants" and "normal viewers" when doing audience research.[26] Writing about broadcasts from Britain's Open University—an institution founded in 1971 to help nontraditional adults earn degrees from home and supplemented reading and written work with some television—Allan Jones theorizes that "it is likely that most ... viewers would not have been students."[27] Of the three goals, distance education is the one that arguably kept ITV, and by extension televised music instruction, relevant beyond the 1980s despite the advent of computers and the Internet. Lack of access to Internet (and now broadband) in "developing" countries, and many rural areas within wealthier countries, caused government and educational leaders to turn to ITV to educate underserved populations.[28] Finally, it is worth noting that the two methods of transmitting signals—broadcasting and closed circuit—could be put to different uses. Broadcasting worked to standardize within a given reception area, whereas closed circuit allowed tailoring of music lessons to meet specific student needs within a system.[29]

A BRIEF REVIEW OF EDUCATIONAL IMPACT

Much of the research on ITV conducted during the 1950s and 1960s tended to compare the effectiveness of televised and traditional instruction in general, occasionally but seldom including music courses in the data. These studies overwhelmingly found no statistically significant differences between the two modalities.[30] University-level music appreciation classes were included in at least one such study at Pennsylvania State University in 1954, and test results showed no difference between televised and traditional instruction.[31] Speaking of these early studies collectively, Carpenter cautions readers that

> the comparability of control and experimental subjects, the comparability of the effectiveness and personality of the teachers, the lack of agreement on a definition of conventional classroom teaching, and imprecise and invalid measuring instruments and techniques are all factors that have cast doubt on the validity of many of these studies.[32]

Moreover, the early consensus of "no difference" should be interpreted especially carefully when applied to music for two reasons. First, most early research focused on retention of information as measured by traditional standardized tests. This is different from measuring the effectiveness of learned *procedural* knowledge such as listening and performing. In the early 1950s, for example, the abovementioned students at Western Reserve University taking televised music appreciation scored below average on only one component of the exam: required listening.[33] Several years of comparison within six elementary schools in the northwestern United States showed that young students taught to sing through ITV had difficulty matching pitch compared to their cohorts taught traditionally.[34] Second, and perhaps more importantly, because television teachers of young students were musically trained specialists whose work either assisted with or substituted for general classroom instruction not normally delivered by specialists, it is difficult to see how an "apples-to-apples" comparison of the two modalities would have been possible in those cases.

The 1970s saw more research on televised music instruction conducted, much of it continuing to find no appreciable differences between it and traditional instruction. One 1978 study found no significant differences among the experimental (television) group and two control groups for either gains in musical skills or attitudes toward music.[35] Interestingly though, the researcher speculated that this result may have been linked to the fact that students in the study had been conditioned to think of television viewing in school as "a reward for good behavior" rather than a normal part of "structured learning."[36] But even instructional television used as a reward can have incidental learning benefits, which Clifford Madsen demonstrated in a 1981 study. Televised music lessons were offered to students as rewards for correct math responses, and the lessons not only indirectly raised math scores but also improved music scores.[37]

Regarding televised music instruction designed to be viewed by children alone at home, as late as 2002, the authors of a study examining its impact on children's musical skill acquisition claimed that no such prior study existed.[38] They found that when children viewed and participated in a televised musical activity repeatedly, they could more easily reproduce "relatively short song phrases." The results were by no means impressive enough to suggest, however, "that televised music instruction is an adequate substitute for human music teaching."[39] As for distance learning involving older or adult music students, beyond the early results on music appreciation courses cited above, there is a paucity of research on its effectiveness.[40] Students who enrol in distance courses may differ in kind from those who enrol in conventional courses, and instructors may evaluate students differently in distance courses, making such research challenging.

A HARBINGER OF CHANGING CONCEPTIONS

If television failed to prove itself a more effective medium for teaching music, one might wonder if its sole contribution to the historical development of music education was as a model for improved efficiency. But television did much more than this. It represented, and probably helped facilitate, a "slow revolutionary turn" in how music education is both structured and perceived. At some unspecifiable point between its introduction in 1948 and its zenith in the late 1970s, ITV began to blur the boundaries between the previously formal, sequential, and focused world of music education and the vernacular, visual, and distracted world of music entertainment. People began to see television not only as a means to disseminate musical information but also as a means of enhancing visual interest and enjoyment as integral parts of music teaching and learning. Although Carpenter notes that in the United States, the "conventions of studio production" often limited experimentation and creativity in telelessons, there came a point in time where "no effort [was] spared to make the lessons visually interesting."[41] He cites several differences between televised music lessons and traditional classroom music instruction that had surfaced by the early 1970s. These include less emphasis on sequential song teaching using patterns; more focus on entertainment, interest, and enjoyment; and, significantly, a shift away from the lecture-demonstration format.[42]

Televised music instruction, in other words, appears to have enabled or, if simply a hallmark of larger cultural changes, at least represented an important perceptual shift in what music teaching and learning could look and sound like, for better or worse, in the future. It did not so much mark a rejection of traditional pedagogy as indicating a broadening of perspectives on how music learning and teaching constantly cross over what were thought to be firm boundaries between so-called direct teaching and the pedagogy of mass media, which now includes, crucially, social media. As televised music instruction, often blended with performance presentations, seeped into the vernacular lives of children and adults, music instruction itself became more vernacular. This did not happen suddenly. As Carpenter notes, in its early years of use, a television camera often simply showed the perspective of a phantom student sitting in the back of a classroom.[43] The pedagogical approach, in other words, would often have been indistinguishable from traditional face-to-face teaching as it looked in the 1950s. But that was soon to change. By 1977, an article in the widely read *Journal of Teacher Education* argued for more ITV in teacher training based on "television's motivational appeal for youngsters," who were by then viewing television more hours per week than they were spending in school.[44]

This marked a significant shift away from economic or convenience arguments—which seemed to proliferate in the 1950s and early 1960s—and toward the idea that television might represent a key link between formal education and the concrete, vernacular world of students' lived experiences. The argument that televised music instruction should "fight fire with fire" by incorporating entertaining elements to compete for students' attention using a medium that was well-known to attract it marked a decided change in attitude for some educators and scholars. Some of the pushback against television's use in music education likely stemmed from discomfort with blurring traditional boundaries between instruction and entertainment, blurring that resulted from emphasizing visual elements that might stimulate interest in something other than pure musical sounds. Additionally, perceived tensions between an instructional delivery method that purportedly encourages focused attention (traditional teaching) and one that purportedly encourages distraction (televised instruction using commercial television strategies) mirrored parallel concerns about blurring the boundaries between the public and commercial spheres. Consider Skornia's 1955 plea that educators embrace television's educational potential in which he nevertheless cautions that "education shouldn't have to put on commercial packaging to justify itself."[45]

This gradual blurring of boundaries between the worlds of public education and private entertainment may have been facilitated in some countries by the blending of commercial, school, and not-for-profit production that comprised the various forms of televised music education, since commercial and even not-for-profit television that is not fully government-funded must be sufficiently entertaining to motivate viewers to continually tune in.[46] Even as regards government funding, shifting historical priorities in the United States are instructive. In 1967, federal funding shifted from ITV to "educational television (ETV) meaning informative, cultural programming, and eventually to stations carrying public television (PTV) meaning cultural, entertaining programming."⁴⁷ In other words, there was a gradual shift from the idea that the public had an obligation to support televised content that offered direct instruction to the idea that culturally enriching *and* entertaining content deserved support.

Donald Pash, a prolific music television producer with credentials in both fields, agreed, arguing in 1971 for "the broadest possible concept of music education in television."⁴⁸ Pash criticized the narrow view that music education was only served through televised *instruction*. In fact, he went so far as to "seriously question the so-called educational values of [purely instructional] programs" while bemoaning the overlooked educational potential of television that presents superior musical performances without explicit pedagogical content.⁴⁹ The suggestion that high-quality musical performances can be stand-alone forms of education owes something to the theory of presentational knowledge. The term was coined by the philosopher Suzanne Langer to indicate a type of artistic or intuitive understanding that "presents" itself directly to human consciousness without the intervention of language.⁵⁰ Although not without controversy, the idea that musical learning may proceed this way has many advocates. Significantly, however, Pash argued that the key to television viewers receiving maximal educational benefits from such presentations "lies in the production of the program itself in every phase, including the camera work, the settings, the lighting, and the supplementary visual content."⁵¹ He also reasoned that "if we are to develop audiences for contemporary music, we must present it in such a manner that it will be attractive . . . we must induce [potential audiences] to listen . . . the artistic staging of such presentations on television can assist in accomplishing this."⁵²

Pash's words here represent one side of an important musical debate that is distinct from the one about instruction versus entertainment. There was (and still is) active pushback against the pairing of television with not only music instruction but also music more generally because that pairing often blurs the boundaries between focused listening and visual distraction. Around the time that Pash was advocating to broaden music education's approach to ITV, the composer Benjamin Britten expressed concerns about TV viewers not taking music presentations seriously enough because of the medium.⁵³ More recently, Keith Negus argued that television is more conducive to different aesthetic practices than the "culturally specific" type of "respectful viewing and concentrated listening" to which Britten hoped audiences would aspire.⁵⁴ This is supported by television reception research suggesting "a highly active, but not necessarily fully attentive, audience, engaged in all manner of viewing strategies."⁵⁵ These diametrically opposed ways of attending to stimuli invite divergent views on how television images alter our experiences of music. Negus explains that "a belief in the purity of music, uncontaminated by the visual, was applied not just to art music" but also to jazz and rock ideology. And importantly, musicians, scholars, and audience members who have upheld this view have often pointed to the "distracting" aesthetic of television as a counterexample.[56] He also notes that although "concerns about the physical appearance of musicians when performing" predated television, televised music performances "exaggerated, accentuated, and focused" those concerns.[57]

THE BERNSTEIN EFFECT

Between 1958 and 1972, the famed conductor and composer Leonard Bernstein presented a series of educational telecasts, his *Young People's Concerts*, specifically designed for children that the show's producer called "probably the most unconventional programs on television" at the time.[58] Bernstein's lasting accomplishment was not to transform television into a means through which ordinary people could be "uplifted" through exposure to and education about symphonic art music, which today represents a niche television market at best.[59] What Bernstein did instead was to maximize the presentational power of television to demonstrate that music learning not only could be accessible but also need not be disconnected from the immediacy of musical performance, including its visual, processual, and embodied aspects. Musical learning while not singing or playing an instrument could be more than a disconnected academic pursuit. It could be experienced alongside those presentational aspects of musical performance that were captured and transmitted to screens. It was perhaps ironic, then, that Bernstein used the first installment of his series to teach children the formalist lesson that music's significance is unrelated to any ostensibly extra-musical ideas, even as the televisions they were watching presented a new and powerful comingling of music and visual content.[60]

The pedagogical implications of this comingling may be easily overlooked in today's multimedia-saturated environment. It is worth remembering, though, that early general music instruction was often quite separated from its performative aspects, perhaps implying a perceived separation between the worlds of musicians and music scholars.[61] Yet in Bernstein viewers saw a highly esteemed artist who taught *about* music as it was performed in real time (relative to his commentary) by a real orchestra. When millions of children and their parents experienced this phenomenon, it was an important step in broadening at least some popular conceptions of formal music learning into something that could be systematic but also presentational *and* entertaining.

YOUTUBE AND BEYOND

Now, at least fifty years into the computer age, the pathway forged by educational and instructional television is taken up by countless websites that can perform similar roles. Of these, the so-called Web 2.0 sites, those that offer opportunities for user feedback and/or multidirectional communication, represent particularly powerful educational opportunities for formal and informal music learning that extend well beyond what was possible with ITV. For example, Janice Waldron shows how "participatory culture" is enabled by such websites through their encouragement of user-generated content, which then accelerates informal music learning.[62] There is also now an unimaginable amount of music education content available on computer screens. When delayed, videotaped transmission led to greater sharing of televised resources among music teachers in the 1960s, and it was a portent of what would be possible in the age of social media. Social network sites like Facebook, with billions of monthly users now, provide constant opportunities for collaboration and resource sharing among music teachers.[63]

YouTube, in particular, facilitates a unique convergence of the physical and virtual worlds of learning and is sufficiently ubiquitous to resemble or even surpass broadcast television in potential reach. Beyond its many "television-like" uses in direct or supplemental music instruction, YouTube offers an additional dimension: its users often acquire sophisticated music creation skills through producing their own video content.[64] In an important sense, this is turning traditional televised music instruction—where the experts were behind the cameras and the learners in front—on its head. Television's most pronounced impact on music education was the cultural and perceptual shift that it helped usher in. Much like the burnt-in "ghost images" on early TV screens that resulted from static projection for extended periods of time, ITV's influence is not immediately noticeable, but it is certainly long-lasting.

NOTES

1. Developed in an international, piecemeal fashion, television has been called "probably the first invention by committee." Albert Abramson, "The Invention of Television," in *Television: An International History*, ed. Anthony Smith (New York: Oxford University Press, 1998), 9.

2. This began in 1936 in Britain and 1939 in the United States. The German postal service began televised broadcasts in 1935, but the experiment was unsuccessful and television receivers were not marketed to the German public at that time.

Albert Abramson, *Television: An International History* (Jefferson, NC: McFarland and Co., 2003), 18–19.

3. The terms "open-circuit broadcasting" and "closed-circuit broadcasting" have largely fallen out of use in favor of the less confusing "broadcast TV" and "closed-circuit TV" (CCTV).

4. Thomas H. Carpenter, *Televised Music Instruction* (Washington: MENC, 1973), 26–27.

5. Robert A. Levine and Laurie Moses Hines, "Educational Television, Fred Rogers, and the History of Education," *History of Education Quarterly* 43, no. 2 (Summer, 2003): 265.

6. Report, "Educational Television in Britain," prepared for the Central Office of Information (London, UK., 1967), 1–2.

7. "Educational Television in Britain," 3.

8. Susan Swan, "Educative Activities of the Canadian Broadcasting Corporation and the National Film Board of Canada. New Technologies in Canadian Education Series. Paper 8," (Toronto: TV Ontario, 1984), 4; Educational television for the wider public did not begin until the 1970s.; Marc Raboy, "Canada," in *Television: An International History*, eds. Anthony Smith, and Richard Paterson (Oxford: Oxford University Press, 1998), 163.

9. Dorothy Krynatonos and Renate Vonhoff, "Multi-media Systems in Adult Education: Twelve Project Descriptions in Nine Countries" (Munich: International Central Institution for Youth and Educational Television, 1971), 138.

10. Leo H. Larkin, "Instructional Television in Southeast Asia," *Philippine Studies* 14, no. 3 (July 1966): 469.

11. Allen Britton, Arnold Broido, and Charles Grey, *The Tanglewood Declaration*, December 31, 1967. http://tanglewoodsymposium.blogspot.com/p/the-tanglewood-declaration.html Originally published in Robert A. Choate, *Music in American Society: Documentary Report of the Tanglewood Symposium* (Bordertown, NJ: Alliance for Arts Education New Jersey, 1967).

12. Carpenter, "Televised Music Instruction," 77.

13. In the late 1960s, Carpenter received a government grant to research and report on the state of ITV use in music education in the United States. See Thomas H. Carpenter, "The Utilization of Instructional Television in Music Education." U.S. Department of Health, Education, and Welfare, Office of Education, Bureau of Research, 1969.

14. Thomas Carpenter, "Television and Video Recording in Music Education," *Educational Technology* 11, no. 8 (August 1971): 15.

15. Harry J. Skornia, "What Can You Do About Educational Television?" *Audio Visual Communications Review* 3, no. 2 (Spring, 1955): 85; Skornia worried that television frequencies reserved for education would not be put to that use in private sector hands.

16. Carpenter, "Televised Music Instruction," 48.

17. In 1967 in the United States, 94 percent of all music telecourses were intended for elementary music instruction; Jack Watson, "Television in Music Education," *Music Educators Journal* 53, no. 8 (April, 1967): 64–65.

18. Carpenter, "Televised Music Instruction," 37–38.
19. Carpenter, "Televised Music Instruction," 41, 43, 46, 52, 58, 87.
20. Carpenter, "Televised Music Instruction," 87.
21. George Comstock and Nathan Maccoby, "The Day-to-Day Job of the Utilization Volunteer: Structure, Problems, and Solutions. The Peace Corps Educational Television (ETV) Project in Columbia: Two Years of Research" (The Institution for Communication Research, Stanford University, 1966), 78.
22. Carpenter, "Televised Music Instruction," 44.
23. Carpenter, "Televised Music Instruction," 44.
24. Although unlikely to have significantly impacted music instruction, another early form of distance education was teletext. This was a "pseudo-interactive medium" in which information in text form originating on a computer was broadcast on unused TV signals; Aliza Duby, "Teletext: A Distance Education Medium," *Educational Technology* 28, no. 4 (April, 1988): 54.
25. Carpenter, "Televised Music Instruction," 30–31.
26. Kyatonis and Vonhoff, "Multi-media Systems in Adult Education," 38, 46.
27. Allan Jones, "The Rises and Falls of Adult Education on the BBC" *French Journal of British Studies* 26, no. 1 (2021): 8.
28. Charles M. Lyons, Pamela MacBrayne, and Judith L. Johnson "Interactive Television as a Vehicle for the Delivery of Higher Education to Rural Areas," *Journal of Educational Technology Systems* 23, no. 3 (1993–1994): 205–211; Sung-Wan Kim, "Effectiveness of a Satellite Educational Television Program for Ethiopian Secondary Education," *Distance Education* 36, no. 3 (2015): 420.
29. Carpenter, "Televised Music Instruction," 68.
30. Taher A. Razik, "What Instructional Television Research Tells Us," *Educational Technology* 7, no. 8 (1967): 10–15.
31. The study was made possible by the Fund for the Advancement of Education. Carpenter; "Televised Music Instruction," 121.
32. Carpenter, "Televised Music Instruction," 78.
33. Carpenter, "Televised Music Instruction," 30–31.
34. Carpenter, "Televised Music Instruction," 52.
35. Amy Brown, "Effects of Televised Instruction on Student Music Selection, Music Skills, and Attitudes," *Journal of Research in Music Education* 26, no. 4 (Winter, 1978): 449.
36. Brown, "Effects of Televised Instruction," 452.
37. Clifford K. Madsen, "Music Lessons and Books as Reinforcement Alternatives for an Academic Task," *Journal of Research in Music Education* 29, no. 2 (Summer, 1981): 103–110.
38. The authors do note that previous research had examined how the music content of children's educational programs affect musical preferences. John M. Feierabend, T. Clark Saunders, and Barbara N. Flagg, "The Effects of Television Music Instruction on Kindergarten Students' Music Performance Skills," *Bulletin of the Council for Research in Music Education* 152 (Spring, 2002): 65.
39. Feierabend, Saunders, and Flagg, "The Effects of Television," 71, 72.
40. Feierabend, Saunders, and Flagg, "The Effects of Television," 65.

41. Carpenter, "Televised Music Instruction," 85.
42. *Carpenter* "Televised Music Instruction," 84.
43. *Carpenter* "Televised Music Instruction," 83.
44. Pauline B. Gough, "Instructional Television's Time Has Come," *Journal of Teacher Education* 28, no. 5 (1977): 33.
45. Skornia, "Educational Television?" 86.
46. In the United States, for example, the Public Broadcasting System is a nongovernmental entity that relies heavily on viewer donations, which in turn clearly requires engaging programming.
47. Randy William Maule, "A History of K-12 Instructional Television" (PhD diss., University of Florida, 1987), 4.
48. Donald A. Pash, "Music Education on Television," *The World of Music* 13, no. 4 (1971): 3.
49. Pash, Music "Education on Television," 3, 4.
50. See, for example, Suzanne K. Langer, *Feeling and Form* (New York: Charles Scribner's Sons, 1953), 378.
51. Pash, "Education on Television," 4.
52. Pash, "Education on Television," 5–6.
53. From a 1970 *Grammophone* interview quoted in Keith Negus, "Musicians on Television: Visible, Audible, and Ignored," *Journal of the Royal Musical Association* 131, no. 2 (2006): 325.
54. Negus, "Musicians on Television," 325.
55. Negus, "Musicians on Television," 326.
56. Negus, "Musicians on Television," 316.
57. Negus, "Musicians on Television," 310.
58. Roger Englander, quoted in Réal La Rochelle, *Leonard Bernstein: L'oeuvre Télévisuelle* (Quebec City: Université Laval, 2010), 73 (my translation).
59. Simon Frith, "Look! Hear! The Uneasy Relationship of Music and Television," *Popular Music* 21, no. 3 (October 2002): 279.
60. La Rochelle, "Bernstein: L'oeuvre Télévisuelle, " 71.
61. Marguerite V. Hood, "Non-performance Music Classes in Secondary Schools," *Music Educators Journal* 53, no. 9 (May 1967): 75. This attitude can be traced back to Lowell Mason's division of musical goals into base pleasures, such as performance, and higher intellectual pursuits, such as learning music theory and history; Mary Browning Scanlon, "Lowell Mason's Philosophy of Music Education," *Music Educators Journal* 28, no. 3 (January 1942): 24–25, 70.
62. Janice Waldron, "An Alternative Model of Music Learning and 'Last Night's Fun': Participatory Music Making in/as Participatory Culture in Irish Traditional Music," *Action, Criticism and Theory for Music Education* 15, no. 3 (June 2016): 86–112. Waldron draws on Henry Jenkins' concept of 'participatory culture' here.
63. Radio Cremata and Bryan Powell, "Online Collabortion in Suporting Music Teaching and Learning," in *The Oxford Handbook of Social Media and Music Learning*, eds. Janice L. Waldron, Stephanie Horsley, and Kari K. Veblen (New York: Oxford University Press, 2020), 153–176.

64. Christopher Cayari, "Connecting Musical Education and Virtual Performance Practices from YouTube," *Music Education* Research 20, no. 3 (2018): 364, 371.

BIBLIOGRAPHY

Abramson, Albert. "The Invention of Television." In *Television: An International History*. Edited by Anthony Smith, 9–22. New York: Oxford University Press, 1998.

Brown, Amy. "Effects of Televised Instruction on Student Music Selection, Music Skills, and Attitudes." *Journal of Research in Music Education* 26, no. 4 (Winter, 1978): 445–455.

Carpenter, Thomas H. *Televised Music Instruction*. Washington, DC: Music Educators National Conference, 1973.

Carpenter, Thomas H. "Television and Video Recording in Music Education," *Educational Technology* 11, no. 8 (August, 1971): 15–18.

Carpenter, Thomas H. "The Utilization of Instructional Television in Music Education." U.S. Department of Health, Education, and Welfare, Office of Education, Bureau of Research, 1969.

Cayari, Christopher. "Connecting Musical Education and Virtual Performance Practices from YouTube," *Music Education* Research 20, no. 3 (2018): 360–376.

Choate, Robert A. *Music in American Society: Documentary Report of the Tanglewood Symposium*. Bordertown, NJ: Alliance for Arts Education New Jersey, 1967.

Comstock, George and Nathan Maccoby. "The Day-to-Day Job of the Utilization Volunteer: Structure, Problems, and Solutions. The Peace Corps Educational Television (ETV) Project in Columbia: Two Years of Research." The Institution for Communication Research, Stanford University, 1966.

Cremata, Radio and Bryan Powell. "Online Collabortion in Suporting Music Teaching and Learning." In *The Oxford Handbook of Social Media and Music Learning*, edited by Janice L. Waldron, Stephanie Horsley, and Kari K. Veblen, 153–176. New York: Oxford University Press, 2020.

Duby, Aliza. "Teletext: A Distance Education Medium," *Educational Technology* 28, no. 4 (April 1988): 54–57.

Feierabend, John M, T. Clark Saunders, and Barbara N. Flagg, "The Effects of Television Music Instruction on Kindergarten Students' Music Performance Skills," *Bulletin of the Council for Research in Music Education* 152 (Spring, 2002): 64–73.

Frith, Simon. "Look! Hear! The Uneasy Relationship of Music and Television." *Popular Music* 21, no. 3 (October 2002): 277–290.

Gough, Pauline B. "Instructional Television's Time Has Come," *Journal of Teacher Education* 28, no. 5 (1977): 32–36.

Jones, Allan. "The Rises and Falls of Adult Education on the BBC" *French Journal of British Studies* 26, no. 1 (2021). Accessed April 5, 2021. DOI: https://doi.org/10.4000/rfcb.7377

Hood, Marguerite V. "Non-performance Music Classes in Secondary Schools," *Music Educators Journal* 53, no. 9 (May 1967): 75–77, 79.

Kim, Sung-Wan. "Effectiveness of a Satellite Educational Television Program for Ethiopian Secondary Education." *Distance Education* 36, no. 3 (2015): 419–436.

Krynatonos, Dorothy and Renate Vonhoff. "Multi-media Systems in Adult Education: Twelve Project Descriptions in Nine Countries." Munich: International Central Institution for Youth and Educational Television, 1971.

La Rochelle, Réal. *Leonard Bernstein: L'oeuvre Télévisuelle.* Quebec City: Université Laval, 2010.

Langer, Suzanne K. *Feeling and Form.* New York: Charles Scribner's Sons, 1953.

Larkin, Leo H. "Instructional Television in Southeast Asia." *Philippine Studies* 14, no. 3 (July 1966): 460–470.

Levin, Robert A. and Laurie Moses Hines. "Educational Television, Fred Rogers, and the History of Education." *History of Education Quarterly* 43, no. 2 (Summer, 2003): 262–275.

Lyons, Charles M., Pamela MacBrayne, and Judith L. Johnson "Interactive Television as a Vehicle for the Delivery of Higher Education to Rural Areas," *Journal of Educational Technology Systems* 23, no. 3 (1993–1994): 205–211.

Madsen, Clifford K. "Music Lessons and Books as Reinforcement Alternatives for an Academic Task." *Journal of Research in Music Education* 29, no. 2 (Summer, 1981): 103–110.

Maule, Randy William. "A History of K-12 Instructional Television." PhD diss., University of Florida, 1987.

Negus, Keith. "Musicians on Television: Visible, Audible, and Ignored." *Journal of the Royal Musical Association* 131, no. 2 (2006): 310–330.

Pash, Donald A. "Music Education on Television." *The World of Music* 13, no. 4 (1971): 3–19.

Raboy, Marc. "Canada." In *Television: An International History.* Edited by Anthony Smith, 162–168. New York: Oxford University Press, 1998.

Razik, Taher A. "What Instructional Television Research Tells Us." *Educational Technology* 7, no. 8 (1967): 10–15.

Report, "Educational Television in Britain." Prepared for the Central Office of Information, London, UK., 1967.

Scanlon, Mary Browning. "Lowell Mason's Philosophy of Music Education," *Music Educators Journal* 28, no. 3 (January, 1942): 24–25, 70.

Skornia, Harry J. "What Can You Do About Educational Television?" *Audio Visual Communications Review* 3, no. 2 (Spring, 1955): 83–90.

Swan, Susan. "Educative Activities of the Canadian Broadcasting Corporation and the National Film Board of Canada. New Technologies in Canadian Education Series. Paper 8." Toronto: TV Ontario, 1984.

Waldron, Janice. "An Alternative Model of Music Learning and 'Last Night's Fun': Participatory Music Making in/as Participatory Culture in Irish Traditional Music." *Action, Criticism and Theory for Music Education* 15, no. 3 (June 2016): 86–112.

Watson, Jack. "Television in Music Education," *Music Educators Journal* 53, no. 8 (April, 1967): 64–65.

Chapter 9

Subverting the Hegemony
The Popular Music Revolution
Geoffrey M. Lowe

A relatively recent "revolution" has been a growing inclusion of popular music in schools. This has not been without controversy as evidenced by Brocklehurst's condemnation of its use in English schools in 1962:

> The primary purpose of musical appreciation is to inculcate a love and understanding of good music. It is surely the duty of teachers to do all they can to prevent young people falling ready prey to the purveyors of commercialized 'popular' music, for these slick, high pressure salesmen, have developed the exploitation of teenagers into a fine art.[1]

The inclusion of popular music has not been uniform across countries, and despite the recent advent of dedicated scholarly publications, its impact remains underresearched.[2] Notwithstanding increasing acceptance, equity issues remain between the treatment of popular and classical music,[3] and despite its popularity among students, it remains a fringe activity in some jurisdictions.[4] Engendering fierce debate upon its first emergence in music programs in the 1960s, the popular music discourse has coalesced around issues of legitimacy, repertoire issues, and pedagogical implications.

This chapter commences with an operational definition before briefly outlining popular music in education across the United Kingdom, the United States, and Australia. The chapter then focuses on the social context and in particular the discourse surrounding worthiness, relevance, and motivational value before considering the pedagogical implications and the impact of technology.

DEFINITION

The term "popular music" is problematic because it offers no clear definition or boundaries of application, and cultural context changes over time.[5] Some authors define it by contrasting it with folk or classical music,[6] others by its production,[7] mass appeal,[8] high consumption,[9] social influence,[10] or appeal to embodied experience.[11] Most define it as genres within an umbrella term that includes rock, country, jazz, folk, and soul.[12] Acknowledging definitional dilemmas and that "popular music" sits in an evolving sociomusical space,[13] this chapter utilizes Woody's umbrella term comprising Western popular music genres originating from 1950's rock and roll.

Popular Music in Education

United Kingdom

Early debate in the UK centered around the cultural and moral value of popular music. According to Rainbow,[14] music education's mission was to "wean students away from the raucous notes of course music hall songs." However, as early as 1955, the Scottish Education Department declared that "the interest of the pupils in contemporary popular music should not be ignored."[15] As the scale of popular youth culture became apparent in the 1960s, many teachers sought to tap into the music. Conversely, some teachers declared popular music an unhealthy influence to be counteracted at all costs, while others saw it as a steppingstone to "good" (classical) music.[16,17]

Vulliamy and Lee[18] countered claims of commercialism and low musical worth were based on lack of knowledge and misunderstanding of popular music's function. They argued that music education reflected the establishment's assumptions about what constituted "good" music, that is, European classical music, and that dismissal of popular music was flawed because it was premised upon classical music standards.

Early discourse into popular music's legitimacy took place against a backdrop of educational change including moves toward a creative and practical curriculum,[19] a more experimental curriculum,[20] and a general movement toward student-centered learning which Vulliamy and Lee described as ideally suited to popular music teaching.[21] Simmering tension erupted into a "culture war" surrounding the development of the English National Curriculum (ENC) in the early 1990s.[22] A working party of eminent musicians and music educators developed a draft practical curriculum which drew upon a wide variety of genres including popular music. However, the draft drew bitter criticism from conservative commentators largely unassociated with music education who lamented popular music's inclusion as undermining cultural tradition. Restorationist commentor Sir Roger Scruton declared:

> in its 117 page document you'll find only one mention of a classical composer—Mozart—and scarcely a reference to the tradition of Western music, although pop, reggae, flamenco, mambo, salsa and a thousand other ephemera are constantly paraded for consideration.[23]

Disturbingly Ball stated: "The restorationists reduced a set of complex issues to a matter of Beethoven versus steel bands"[24] as intense vitriol was directed not just against popular music but the draft practical curriculum with opponents advocating a return to a prescriptive "music appreciation" curriculum.

A degree of compromise was reached in the first iteration of the ENC in 1992, and the UK has since witnessed the widespread incorporation of popular music into mainstream teaching programs. Discourse has evolved from legitimacy to pedagogy because, according to Green[25] and Lamont et al.,[26] despite different pedagogical implications, teaching methods have remained largely changed. However, while discussion continues around pedagogy, UK music education is currently facing greater challenges presented by Covid-19 and the changing arts landscape on student enrollments and retention.[27]

United States

By contrast, popular music was not formally acknowledged as being worthy of study until the 1967 Tanglewood Declaration[28] which defined the role of music education in contemporary American society. Of the eight Tanglewood recommendations, the second stated:

> Music of all periods, styles, forms and cultures belongs in the curriculum. The musical repertory should be expanded to involve music of our time in its rich variety, including currently popular teenage music and avant-grade music, American folk music and the music of other cultures.[29]

The Tanglewood Declaration was succeeded in 1970 by thirty-five published MENC goals and objectives which included priority objective 4: "Advance the teaching of music of all periods, styles, forms and cultures." The MENC goals appeared at a time when little popular music was taught in schools and was widely dismissed as inappropriate.[30] In 1970, Fowler denounced popular music as "aesthetically inferior music, if music at all, damaging to youth both physically and morally, and school time should not be expended on what could learned in the vernacular."[31] In their 2000 review of popular music in U.S. schools, Hebert and Campbell identified three major impediments including lack of substantial teacher training in popular music, general dismissal of popular music as rebellious and anti-educational, and a lack of an effective instructional curriculum.[32]

Fifty years after Tanglewood, Cutietta[33] noted that few teach popular music in a substantive way. Rinsema noted that music teachers still feel the need to justify its inclusion,[34] while Cutietta described a general fear that the introduction of popular music would diminish existing programs.[35] Powell et al. noted that where it is taught, courses often focus on history and reside in social studies, history, English, and, to a lesser extent, general music curricula.[36] Practical programs are frequently tokenistic, comprising arrangements played by bands and choirs as part of "bait-and-switch" programs.[37] As in the UK, tokenism appeared in much of the early literature. For example, Smith argued for limited inclusion on the grounds of student alienation,[38] Landeck on musical compromise[39] and Fox as a hook to studying the "great" music of the past.[40] Sadly, Cutietta noted that while around 20 percent of U.S. students engage in school music, the majority who are interested in popular music do not,[41] and Mantie[42] notes that U.S. music education has been effectively immune to discourse from non-American countries.

Australia

Music education in Australia operates on the UK model, but popular music crept into Australian syllabuses from the 1970s without the same controversy. Dunbar-Hall and Wemyss state that it first settled into primary schools because of its simplicity, popularity, and practicability.[43] It also coincided with the shift toward practical curricula and student-centered learning and a general move toward multiculturalism in schools whereby it became acceptable to teach music from non-Western sources.[44] While accepted into classroom practice, its inclusion into national and state curricula has not been entirely seamless. For example, curriculum reform in Western Australia in the late 2000s and music teacher desire to include popular music in a previously exclusively classical curriculum saw intense and ill-informed public debates.[45] Unlike the UK, disquiet did not center around moral or cultural value but practice and, in particular, the place of notation. A compromise saw the division of the senior secondary curriculum into three "contexts"—Western Art Music, Jazz and Contemporary Music—with schools choosing one context exclusively. The result was a balkanization of school programs and philosophical division rather than inclusion.[46] This situation is under review with a single inclusive course proposed from 2023.

THE SOCIAL CONTEXT OF POPULAR MUSIC EDUCATION

Legitimacy

In defending popular music, Vulliamy and Lee countered its moral and cultural dismissal by claiming that the application of classical music evaluative criteria created a false dichotomy between "serious" and popular music.[47] Drawing upon Adorno,[48] opponents including Routh decried popular music for not demanding listeners' attention and being chiefly commercial in nature,[49] while Parker dismissed it as a homogenous product, commercially motivated and exploitative.[50] Vulliamy and Shepherd's response was that popular music was not homogenous; like classical music, it comprised of a huge range of subgenres and styles, and young people in turn saw classical music as homogenous. They defended popular musicians' motivation as primarily artistic but acknowledged a commercial imperative to survive, whereas classical music was heavily state-subsidized, allowing greater artistic freedom. Further, they countered exploitative claims by stating that no one forced people to purchase music; record companies reacted to changes in taste, rather than the reverse.[51] Hebert and Campbell have summarized legitimacy objections as either elitist, naive, or lacking in historical consciousness.[52] The latter in particular alludes to a sociocultural/contextual shift as the discourse has progressed from defense to justification as a product of place and time.

Frith was among the first to articulate a sociocultural repositioning.[53] According to Frith, popular music answers questions about personal identity and social standing, manages the relationship between public and private emotional lives, and shapes a sense of time and popular memory. Hebert and Campbell stated that every generation creates a powerful sense of identity, with music among the most personal and meaningful. They cited Frith: "we absorb songs into our own lives and rhythm into our own bodies."[54] Downey proposed "for young people, 'their culture' is frequently construed as the popular music culture of their time."[55] Repositioning was well articulated by Spruce who described society as a collection of disparate social groupings rather than a homogenous entity; the way disparate groups use and practice music is one way they create and express their identity. By extension, as schools are social arenas where music is culturally and socially rooted, music education should develop understanding of how music operates in social settings.[56] The sociocultural rationale has been generally accepted in a movement away from what Green describes as music "autonomy" whereby music rises above the mundane (social and political context) to music as part of everyday life (a product of time and place) and is not context-free.[57] While this assumes all music to be worthy of study, it has been particularly powerful in legitimizing popular music in schools.

Relevance to the Student Experiential World

Drawing upon sociocultural context, popular music advocates note its centrality in young people's lives, namely in identity development and social experience[58,59] and emotional connection to the music.[60] Music may be the single most important adolescent leisure activity,[61] and positive attitudes to popular music may be accompanied by lack of interest in "traditional" forms such as classical music.[62] For Hebert and Campbell, not including popular music serves to alienate students.[63] Vulliamy and Lee cited a Director of Music's justification for inclusion as "I use it not because they like it, but because they understand it."[64] More recently, positioning within the student experiential world is backed by general neurological research whereby students are more motivated when there is an emotional connection to learning and materials are deemed relevant.[65]

Motivational Positioning

Closely linked to relevance has been discourse surrounding the motivational value of popular music. Much has been written about the "real music" versus "school music" divide[66] and student dislike of school music.[67,68,69] Many have noted high levels of adolescent musical engagement outside school not reflected in attitudes or retention in senior secondary school music programs,[70,71,72] and negative attitudes toward music in schools pose serious challenges.[73] Research has demonstrated empirical links between student valuing of a subject and subsequent enrolment decisions,[74] while Vulliamy and Lee stated that popular music inclusion "enlarged student interest as a result of their present tastes being taken seriously."[75] However, Green cautioned that while popular music may appear motivating for students, perceptions that it is less rigorous than classical music effectively downgrades it, potentially undermining its educational potential.[76]

The motivational literature includes not just what is studied but also how it is experienced. Boal-Palheiros and Hargreaves reported correlations between out-of-school music listening and enjoyment and positive moods, as opposed to in-school association with learning and information.[77] Motivation to engage is enhanced when learning includes autonomy, creativity, personal expression, ownership, and attendant social benefits,[78] and "real world" tasks which encourage ownership can be significant student motivators.[79] Lamont et al. reported that when teacher attitudes to active popular music-making shifted, there was a corresponding increase in positive student attitudes.[80]

Ozdemir and Ciftcibasi reported improved motivation when popular music repertoire was included, but only when combined with practical learning experiences and technology.[81]

Impediments to Popular Music Education

Early opposition coalesced around perceived lowering of musical standards and formed the dominant ideology:

> The "pop" disease is so widespread these days that no child seems to escape it . . . one good defense is to say to the pupil who asks for pop: what has it to do with a music lesson? Do you ask your English teacher for Superman comics? Do you expect to play marbles in P.E. lessons?[82]

However, as McPhail noted, changing context sees discourse coalesce around a new dominant ideology.[83] For the past fifty years (with the exception of the United States), ideology has been reshaped by popular music as a social and cultural force in adolescent life. As music teachers seek to affirm student interest and skills, it creates challenges for those trained in classical traditions around perceived loss of control and lack of knowledge and resources. For example, Bresler described many music educators still believing in a past paradigm of formally cultivating mind and spirit.[84] This implies imposing values and beliefs on students rather than guiding them toward formation of their own.

Practical curricula can elicit a fear of student-centered learning leading to loss of teacher control[85] and is central to popular music pedagogies. Woody noted that it was not that many teachers rejected popular music but rather feared not knowing how to teach it.[86] Fear could be compounded by lack of resources[87] as well as lack of training.[88,89,90] Additionally, Vulliamy and Lee identified staffing as an impediment due to the reluctance of school authorities to hire staff with the requisite skills.[91] In terms of time and space, counterarguments have included a crowded music curriculum[92,93] and insufficient teaching space with appropriate soundproofing and safety concerns. Indeed, safety fears led some UK local authorities in the 1970s to ban the use of electric instruments entirely.[94] While many appear as impediments of convenience, there is no doubt of the broader challenge posed by effective pedagogy.

Negotiating the Pedagogy of Popular music

There has long been recognition of problems when employing pedagogies from classical music traditions. For Green, "the question is not one of content but of pedagogy."[95] Sloboda concurred, "one cannot just insert a popular genre into a set of classroom practices that have been developed with classical music."[96] Woody has called for reframed popular music pedagogical models focused on emotional/expressive qualities and social/cultural context rather than merely analysis of musical elements.[97] A compelling pedagogical conundrum was presented by Green who described two musical states, one based upon inherent meaning as response to sound and silence and the other, delineated meaning surrounding social, cultural, and political context.[98] Both are influenced by familiarity and identity. For Green, when popular music is brought into the classroom, delineated meaning is inadvertently changed for students because of the change of context; in essence, popular music taught in a classical way turns it into "new classical." Recognizing this conceptual challenge, many have proposed broad pedagogical frameworks including cooperative informal learning approaches associated with social skill development,[99] "vernacular musicianship" driven by listening, improvisation, collaborative composing, shared musical tastes, ownership and personal expression,[100] and the nurturing of musical process over polished product.[101] Cloonan[102] and Till[103] advocate broadening pedagogy to cover musical (creating and performing), vocational (music business), critical (cultural study and analysis), and technical (recording, production, and programming) elements. Understanding the learning processes of popular musicians is central.

Informal Learning

Green was among the first to discuss informal learning practices associated with popular music creation.[104] She described five processes: (1) choosing the music, (2) copying recordings by ear, (3) self-learning in groups, (4) trial and error, and (5) integration of listening, performing, creating, and improvising. She noted that convergent analysis of popular music did not necessarily engage students and bore little resemblance to how popular musicians created music. Green advised focusing on the process of generation and in particular inherent meaning derived through engagement with sound in a largely context-free environment. She reported no issues for students when emphasis was placed on the authenticity of the learning process. Green's research has been highly influential and, although recently challenged,[105] is still cited as the pedagogical basis for many popular music programs.

Issues Surrounding Repertoire Selection

While popular music potentially encourages a more democratic repertoire selection process, issues can arise surrounding suitability for classroom use.

For example, Kallio noted that certain songs can conflict with educational values.[106] Defined by Kallio as "deviant music," these songs may not conform to social norms, but students often identify with them. Rejecting these songs makes the students outsiders. For Kallio, despite music education increasingly welcoming diversity, exclusion becomes more difficult to justify against the ideals of democratic schooling and inclusion. In addition, while acknowledging the motivational merits of "student agency," there are caveats in terms of reduced rather than expanded repertoire range.[107]

The unsuitability of some song lyrics has also drawn public attention. Hebert and Campbell described attempted censorship in the United States in the 1980s by the Parents Music Resource Centre which resulted in warning labels on some music.[108] Rather than shunning popular music (and especially its lyrics) as antisocial, Hebert and Campbell advocated utilizing its power to advantage. They also noted hypocritical polarization over the lifestyle or political views of popular music artists because classical musicians are not held to the same levels of scrutiny. They questioned whether this was because popular music studies in the United States tend to be socially rather than practically embedded in schools.

Finally, the early discourse described student "taste cultures" operating along sociocultural lines, with, for example, working-class students preferring hard rock and upper-class students preferring progressive rock.[109] Vulliamy and Lee stressed the importance of breaking down barriers within popular music as much as between it and classical music. Sloboda reported popular music subcultural issues to be as important to students as the music itself.[110] Labeled "badge identity" by Tarrant et al., they reported student ownership of not just the music but the subculture.[111] This requires careful negotiation for teachers as "outsiders," as music may be jealously guarded by taste culture "insiders" who resent "outside" assessment of their music. Conversely, students not in the selected taste culture may resent use of the former group's music in preference to their own.[112]

Listening to Popular Music

Of importance has been how to meaningfully engage students in listening given that they are critically appreciative of popular music subgenres. According to Kratus,[113] classical music listening processes are largely convergent, that is, deconstructing using musical elements. Convergent thinking is not authentic to popular music appreciation and fuels the divide between "real" music and "school" music. Dunbar-Hall was among the first to present a listening model utilizing etic/emic interplay between analyzable facts and interpreted meanings.[114] For Dunbar-Hall, the etic (objective and autonomous) employed convergent thinking which was based around "how does this piece function" whereas the emic (the product of cultural knowledge) was divergent by drilling into subcultural associations of musical style, subculture, lifestyle, and beliefs. Parallels with Green's inherent and delineated states are evident.

More recently, Rinsema has advocated a hermeneutic listening approach as an expressive act interpreted through reflection.[115] Rinsema described three windows: (1) media integration to explore links between songs, accompanying videos, artwork, and text; (2) allusions which encompass indirect, passing, or unspoken references; and (3) actions which incorporate investigation of the when, why, where, and who of music listeners and creators, including the changing contexts in which music might be experienced. Rinsema argued that this approach can bring popular music listening into the classroom on its own terms rather than in terms of another tradition, validates student engagement with music in their everyday lives as listeners, and facilitates exploration in settings with limited resources.

Practical Pedagogy

Practice remains a recurring issue. Colquhoun has addressed the role of producers in song creation and the place of song covers,[116] Tobias addressed pedagogical approaches to recording, engineering, mixing, and producing, and DJing[117,118] and Kruse addressed hip-hop music learning.[119] Springer,[120] Dunbar-Hall,[121] Dunbar-Hall and Wemyss[122] and Woody[123] have noted similarities between informal popular music practical pedagogies and Orff-Schulwerk. Both emphasize creativity, experiential learning, and a pedagogical approach of observe-imitate-experiment-create. Further, Dunbar-Hall cites the use of similar musical materials including pentatonic scales, modes, ostinatos, and emphasis on poetry/lyrics, natural speech, and expressive movement,[124] while Woody notes the role of listening and copying (echoing).[125] Woody stated: "teachers who use Orff Schulwerk recognize the value of giving up absolute control of a classroom so that students may employ their own creativity and natural musicianship."[126]

Reconciling Pedagogical Tensions

While music teacher attitudes have largely changed, McPhail described two remaining dilemmas: reconciliation of the challenges presented by the inclusion of both classical and popular music in the curriculum and understanding what the change in dominant ideology toward popular music represents.[127] For McPhail, tension exists between different forms of knowledge and its relation to cultural transmission such as the desire to broaden student experience by exposing them to classical music while also affirming student interests and preexisting skills/knowledge. In exploring these tensions, McPhail described a tacit belief that classical and popular pedagogies function in binary opposition. In an attempt at reconciliation, he has argued for Bernstein and his horizontal/vertical discourse model, whereby horizontal discourse comprises the everyday and facilitates broad access, whereas vertical discourse is associated with higher-order conceptual understanding.[128] McPhail argues the need for balance between student interest and rounded education, knowledge differentiation between "knowing about music" in the classical tradition, "music as knowledge" in the popular music-making tradition, and theoretical knowledge enhancing other music learning to broaden students' creative and expressive potential. He claimed that with time and thought, the pedagogical divide can blur as teachers affirm, legitimize, and accommodate student interests through the lens of educational values.

Technology and Popular Music Education

This chapter cannot conclude without passing reference to music technology. While not exclusive to popular music, it is central to popular music creation and distribution, and contemporary genres such as EDM are the exclusive preserve of music technology. Dunbar-Hall and Wemyss advocate based upon digital technology's ability to manipulate sound, new instruments, and new effects[129] but caution that the effect of technology on music should be the focus of study, not technology itself. They argued its potential on pedagogical grounds, including its ability to enhance basic music principles such as sound before symbol, its functionality for trial and error, its ability to focus on multiple concepts simultaneously with immediacy, and its potential to bypass barriers presented by pen-and-paper transcription. Similarly, Parasiz noted the value of technology in offering fluency, reducing the classical versus popular music notation debate through instant playback options.[130]

However, the lag between new technology and the ability of teachers to recognize its potential and implement remain. Both Gall[131] and Gilbert[132] reported physical barriers to technology adoption in classrooms due to lack of availability, technical competence, staff support, and lack of set-up time, while Kassner listed a range of personal fears for teachers including fear of the unknown, personal costs, failure, unemployment, computerized teaching, limited budgets, wasted time, and poor materials, along with fear of random sounds, losing aesthetics, and of limited transfer.[133] For Waddell and Williamon it is primarily a question of ease of use.[134] Parasiz has called for greater inclusion in music teacher training[135] and examination of the way students access music technology outside school.[136]

Despite reticence in technology uptake, Savage noted that music services and providers moved online at breakneck speed at the onset of the Covid-19 crisis.[137] The use of video technologies and streaming media are forcing a reassessment of music education, as are mobile smartphones, Cloud applications and tablets.[138] Emergent music education technology issues now revolve around assessment and teacher professional development. Finally, Challis has discussed popular music technology application in terms of accessibility for students with disabilities[139] including the value of Sunbeam software and the Benemin in providing practical access to music performance. For Waddell and Williamon, while technology is the new pedagogical frontier, few use it effectively.[140]

CONCLUSION

The inclusion of popular music has presented unique challenges. It has polarized as perhaps no other "revolution" before or since. Issues surrounding ideology, pedagogy, and application remain unresolved for many and are now compounded by the technology "revolution." Despite initial fears that popular music would "subvert the hegemony" of classical music and debase music education, it has developed into a powerful and vibrant addition to the music education collective consciousness, forced a re-evaluation of music education's purpose, and forged a closer alignment between educational goals and the student experiential world.

NOTES

1. John Brocklehurst. *Music in Schools* (London: Routledge & Kegan Paul, 1962): 55.
2. Rupert Till. "Popular music education: A step into the light," In *The Routledge research companion to popular music education* edited by Gareth Smith (2017): 15–29.
3. Phillip Tagg. "Caught on the back foot: Epistemic inertia and visible music," *IASPM Journal* 2, no. 1–2 (2012): 3–18.
4. Till, "Popular music education," 2017.
5. Richard Middleton, "Popular music." Grove Music Online (2015).
6. Simon Frith, *Music and Society: The Politics of Consumption, Performance and Reception* (Cambridge: Cambridge University Press, 1987): 131–151.
7. Wayne Bowman, "Pop" goes . . . ? Taking popular music seriously," in *Bridging the gap: Popular music and music education* edited by Carlos Rodriguez, 29–50. Reston, VA: MENC, 2004.
8. Gracyk, "Popular music: The very idea of listening to it," 2004.
9. Carlos Rodriguez, "Popular music in music education: Towards a new conception of musicality," In *Bridging the gap: Popular music and music education* edited by Carlos Rodriguez. Reston, VA: MENC, 2004.

10. Sharon Davis, and Deborah Blair, "Popular music in American education: A glimpse into a secondary methods course," *IJME Journal* 29 (2011): 124–140.

11. Bowman, "Pop" goes . . . ? Taking popular music seriously," 2004.

12. Robert Woody. "Willing and able: Equipping music teachers to teach with popular music," *Orff Echo Journal 43*, no. 4 (2011), 14–17.

13. Middleton, "Popular music," 2015.

14. Bernarr Rainbow, "Onwards from Butler," in *Teaching Music*, ed. Gary Spruce (Routledge: London, 1996): 9–20: 14.

15. Scottish Education Department. *Junior Secondary Education*. Edinburgh: HMSO, 1955: 218.

16. Keith Swanwick, *Popular Music and the Teacher* (London: Elsevier, 1968).

17. Graham Vulliamy and Ed Lee. *Pop Music in Schools* (Cambridge: Cambridge University Press, 1976).

18. Vulliamy and Lee, *Pop Music in Schools*.

19. Keith Swanwick, *A Basis for Music Education* (London: Routledge, 1979).

20. John Paynter, & Peter Aston, *Sound and Silence: Class Projects in Creative Music* (Cambridge University Press: Cambridge, 1970).

21. Vulliamy and Lee, *Pop Music in Schools*.

22. Vic Gammon, "Cultural politics of the English National Curriculum for music, 1991 – 1992." *Journal of Educational Administration and History*, 31, no. 2 (1999): 130–147.

23. Gammon, "Cultural politics," 136.

24. Stephen Ball, *Education Reform: A Critical and Post Structural Approach* (Buckingham: Open University Press, 1994).

25. Lucy Green, *How Popular Musicians Learn: A Way Ahead for Music Education* (London: Routledge, 2001).

26. Alexandra Lamont, David Hargreaves, Nigel Marshall, and Mark Tarrant, "Young people's music in and out of school," *British Journal of Music Education* 20, no. 3 (2003): 229–241.

27. Karen Burland, "Music for all: Identifying, challenging and overcoming barriers," *Music & Science*, 3 (2020): 1–6.

28. Jere Humphreys, "Popular music in the American schools: What history tells us about the present and the future," in *Bridging the Gap: Popular Music and Music Education* ed. Carlos Rodriguez (Music Educator's National Conference, Reston, VA, 2004): 91–106.

29. "The Tanglewood Declaration," in *Documentary Report of the Tanglewood Symposium* ed. Robert Choate (Music Educators National Conference, Washington DC, 1968): 139.

30. Bryan Powell, Andrew Krikun, and Joseph Pignato, "Something's happening here!": Popular Music Education in the United States," *Journal of the International Association for the Study of Popular Music* 5, no. 1 (2015): 5–22.

31. Charles Fowler, "The case against rock: A reply," *Music Educator's Journal* 57, no. 1 (1970): 38–42.

32. David Hebert, and Patricia Shehan-Campbell, "Rock music in American Schools: Positions and practices since the 1960s." *International Journal of Music Education* 36 (2000): 14–22.

33. Robert Cutietta, "Forward to the 2019 special focus issue on popular music education," in *Popular Music Education: A Call to Action*, ed. Bryan Powell, Gareth Smith, Chad West and John Kratus. *Music Educator's Journal*, 2019: 21–24.

34. Rebecca Rinsema, "Opening the 'hermeneutic window' in popular music," in *Coming of Age: Teaching and Learning Popular Music in Academia* ed. Carlos Rodriguez (Ann Arbor, MI: Michigan Publishing, 2017).

35. Cutietta, "Popular music education—a call to action," 2019.

36. Bryan Powell, Andrew Krikun and Joseph Pignato, "'Something's happening here!': Popular Music Education in the United States," *Journal of the International Association for the Study of Popular Music* 5, no. 1 (2015): 5–22.

37. Robert Woody, "Popular music in school: Remixing the issues," *Music Educators Journal* 93, no. 4 (2007): 32–37.

38. Stuart Smith, "Rock: Swim in it or sink," *Music Educator's Journal* 56, no. 5 (1970): 86.

39. Beatrice Landeck, "A happy alternative to embracing rock," *Music Educators Journal* 55, no. 4 (1968): 35–36.

40. Sydney Fox, "From rock to Bach: Youth music on our terms," *Music Educator's Journal* 56, no. 9 (1970): 52.

41. Cutietta, "Popular music education—a call to action," 2019.

42. Mantie, "A comparison of 'popular music pedagogy' discourse," 2013.

43. Peter Dunbar-Hall, and Kathryn Wemyss, "The effects of the study of popular music on music education," *International Journal of Music Education* 36 (2000): 23–34.

44. Dunbar-Hall and Wemyss, "The effects of the study of popular music," 26.

45. Geoffrey Lowe, and Andrew Sutherland, "Western Australian music teachers and the WACE Music syllabus five years down the track: where are we now?" *Australian Journal of Teacher Education* 39, no. 11 (2014): 162–177.

46. Lowe and Sutherland, "Western Australian music teachers."

47. Vulliamy and Lee, *Pop Music in Schools*.

48. Theodor Adorno, "On Popular Music," *Studies in Philosophy and Social Sciences*, 9 (1941): 17–18.

49. Francis Routh, *Contemporary British Music: The Twenty-Five Years from 1945 to 1970* (London: McDonald, 1972).

50. Charles Parker, "Pop Song, The Manipulated Ritual," in *The Black Rainbow* ed. Paul Abbs (London: Heinemann Educational, 1975).

51. Graham Vulliamy, and John Shepherd, "The application of a critical sociology to music education," *British Journal of Music Education* 1, no. 3 (1984): 247–266.

52. Hebert and Campbell, "Rock music in American Schools."

53. Simon Frith, *Music and Society: The Politics of Consumption, Performance and Reception* (1987): 131–151.

54. Hebert and Campbell, "Rock music in American Schools," 273.

55. Jean Downey, "Informal learning in music in the Irish secondary school context," *Action, Criticism and Theory for Music Education* 8, no. 2 (2009): 46–59.

56. Gary Spruce, "Culture, society and musical learning," in *Learning to Teach Music in the Secondary School*, 3rd ed, ed. Carolyn Cooke, Keith Evans, Chris Philpott and Gary Spruce (London: Routledge, 2016).

57. Lucy Green, "Popular music education in and for itself, and for 'other' music: Current research in the classroom," *International Journal of Music Education* 24, no. 2 (2006): 101–118.

58. D. Gregory Springer, "Teaching popular music: Investigating music educators' perceptions and preparation," *International Journal of Music Education* 34, no. 4 (2016): 403–415.

59. Davis and Blair, "Popular music in American education."

60. Mark Tarrant, Adrian North and David Hargreaves, *Social categorization, self-esteem, and the estimated musical preferences of male adolescents: A Reader* (London: Routledge Falmer, 2001).

61. Michael Fitzgerald, Anil Joseph, Mary Hayes and Myra O'Regan, "Leisure activities of adolescent children," *Journal of Adolescence*, 18 (1995): 349–358.

62. Adrian North, David Hargreaves and Susan O'Neill, "The importance of music to adolescents," *British Journal of Educational Psychology* 70 (2000): 255–272.

63. Hebert and Campbell, "Rock music in American Schools," 2000.

64. Vulliamy and Lee, "Pop music in schools," 53.

65. Michael Nagel, "Student learning," in *Teaching Making a Difference, 3rd ed*, ed. Rick Churchill (Milton, QLD: John Wiley, 2016), 118–150.

66. Vulliamy and Shepherd, "The application of a critical sociology to music education."

67. Malcolm Ross, "What's Wrong with School Music," *British Journal of Music Education*, 12, 1995: 185–201.

68. Malcom Ross, "Missing Solemnis: Reforming music in schools," *British Journal of Music Education*, 15, no. 3 (1998): 255–262.

69. John Harland, Kay Kinder, Pippa Lord and Ian Schagen, *Arts Education in Secondary Schools: Effects and Effectiveness* (Slough: National Foundation for Educational Research, 2000).

70. Cutietta, "Popular music education—a call to action," 2019.

71. Geoffrey Lowe. *A study in Year 8 student motivation to continue class music in Perth, Western Australia* (PhD diss., Edith Cowan University, 2008).

72. Jennifer Rosevear, *Attitudes of High school Students towards Learning Music: Love ensemble, hate theory*. Paper presented at the Australian Society for Music Education XIV National Conference (Darwin, Northern Territory, 2003).

73. Alexandra Lamont, and Karl Maton. "Unpopular music: Beliefs and behaviours towards music in Education," in *Sociology and Music Education*, ed. Ruth Wright, 63–80 (London: Ashgate, 2010).

74. Geoffrey Lowe, "Class music learning activities: Do students find them important, interesting and useful?," *Research Studies in Music Education* 33, no. 2 (2011): 143–159.

75. Vulliamy and Lee, "Pop music in schools," 57.

76. Green, "Popular music education," 2006.

77. Graca Boal-Palheiros, and David Hargreaves, "Listening to music at home and at school," *British Journal of Music Education* 18, no. 2 (2001): 103–118.

78. Woody, "Willing and able," 2011.

79. Jacalyn Lund, and Mary Fortman-Kirk, *Performance-Based Assessment for Middle and High School Physical Education* (Leeds: Human Kinetics, 2010).

80. Lamont et al., "Young people's music," 2003.

81. Gokhan Ozdemir, and M. Can Ciftcibasi, "Effect of pop music on students' attitudes to music lessons," *Educational Research and Reviews* 12, no. 18 (2017): 884–890.

82. Terrence Dwyer, *Teaching Musical Appreciation* (Oxford: Oxford University Press, 1967): 115.

83. Graham McPhail, "The canon or the kids: Teachers and the recontextualization of classical and popular music in the secondary school curriculum," *Research Studies in Music Education* 35, no. 7 (2013): 7–20.

84. Liora Bresler, "The genre of school music and its shaping by meso, micro and macro contexts," *Research Studies in Music Education* 11, no. 2 (1998): 2–18.

85. Vulliamy and Lee, *Pop Music in Schools*.

86. Woody, "Popular music in schools: Remixing the issues."

87. Hebert and Campbell, "Rock music in American Schools."

88. Hebert, "Originality and institutionalization."

89. Powell et al., "Something's happening here!," 2015.

90. Springer, "Teaching popular music."

91. Vulliamy and Lee, *Pop Music in Schools*.

92. Springer, "Teaching popular music."

93. Davis and Blair, "Popular music in American education."

94. Vulliamy and Lee, *Pop Music in Schools*.

95. Lucy Green, *Music, Gender, Education* (Cambridge: Cambridge University Press, 1997): 145.

96. John Sloboda, "Generative processes of music: The psychology of performance, improvisation and Composition," *Psychology of Music* 17, no. 2 (2001): 158–164.

97. Woody, "Popular music in schools: Remixing the issues."

98. Green, "Popular music education."

99. Vulliamy and Lee, *Pop Music in Schools*.

100. Woody, "Popular music in schools: Remixing the issues."

101. Bryan Powell, Gareth Smith, Chad West and John Kratus, "Popular Music Education: A Call to Action," *Music Educators Journal* 106, no. 1 (2019): 21–24.

102. Martin Cloonan, "What is popular music studies?," *British Journal of Music Education* 22, no. 1 (2005): 77–93.

103. Till, "Popular music education."

104. Green, "Popular music education."

105. Adam Kruse, "Hip-hop wasn't something a teacher ever gave me'; exploring hip-hop musical learning," *Music Education Research* 20, no. 3 (2018): 317–329.

106. Alexis Kallio, "Popular 'problems': Deviantization and teachers' curation of popular music," *International Journal of Music Education* 35, no. 3 (2017): 319–332.

107. Ofsted, 2010.
108. Hebert and Campbell, "Rock music in American Schools."
109. Vulliamy and Lee, *Pop Music in Schools*.
110. Sloboda, "Generative processes of music."
111. Tarrant et al., "Musical preferences of male adolescents."
112. David Hargreaves, and Adrian North, *The Social Psychology of Music* (Oxford: Oxford University Press, 1996).
113. John Kratus, "Music listening is creative," *Music Educators Journal*, 103, no. 3 (2017): 46–51.
114. Peter Dunbar-Hall, "Designing a teaching model for popular music," in *Teaching Music*, ed. Gary Spruce, 216–226 (London: Routledge, 1996).
115. Rinsema, "Opening the 'hermeneutic window.'"
116. Shane Colquhoun, "Popular song genres, music producers and song creation in the general music classroom," *General Music Today*, 31, no. 2 (2018): 17–20.
117. Evan Tobias, "Composing, song writing and producing: Informing popular music pedagogy," *Research Studies in Music Education*, 35, no. 2 (2013): 213–237.
118. Evan Tobias, "From musical detectives to DJs: Expanding aural skills and analysis through engaging popular music and culture," *General Music Today*, 28, no. 3 (2015): 23–27.
119. Kruse, "Hip-hop wasn't something a teacher ever gave me."
120. Springer, "Teaching popular music."
121. Peter Dunbar-Hall, "World music, creativity and Orff Schulwerk methodology," in *Many Seeds, Different Flowers: The Music Education Legacy of Carl Orff*, ed. Andre De Quadros (Perth, WA: CIRCME, 2000), 58–67.
122. Dunbar-Hall and Wemyss, "The effects of the study of popular music."
123. Woody, "Willing and able."
124. Dunbar-Hall, "World music and creativity."
125. Woody, "Willing and able."
126. Woody, "Willing and able," 17.
127. McPhail, "The canon or the kids."
128. Basil Bernstein, *Pedagogy, symbolic control and identity: Theory, research, critique* (New York: Rowman and Littlefield, 2000).
129. Dunbar-Hall and Wemyss, "The effects of the study of popular music."
130. Gokalp Parasiz, "The use of music technologies in field education courses and daily lives of music education department students," *Universal Journal of Educational Research* 6, no. 5 (2018): 1005–1014.
131. Marina Gall, "Trainee teachers' perceptions: factors that constrain the use of music technology in teaching placements," *Journal of Music Technology and Education* 6 (2013): 5–27.
132. Ashley Danielle Gilbert, *An Exploration of the Use of and the Attitudes Toward Technology in First-Year Instrumental Music* (PhD diss., The University of Nebraska-Lincoln, 2015).
133. Kirk Kassner, "RX for technophobia," in *Teaching Music*, ed. Gary Spruce (London: Routledge, 1996): 193–198.

134. George Waddell, and Aaron Williamon, "Technology use and attitudes in music learning," *Frontiers in ICT*, 6, no. 11 (2019): 1–13.

135. Parasiz, "The use of music technologies."

136. Duncan Mackrill and Alison Daubney, "Framing conceptions of technology for learning in music-implications for pedagogy," in *Learning to Teach Music in the Secondary School, 3rd ed*, ed. Carolyn Cooke, Keith Evans, Chris Philpott and Gary Spruce (London: Routledge, 2016).

137. Savage, "Teaching music in England today."

138. Mackrill and Daubney, "Framing conceptions of technology for learning in music."

139. Ben Challis, "Technology, accessibility and creativity in popular music education," *Popular Music* 28, no. 3 (2009): 425–431.

140. Waddell and Williamon, "Technology use and attitudes."

BIBLIOGRAPHY

Adorno, Theodor. "On popular music." *Studies in Philosophy and Social Sciences* 9, no. 1 (1941): 17–18.

Allsup, Randall. "Popular music and classical musicians: Strategies and perspectives." *Music Educators Journal* 97, no. 3 (2011): 30–34. doi: 10.1177/0027432110391810

Ball, Stephen. *Education Reform: A Critical and Post Structural Approach*. Buckingham: Open University Press, 1994.

Bernstein, Basil. *Pedagogy, Symbolic Control and Identity: Theory, Research, Critique*. New York: Rowman and Littlefield Publishers, 2000.

Boal-Palheiros, Graca, and David Hargreaves. "Listening to music at home and at school." *British Journal of Music Education* 18, no. 2 (2001): 103–118.

Bowman, Wayne. ""Pop" goes . . .? Taking popular music seriously." In *Bridging the gap: Popular music and music education*, edited by Carlos Rodriguez, 29 – 50. Reston, VA: MENC, 2004.

Bray, David. "An examination of GCE music uptake rates." *British Journal of Music Education* 17, no. 1 (2000): 79–89.

Bresler, Liora. "The genre of school music and its shaping by meso, micro and macro contexts." *Research Studies in Music Education* 11, no. 2 (1998): 2–18.

Brocklehurst, John. *Music in Schools*. London: Routledge & Kegan Paul, 1962.

Burgess, Barry. "The changing face of music education in Ireland." *Journal of Music Education*. 2001. Retrieved from http://journalofmusic.com/focus/changing-face-music-education-Ireland. Accessed 11 August, 2021.

Burland, Karen. "Music for all: Identifying, challenging and overcoming barriers." *Music & Science* 3 (2020): 1–6. doi: 10.1177/2059204320946950

Challis, Ben. "Technology, accessibility and creativity in popular music education." *Popular Music* 28, no. 3 (2009): 425–431. doi: 10.0117/S0261143009990158

Chester, Andrew. "Second thoughts on a rock aesthetic: The Band." *New Left Review* 62 (1970).

Cloonan, Martin. "What is popular music studies?" *British Journal of Music Education* 22, no. 1 (2005): 77–93.

Colquhoun, Shane. "Popular song genres, music producers and song creation in the general music classroom." *General Music Today* 31, no. 2 (2018): 17–20. doi: 10.1177/1048371317711031

Cutietta, Robert. Forward to the 2019 special focus issue on popular music education. In *Popular Music Education: A Call To Action* edited by Bryan Powell, Gareth Dylan Smith, Chad West and John Kratus, 21–24. *Music Educator's Journal*, 2019. doi: 10.1177/0027432119861528

Cutietta, Robert, and Thomas Brennan. "Coaching a pop'rock ensemble." *Music Educator's Journal* 77, no. 8 (1991): 40. doi: 10.2307/3398152

Davis, Sharon. and Deborah Blair. "Popular music in American education: A glimpse into a secondary methods course." *International Journal of Music Education* 29 (2011): 124 – 140. doi: 10.1177/0255761410396962

Downey, Jean. "Informal learning in music in the Irish secondary school context." *Action, Criticism and Theory for Music Education* 8, no. 2 (2009): 46–59.

Dunbar-Hall, Peter. "Designing a teaching model for popular music." In *Teaching Music*, edited by Gary Spruce, 216–226. London: Routledge, 1996.

Dunbar-Hall, Peter. "World music, creativity and Orff Schulwerk methodology." In *Many seeds, different flowers: The music education legacy of Carl Orff* edited by Andre De Quadros, 58–67. Perth, WA: CIRCME, 2000.

Dunbar-Hall, Peter. "Designing a teaching model for popular music." In *Aspects of teaching secondary music* edited by Gary Spruce, 173–181. London, UK: Routledge/Falmer, 2002.

Dunbar-Hall, Peter, and Kathryn Wemyss. "The effects of the study of popular music on music education". *International Journal of Music Education* 36 (2000): 23–34.

Dwyer, Terrence. *Teaching Musical Appreciation.* Oxford University Press: Oxford, 1967.

Eccles, Jacqueline, and Alan Wigfield. "From expectancy-value theory to situated expectancy-value theory: A developmental, social cognitive, and sociocultural perspective on motivation." *Contemporary Educational Psychology* 61 (2020): 101859. doi: 10.1016/j.cedpsych.2020.101859

Edexcel. *Specification: GCE Music.* 2004. Retrieved from http://qualifications.pearson.com/content/dam/pdf/A%20Level/Music/2013/Specification%20and%20sample%assessments/UA035245_GCE_Lin_Music_Issue_5.pdf

Finney, John. "The place of music in the secondary school: Ideology-history-justification." In *Learning to Teach Music in the Secondary School, 3rd ed* edited by Carolyn Cooke, Keith Evans, Chris Philpott and Gary Spruce, 4–16. London: Routledge, 2016.

Fitzgerald, Michael, Anil Joseph, Mary Hayes and Myra O'Regan. "Leisure activities of adolescent children." *Journal of Adolescence*, 18 (1995): 349–358. doi: 10.1006/jado.1995.1024

Ford, Lynsey. Teachers blame EBacc for decline in Music student numbers. 2018. http://www.sussex.ac.uk/broadcast/read/39525

Fowler, Charles. "The case against rock: A reply." *Music Educator's Journal* 57, no. 1 (1970): 38–42.

Fox, Sidney. "From rock to Bach: Youth music on our terms." *Music Educator's Journal* 56, no. 9 (1970): 52.

Frith, Simon. *Music and Society: The Politics of Consumption, Performance and Reception.* Cambridge: Cambridge University Press, 1987.

Gammon, Vic. "Cultural politics of the English National Curriculum for music, 1991 – 1992." *Journal of Educational Administration and History* 31, no. 2 (1999): 130–147. doi: 10.1080/0022062990310204

Gall, Marina. "Trainee teachers' perceptions: factors that constrain the use of music technology in teaching placements." *Journal of Music Technology and Education* 6 (2013): 5–27. doi: 10.1386.jmte.6.1.5_1

Garnett, James. "Beyond a constructivist curriculum: A critique of competing paradigms in music education." *British Journal of Music Education* 30, no. 2 (2013): 161–175. doi: 10.1017/S0265051712000575

Gilbert, Ashley. *An Exploration of the Use of and Attitudes Towards Technology in First-Year Instrumental Music.* Unpublished PhD thesis, University of Nebraska, 2015.

Gracyk, Theodore. "Popular music: The very idea of listening to it." In *Bridging the Gap: Popular Music and Music Education,* edited by Carlos Rodriguez, 51 – 70. Reston, VA: MENC, 2004.

Green, Lucy. *Music, Gender, Education.* Cambridge: Cambridge University Press, 1997.

Green, Lucy. *How Popular Musicians Learn: A Way Ahead for Music Education.* London: Routledge, 2001.

Green, Lucy. "Popular music education in and for itself, and for 'other' music: Current research in the classroom." *International Journal of Music Education* 24, no. 2 (2006): 101–118. doi: 10.1177/0255761406065471

Hallam, Susan, Andrea Creech and Hilary McQueen. *Musical Futures: A case study investigation.* Final Report from Institute of Education, University of London for the Paul Hamlyn Foundation, 2011. Retrieved from https://www.musicalfutures.org/wp-content/uploads/2012/12/musicalfutureslongitudinalstudy.pdf

Hargreaves, David, and Adrian North. *The Social Psychology of Music.* Oxford: Oxford University Press, 1996.

Harland, John, Kay Kinder, Pippa Lord and Ian Schagen. *Arts Education in Secondary Schools: Effects and Effectiveness.* Slough: National Foundation for Educational Research, 2000.

Hebert, David. "Originality and institutionalization: Factors engendering resistance to popular music pedagogy in the U.S.A." *Music Education Research International* 5 (2011): 12–21.

Hebert, David, and Patricia Shehan-Campbell. "Rock music in American Schools: Positions and practices since the 1960s." *International Journal of Music Education* 36 (2000): 14–22.

Humphreys, Jere. "Popular music in the American schools: What history tells us about the present and the future." In *Bridging the Gap: Popular Music and Music Education,* edited by Carlos Rodriguez, 91–106. Reston, VA: MENC, 2004.

Kallio, Alexis. "Popular 'problems': Deviantization and teachers' curation of popular music." *International Journal of Music Education* 35, no. 3 (2017): 319–332. doi: 10.1177/0255761417725262

Kassner, Kirk. "RX for technophobia." In *Teaching Music* edited by Gary Spruce, 193–198. London: Routledge, 1996.

Keil, Charles. "Motion and feeling through music." *Journal of Aesthetics and Art Criticism* 24, no. 3 (1966): 337–349.

Kratus, John. "Music listening is creative." *Music Educators Journal* 103, no. 3 (2017): 46–51. doi: 10.1177/0027432116686843

Kruse, Adam. "Hip-hop wasn't something a teacher ever gave me'; exploring hip-hop musical learning." *Music Education Research* 20, no. 3 (2018): 317–329. doi: 10.1080/14613808.1445210

Lamont, Alexandra, David Hargreaves, Nigel Marshall, and Mark Tarrant. "Young people's music in and out of school." *British Journal of Music Education* 20, no. 3 (2003): 229–241. doi: 10.1017/S0265051703005412

Lamont, Alexandra and Karl Maton. "Unpopular music: Beliefs and behaviours towards music in education." In *Sociology and Music Education* edited by Ruth Wright, 63–80. London: Ashgate, 2010.

Landeck, Beatrice. "A happy alternative to embracing rock." *Music Educators Journal* 55, no. 4 (1968): 35–36.

Lowe, Geoffrey. *A Study in Year 8 Student Motivation to Continue Class Music in Perth, Western Australia.* Unpublished PhD thesis, Edith Cowan University, 2008.

Lowe, Geoffrey. "Class music learning activities: Do students find them important, interesting and useful?" *Research Studies in Music Education* 33, no. 2 (2011): 143–159. doi: 10.1177/1321103X11422768.

Lowe, Geoffrey, and Andrew Sutherland. "Western Australian music teachers and the WACE Music syllabus five years down the track: where are we now?" *Australian Journal of Teacher Education* 39, no. 11 (2014): 162–177. http://ro.ecu.edu.au/ajte/vol39/iss11/10

Lund, Jacalyn, and Mary Fortman-Kirk. *Performance-Based Assessment for Middle and High School Physical Education.* Leeds: Human Kinetics, 2010.

McCarthy, Carrie, Joanne O'Flaherty, and Jean Downey. "Choosing to study music: Student attitudes towards the subject of music in second-level education in the Republic of Ireland." *British Journal of Music Education* 36 (2019): 139–153. doi: 10.1017/S02650517190000093

McPhail, Graham. "The canon or the kids: Teachers and the recontextualization of classical and popular music in the secondary school curriculum." *Research Studies in Music Education* 35, no. 7 (2013): 7–20. doi: 10.1177/1321103X13483083

Mackrill, Duncan, and Alison Daubney. "Framing conceptions of technology for learning in music-implications for pedagogy." In *Learning to Teach Music in the Secondary School, 3rd ed*, edited by Carolyn Cooke, Keith Evans, Chris Philpott and Gary Spruce, 157–172. London: Routledge, 2016.

Mantie, Roger. "A comparison of "popular music pedagogy" discourse." *Journal of Research in Music Education* 61, no. 3 (2013): 334–352. doi: 10.1177/0022429413497235

Mark, Michael. "MENC: From tanglewood to the present." 2015. Retrieved from https://nafme.org/wp-content/uploads/2015/12/5-MENCFromTanglewood.pdf

Meyer, Leonard. *Emotion and Meaning in Music*. Cambridge: Cambridge University Press, 1956.

Middleton, Richard. "Popular Music." *Grove Music Online*, 2015. doi: 10.1093/gmo/9781561592630.article.43179. Retrieved from https://www.oxfordmusiconline.com/grovemusic/view/10.1093/gmo/9781561592630.001.0001/omo-9781561592630-e-0000043179

"Music Manifesto." 2007. Retrieved from http://www.musicmanifesto.co.uk/key-aims.html

Nagel, Michael. "Student learning." In *Teaching Making a Difference, 3rd ed* edited by Rick Churchill, 118–150. Milton, QLD: John Wiley, 2016.

North, Adrian, David Hargreaves and Susan O'Neill. "The importance of music to adolescents." *British Journal of Educational Psychology* 70 (2000): 255–272.

Ozdemir, Gokhan, and M. Can Ciftcibasi. "Effect of pop music on students' attitudes to music lessons." *Educational Research and Reviews* 12, no. 18 (2017): 884–890. doi: 10.5897/ERR2017.3321

Ofsted. *Research Review Series: Music*. 2021. Retrieved from: https://www.gov.uk/government/oublications/research-review-series-music/research-review-series-music

Parasiz, Gokalp. "The use of music technologies in field education courses and daily lives of music education department students." *Universal Journal of Educational Research* 6, no. 5 (2018): 1005–1014. doi: 10.13189/ujer.2018.060521

Parker, Charles. "Pop song, the manipulated ritual." In *The Black Rainbow* edited by Paul Abbs. London: Heinemann Educational, 1975.

Paynter, John. & Peter Aston. *Sound and Silence: Class Projects in Creative Music*. Cambridge University Press: Cambridge, 1970.

Pignato, Joseph. *An Analysis of Practical Challenges Posed by Teaching Improvisation: Case Studies in New York State Schools*. DMA. Boston University, Boston, 2010. Retrieved from ProQuest Digital Dissertations database. Publication No. 3430429.

Pleasants, Henry. *Serious Music and all that Jazz: An Adventure in Music Criticism*. London: Simon and Schuster, 1969.

Powell, Bryan, Andrew Krikun, and Joseph Pignato. "Something's happening here!: Popular Music Education in the United States." *Journal of the International Association for the Study of Popular Music* 5, no. 1 (2015): 5–22. doi: 10.5429/20793871(2015)v5i1.2en

Powell, Bryan, Gareth Smith, Chad West and John Kratus. "Popular music education: A call to action." *Music Educators Journal* September, 2019. doi: 10.1177/0027432119861528

Rainbow, Bernarr. "Onwards from butler." In *Teaching Music* edited by Gary Spruce, 9–20. London: Routledge, 1996.: London.

Rinsema, Rebecca. "Opening the "hermeneutic window" in popular music." In *Coming of Age: Teaching and Learning Popular Music in Academia* edited by Carlos Rodriguez. Ann Arbor: Michigan Publishing, 2017. doi:

10.3998/mpub.9470277. Retrieved from https://quod.lib.umich.edu/m/maize/mpub9470277/1:14/--coming-of-age-teaching-and-learning-popular-music?rgn=div1;view=fulltext

Rodriguez, Carlos. "Popular music in music education: Towards a new conception of musicality." In *Bridging the gap: Popular music and music education*, edited by Carlos Rodriguez. Reston, VA: MENC, 2004.

Rosevear, Jennifer. *Attitudes of High school Students towards Learning Music: Love ensemble, hate theory*. Paper presented at the Australian Society for Music Education XIV National Conference, Darwin, Northern Territory, 2003.

Ross, Malcolm. "What's wrong with school music." *British Journal of Music Education* 12 (1995): 185–201.

Ross, Malcom. "Missing Solemnis: Reforming music in schools." *British Journal of Music Education* 15, no. 3 (1998): 255–262.

Routh, Francis. *Contemporary British Music: The Twenty-Five Years from 1945 to 1970*. London: McDonald, 1972.

Savage, Jonathan. "Teaching music in England today." *International Journal of Music Education* (2020): 1–13. doi: 10.1177/0255761420986213

Scholten, James. "Born in the USA: Vernacular music and public education." *Music Educator's Journal* 74, no. 5 (1988): 22–25. doi: 10.2307/3397976

Scottish Education Department. *Junior Secondary Education*. Edinburgh: HMSO, 1955.

Shepherd, John. "Music and the last intellectuals." *Journal of Aesthetic Education* 25, no. 3 (1991): 95–114. doi: 10.2307/3332997

Sloboda, John. "Generative processes of music: The psychology of performance, improvisation and composition." *Psychology of Music* 17, no. 2 (2001): 158–164.

Smith, Stuart. "Rock: Swim in it or sink." *Music Educator's Journal* 56, no. 5 (1970): 86. doi: 10.2307/3392697

Springer, D Gregory. "Teaching popular music: Investigating music educators' perceptions and preparation." *International Journal of Music Education* 34, no. 4 (2016): 403–415. doi: 10.1177/0255761415619068

Spruce, Gary. 2016. "Culture, society and musical learning." In *Learning to Teach Music in the Secondary School*, 3rd ed., edited by Carolyn Cooke, Keith Evans, Chris Philpott and Gary Spruce, 17–31. London: Routledge, 2016.

Stevens, Robin. *Music in State-Supported Education in New South Wales and Victoria, 1848 – 1920*. Unpublished PhD thesis, University of Melbourne, 1978.

Swanwick, Keith. *Popular Music and the Teacher*. London: Elsevier, 1968.

Swanwick, Keith. *A Basis for Music Education*. London: Routledge, 1979.

Swanwick, Keith. "Music education before the National Curriculum." In *Teaching Music* edited by Gary Spruce, 21–48. London: Routledge, 1996.

Tagg, Phillip. "Caught on the back foot: Epistemic inertia and visible music." *International Association for the Study of Popular Music* 2, no. 1 (2012): 3–18. doi: 10.5429/2079-3871(2011)v2i1-2.2en

"The Tanglewood Declaration," in Documentary Report of the Tanglewood Symposium (R. Choate, Ed.). Music Educators National Conference, Washington DC, 1968, 139.

Tarrant, Mark, Adrian North and David Hargreaves. *Social Categorization, Self-esteem, and the Estimated Musical Preferences of Male Adolescents: A Reader.* London: Routledge Falmer, 2001.

Till, Rupert. "Popular Music Education: A Step Into the Light." In *Routledge Research Companion to Popular Music Education* edited by Gareth Dylan Smith, Zack Moir, Matt Brennan, Share Rambarran, Phil Kirkman, chapter 3. London: Routledge, 2017.

Thompson, Dick. "Plugging into pop at the junior high level." *Music Educator's Journal* 66, no. 4 (1979): 54–58.

Tobias, Evan. "Composing, song writing and producing: Informing popular music pedagogy." *Research Studies in Music Education* 35, no 2 (2013): 213–237. doi: 10.1177/1321103X13487466

Tobias, Evan. "From musical detectives to DJs: Expanding aural skills and analysis through engaging popular music and culture." *General Music Today* 28, no. 3 (2015): 23–27. doi: 10.1177/1048371314558293

Vulliamy, Graham, and Ed Lee. *Pop Music in Schools,* edited by Graham Vulliamy and Ed Lee. Cambridge: Cambridge University Press: 1976.

Vulliamy, Graham, and John Shepherd. "The application of a critical sociology to music education." *British Journal of Music Education* 1, no. 3 (1984b): 247–266.

Waddell, George, and Aaron Williamon. "Technology use and attitudes in music learning." *Frontiers in ICT* 6, no. 11 (2019): 1–13. doi: 103389/fict.2019.00011

Woody, Robert. "Popular music in school: Remixing the issues." *Music Educators Journal* 93, no. 4 (2007): 32–37. doi: 10.1177/002743210709300415

Woody, Robert. "Willing and able: Equipping music teachers to teach with popular music." *Orff Echo,* 43, no. 4 (2011): 14–17.

Chapter 10

Progressing Multicultural Music Education from Colonialism, Othering, and Tokenism

Andrew Sutherland

Multicultural music education should be considered through perspectives that consider both the complex and multifaceted aspect of how "education" and "multiculturalism" is understood. Music educators remain challenged to engage authentically with the global multiplicity of musics, and there remains an all-too-common undertone of the old hegemony of "West is best" when it comes to music education. Influenced by the long tradition of ethnomusicology, and the more recent rise of globalization and "world music," musics of diverse cultures have and will continue to find their way into music classrooms, as nations reconceptualize themselves as multicultural societies.[1]

The deep-rooted traditions of teaching Western Art music in countries such as the United States, Great Britain, Australia, and Canada are challenged by a more globally aware and inward/outward-looking view of culture. Changing understandings have evolved slowly with varying considerations to Indigenous musics, integration of diasporic and migrant cultures, and prevailing political and sociocultural tendencies. Locally developed practices involving some degree of transmission of multicultural musics became increasingly evident. Such musics were understood as "other" to the prevailing dominant culture. The flow-on effect was the increasing introduction of alternative musical systems and traditions into music classrooms, constrained by contextualizing social contexts, teacher/facilitator expertise, resources, and understandings. Emphasizing the political "press" evident in societies, though we now live in a "socio-culturally, fluid, politically dynamic, and highly interconnected global environment,"[2] it is important to acknowledge that this was not always the case.

This chapter does not offer a comprehensive chronological examination but rather an overview of developments in music education with examples from different cultures and locations. Further complicated by notions of colonialism, nationalism, and evolving cultural identities, we feel comprehensive accounts of particular musics and their threadiness within multiculturalist educational aims would necessitate details of cultural exchanges in greater detail than can be afforded here. What I address here are certain music education approaches which hold a multicultural perspective. Much of this development has emerged from processes initially influenced by ethnomusicology and increasingly supported by increasing availability of authentic materials facilitated by technologies. This carries implications for responsible and ethical engagement and requires the visionary thinking of individuals willing to challenge an all too often entrenched view of Western cultural supremacy. Applied to music education, adopting a multicultural approach implies "the understanding that there are many different but equally valid forms of musical and artistic expression [that] encourages students to develop a broad perspective based on understanding, tolerance, and respect for a variety of opinions and approaches."[3]

The tokenistic inclusion of non-Western music in much of the music teaching material in western educational systems, particularly in the first half of the twentieth century, meant that cultural meaning and textual accuracy were most often lost or sometimes bowdlerized. Schippers' observation that "almost all music is transmitted out of context"[4] underscores issues of authenticity and transmission context provided with well-intentioned but practically tokenist applications with reductivist outcomes. For decades, the addition of Westernized piano accompaniments to many non-Western songs made music accessible but unauthentic. For example, the folk songs from Eastern Europe accepted into U. S. school curricula in the 1930s that were frequently inaccurately translated, rhythmically adjusted with unauthentic piano accompaniments and harmonization in some cases, bore little resemblance to the original, in order to make it possible for nonculture bearers to teach and accord with contemporary mores.[5]

The American experience saw by 1936 publications of music songbooks include material from Bulgaria, Czechoslovakia, Greece, Hungary, Russia, Ukraine, and Yugoslavia[6] that contrasted to preceding decades. Folk musics from North and South America were largely ignored, and broad disinterest in musics from African, Asian, and Middle Eastern cultures reflected the Eurocentric view. Nevertheless, some publications designed for class music instruction in the United States, such as New Music Horizons and The World of Music, gradually introduced songs from these countries. The problem remained of presenting non-Western music to Western music educators. In

1943 the authors of "The Flower Drum and Other Chinese Songs" grappled with the problem, as Pearl S. Buck explained:

> To discover the original, so far as there is an original, to catch the essential rhythms under the changes, is not easy. Even more difficult, perhaps, is to convey to western ears the effect of the accompaniments upon instruments foreign to those ears. Harmonization in the western sense destroys the songs.[7]

This collection was unusual as the accompaniments were created with considerable cultural sensitivity, "not harmonized in the western sense."[8]

By the 1940s, Western countries began to introduce music from countries that broadly reflected contemporary patterns of migration.[9] Again, much of this material represented egregious misrepresentations, cultural misappropriations based on cultural ignorance and a colonial perspective. As late as 1969, the first purportedly African song appeared in the nationally distributed school singing books, which was actually a version of an English marching song from the Zulu War (1879), titled "The Swazi Warrior."[10] Such practices had to change. The inclusion of multicultural music in music teaching and learning required deeper, holistic thinking and practice, such as greater exploration of the source culture[11] and, as Nethsinghe suggests, fore-fronting a "culture bearer" as an owner and sharer of knowledge and practice to meaningful and authentic guidance.[12]

Music education organizations acted in positive ways to politically and socially drive development and change. For example, in the 1950s the work of MENC and "American Unity Through Music" promoted Latin American music and inter-Americanism in schools in line with sociopolitical ideals echoed in the federal "Good Neighbour" Policy. A two-part program, "American songs for American Children," emphasized American folk songs, whereas "Music to Unify the Americas" incorporated international repertoire with emphasis on Latin American music.[13] These early steps introduced adapted material but did little to attach any cultural meaning to the songs, and it would be several decades before such meaning would be viewed as important to music education.

Work in the United States continued, and the 1960s witnessed an increasing interest in ethnic, creating a momentum of interest in ethnic diversity that developed a general focus on multiculturalism in the 1970s which moved toward a more active role in promoting social justice issues with ethnic minorities. In 1977, multicultural education became a focus for many colleges and universities following an initiative from the National Council for Accreditation of Teacher Education (NCATE). Standards for Accreditation of Teacher Education included multicultural education requirements for accreditation.[14] Throughout the following decade, the movement which espoused intergroup education as a means of promoting harmony in human relations became a growing voice in the United States.

The reality of teaching authentic and varied multicultural musics in classrooms throughout the country did not always match the rhetoric espoused by umbrella organizations. David Elliot found in 1995 that music educators were not uniformly focused on delivering a culturally diverse musical experience for their students. Based on Richard Pratte's philosophy of multiculturalism, Elliot considered six levels of multicultural engagement: (a) assimilationist, (b) amalgamationist, (c) open-society view of multiculturalism, (d) insular multiculturalism, (e) modified multicultural curriculum, and (f) dynamic multicultural curriculum.[15] The lowest level, assimilation, involved teachers who maintained an exclusively Western European repertoire for their students which they considered to be superior in structure and content with no inclusion of music from non-Western cultures.

Britain (later the United Kingdom) has always been comprised of people from different cultures whose music was to varying degrees assimilated within the English class music materials. For example, in 1893 Harold Boulton edited "Songs of the Four Nations" with music arranged by Arthur Somervell. This extensive collection included "Old Songs of the People of England, Scotland, Ireland and Wales."[16] This repertoire became a staple in classrooms and community singing; sung in English (not Welsh or Gaelic) with robust piano accompaniments, these different cultures were Anglicized. By 1911, J. Spencer Curwen's "Folk Songs of Many Lands" was commonly used across the empire and dominions.[17] This comprised songs from Europe (France, Italy, and so forth) and one offering from Mexico. The "Many Lands" did not spread far from England. Since the 1930s, changes to the cultural landscape of British music education largely occurred through class engagement in singing and the folk song movement that relied on European traditional songs adjusted with Anglicized lyrics. This was maintained throughout the 1950s and 1960s.

Despite Britain experiencing massive levels of immigration from the Commonwealth, including West India and India, classical western musicianship and musical appreciation continued to forefront curriculum and delivery of music education.[18] Increasingly music texts were prepared for teachers about Indian classical music, Steel Bands, and so forth.

In the United Kingdom, from an immigrant perspective, music collectivized complex histories of displacement, slavery, and civil rights through which the assertion of history, place, and community was through music. The lack of adaptation of educational approaches to changing societal needs from imported contemporary music marks a seismic shift in the music that was taught in schools, from the music that was heard and enjoyed socially, that "soundtracked everyday lives in youth clubs, school dances, coffee bars, that offered perspectives and narratives related to notions of love, loss, belonging and solidarity,"[19] for a generation of students, a schism that arguably continues in music education to this day.

The early 1980s saw government enquiries[20] and publication resources for multicultural education by addressing the concern for racism and the development of cultural pluralism being represented in curriculum documents. It was not until Lucy Green's longitudinal study involving music teachers from predominantly mixed comprehensive schools across England[21] provided evidence that a seismic shift had occurred in the perception of world music in the UK.

The first survey in 1982 was followed by another in 1998, following the widespread implementation of the new curriculum. Green observed a discernible change in conventional use of terminology between the early 1980s and late 1990s as well as a relative estimation of diverse musical styles. Although teachers indicated that Western Art music maintained the greatest emphasis of all genres, world music, which had played an obscure role in the curriculum only sixteen years before, effectively took equal second place alongside classical music. Jazz and twentieth-century classical music followed, with folk music lagging behind.

Green noted that in 1982, the term "folk music" was assumed to mean geographically proximate material; however, by 1998, many teachers suggested in their responses to consider a more general world view of folk music. In addition, a greater emphasis on teaching world music was evident in many of the written responses which indicated that it raised awareness and improved the understanding and appreciation of non-European cultures. Indian, Gamelan, Chinese, Caribbean, Latin-American, and some African musics had become important components of the classroom music experience for students studying Graduate Certificate of Secondary Education (GCSE), and many teachers began introducing it earlier to prepare students in advance. Music examination boards have since routinely included a variety of culturally diverse musics among their curriculum documents.

While the UK has experienced a significant sea change in actualizing a genuinely effective world music curriculum, other countries have had a more gradual and uneven approach. In Canada, the focus remains largely on the teaching of Western classical music and Western notation. Hess noted in 2015 that the Canadian curriculum documents actually reinforced notions of Eurocentricity and Western cultural and power dominance.[22] The Grade 52 music curriculum in Ontario creates a binary position through its linguistic choices of Western music and "others." Furthermore, students are asked to "sing and/or play, in tune, from musical notation, unison and two-part music with accompaniments, from a wide variety of cultures, styles, and historical periods."[23] The implied message that non-Western tuning systems and notation is difficult to reconcile with nonspecified ideals of a wide variety of cultures. Although tokenistic references to "other" kinds of music can be found in the curriculum document, there is little to encourage a comprehensive approach.

The impact of colonialization can be further examined in *Aotearoa* (New Zealand). The Māori culture has played a critical role throughout New Zealand society for many years, and the Māori *waiata* (song) has been woven into the cultural identity of the nation. The *waiata* in its various forms was used as a didactic tool in which Māori traditions history could be propagated. The introduction of colonial rule brought Western alterations to much of the musical characteristics. Graham Parsons observes that the *waiata*'s unregimented beat and unison drone punctuated by melodic inflections were replaced by uniformed phrases, rich harmonies, and steady pulse found in the Western traditions. Much of the Maori music presented to international audiences since around fifty years following colonialization has been largely Europeanized.[24]

The relegation of multicultural music to that of "other" may not reflect what is a broadly tolerant nation; Alibhai-Brown points to the limitation of cultural tolerance through the "3S" model of multiculturalism comprised of saris, samosas, and steel drums.[25] This metaphor places music within the essentialization, trivialization, and marginalization of non-Western cultures. This model elucidates the superficiality of selective ethnic referencing by reinforcing Anglo-Canadian culture as the dominant presence which "tolerates" multiculturalism through a carefully arranged hierarchy.[26]

In multicultural Australia, the development of positive intercultural attitudes has been essential in the creation and development of a harmonious, integrated society. Despite multiculturalism being acknowledged firmly as a part of the Australian tapestry for sixty years, it has only been the past thirty that Green acknowledges "a sea-change in music education, inspired by new practices, values and identities in the globalised and localised musical world we all inhabit" occurred.[27] In Australia, school music can encompass a wide range of approaches to teaching and learning. In general, music ensembles (bands, choirs, orchestras, and so forth) take place outside the scheduled school timetable. Class music lessons employ a wide range of content and styles that depend on school context and teacher competence. A music classroom may include a huge diversity of cultures that can include European, Asian, American, and African populations. This is where there would be considerable opportunities for inclusion and "the understanding that there are many different but equally valid forms of musical and artistic expression [that] encourages students to develop a broad perspective based on understanding, tolerance, and respect for a variety of opinions and approaches."[28]

STEPS FORWARD THROUGH TECHNOLOGY

Globally, increasingly sophisticated and accessible forms of technology have enabled deeper and more personalized engagement with musics of diverse cultures. Earlier forms of technology such as gramophones and records allowed multicultural music enthusiasts access to authentic performance examples, albeit often captured outside of the cultural context. However, such materials were not easily available to teachers. Concurrent with the exponential globalization and the rapid development of music-related technologies was the access to expansive regional and transnational recordings. With this came a diversification of music consumption which allowed regional and popular musics to flourish.

Readily available, quality materials such as Smithsonian Folkways Tools for Teaching and Oxford University's Global Sound materials and Global Music Series allowed music teachers to maintain an affinity with Westernized repertoire.[29]

With the advent of cassette technology by the late 1970s, came a process of democratization of production, allowing in situ school classroom recordings to be used as credible audio models and archives but also for creative outcomes. The emergence and accessibility for school children to utilize synthesizers may have been prophesized as the ultimate threat to the use of traditional instruments. However, the imitation of indigenous instruments from around the world allowed synthetically soundscapes that could be utilized within multicultural educative aims. Technology played a significant part in widely disseminating ethnographic timbres to a more global audience, encouraging a growing interest in musics from multiple cultures.[30]

ENACTING CULTURAL AWARENESS THROUGH MUSIC CURRICULUM

For many decades, there has been an increasing emphasis on the acknowledgment of nondominant cultures. Many nations have particularly responded to the label of "the melting pot" to denote an assumed blending and coalescing of cultures and how they actually may respond to significant music education declarations.

The first major turning point for the incorporation of multicultural music education was the Tanglewood Symposium that took place from July 23 to August 2, 1967, in Tanglewood, Massachusetts. Three broad questions formed the basis for discussion:

- What are the characteristics and desirable ideologies for an emerging and postindustrial society?

- What are the values and unique functions of music and other arts for individuals and communities in such a society?
- How may these potentials be attained?

The Tanglewood Declaration was designed to provide a way forward for a modernized music curriculum with greater efficacy and relevance for American students. One of the points stated that "Music of all periods, styles, forms, and cultures belongs in the curriculum. The musical repertory should be expanded to involve music of our time in its rich variety, including currently popular teenage music and avant-garde music, American folk music, and the music of other cultures."[31] As important as this was, the declaration was nevertheless a recommendation, and the practical implementation of a wide range of culturally specific musics would require significant production of resources and teacher training to be effective.

In 1972, the National Association for Schools of Music (NASM) took the necessary step of mandating multicultural music training for all undergraduate music teaching programs.[32] Many teachers expressed feeling unprepared to effectively deliver a range of world music concepts upon graduating, despite the NASM mandate.[33] Further progress came in 1990 with the introduction of the "Educate America Act" and the subsequent implementation of standards-based education. MENC responded to this initiative by publishing the National Standards for Arts Education in 1994. Point nine in the list of standards was the requirement that students should understand "music in relation to history and culture."[34] With the demand for students to understand the culture associated with musical understanding, tokenism became harder to justify. Although each state enacted their own standards, they were required to reflect the content laid out in the national standards document.

The Tanglewood Symposium viewed the year 2000 as a time to re-evaluate progress in achieving the original objectives as well as strategizing new strategic goals for the future, and Vision 2020: The Housewright Symposium on the Future of Music Education was convened to do just that. It was held at Florida State University in late 1999, and a formal presentation of recommendations was made at the MENC National Conference the following year. With the dramatic diversification of the United States population since the 1960s, the fourth recommendation stated, "All music has a place in the curriculum. Not only does the Western art tradition need to be preserved and disseminated, music educators also need to be aware of other music that people experience and be able to integrate it into classroom music instruction."[35]

While some music curricula made broad suggestions about music from different cultures being included, allowing for a Westernized perspective or lip service being paid by underresourced and underskilled teachers, exam boards in the UK mandated world music through explicit focus on topics. In 1995, the Department for Education (DFE) introduced new legal requirements that necessitated the inclusion of "music in a variety of styles from the European 'classical' tradition . . . , from folk and popular music, from the countries and regions of the British Isles, from cultures across the world, by well-known composers and performers, past and present."[36] Examination boards, vying for schools across the country to adopt their syllabi, adopted the position of including music from cultures across the world with in-depth study guides, aural activities, and, importantly for teachers, useful resources that provided authentic examples of a wide range of musics and their cultural context.

PATHWAYS TO AUTHENTIC MULTICULTURAL PRACTICES

The pathway to authentic practice in the music classroom is rarely straightforward. In order to achieve what some might consider to be a proximal authenticity, inadequate materials and processes are initially introduced that require revision and improvement. This conundrum is compounded with two important points, the first being the issue of the absence of a culture bearer, and the second concerns the notion of reproduction being linked to authentic practice. By definition, most teachers attempting multicultural music in the classroom are not culture bearers.[37] In 1992, in consultation with the Society for Ethnomusicology Education Committee, Judith Tucker devised a checklist to be used to achieve cultural authenticity. The checklist included the preparation of all materials with the involvement of someone within the culture, minimal or no adaptations (such as arrangements or accompaniments), lyrics should be in the original language, and the inclusion of cultural context.[38]

For many music educators, introducing musical material to listen to from other cultures presents little difficulty, but actually performing the musics of other cultures can be problematic. To accommodate music educators untrained in particular musics, music is often presented in a format recognizable in Western contexts and simplified to be within the abilities of classroom educators. Altering timbre, tuning systems, harmony, and instrumentation, so that the musical experience is "comfortable" means that a nod to different styles can be given without having to add teaching details that are unfamiliar. Such tokenism frequently includes the addition of piano or guitar accompaniment, the poor translation of texts, and the removal of original rhythmic and tonal characteristics in an attempt to make pieces more easily digestible.[39] Whether material which has only the title or melodic line remaining can be considered "world musics," given the lack of cultural values or authenticity, is very much in question.[40]

The work of the International Society for Music Education (ISME) has increased understanding of the world's diverse cultures and associated musics. Since its inception in 1953, and regular world conferences since, ISME has forged the need for teacher training as well as the inclusion of world musics in curricula. ISME's advocacy for multicultural music education has contributed to the "Policy on Musics of the World's Cultures," leading to several publications, including "Musics of the World's Cultures: A Source Book for Music Educators,"[41] "Traditional Songs of Singing Cultures,"[42] and "Canciones de America Latina: De Origen a la Escuela,"[43] providing a range of varied, culturally informed materials.[44] The view of promoting diverse musical cultures as well as local cultures and the refuting of Western cultural supremacy has urged the importance of a global view and with it an important revolution in music education.

CODA

Music provides a visceral expression of culture and advocates for a multicultural approach to education have made the case for the need to challenge separatist agendas, both institutional and community-oriented. Systemic changes to our institutions have been espoused by researchers to wrestle with these injustices, such as representation of minority groups in staffing, emphasizing multiculturalism in teaching, content, and engagement that counters a Western-dominated perspective.[45] These views are far from universally accepted, and, as traditional paradigms of approach are revised along lines reflective of our current *epistime*, the discourse is characterized by considerable friction. Within the music education teaching fraternity, a disparity remains between the widely accepted practice of a multicultural approach and at times prevailing practices.[46] This disparity manifests largely in the gulf between content and process, an essential component in allowing for authentic understanding of cultural practice.

Despite our increasing understanding, tolerance, and respect of music and the cultures it emanates from, we have problems introducing a broad range of multicultural musics in classrooms because of the enormously varied range of skills this requires. Music teachers who have upskilled in one nonlocal music system have in some cases achieved the equivalent of learning a new language. This problem is in many ways unique to the arts, combining cultural understanding with skills-based and language-based issues. Additionally, our localized and varied definitions of multicultural music are fundamentally guided by our own emic perspective, providing an additional complexity in achieving a universal notion of multicultural music education and how localized responses may be more dynamic and effective.

There are many examples of institutions which, despite a general marginalization of intercultural representation in the local music curriculum, serve as positive exemplars. My own school incorporates African djembe drumming, Balinese Gamelan ensemble, Zimbabwean xylophone playing, and Chinese guzheng ensembles into the curriculum and cocurricular programs. These activities not only allow for a more global musical perspective for students but also provide excellent internalization of fundamental musical skills. With the fast pace and democratization of technological developments, transmission and engagement via recordings, authentic performance, interviews, documentaries, and instructional videos are readily available to music educators at all levels. Exposure to these materials, along with efforts to respect source cultures, offers a touchstone to facilitating meaningful music experiences that acknowledge the cultural contexts from which they emanate.

NOTES

1. Patricia Shehan Campbell, *Music, education, and diversity: Bridging cultures and communities* (Teachers College Press, 2017).

2. Fethi, Mansouri, and Tariq Modood, "The complementarity of multiculturalism and interculturalism: theory backed by Australian Evidence," *Ethnic and Racial Studies* 44, no. 16 (2021): 1–20: 1.

3. William M. Anderson, and Patricia Shehan Campbell, "Teaching music from a multicultural perspective." In *Multicultural perspectives in music education*, eds. William M. Anderson and Patricia S. Campbell, 1–7. Reston VA: MENC, 1989, 1.

4. Huib, Schippers, "Tradition, authenticity and context: The case for a dynamic approach," *British Journal of Music Education* 23, no. 3 (2006): 333–349: 347.

5. Melissa Cain, Shari Lindblom, and Jennifer Walden, "Initiate, create, activate: practical solutions for making culturally diverse music education a reality," *Australian Journal of Music Education* 2 (2013): 79–97.

6. Terese M. Volk, "'Music speaks to the hearts of all men': The international movement in American Music Education: 1930–1954," *Bulletin of the Council for Research in Music Education* (1997): 143–152.

7. Pearl S. Buck, Foreword, Chin-Hsin Yao Chen and Shih-Hsiang Chen (1943) *The flower drum and other Chinese songs*. New York: The John Day Company, p. 5.

8. Ibid.

9. Stefanie L. Cash, *The use of world music in high school choral classrooms* (PhD Diss. The Florida State University, 2012).

10. Jane Southcott, and Dawn Joseph, "Integration and multiculturalism in music in Australian schools: Has/can/should the leopard change its spots?" *Proceedings of the XXVIIth Annual Conference, Australian Association for Research in Music Education*, 2005, 150–156.

11. Karen Howard, "Equity in music education: Cultural appropriation versus cultural appreciation—Understanding the difference," *Music Educators Journal* 106, no. 3 (March 2020): 68–70.

12. Rohan Nishantha Nethsinghe, "The notion of authenticity in multicultural music: Approaching proximal simulation," *International Journal of Multicultural Education* 15, no. 2 (2013).

13. Carolyn Livingston, "Charles Faulkner Bryan's legacy for general music," *Journal of Research in Music Education* 46, no. 2 (1998): 223–238.

14. James A. Banks, "Multicultural education: Historical development, dimensions, and practice," *Review of research in education* 19 (1993): 3–49.

15. David James Elliott, "Music matters a new philosophy of music education," (New York, Toronto: Oxford University Press, 1995).

16. Harold Boulton and Arthur Somervell, *Songs of the four nations*. London, J. B. Cramer & Co. Title page.

17. John Spencer Curwen, *Folk songs from many lands*, London: J. Curwen & Sons.

18. John Finney, *Music education in England, 1950–2010: The child-centred progressive tradition*. London: Routledge, 2016.

19. Paul Gilroy, *The black Atlantic: Modernity and double consciousness* (Cambridge, MA: Harvard University Press, 1993): 23.

20. Rampton Committee, *West Indian children in our schools*, Interim Report (London: HMSO, 1981).

21. Lucy Green, "From the Western classics to the world: secondary music teachers' changing attitudes in England, 1982 and 1998," *British Journal of Music Education* 19, no. 1 (2002): 5–30.

22. Juliet Hess, "Decolonizing music education: Moving beyond tokenism," *International Journal of Music Education* 33, no. 3 (2015): 336–347.

23. Government of Ontario. The Ontario curriculum grades 1–8: The arts (Rev.) (2009). Retrieved from http:// www.edu.gov.on.ca/eng/curriculum/elementary/arts18b09curr.pdf

24. Graham Parsons, "Songs old and new: The survival of the New Zealand Maori waiata in a changing world," in *Music education entering the 21st Century*, ed. Patricia Martin Shand (ISME, 2004): 67–71.

25. Yasmin Alibhai-Brown, *After multiculturalism* (London: Foreign Policy Centre, 2000).

26. Himani Bannerji, *The dark side of the nation: Essays on multiculturalism, nationalism and gender* (Toronto, Canada: Canadian Scholars' Press, 2000).

27. Green, "From the Western classics" 29.

28. Anderson and Campbell, "Teaching music from a multicultural perspective," 1.

29. Sangmi Kang, and Hyesoo Yoo, "Effects of a westernized Korean folk music selection on students' music familiarity and preference for its traditional version," *Journal of Research in Music Education* 63, no. 4 (2016): 469–486.

30. Cathy Ragland, "Mexican deejays and the transnational space of youth dances in New York and New Jersey." *Ethnomusicology* 47, no. 3 (2003): 338–354.

31. Robert A. Choate, *Documentary report of the Tanglewood Symposium* (Washington, DC: Music Educators National Conference, 1968), 139.

32. David G. Klocko, "Multicultural music in the college curriculum." *Music Educators Journal* 75, no. 5 (1989): 38–41.

33. Sharon Marlene Young, *Music teachers' attitudes, classroom environments, and music activities in multicultural music education* (PhD Diss. The Ohio State University, 1996).

34. Michael Blakeslee, "National standards for arts education," (Reston, VA: Music Educators National Conference, 1994), 63.

35. Clifford Madsen, ed. *Vision 2020: The Housewright symposium on the future of music education* (Lanham, MD: Rowman & Littlefield Publishers, 2020), 206.

36. Department for Education (DFE). "Music in the National Curriculum" (England), 1995, DFE.

37. Rohan Nishantha Nethsinghe, "Attaining proximal simulation in multicultural music education" (PhD diss., Monash University, 2012).

38. Judith Cook Tucker, "Circling the globe: multicultural resources," *Music Educators Journal* 78, no. 9 (1992): 37–40.

39. Barbara Reeder Lundquist, "Music, culture, curriculum and instruction," in *The new handbook of research on music teaching and learning: A project of the Music Educators National Conference* (Oxford: Oxford University Press, 2002), 626–647.

40. Anthony J. Palmer, "World musics in music education: The matter of authenticity," *International Journal of Music Education* 1 (1992): 32–40.

41. Elizabeth Oehrle, "Musics of the world's cultures: A source book for music educators," eds., Barbara Lundquist and CK Szego with Bruno Nettl, Ramon Santos and Einar Solbu (Callaway International Resource Centre for Music Education, for the International Society for Music Education, 1998).

42. Patricia Shehan Campbell, Sue Williamson, and Pierre Perron. *Traditional songs of singing cultures: a world sampler* (Alfred Music Publishing, 1996).

43. Campbell, Patricia Shehan, and Ana Lucía Frega. *Songs of Latin America: From the field to the classroom: Canciones de América Latina: de sus orígenes a la escuela* (Miami, FL: Warner Bros. Publications, 2001).

44. Cash, "World music in high school choral classrooms."

45. Geoffrey Short, "Retain, relinquish or revise: The future for multicultural education," *Journal of Multilingual & Multicultural Development* 15, no. 4 (1994): 329–344.

46. Katherine Norman, "Music faculty perceptions of multicultural music education," *Bulletin of the Council for Research in Music Education* (1999): 37–49.

BIBLIOGRAPHY

Alibhai-Brown, Yasmin. *After multiculturalism*. London: Foreign Policy Centre, 2000.

Anderson, William M., and Patricia Shehan Campbell, "Teaching music from a multicultural perspective." In *Multicultural perspectives in music education*, edited by William M. Anderson and Patricia S. Campbell, 1–7. Reston VA: MENC, 1989.

Banks, James A. "Multicultural education: Historical development, dimensions, and practice." *Review of research in education* 19 (1993): 3–49.

Bannerji, Himani. *The dark side of the nation: Essays on multiculturalism, nationalism and gender.* Toronto: Canadian Scholars' Press, 2000.

Bennett, Christine, Timothy Niggle, and Frances Stage. "Preservice multicultural teacher education: Predictors of student readiness." *Teaching and teacher education* 6, no. 3 (1990): 243–254.

Blakeslee, Michael. "National standards for arts education." Reston, VA: Music Educators National Conference, 1994, 63.

Bohlman, Philip V., ed. *The Cambridge history of world music.* Cambridge University Press, 2013.

Boulton, Harold, and Arthur Somervell. *Songs of the four nations.* London: J. B. Cramer & Co., 1893.

Brown, Vincent. *The reaper's garden: Death and power in the world of Atlantic slavery.* Harvard University Press, 2008.

Campbell, Patricia Shehan, and Ana Lucía Frega. *Songs of Latin America: From the field to the classroom: Canciones de América Latina: de sus orígenes a la escuela.* Miami, FL: Warner Bros. Publications, 2001.

Campbell, Patricia Shehan, Sue Williamson, and Pierre Perron. *Traditional songs of singing cultures: a world sampler.* Alfred Music Publishing, 1996.

Cash, Stefanie L. *The use of world music in high school choral classrooms.* PhD Diss. The Florida State University, 2012.

Chen, Chin-Hsin Yao, and Shih-Hsiang Chen. *The flower drum and other Chinese songs.* New York: The John Day Company, 1943.

Choate, Robert A. *Documentary Report of the Tanglewood Symposium.* Washington, DC: Music Educators National Conference, 1968, 139.

Curwen, John Spencer. *Folk songs from many lands.* London: J. Curwen & Sons.

Department for Education (DFE). "Music in the National Curriculum" (England), 1995, DFE.

Diamond, Beverley, and Anna Hoefnagels, eds. *Aboriginal music in contemporary: Echoes and exchanges.* McGill-Queen's Press-MQUP, 2012.

Elliott, David James. *Music matters a new philosophy of music education.* New York; Toronto: Oxford University Press, 1995.

Finney, John. *Music education in England, 1950–2010: The child-centred progressive tradition.* London: Routledge, 2016.

Gilman, Benjamin Ives. "The science of exotic music." *Science* 30, no. 772 (1909): 532–535.

Gilroy, Paul. *The black Atlantic: Modernity and double consciousness.* Cambridge, MA: Harvard University Press, 1993.

Government of Ontario. The Ontario curriculum grades 1–8: The arts (Rev.), 2009. Retrieved from http:// www.edu.gov.on.ca/eng/curriculum/elementary/arts18b-09curr.pdf

Green, Lucy. "From the Western classics to the world: secondary music teachers' changing attitudes in England, 1982 and 1998." *British Journal of Music Education* 19, no. 1 (2002): 5–30.

Hess, Juliet. "Decolonizing music education: Moving beyond tokenism." *International Journal of Music Education* 33, no. 3 (2015): 336–347.
Johnson, Byron Gordon. *Presenting Jamaican folk songs on the art music stage: Social history and artistic decisions.* The University of Southern Mississippi, 2010.
Kang, Sangmi, and Hyesoo Yoo. "Effects of a westernized Korean folk music selection on students' music familiarity and preference for its traditional version." *Journal of Research in Music Education* 63, no. 4 (2016): 469–486.
Klocko, David G. "Multicultural music in the college curriculum." *Music Educators Journal* 75, no. 5 (1989): 38–41.
Lavezzoli, Peter. *The dawn of Indian music in the West.* London: A&C Black, 2006.
Legette, Roy M. "Multicultural music education attitudes, values, and practices of public school music teachers." *Journal of Music Teacher Education* 13, no. 1 (2003): 51–59.
Lidskog, Rolf, "The role of music in ethnic identity formation in diaspora: A research review," *International Social Science Journal* 66, no. 219–220 (2016): 23–38.
Livingston, Carolyn. "Charles Faulkner Bryan's legacy for general music." *Journal of Research in Music Education* 46, no. 2 (1998): 223–238.
Lowe, Geoffrey M., and Andrew Sutherland. "Western Australian music teachers and the WACE Music syllabus five years down the track: Where are we now?" *Australian Journal of Teacher Education (Online)* 39, no. 11 (2014): 162–177.
Lundquist, Barbara Reeder. "Music, culture, curriculum and instruction." In *The new handbook of research on music teaching and learning: A project of the Music Educators National Conference*, edited by Richard Colwell, and Carol Richardson, 626–647. Oxford: Oxford University Press, 2002.
Madsen, Clifford, ed. *Vision 2020: The Housewright symposium on the future of music education.* Lanham, MD: Rowman & Littlefield Publishers, 2020, 206.
Mansouri, Fethi, and Tariq Modood. "The complementarity of multiculturalism and interculturalism: theory backed by Australian Evidence." *Ethnic and Racial Studies* 44, no. 16 (2021): 1–20.
McCarthy, Marie. "Toward a global community: The international society for music education." *Perth: International Society for Music Education* (2004).
Nethsinghe, Nishantha Rohan. "Attaining proximal simulation in multicultural music education." PhD diss., Monash University, 2012.
Nethsinghe, Nishantha Rohan. "The notion of authenticity in multicultural music: Approaching proximal simulation." *International Journal of Multicultural Education* 15, no. 2 (2013).
Nettl, Bruno. *The study of ethnomusicology: Twenty-nine issues and concepts.* Champaigne IL: University of Illinois Press, 1983, 2.
Norman, Katherine. "Music faculty perceptions of multicultural music education." *Bulletin of the Council for Research in Music Education* (1999): 37–49.
Oehrle, Elizabeth. "Musics of the world's cultures: A source book for music educators," in *Callaway International Resource Centre for Music Education, for the International Society for Music Education*, edited by Barbara Lundquist and CK Szego with Bruno Nettl, Ramon Santos and Einar Solbu (1998).

Palmer, Anthony J. "World musics in music education: The matter of authenticity." *International Journal of Music Education* 1 (1992): 32–40.
Parsons, Graham. "Songs old and new: The survival of the New Zealand Maori waiata in a changing world." *Music education entering the* 21 (2004): 67–71.
Petersen Jr, Gerald Anthony. *Factors contributing to Arizona elementary general music teachers' attitudes and practices regarding multicultural music education.* PhD diss., The University of Arizona, 2005.
Pohlit, Stefan. "Musical life and westernization in the Republic of Turkey schismogenesis and cultural revisioning in contemporary music." In *Conference "Europe in Opera—Musical Compositions of an Identity" at Casa de Mateus (Porto/Portugal).* 2010.
Ragland, Cathy. "Mexican deejays and the transnational space of youth dances in New York and New Jersey." *Ethnomusicology* 47, no. 3 (2003): 338–354.
Rampton Committee, *West Indian children in our schools, Interim Report* (London: HMSO, 1981).
Romero, Ral. "Popular Music and the Global City." *Huayno, Chicha, and* (2002).
Schippers, Huib. "Tradition, authenticity and context: The case for a dynamic approach." *British Journal of Music Education* 23, no. 3 (2006): 333–349: 347.
Schneider, Eta Harich. "Renaissance Europe through Japanese eyes: Record of a strange triumphal journey." *Early Music* 1, no. 1 (1973): 19–26.
Short, Geoffrey. "Retain, relinquish or revise: The future for multicultural education." *Journal of Multilingual & Multicultural Development* 15, no. 4 (1994): 329–344.
Sutherland, Andrew. "The developing timbre palette of film music: The emergence of world instruments for non-ethnographic association." *The International Journal of Arts Theory and History* 13, no. 2 (2018), 19–31.
Thielen-Gaffey, Tina L. "David Fanshawe's African Sanctus: One work for one world [approx] through one music." PhD diss., The University of Iowa, 2010.
Toner, Peter G. "The gestation of cross-cultural music research and the birth of ethnomusicology." *Humanities Research* 14, no. 1 (2007): 85–110, 86.
Volk, Terese M. "'Music speaks to the hearts of all men': The international movement in American Music Education: 1930–1954." *Bulletin of the Council for Research in Music Education* (1997): 143–152.
Von Hornbostel, Erich Moritz. "African negro music." *Africa* 1, no. 1 (1928): 30–62.
Woodfield, Ian. *English musicians in the age of exploration.* Vol. 8. Hillsdale NY: Pendragon Press, 1995.
Young, Sharon Marlene. *Music teachers' attitudes, classroom environments, and music activities in multicultural music education.* PhD Diss. The Ohio State University, 1996.

Part 3

ADVANCING PEDAGOGY WITH TECHNOLOGY AND CREATIVE REVOLUTIONS

The final section of this book contains six chapters that describe diverse revolutions, some comparatively recent. Some revolutionary ideas begin well before the technologies that we know today evolve. In "Class Piano—Democratizing a Nineteenth-Century Status Symbol," Timothy J. Groulx explores the beginnings and evolutions of the idea that the piano could be taught in a group. It was some time before the technology caught up with the basic premise advanced to what we recognize today. Contemporary music educators would find early applications of this idea shocking, for example, a class of adolescents "playing" a cardboard replica of a keyboard. Even more recently, early keyboard laboratories were large and cumbersome, with classrooms looking a little like mission control in the early space race with a clear hierarchy of teacher (with microphones and headphones) directing the individual and partnered work of students at their silent work station. Even with the advent of Musical Instrument Digital Interface (MIDI) the keyboard laboratory classroom remained a relatively silent place. To the observer, there was no overt music making, just the sound of the teacher's voice, the quiet tapping of keyboards, and the occasional rustle of pages being turned. Current practice allows far less regimented engagement via ever-changing music technologies, with students able to engage in individually paced learning and creative exploration.

Other revolutions are such that they almost burst upon our understanding. Such was the case with the work of R. Murray Schafer. Ros McMillan discusses Schafer's work and offers exploration of its impact on Australian music education as an example of what occurred in other places. We also note that revolutions often abut, impinge, transgress, and sometimes infiltrate others. For example, Schafer's work seemed to appear from nowhere in the early 1970s, galvanizing a generation of receptive Australian educators. Schafer's impact was immediate because, unlike many other charismatic musicians and educators, he came to Australia. Under the auspices of the Australian Society for Music Education (ASME), Schafer presented to groups of current and future music educators in workshops, at universities, and at residential weekends. Having direct contact with Schafer was inspirational and his work more impactful because he was present in person. For all revolutions in this book, personal experience with inspirational figures seems to drive the explosions of ideas. Once unfolded and disseminated by Schafer, his work spread further appearing sometimes in what might be unlikely places. For example, in 1990 Jane Southcott observed a workshop for Orff educators at the Orff Institut in Salzburg that began with a discussion of Schafer's "Moonlight" that evolved into an improvisation workshop based on the weather over the mountains seen from the windows using words such as *schnee* (snow), *hagel* (hail), *regen* (rainbow), and *nebel* (fog).

Next, Patrick Horton explores the development of music notation software. In a way, he explores the ongoing revolutions that began with the conceptions of solmization and music notation *per se*. These notational software evolutions permeate all aspects of music and music education praxis today. In the space of one lifetime, notating music has moved from a slow paper-and-pencil practice closely linked to music making and music imagining remembered by many to one in which students can notate and record their musical creations, share them with their immediate colleagues, and then disseminate them to the world with consummate ease. This has made the work of the class music educator and school music director far easier. For example, gone are the days when student clarinetists need to learn to sight transpose in case a Bb ensemble part was not available.

In the next chapter of this collection, Hilary McQueen discusses one of the most recent revolutions in school music education included in this collection, Musical Futures. This approach has permeated middle school and high school music classrooms in many countries. Heralded by many as a solution to the long-recognized separation of school music from the music valued and made by adolescents, Musical Futures has been heralded both as a salvation and as a challenge to established practice. Based on the premise that nonformal teaching and informal learning best support students who prefer popular music making, the practices of Musical Futures advocates and practitioners offer provocation to curriculum designers seeking to cater for all students.

Corollary to the preceding chapter, Andrew Brown addresses another contemporary revolution, digital technologies, and interfaces as maker spaces that facilitate musical expression in music learning. Tracing the evolution of electronic music instruments in classrooms, Brown begins with early inventions that supported compositional practices such as musique concrète that gradually appeared in school music classrooms. Beginning with the tape recorder, school students were able to record and manipulate found sounds to create musical artifacts. With the appearance of early synthesizers in schools, this horizon expanded to the school studio recording suite that we find in many schools. These developments entwine with those of keyboard technologies and music notation software discussed in preceding chapters creating a world of musical possibilities for making, recording, and sharing music that we now expect to find in school music programs in many contexts.

In the final chapter of this book, Renée Crawford offers an overview of the relationship between technology and music and its revolutionary impact on music education. Thus, she brings together the revolutions already described. Musicians and music educators have always taken full advantage of whatever technological advancements are available. School music praxis will always lag behind industry, but once technologies become affordable, they are quickly adopted, becoming part of our quotidian music classroom landscape. Once schools could afford gramophones, a world of music became accessible via music recordings; other vistas opened as inventions were mass-marketed, and there has been a long line of additions to school music resources.

Overall, this chapter has captured a number of technological revolutions that have permeated our practice as music educators—we now have available the resources to evolve our practice and the music making of our students in ways unthought and at a standard unimaged by our forebears.

Chapter 11

Class Piano—Democratizing a Nineteenth-Century Status Symbol

Timothy J. Groulx

To own a piano was to have social status, particularly in the early nineteenth century.[1] It suggested cultural refinement and that its owner could afford the instrument's expense as well as the time to learn to play it. The period between 1850 and 1914 was a time of great economic growth and expansion of the middle class, and the piano was highly sought-after. It "provided entertainment and decoration, being both a musical instrument and a substantial piece of furniture. Its ownership conferred status, symbolic as it was of gentility, family life, taste, and wealth."[2] Approximately a century and a half after Bartolomeo Cristofori developed the modern piano,[3] when the instrument had become increasingly available and less expensive, it seemed natural for people to want to learn to play it as it was rapidly becoming the "most universal and indispensable medium of music."[4] People appreciated that the piano was capable of melody and harmony across an extensive range and was relatively easy to play. For many centuries, learning to play the piano typically required a private teacher.[5] The teaching of piano in groups, rather than individually, was therefore a significant step forward in democratization of a symbol of privilege and wealth as it was often affordable to most strata of society.[6]

The focus of this research was the evolution and growth of class piano in public schools, though this historical perspective includes roots in private instruction and is interconnected with postsecondary education. The body of research on class piano also included group instruction by composers such as Chopin and Liszt. This falls outside the purview of this study as these composers were using what they called a "master class" model, where they were teaching almost exclusively mature musicians, or at least advanced students.[7]

PIONEERS OF CLASS PIANO

The first documented instance of piano being taught in groups, rather than individually, is associated with Johann Bernhard Logier (1777–1846). Born in Germany, his father taught him to play flute and piano at a young age. His parents both died when he was very young, and a visiting Englishman who was impressed by Logier's musical talents brought him to London and raised him. Settling in Dublin in 1807, Logier became the orchestra director of the Dublin Theater where he also managed a music shop and taught lessons.[8] It should be noted that group piano classes probably did exist prior to this, though the only known documentation of such is a comment made by George Farquhar Graham, a critic of Logier: "Teachers of music in England and Scotland had taught their pupils in classes, but upon a better plan than Mr. Logier's before that musician's system was heard of."[9]

Logier began developing his methods and an apparatus he called a "chiroplast" (patented in 1814) while teaching his young daughter to play piano. The chiroplast was essentially an arrangement of dowels, rods, and finger guides to keep the hands in an ideal piano playing position. Logier claimed that his chiroplast would reduce the amount of time a teacher would spend adjusting hand and finger positions, which he described as "the most tedious part of professional labor" and "wearisome drudgery."[10] Logier published testimonials of the chiroplast that he had solicited from prominent pianists such as Muzio Clementi.[11]

Using the chiroplast, Logier did not have to closely monitor the hands of every pianist, and he began teaching piano in groups of twelve to thirty students, playing eight to ten instruments simultaneously, with a smaller room for individual attention and instruction. Indeed, his classes were not limited to only beginners but also students of varying skill levels. To do this, each student was playing a different part of the same composition, with the beginners playing technically simple parts and advanced students playing more demanding parts.[12] Logier's system benefitted from its similarity to the Lancastrian, or monitorial system of classroom education, where more advanced students coached or tutored novices. Logier also taught elementary harmony as an integral part of his system.[13]

An advertisement in support of Logier's system appeared in London newspapers in December 1817 which enticed many piano teachers to adopt it, though it required training directly from Logier at a "not inconsiderable fee" of 100 guineas.[14] These new teachers were sworn to maintain secrecy.[15] Logier Academies quickly spread across Ireland, Scotland, and England and within a few years had spread to Spain, India, France, and the United States (Philadelphia and New York City). The majority of those who actually witnessed the pedagogical system in practice were impressed, including German conductor Louis Spohr whose commendations led the Prussian government to induce Logier to establish academies in seven of their cities in 1822.[16] Johann's son Frederick Augustus Logier (1801–1867) emigrated to Cape Town, South Africa, in 1826 to establish a Logierian piano school with his partner and colleague Edward Knollys Green, who died just two years later. Frederick Logier was unable to run the piano school alone, went bankrupt, and the school had its very last public examination of pupils in 1833.[17]

Many private piano instructors were critical of Johann Bernhard Logier's system, often out of fear that group piano lessons would be detrimental to their livelihood. Multiple letters to the editor criticizing him in Scottish newspapers (to which he responded) took place over the ensuing years. Critics asserted that an instructor would have to divide their attention among the members of the class so much that no one student would receive sufficient individual attention. They also complained that the classical compositions which he included in his three volumes of studies were not true to the originals and had been altered in what they found to be a disagreeable fashion. Ultimately, these debates advertised his method and helped him attract more students and teachers.[18]

Group piano instruction spread to North America throughout the 1800s. An anonymous article in *New York Musical World*, dated September 27, 1856, and entitled "Gottschalk's New Enterprise," describes a class of eight piano students sight-reading Beethoven's C Minor symphony, with parts distributed based on individual ability. The author commented on the success of the class and that this method had made a fortune for one teacher of this method in Paris which Gottschalk should expect.[19] An anonymous letter to the editor was published in the *Canadian Musical Review* in October 1856, where the author rhetorically asked the school superintendent how students can learn music effectively with twelve pianos and an organ being played simultaneously in a public school.[20] Another anonymous letter to the editor complaining about group piano lessons appeared in *The Etude* in 1860 from a group of annoyed private piano teachers in Holly Springs, Mississippi. They described a teacher employed at some "female schools" who gave three thirty-minute group lessons per week and another in southern Tennessee who used a piano method which taught "neither notes nor keys . . . but numbers."[21] In a second letter in the same journal later that same year, a different author complained about group teaching from the state of Virginia.[22] Group piano had spread west to Utah by 1869 in a music boarding school.[23]

Calvin Bernard Cady, a professor at the University of Michigan, began to advocate class piano in 1887 and established a philosophy of group instruction that capitalized on the benefits of a shared thought process which gained him the reputation as the father of class piano in the United States. Cady focused on the spirit and motivation that was only possible with a group dynamic.[24] The goals of every piano class were to develop musical ideas, the power to express those ideas, and to experience music making. Unlike Logier's system, Cady's system did not have students spending the majority of class playing simultaneously. It was important for the students to also actively listen to each other. His class size was typically four students, far less than Logier's sixteen to thirty member classes, and he divided groups by ability level, rather than having all levels playing simultaneously.[25]

Just prior to the turn of the twentieth century, public attitude toward group piano had grown substantially more positive. Constantine Sternberg, a piano teacher in Philadelphia, wrote that piano classes were beneficial as the lower tuition fees made piano accessible to the average family. While he felt that piano classes were not the ideal forum to develop musical artists, he felt that they introduced artistic concepts and aesthetic values to those who otherwise would not have had access. His piano classes were reported to be very large.[26] Another group piano teacher, B. Hella Prince Stockey, made a practice of starting all new pianists in groups for ten weeks prior to starting private lessons.[27] James C. Fillmore in the U. S. Office of Education was a vocal advocate of class piano. His philosophy favored a group of eight or more students. Under all circumstances, the teacher must take what time is necessary to ensure student growth takes place. Further, he believed that lessons were not the place for a student to practice and that should take place exclusively at home.[28]

CLASS PIANO ENTERS PUBLIC SCHOOL CLASSROOMS

The class piano model began entering public schools in the United States around the time of World War I. Karl Gehrkins noted the connection between public school class piano instruction and class violin instruction, both of which came to the United States from England. He envisioned group instrument pedagogy where the teacher was employed full-time by a school district and thereby enabling all students to learn to play an instrument. This was significant because in the early 1900s most public school music teachers taught only vocal music.[29]

The first record of curricular piano classes in a public school in the United States was in Boston in 1913. H. S. Wilder left his teaching post at the New England Conservatory, where he had taught piano since 1904, to go into local elementary schools where he would enter a classroom and teach piano skills to the entire class of approximately twenty students. Wilder used tables for hand culture and rhythmic work, flash cards for intervals, chords, and short phrases, dummy keyboards for technique and to aid in memorization, and one actual piano for ear training and student performance.[30]

School-based piano classes appeared in Milwaukee, Wisconsin, the year after they appeared in Boston, and in 1915 they appeared in three more cities in the United States. Blanche E. K. Evans of Cincinnati, Ohio, may have been the first to institute class piano at the high school level. Children in the public schools of Schenectady, New York, had violin classes and began demanding piano classes as well. Music supervisor Inez Field instituted weekly one-hour lessons with six to twenty students per class and advanced classes of four to six. Thaddeus P. Giddings, music supervisor of schools in Minneapolis, Minnesota, was asked to implement class piano for the students which contained usually sixteen to twenty students. Most classrooms had one piano and several keyboards printed on cloth, cardboard, or paper for students to learn fingering patterns.[31] Students learned to play songs on the piano that they already knew how to sing and were instructed to sing while playing at the piano or at a paper keyboard "in order to tell [their] fingers what to do." Little piano music was published within the singing range of children, so the school's second-grade songbook became the source material for the class. Since the students already knew the songs, the only cognitive demand was learning the keyboard.[32]

One of the biggest challenges in implementing piano classes in public schools was finding a suitable teacher. Piano had traditionally been taught privately, so piano teachers were largely unfamiliar with managing large groups of students and making the most of group dynamics. Occasionally, classroom teachers could be found who had learned to play the piano, but even these teachers lacked the pedagogical knowledge for effectively implementing piano curriculum. In the earliest days, different communities used both of these approaches with varying levels of success. In Schenectady, classroom teachers taught piano classes with weekly support and training from the music supervisor who later developed a course to prepare classroom teachers to teach piano. In Minneapolis, Giddings (the music supervisor) hired piano teachers to teach class piano, and the result was considered far more successful than in Schenectady. Giddings met with the piano teachers to discuss classroom procedures and group materials. They were required to attend training with Giddings and his staff every five to six weeks, during which each piano teacher taught the group of peer teachers which allowed everyone to share their best practices efficiently. As a result, classes district-wide progressed uniformly.[33]

In addition to the lack of appropriate teachers was the lack of curricular materials. One of the earlier published beginning piano methods book was *The Burrowes' Piano Primer*, published in 1904 and selling over one million copies prior to revision. Logier's practice of having multiple levels of achievement taught simultaneously in one room is evident in the Burrowes method. Giddings, mentioned above, combined the singing of familiar songs with piano playing, which he later compiled into his *Piano Class Readers*, and in 1919 published the *Giddings Public School Class Method for Piano*. Calvin Cady had referenced this "song approach" earlier in his 1904 book, *Music Education (An Outline)*.[34]

There was little expansion of class piano during World War I, but in 1919 piano classes began spreading again, this time to public schools in Lincoln, Nebraska, and Rochester, New York, with further growth to nine additional cities in the early 1920s. Will Earhart of the U. S. Office of Education stated in 1923 that thousands of children are now receiving, at the very least, exploratory courses in piano, violin, and other orchestral instruments during school hours, either at minimal expense or publicly funded.[35]

RAPID EXPANSION AND THE NATIONAL BUREAU FOR THE ADVANCEMENT OF MUSIC

As class piano had begun to take hold in schools across the country, its associated advantages and problems had become well known. Educators had seized upon the benefit of the democratizing effects of class piano, which made instruction accessible to nearly every student, its efficiency and economy of scale, and the benefits of the group dynamics it fostered. The problems of incompetent teachers, unsatisfactory equipment, poorly grouped students, poor quality music, and over-commercialization had continued to grow rather than abate.[36]

The National Bureau for the Advancement of Music (NBAM) was a potent force for the growth of music in schools, especially instrumental music. C. M. Tremaine founded NBAM on September 1, 1916, with other large corporations, having determined that working through a central agency for the promotion of music would increase profits. NBAM promoted all areas of music, though two-thirds of their budget was dedicated toward promoting piano classes.[37]

Tremaine noted in April 1928 that class piano had made its way into schools in all parts of the country and that it was steadily growing alongside bands, orchestras, and other instrumental music classes. Many schools awaited qualified teachers so they could offer it, and several colleges and universities had introduced group piano methods. It was argued that school choral programs benefitted when a school offered class piano.[38]

In 1929, NBAM undertook a national survey to determine the status of school piano classes in the United States. They found that there were five hundred and fifty-seven municipalities with operational piano classes, which increased to eight hundred and seventy-three in a 1930 survey. Only 6 percent of the sample reported that piano classes had been started and discontinued, which usually was due to losing the teacher. Most class sizes were around twelve and were usually grouped by ability. Program cost was usually minimal, with 69 percent of the sample reporting $0.25, and several stating lessons were fully paid for by their board of education. Retention rates were reportedly very high for class piano, while the dropout rate for private piano instruction was 41 percent. Piano classes were initially offered primarily to students in grades three to six, but later many schools added junior high grades.[39]

NBAM produced a pamphlet which was a detailed guide for the implementation, teaching, and management of class piano in a school system entitled *A Guide for Conducting Piano Classes in the School*, first published in the 1928 *Journal of the Music Supervisors National Conference*. There were 8,210 requests in the first year, representing 3,779 different towns and cities across the world (up to 4,853 in 1930). Ten inquiries came from Canada and stated that piano classes were operational. Ninety-one inquiries came from Egypt, Turkey, Hawaii, Japan, Korea, and South Africa, of which ten confirmed existing piano classes.[40]

The *Guide* contained a great deal of valuable information for those wishing to offer piano classes or to maximize the effectiveness of piano classes already established. It included a discussion of the need for qualified teachers and directed private piano teachers to find a list of institutions offering class piano pedagogy courses. The *Guide* recommended starting piano around third or fourth grade, allowing for at least two years of vocal experience prior to class piano, and that initial piano materials should consist of songs familiar to the student as Giddings had promoted previously in Minneapolis.[41]

The *Guide* contained a great deal of additional recommendations, policies, and guidelines for success. It recommended that teachers of class piano should be paid by the board of education, as with every other subject. If students are charged tuition, they should be expected to pay in advance (to ensure attendance) $0.25 to $0.50 per lesson. Boards of education were advised to use tuition for personnel, instrument purchase and maintenance, and instructional materials. Lessons should be organized as pull-out classes on a rotation during the school day so that they only miss one subject per month. The *Guide* contained advice on publicity and advertising, communication with parents, as well as testimonials regarding best practices from music supervisors and administrators from school districts across the United States.[42]

Alice Colvin also undertook a national survey in the early 1930s to determine the status of music in the secondary schools in U. S. cities (with populations over 100,000). Survey responses indicated that there were piano classes operating in 35.1 percent of seventh and eighth grades, 64.3 percent of ninth grades, 27 percent of tenth grades, and 18.9 percent of the eleventh and twelfth grades. Students could earn credit for piano study at most schools: 54 percent of schools gave credit for piano instruction whether it was within or outside of school, 21.6 percent only gave credit for piano outside of school, 13.5 percent only gave credit for piano within school, and only 10.8 percent offered piano but did not offer credit. The majority (80 percent) of classrooms had only one piano in each classroom, while the remaining 20 percent had more than one piano. The remaining students who were not playing at the piano used cardboard keyboards for practice in 75 percent of classrooms, though every instructor indicated that each student had regular opportunities to use the piano.[43]

W. Otto Miessner also contributed to advancing class piano during this period. Miessner taught piano, band, chorus, and orchestra for several years and in 1914 became the director of the newly organized School Music Department at the State Teachers College in Milwaukee. In addition to other music courses, he designed and taught methods to teach group piano, group voice, and orchestral instruments. In 1918, he developed a small, portable piano which was the predecessor to the spinet, called the Miessner piano. He founded the Miessner Institute in 1924 to publish and promote his pedagogical and instructional materials, and in 1929 he moved to Chicago, where he began teaching elementary music methods since no colleges offered such methods yet. One of the instructional materials he published through his institute was the highly popular and influential series *The Melody Way*, based on Giddings' *Class Piano Readers* which based piano instruction on songs that were already familiar to children. Alice Colvin found in her survey (above) that *The Melody Way* was the most commonly used instructional method (used by 31.25 percent of respondents), followed by the Oxford methods (18.75 percent).[44]

The *Oxford Piano Course* series, developed by four authors and published in 1929, was among the most influential class piano curricula. The teacher's manual included detailed lesson plans and also discussed the sociological, educational, and artistic factors involved in a successful piano class. Another section focused on classroom management and fostering effective teacher-student relationships.[45] In a detailed analysis, which evaluated and compared piano method books, Lewison (1933) found the *Oxford Piano Course* to be the most suitable and effective instructional method for class piano.[46]

Robert Pace developed a successful group piano method called *Contemporary Group Piano*. He established biweekly lessons, including music fundamentals, theory, improvisation, and ear training for a group of eight-twelve students, and then in a second lesson of two or three students who worked on individual music and repertoire. What made Pace's work particularly notable was its grounding in the psychological theories of Piaget,

Bruner, Maslow, and Mursell. He sought to develop sensitivity, believing that aesthetic experiences and peak experiences through music helped people become more self-actualized. He fostered the group dynamic, believing that social interactions such as encouragement and students helping other students were important for motivation and growth.[47]

Aside from the democratic nature of class piano instruction, a number of researchers found lasting benefits of class piano instruction that support the ideas of early class piano pioneers such as Tremaine, Miessner, and Pace. Burtness (1933) found that teachers who took advantage of the group dynamic, including motivation and socialization were most successful. Other advantages of group instruction included development of listening habits and opportunities to perform, especially for an appreciative peer group.[48] Diehl found no significant difference in achievement scores between private piano students and group piano students in aural discrimination, knowledge of musical symbols, public performance, and transposition, but significantly higher sight-reading scores from group piano students than private piano students.[49] Hutcherson also found a greater success rate with sight-reading in group piano students.[50]

By the end of World War II, the piano class instructor had evolved to become more of a guide and moderator, and the students had become vital contributors. It had become clear that class piano could develop musical ideas and the power to express those ideas at a level commensurate with individual instruction (particularly during early stages of instruction) but that the musical experience was much richer in group instruction as students were able to not only experience their own playing and literature but were able to learn from others as well. On average, group piano students learned three times as many pieces. Group piano also had the capacity for students to play piano ensembles, which cannot be replicated in private study. Class piano instructors had also become adept at reclassifying learners to find the most appropriately paced instruction as the students developed.[51]

CHALLENGES OF CLASS PIANO

The supply of qualified class piano teachers did not keep up with the pace of the rapid expansion of piano classes in schools. Most school administrators recognized that the piano teacher untrained in classroom dynamics was the better candidate than the classroom teacher untrained in piano. Many employers opted not to offer a program at all, rather than starting one with an unprepared teacher, though unwilling private piano teachers were occasionally convinced to teach in schools. Large school systems could offer training, but in smaller communities lacking this resource, these private teachers were unsuccessful as often as they were successful. Prudent teachers would seek workshops, read literature, or go to a nearby college for professional development. Class piano pedagogy at colleges had grown significantly from forty-three in 1929 to one hundred and thirty-two in 1930. This problem was largely resolved by 1930, with the majority of class piano courses being instructed by piano teachers trained to work with classes.[52]

One reason that class piano did not proliferate in some countries may have been because of its status in public education. Class piano had not been accepted as a curricular subject in the United Kingdom as it had in many parts of the United States, even though Logier's system originated in this region over a century earlier. Jevons (1937) had described how piano teaching was not new to the United Kingdom and how it had been implemented in Germany and the United States as a curricular subject. He stated, "Above all, music teachers must be able to show convincingly that as an aid in character-training, and in developing the physical, mental and imaginative powers, playing an instrument surpasses some subjects which are fully recognized by the Board of Education."[53] Japan and Korea both adopted class piano instruction around the year 1930, although it abruptly stopped in Korea in 1950 with the outbreak of domestic war and was forgotten for several decades.[54] Egyptian educators first recognized the importance of music education for every citizen in 1932. Since piano was the primary instrument of so many music educators, a solution was to promote group piano in schools to foster more students to enter the music education profession.[55]

There were a number of problems that began to arise within the realm of class piano. Private piano teachers complained about class piano students having bad technique due to what they perceived as inadequate individual instruction. Piano classes tended to fail when the teacher was not properly prepared, there were too many students, or facilities were inadequate. Many piano dealers offered free piano classes, which were often unsuccessful as their primary goal was to sell pianos not to raise the standards of musicianship.[56] NBAM surveyed reasons why students were discontinuing piano instruction in 1936 and found that the primary reason was unemployment and financial hardship resulting from the Great Depression. The second most common reason was that students were distracted by the radio, phonographs, and other forms of "passive enjoyment." Following closely behind these reasons were parents failing to recognize the value of music, poor-quality instructors, surfeit of extracurricular activities competing for students' attention, and a lack of public taste for good music.[57]

A source of contention among class piano and private piano teachers was the appropriate size of groupings. Logier was roundly criticized for his groups of sometimes thirty students, and there was much debate about the most appropriate group size, referenced above. One study examined student achievement when taught in pairs, groups of four, groups of six, or groups of eight and found no significant difference among student achievement based on these group sizes.[58]

One other difficulty encountered in piano classes was the issue of access to a piano. Pianos were expensive, consumed a great deal of space, and even if a teacher had one piano for each student, the resulting cacophony of ten to twenty students all practicing simultaneously presented problems. The universally adopted solution was to use "dummy keyboards," which were exploited by the piano class teacher with little effectiveness. The results indicated that students were kept busy at the keyboards and sacrificed real areas of learning. All types of keyboards were manufactured; cardboard keyboards, oilcloth keyboards, and far more expensive keyboards with key actions were available.[59]

The problem of "dummy keyboards" was to remain a significant problem until the advent of electronic keyboards with headphones in the 1950s. The first electronic piano laboratory was installed and implemented at Ball State University in Muncie, Indiana, in 1956. Electronic pianos were an ideal medium for class piano instruction as the instruments are smaller, enable both individual and class work, were less expensive than an acoustic piano laboratory,[60] and had virtually no maintenance costs associated.[61] Students can be actively engaged in music-making at the piano for the entirety of a class period with electronic pianos, and the instructor can engage the entire class or an individual student without interrupting others through the aid of communications controllers and student earphones.[62] Technological developments, like the concept of group piano instruction itself, had a mixed reception by music educators. Many refused to accept electronic keyboards as acceptable substitutes for acoustic pianos.[63]

Class piano instruction grew rapidly in the 1920s and was at its strongest in public schools until the early 1940s. Despite the invention of the electronic piano and its increased ease of access, class piano declined significantly in public schools over time.[64] Class piano was in 71.2 percent of U.S. elementary schools in 1949,[65] but only 13.4 percent in 1963.[66] A 1989 study identified that approximately 16 percent of secondary schools in Florida offered class piano and were almost exclusively using electronic keyboards.[67]

Class piano went through a great deal of development in the past two centuries since Logier's first published endeavors with his chiroplast. While there is clear evidence that the class piano model had spread internationally, there is a marked lack of published research on its development or status since Logier's disciples went forth to spread his pedagogical method except in the United States, where the subject became a curricular offering early and remained so until the present. Class piano had become a growing curiosity in the late nineteenth century, and by 1913 the subject had secured a foothold in public school curricula. The growing pains of the early 1920s led to rapid growth and expansion, a proliferation of instructional materials and methods, and an appreciation of the unique benefits of group piano instruction. Educators and administrators also arrived at a consensus that the best instructor is a musician trained as an educator and not the other way around. The Great Depression had a significant negative impact on class piano. By the time electronic keyboards arrived, the tidal wave of interest had subsided to a small but steady stream in elementary and secondary education. Notably, class piano's most constant presence at present is in higher education. The primary accrediting body for music degrees in U.S. colleges and universities established keyboard skills as a core competency for all undergraduate degrees in music, and most institutions achieve this through the efficiency of class piano.[68] This suggests concurrence with the previous assertion that piano was indeed "the most universal and indispensable medium of music."

NOTES

1. Francesca Carnevali, and Lucy Newton, "Pianos for the People: From Producer to Consumer in Britain, 1851–1914," *Enterprise & Society* 14, no. 1 (2013): 37–70. https://www.jstor.org/stable/23701647.

2. Carnevali and Newton, "Pianos for the People," 39.

3. Michael O'Brien, "Cristofori, Bartolomeo," *Grove Music Online*. 2001. Accessed June 15, 2021. https://www.oxfordmusiconline.com/grovemusic/view/10.1093/gmo/9781561592630.001.0001/omo-9781561592630-e-0000006835.

4. Lily P. Diehl, "An Investigation of the Relative Effectiveness of Group and Individual Piano Instruction on Young Beginners in an Independent Music Studio Utilizing an Electropiano Laboratory" (DMA Diss., University of Southern California, 1980), 2.

5. William Henry Richards, "Trends of Piano Class Instruction, 1815–1962." (PhD diss., University of Missouri at Kansas City, 1962), 6.

6. Richards, "Piano Class Instruction," 40.

7. Gladys Manigault Watkins, "An Analysis of Contemporary Class Piano Methods and the Establishment of Norms for their Evaluation" (DMA Diss., The Catholic University of America, 1979), 2.

8. Bernarr Rainbow, 1990. "Johann Bernhard Logier and the Chiroplast Controversy," *The Musical Times* 131 (1766): 193–196; Richards, 6.

9. George Farquhar Graham, *General Observations upon Music, and Remarks on Mr. Logier's System of Musical Education* (Edinburgh: Duncan Stevenson and Co., 1817), 5.

10. Bernhard Logier, Johann. 1815. *The First Companion to the Royal Patent Chiroplast; or Hand-Director* (London: I. Green, 1815). https://id.lib.harvard.edu/curiosity/digital-scores-and-libretti/37-990058931840203941, 1–2.

11. Logier, "Royal Patent Chiroplast" 9.
12. Rainbow, "Johann Bernhard Logier," 193; Richards, 8.
13. Rainbow, "Johann Bernhard Logier," 196; Richards, 8.
14. Rainbow, "Johann Bernhard Logier," 194.
15. Richards, "Piano Class Instruction," 12.
16. Rainbow, "Johann Bernhard Logier," 194; Richards, 7.
17. Nuala McAllister Hart, "Logier, Frederick." *Dictionary of Irish Biography*, 2009. Accessed August 11, 2021. https://www.dib.ie/index.php/biography/logier-frederick-a9281.
18. Richards, "Piano Class Instruction," 14–15.
19. *New York Musical World.* "Gottschalk's New Enterprise," (September 27, 1856): 450.
20. Richards, "Piano Class Instruction," 18–19.
21. Richards, "Piano Class Instruction," 23
22. Richards, "Piano Class Instruction," 25.
23. Richards, "Piano Class Instruction," 28.
24. Calvin P. Cady," Certain Educational Aspects of Technical Development." *The Etude* 7, no. 3 (1889): 40.
25. Richards, "Piano Class Instruction," 31.
26. Constantine Sternberg, "Musings on Class-Teaching." *The Etude* 9, no. 2 (1891): 29.
27. Hella Prince B. Stockey, "A Class in Ear Training." *The Etude* 14, no. 11 (1896): 249.
28. James C. Fillmore, "Class Teaching Once More." *The Etude* 7, no. 6 (1889): 91.
29. Karl W Gehrkens *An Introduction to School Music Teaching* (Boston: Birchard, 1919), 43.
30. H. S. Wilder, "How Full Room Piano Classes of Pupils are Conducted in the Boston Public Schools." *Journal of Proceedings of the Music Supervisors' National Conference* (Durham: Music Supervisors' National Conference, 1929), 268.
31. Richards, "Piano Class Instruction," 49–50.
32. Richards, "Piano Class Instruction," 46.
33. Richards, "Piano Class Instruction," 43.
34. Richards, "Piano Class Instruction," 52–54.
35. Will Earhart, "Piano Questionnaire." *Bulletin of the U. S. Bureau of Education* (U. S. Government Printing Office, 21, 1923): 8.
36. Leland A. Coon, "The Values and Dangers of Class Piano Instruction." *Music Supervisors' Journal* 14, no. 5(1928): 57–63.
37. Richards, "Piano Class Instruction," 56–58.
38. Charles M. Tremaine, "The School Piano Class." *The Journal of Education* 107, no. 16 (1928): 469–470. https://www.jstor.org/stable/42836436.
39. Charles M. Tremaine, and Ella M. Ahearn 1928. *National Survey of Piano Classes in Operation* (New York: National Bureau for the Advancement of Music, 1928); Charles M. Tremaine, and Ella M. Ahearn, *Supplement to the National Survey of Piano Classes in Operation* (New York: National Bureau for the Advancement of Music, 1930).

40. Richards, "Piano Class Instruction," 65.
41. Richards, "Piano Class Instruction," 67.
42. Paul J. Weaver, ed. Subcommittee on Class Piano Instruction. "A Guide for Conducting Piano Classes in the Schools." *Journal of the Music Supervisors National Conference* (Seeman Printery Incorporated, 1928), 325–344.
43. Alice J. Campbell Colvin, "Status of Music in the Secondary Schools of the United States." (Master's diss., University of Southern California, 1923).
44. John W Beattie, "Meet Mister Miessner." *Music Educators Journal* 42, no. 3 (1956): 24–26; Samuel D. Miller, "The Story of W. Otto Miessner—Visionary of What Might Be." *Journal of Historical Research in Music Education* 2, no. 2 (1981): 21–34. doi:https://doi.org/10.1177/153660068100200201.
45. Richards, "Piano Class Instruction," 77–79.
46. Mildred E. Lewison, "A Comparative Study of Certain Class Piano Methods." (Master's Thesis, University of Southern California, 1922).
47. Eri Hirokawa, "Robert Pace: Music Theorist, Composer, and Educator," *The Bulletin of Historical Research in Music Education* 18, no. 3(1997): 155–172. https://www.jstor.org/stable/40214934; Chungwon Kim, "Nurturing Students Through Group Lessons," *American Music Teacher* 54, no. 1 (2004): 28–31. https://www.jstor.org/stable/43547529.
48. Rhoda Burtness, 1933. "Methods of Instruction in Public School Piano Classes" (Master's diss., University of Southern California, 1933).
49. Diehl, "An Investigation" 97.
50. Rita Johnson Hutcherson, "Group Instruction in Piano: An Investigation of the Relative Effectiveness of Group and Individual Piano Instruction at Beginning Level." (PhD Diss., State University of Iowa, 1955).
51. Richards, "Piano Class Instruction," 110–112.
52. Richards, "Piano Class Instruction," 90–91.
53. Jevons, Reginald. 1937. "Piano Class Teaching: Will it Succeed?" *The Musical Times* 78 (1128): 137.
54. Koga, Midori. 1998/1999. "Early Piano Education in Japan." *American Music Teacher* 48 (3): 28–32; Sung, Jin He. 1984. "A Survey of Secondary Keyboard Training Practices in the National Teachers Colleges in the Republic of Korea with Recommendations for Implementation of a Class Piano Program." PhD Diss, The Ohio State University; Yang, Ji. 2017. "Teaching Methods for Class Piano in South Korea: a Comparison of Group and Private Lessons." *Music and Culture* 36: 93–125.
55. Sabry, Hoda Nicola. 1965. "The Adaptation of Class Piano Methods as Used in the United States of America for Use in the Egyptian Educational System." Ed.D. Diss., Indiana University.
56. Richards, "Piano Class Instruction," 98–101.
57. Tremaine, Charles M., and Ella Mason Ahearn. 1936. *Summary of Music Conditions Made by Piano Teachers*. New York: National Bureau for the Advancement of Music.
58. Jackson, Anita. 1980. "The Effect of Group Size on Individual Achievement in Beginning Piano Classes." *Journal of Research in Music Education* 28 (3): 162–166.
59. Richards, "Piano Class Instruction," 104.

60. Christopher Fisher, *Teaching Piano in Groups* (Oxford: Oxford University Press, 2010), 5.
61. Jack D. Goltz, "A Survey of Class Piano Laboratories" (PhD Diss., Florida State University, 1975).
62. Carl J. Eberhard, "The Electronic Piano Laboratory," *Educational Technology* 11, no. 8 (1971): 19–20.
63. Marie Shender, "An Evaluation of the Effectiveness of a Group Piano Program Using Electronic Keyboard and Computer Technology" (EdD Diss., Teachers College, Columbia University, 1998), 34.
64. E. L. Lancaster, "The Development and Evaluation of a Hypothetical Model Program for the Education of the College and University Group Piano Instructor" (EdD Diss., Northwestern University, Illinois, 1978).
65. William R. Sur, *Piano Instruction in the Schools* (Chicago: Music Educators National Conference, 1949)
66. Diehl, "An Investigation" 20.
67. David C. McCalla, "The Status of Class Piano Instruction in the Public Secondary Schools of Florida" (PhD Diss., University of Miami, 1989).
68. Jerry E. Lowder, "How Comprehensive Musicianhip Is Promoted in Group Piano Instruction." *Music Educators Journal* 60, no. 3 (1973): 56–58. https://www.jstor.org/stable/3394423; Emanuel. L. Lancaster, "Outstanding Group-Piano Program + Vital Piano-Pedagogy Program = Strong Teacher Training," *American Music Teacher* 30, no. 6 (1981): 36–37. https://www.jstor.org/stable/43535720.

BIBLIOGRAPHY

Beattie, John W. "Meet Mister Miessner." *Music Educators Journal* 42, no. 3 (1956): 24–26.
Burtness, Rhoda. "Methods of Instruction in Public School Piano Classes." PhD diss., University of Southern California, 1933.
Cady, Calvin P. "Certain Educational Aspects of Technical Development." *The Etude* 7, no. 3 (1889): 40.
Carnevali, Francesca, and Lucy Newton. "Pianos for the People: From Producer to Consumer in Britain, 1851–1914." *Enterprise & Society* 14, no. 1 (2013): 37–70. https://www.jstor.org/stable/23701647.
Colvin, Alice J. Campbell. "Status of Music in the Secondary Schools of the United States." Master's diss., University of Southern California, 1932.
Coon, Leland A. "The Values and Danger of Class Piano Instruction." *Music Supervisors' Journal* 14, no. 5 (1928): 57–85.
Diehl, Lily P. "An Investigation of the Relative Effectiveness of Group and Individual Piano Instruction on Young Beginners in an Independent Music Studio Utilizing an Electropiano Laboratory." DMA Diss., University of Southern California, 1980.
Earhart, Will. "Piano Questionnaire." *Bulletin of the U. S. Bureau of Education* (U. S. Government Printing Office) 21 (1923): 8.

Eberhard, Carl J. "The Electronic Piano Laboratory." *Educational Technology* 11, no. 8 (1971): 19–20.

Fillmore, James C. "Class Teaching Once More." *The Etude* 7 no. 6 (1889): 91.

Fisher, Christopher. *Teaching Piano in Groups*. Oxford University Press, 2010.

Gehrkens, Karl W. 1919. *An Introduction to School Music Teaching*. Boston: Birchard, 1919.

Goltz, Jack D. "A Survey of Class Piano Laboratories." PhD Diss., Florida State University, 1975.

Graham, George Farquhar. *General Observations upon Music, and Remarks on Mr. Logier's System of Musical Education*. Edinburgh: Duncan Stevenson and Co., 1817.

Hart, Nuala McAllister. "Logier, Frederick." *Dictionary of Irish Biography*, 2009. Accessed August 11, 2021. https://www.dib.ie/index.php/biography/logier-frederick-a9281.

Hirokawa, Eri. "Robert Pace: Music Theorist, Composer, and Educator." *The Bulletin of Historical Research in Music Education* 18, no. 3 (1997): 155–172. https://www.jstor.org/stable/40214934.

Hutcherson, Rita Johnson. "Group Instruction in Piano: An Investigation of the Relative Effectiveness of Group and Individual Piano Instruction at Beginning Level." PhD Diss., State University of Iowa, 1955.

Jackson, Anita. "The Effect of Group Size on Individual Achievement in Beginning Piano Classes." *Journal of Research in Music Education* 28, no. 3 (1980): 162–166.

Jevons, Reginald. "Piano Class Teaching: Will It Succeed?" *The Musical Times* (1937): 137–137.

Kim, Chungwon. "Nurturing Students Through Group Lessons." *The American Music Teacher* 54, no. 1 (2004): 28. https://www.jstor.org/stable/43547529.

Koga, Midori. "Early Piano Education in Japan." *American Music Teacher* 48, no. 3 (1999): 28–32.

Lancaster, Emanuel. L. "Outstanding Group-Piano Program + Vital Piano-Pedagogy Program = Strong Teacher Training." *American Music Teacher* 30, no. 6 (1981): 36–37. https://www.jstor.org/stable/43535720.

Lancaster, Emanuel. L. "The Development and Evaluation of a Hypothetical Model Program for the Education of the College and University Group Piano Instructor." EdD Diss., Northwestern University, Illinois, 1978.

Lancaster, Emanuel. L. "The Development and Evaluation of a Hypothetical Model Program for the Education of the College and University Group Piano Instructor." EdD Diss., Northwestern University, Illinois, 1978.

Lewison, E. Mildred. "A Comparative Study of Certain Class Piano Methods." Master's Diss., University of Southern California, 1933.

Logier, Johann Bernhard. *The First Companion to the Royal Patent Chiroplast; or Hand-Director*. London: I. Green. 1851. https://id.lib.harvard.edu/curiosity/digital-scores-and-libretti/37-990058931840203941

Lowder, Jerry E. "How Comprehensive Musicianhip is Promoted in Group Piano Instruction." *Music Educators Journal* 60, no. 3 (1973): 56–58. https://www.jstor.org/stable/3394423.

McCalla, David C. "The Status of Class Piano Instruction in the Public Secondary Schools of Florida." PhD Diss., University of Miami, 1989.

Miller, Samuel D. "The Story of W. Otto Miessner: Visionary of What Might Be." *The Bulletin of Historical Research in Music Education* 2, no. 2 (1981): 21–34. doi:https://doi.org/10.1177/153660068100200201.

New York Musical World. 1856. "Gottschalk's New Enterprise." September 27: 450.

O'Brien, Michael. "Cristofori, Bartolomeo." *Grove Music Online*. 2001. Accessed June 15, 2021. https://www.oxfordmusiconline.com/grovemusic/view/10.1093/gmo/9781561592630.001.0001/omo-9781561592630-e-0000006835.

Rainbow, Bernarr. "Johann Bernhard Logier and the chiroplast controversy." *The Musical Times* 131, no. 1766 (1990): 193–196.

Richards, William Henry. "Trends of Piano Class Instruction, 1815–1962." PhD diss., University of Missouri at Kansas City, 1962.

Sabry, Hoda Nicola. "The Adaptation of Class Piano Methods as Used in the United States of America for Use in the Egyptian Educational System." Ed.D. Diss., Indiana University, 1965.

Shender, Marie. "An Evaluation of the Effectiveness of a Group Piano Program Using Electronic Keyboard and Computer Technology." EdD Diss, Teachers College, Columbia University, 1998: 34.

Sternberg, Constantine. "Musings on Class-Teaching." *The Etude* 9, no. 2 (1891): 29.

Stockey, B. Hella Prince. "A Class in Ear Training." *The Etude* 14, no. 11 (1896): 249.

Sung, Jin He. "A Survey of Secondary Keyboard Training Practices in the National Teachers Colleges in the Republic of Korea with Recommendations for Implementation of a Class Piano Program." PhD Diss., The Ohio State University, 1984.

Sur, William R. "Piano Instruction in the Schools." In *Music Education Sourcebook.* Edited by Hazel N. Morgan, 110–118, Chicago: Music Educators National Conference, 1949.

Tremaine, Charles. M. "The School Piano Class." *The Journal of Education* 107, no. 16 (1928): 469–470. https://www.jstor.org/stable/42836436.

Tremaine, Charles. M. *Supplement to the National Survey of Piano Classes in Operation.* New York: National Bureau for the Advancement of Music, 1930.

Tremaine, Charles. M. *Summary of Music Conditions Made by Piano Teachers.* New York: National Bureau for the Advancement of Music, 1936.

Tremaine, Charles. M., and Ella Mason Ahearn. *National Survey of Piano Classes in Operation.* New York: National Bureau for the Advancement of Music, 1928.

Watkins, Gladys Manigault. "An Analysis of Contemporary Class Piano Methods and the Establishment of Norms for their Evaluation." DMA Diss., The Catholic University of America, 1979.

Weaver, Paul J. ed. "A Guide for Conducting Piano Classes in the Schools." *Journal of the Music Supervisors National Conference* (Seeman Printery Incorporated) (1928): 325–344.

Wilder, H. S. "How Full Room Piano Classes of Pupils are Conducted in the Boston Public Schools." *Journal of Proceedings of the Music Supervisors' National Conference.* Durham: Music Supervisors' National Conference, 1929: 268.

Yang, Ji. "Teaching Methods for Class Piano in South Korea: a Comparison of Group and Private Lessons." *Music and Culture* 36 (2017): 93–125.

Chapter 12

R. Murray Schafer—Celebrating a 1960s Visionary

Ros McMillan

AUSTRALIAN MUSIC EDUCATION 1945–1965

In the twenty years following the end of World War II, Australian music education lay in a coma of conservatism. Three of the main means of musical learning, those of studio lessons, school programs, and tertiary courses, were steeped in the music of the post-Renaissance classical tradition. This was despite the broadening of the musical language in the first half of the twentieth century through the development of African American music or jazz, serial music, and electronic music plus the (latent) acknowledgment of world or non-Western music. Profound change was to occur in the next decade, not least in regard to school music with Murray Schafer (1933–2021) playing a leading role.

Throughout the 1950s and 1960s, the idea that musical learning might include students performing music of their own was rarely considered. Creating music was for serious composers; the idea that students might also compose was generally considered an inconsequential occurrence. A notable exception occurred with *The Children's Hour*, an hour-long radio program the ABC broadcast from 1949 to 1972. The program included a daily segment known as *The Argonauts' Club* for children aged from seven to seventeen, each of whom was allocated a Greek ship name and number and who were invited to submit contributions that could include poems, stories, and artwork.[1] Each weekday an expert would talk on his/her particular interest including the Australian composer Lindley Evans (1895–1982) (known as Mr. Melody Man) who played and spoke on music performance and composition.[2] Within the program, there was an annual composition competition that awarded prizes.

Another outlet for student composers, although extremely limited, was in the theory syllabus of the Australian Music Examinations' Board (AMEB). From Grade 2, the course included a section titled "Creative," the so-called creative work at this level requiring a student to "mark the accentuation in a simple couplet of words."[3] By Grade Five, the requirement was "Write a balanced melody to a given rhythm of not more than eight bars."[4] As far back as 1968, Doreen Bridges, a major writer on Australian music education, had commented in relation to public examinations:

> How do we have the nerve to label as "creative activity" the composition of tunes . . . based on pale imitations of "National Songs" but otherwise like no music on earth except similar tunes written for examinations over the last forty years?[5]

I was a school student in the 1950s who gained 100 percent for Grade Five theory because I learnt the formula for writing a "balanced melody" with an upper and lower climax and a modulation at bar four. Equally restrictive for most piano students was the classically based AMEB repertoire, dominated by Bach, Mozart, and Beethoven, with the music of Debussy providing a reprieve from the "great masters" at higher-grade levels. Contemporary piano music was rarely considered, if indeed such repertoire was known to suburban piano teachers.

Classroom music generally had the same focus on classical music, consisting largely of singing, listening, the rudiments of music and aural training. Graham Bartle, writing on the state of music education in Australia in 1967, noted that while some school syllabuses suggested areas of creativity, serious attempts to stimulate creative imagination in students had been "rare in the extreme in past years." "Even now," he wrote, incentive for creativity "is certainly not found in 'write four bars of melody in 3/4 time in F major.'"[6]

This situation was not helped by the lack of creative music-making in teacher training. Indeed, there were no music teachers in secondary schools until these institutions were established in the early-mid twentieth century. Prior to that, primary school teachers were trained in teachers' colleges, where music was part of their curriculum; however, they were not specialist music teachers. Australian universities had no involvement in the training of music teachers until well into the twentieth century, but even when they did, the repertoire of all was invariably "classical," music of any other genre being nonexistent. Indeed, students heard playing anything remotely nonclassical could be reprimanded, as happened to a colleague, then an undergraduate music student in the early 1970s. After practicing his Bach and Beethoven, he began playing the gentle and beautiful *Your Song* by Elton John when a lecturer walked in and said: "I'm sorry you'll have to stop. We don't play that kind of music here." My colleague regrets to this day that he never did play "that kind of music" at his institution again.[7]

Despite the establishment of institutions specifically training teachers, it was possible until the early 1970s to gain employment as a music teacher in both government and independent schools without a teaching qualification. Provided one had an undergraduate degree, this situation continued until the federal government determined that all teachers should have a teaching qualification. Curiously, though, for some music teachers undertaking this there was no method of teaching course, it being considered unnecessary for those already in schools. Thus, the content of music classes was often a matter of choice, with many teaching what they themselves were taught in their own secondary and/or tertiary education. This became a problem to such an extent that in 1970 Doreen Bridges wrote that

> if we go on teaching the way we ourselves were taught . . . we shall find that the 20th century has passed us by, and left us high and dry, isolated from the knowledge explosion, the technological advances and the cultural climate of the times in which we live.[8]

A TIME OF CHANGE

Undeniably the 1960s saw a revolution in many aspects of society, especially social norms regarding clothing, drugs, and sexuality. Politics became an aspect of many people's lives through civil rights and anti-war protests, one of the most significant movements being the emergence of music as a powerful force. Among its leaders were the Beatles, Bob Dylan, especially his poetic lyrics, and performers of folk music including protest music.

A new movement was also fomenting in music education, heralded by the writings of international musician/educators that first appeared in Australian publications in the late 1960s. Peter Maxwell Davies, who visited Australia in 1965 for the UNESCO Conference on Music Education held in Sydney, described his classes in the UK where students composed music for performance by the school's ensembles.[9] Not only was the quality of the work impressive, but it was also evident that the students found their classes stimulating and rewarding. At the same time composers such as Herbert Chappell[10] and Michael Hurd[11] began writing works for school performances that incorporated jazz elements and which proved to be immensely popular with students brought up on an exclusive diet of classical music.

The most significant event in the gradual opening-up of creative practice in Australian music education occurred with the visit to Australia in 1973 by the Canadian composer, R. Murray Schafer. Schafer's books, first published in 1965 but more widely read with his visit to Australia, were breath-taking in their challenge for educators to regard the exploration of sound as the basis of musical learning. He constantly urged educators to teach music as a creative subject, capable of allowing students to be as expressive in the genre as was expected in the visual arts, creative writing, and making of many kinds.

Schafer was a prolific writer, four of his separately published booklets forming the basis of this chapter and written between 1965 and 1975. In a preface to *The Thinking Ear*, published in 1986 and containing the original four plus two more, Schafer noted the volume was not a textbook and made no claims to be one but was a personal account of a music educator rather than the enunciation of a method for slavish imitation. Nothing in the book says "Do it this way." It only says, "I did it this way. It may stimulate you to develop the subject further, and I hope it does that."[12]

Sometimes his writing is acerbic, at other times amusing, particularly when encountering administrators questioning his work. Often reflective and poetic, Schafer is occasionally sad, sometimes hopeful, but all his writing is artistic and elegant. The following sections discuss three of his books directed specifically to teachers, with the year of their first publication noted. Each is introduced by a quotation from the book being discussed, the page numbers referring to the books compiled in *The Thinking Ear*.

THE COMPOSER IN THE CLASSROOM—1965

It is the duty of every composer to be concerned with the creative ability of young people. But one has to be quick to catch it. For our system of music education is one in which creative music is progressively vilified and choked out of existence.[13]

Dealing largely with creativity, which Schafer suggests could be the most neglected subject in Western music education, the content consists of condensed transcriptions of six sessions he conducted with students aged from thirteen to seventeen. A seventh session involves primary school-aged students.

After the first where he questions the students on their likes and dislikes of music, the second session requests answers to the question "What is Music." It is here that Schafer displays his skills at handling the students' predictable answers of "pleasing to the ear" and "sound with rhythm and melody." Most suggestions are disputed with questions that challenge the students' assumptions until the following definition brings partial agreement: "Music is an organization of sounds . . . which is intended to be listened to."[14] Aware of the reluctance of some students to accept this, Schafer displays both his patience for those concerned when their perceptions are challenged and his gentle questioning of views that are clearly contrary to his beliefs.

Sections 3–5 involve students playing musical instruments, the first of these described as an attempt to release students' existing improvisatory abilities. Schafer begins with questions, one of his great strengths as a teacher. Seeking answers to why composers write, one student suggests they might want to describe something or imitate Nature, to which Schafer calls on the class to imitate a variety of sounds including marching into war, laughter, bird-calls, and fog settling over a city. Throughout attempts at producing these sounds, Schafer's ability to help the students listen carefully to the results shows his skill as an educator to gain reactions from his students rather than imposing his ideas.

Graphic notation is introduced in this session, a musical feature that became popular in the 1950s but was seldom used in music education until the 1960s when musicians such as George Self[15] and Brian Dennis[16] published music for classroom performance using this notation. Schafer begins by using his hands to "draw" a bird flying as a guide for the flautists to imitate the movement, followed by discussion as to how other objects can be accurately portrayed musically. These include a stormy sea, a horse standing still, a babbling brook, and a glass of water.

The fourth session, based on textures of sound, begins with a challenge for the students to produce a sound representing anger. Through a discussion of musical elements, Schafer brings the students to an awareness of the music of Debussy, Mussorgsky, and Beethoven and their ability to create moods. As the students improvise emotions, the composer exhorts them to listen (he repeats this three times) and not simply stack sounds on top of each other.

A standard wind quintet provides the basis for the fifth session, one where Schafer hopes the intimacy of the group can provide more challenging experiments in improvising. From the first tentative sounds, described by Schafer as "capricious" and therefore unacceptable, the students are led through tasks that relate their playing to human conversation. Their later efforts he describes as an experience where the listener "begins to sense a kind of intimate communism among the performers," noting that this "could never have been produced an hour before!"[17]

From working with students aged thirteen to seventeen, the book concludes with a project involving primary-aged students. Their teacher begins the session by telling Schafer that her students make up their own music on Orff instruments and then introduces him as a composer who might write something for them. At this, the guest suggests that as the children are composers, they might think it would be more fun if they made up a piece together. Unsurprisingly, the class responds with delight.

The walls of the classroom where the lesson is taking place are covered in student work including a fierce-looking mask that reminds Schafer of a Bertolt Brecht poem titled *The Mask of the Evil Demon*. Inventing a couple of lines that describe the golden mask, Schafer then asks the students how they could replicate the poem musically. Dramatic words, screams, and percussion instruments are produced with Schafer gradually withdrawing from the creative process, as he was pleased to note.

EAR CLEANING: NOTES FOR AN EXPERIMENTAL MUSIC COURSE—1967

> I have always tried to induce students to notice sounds they have never really listened to before. Before ear training . . . we require ear cleaning.[18]

Schafer's ability to produce powerful statements continues in his second book, the strikingly titled *Ear Cleaning*. Introducing a course of study for Year One students at a Canadian university, Schafer soon realized that their musical background was so wildly varied that his primary task was to "open" ears, an important prerequisite for both listening and playing music, he believed.

The book consists of nine workshops, containing course notes followed by exercises, discussions, and assignments. The first eight focus on the elements of noise, silence, tone, timbre, amplitude, melody, texture, and rhythm. The ninth, titled "The Musical Soundscape," is a compilation of the ideas from the previous eight. Although the course notes are each only a single page, they consist of sentences that are both challenging and amusing but always thought-provoking. Over the decades since they were written, they have often incited passionate debates in classes much younger than university students. An example here is from the lecture titled "Noise":

> For the insensitive person, the concept of noise is invalid. A sleeping log hears nothing. Machinery is indifferent to noise because it has no ears. Exploiting this indifference, wired background music was invented for earless humans.[19]

Throughout the book, provocative thinking continues to challenge readers, as the students in Schafer's classes would have experienced. In tone, one reads: "The single tone is two-dimensional. It is like a white line moving steadily across a black, silent time-space. But . . . how does the tone keep from boring itself?"[20] A following exercise requests a class to produce a single tone but try to find how expressive that tone might be by inserting it with silence.

Other art forms, particularly graphic arts, are also utilized. In regard to melody, Schafer employs shapes as notation to depict melodies by drawing lines that include rising, falling, and squiggles. In regard to rhythm, tasks are suggested that have proven to be stimulating for junior secondary students to nonmusical adults, even today. So dominant is the time signature of 4/4 in music that the exercises often provide challenges, a popular one involving polyrhythm with the word chanted together by three different groups, each with one of the time signatures of 3/4, 4/4 and 5/4.

In the introduction to the ninth workshop, titled *The Musical Soundscape*, Schafer suggests that by combining the expressive potential inherent in the first eight the class might consider them as "interacting within a cone of tensions."[21] Seven diverse tasks are provided that include a text by Wassily Kandinsky, graphic scores, and whole-class sound projects designed by the author himself.

For students with a musical background as well as those with little or none, Schafer's ideas would have been extraordinary in the mid-1960s. Arguably, popular music would have been the preferred listening of many in the class; thus, the detailed examination of the basic sounds of music must have been challenging. Yet, for those brought up to believe that the only worthwhile music was that of the post-Renaissance classical tradition, the lack of focus on this music would surely have been liberating.

Reading Schafer, one is constantly amazed at his poetic-like writing, the inventiveness of the tasks he sets and his targeted questioning, always with the purpose of helping the students find their own answers. If he cannot be present in everyone's classroom, his texts provide inspirational ways for teachers to embrace the spirit of his thinking.

WHEN WORDS SING—1970

Just as the architect uses the human body to provide the module for his [sic] living structures, so too is the human voice together with the human ear that must provide the standards in any discussion of the acoustical environment salubrious for human life. Tragically, we have not yet realized this.[22]

When Words Sing is an inspiring publication for classroom music activity, providing enlightened ideas for creative invention by students of all ages, more than fifty years after it was written. In the book's introduction, Schafer notes that its purpose was "to work with raw vocable sound" and that he wishes that he could "sing this book, and chant and whisper and bellow it." He ends the introduction by urging the reader *"to perform this book with your voice.* Out loud."[23]

The book's format is similar to *Ear Cleaning* with chapters on a variety of topics and discussion on each topic followed by exercises that reinforce the message. It is clear, when scanning it, that this is no ordinary textbook, so eye-catching is it with its illustrations and notation, both graphic and conventional. The range of topics is also far-reaching, all concerned with vocal sounds but as varied as James Joyce's "Thunder Word" from *Finnegan's Wake*[24] to "The Biography of the Alphabet," where Schafer provides colorful metaphors to describe each letter. Stating that the sounds should be produced phonemically, as they would appear in a word, the descriptions of those sounds typify his creative thinking. The letter "Z" is described as follows:

> The sound of bees; sound of small aircraft. In the English language "z" appears about 0.7 times per 1000 letters. Airplanes are more frequent.[25]

The topic of onomatopoeia provides ideas for some of the most stimulating lessons for early secondary school students. To begin, students are asked to find a watery-sounding word, then others that are metallic-sounding, bumpy, shaggy and syrupy, a task that students enjoy. It is also an opportunity to ensure that the "rules" of brainstorming are observed, that all suggestions are welcome with no criticism of anyone's choice. This is an important aspect of creative activity, providing an essential support for students at an age where feelings are often close to the surface.

Taking the concept of onomatopoeia further, Schafer asks the students whether the word "gold" glitters or if "war" is adequately ugly for its meaning. From this, they are encouraged to create neologisms that reflect more descriptively the sense of words. Teachers can discover how beautiful vocal pieces can be created by their students through inventing a word to portray a topic such as bell, insect, or raindrops and then finding two ways of pronouncing it such as higher, lower, or sotto voce. As a group, students then create a one-minute piece in ABA form using the two different sounds, the term "ABA," as opposed to "ternary," helping them understand the concept immediately. Whether most students will ever need to know the term "ternary" is unlikely.

There are sixteen discussion notes in total, those from seven to sixteen being ideal for specialist music students. They cover a wide range of topics including vowel sounds, the choruses of ancient Greek dramas, and haiku. This last topic provides the basis for invaluable lessons as it combines poetry, language, and music. It is also suitable for younger students offering the perfect excuse to conduct a lesson outdoors if a nature topic is wanted or to celebrate an occasion such as Halloween.

The last chapter consists of a Schafer vocal composition titled *Epitaph for Moonlight*. Written for youth choir with optional bells, the vocal sounds are neologisms invented by one of his Year 7 classes, including "noorwahm," "shiverglowa," and "lunious." Although deeply concerned with the increasingly noisy world in which we live, Schafer is uncharacteristically pessimistic in his introduction to the piece, noting:

> Why do I call it *Epitaph for Moonlight?* Because I doubt whether a group of young people today asked to produce synonyms for moonlight could find inspiration so easy as did my young poets in 1966. The moon as a numinous and mythogenic symbol died in 1969 [the year of the Moon landing]. It is now merely a piece of property.[26]

THE RHINOCEROS IN THE CLASSROOM—1975

In his introduction to this book, Schafer writes that after publishing his previous books he felt the need to make clearer the concepts espoused in these. A growing interest in integrating music with other art forms was another reason for this publication, consisting of ten reflections covering many topics. So profound are the reflections that it proved difficult to limit these to the three topics that are the basis of this section. Notwithstanding this dilemma, the chosen topics are those at the center of learning, students and teachers, as well as a subject that is often debated by music educators, that of notation.

STUDENTS

Schafer's passion to ensure music education is stimulating and relevant for all students is at the forefront of his thinking, noting that most of his work has been with ordinary rather than exceptional young people. His admiration for primary school students is clear when he writes that he has never met a child incapable of making an original piece of music, stating that he has proven that George Self's method of notating sounds using graphics can be taught to six-year-olds in fifteen minutes.

Another example of Schafer's respect for young children is the title of his third book for teachers, *When Words Sing*. On asking a six-year-old boy for his definition of poetry, the answer was "Poetry is when words sing," an expression that is included in the appendix to the book. This last section, "Texts without comment," provides more material on the power of words to provide creative music-making.

Indisputably one of the saddest comments on students is the following:

> For the child of five, art is life and life is art. Yet as soon as children enter school, art becomes art and life becomes life. They will then discover that "music" is

something which happens in a little bag on Thursday morning while on Friday afternoon there is another little bag called "painting." I suggest this shattering of the total sensorium is the most traumatic experience of a young child's life.[27]

We could do well to question whether the situation has changed in the five decades since Schafer wrote these words. Many schools have timetables where literacy and numeracy subjects are taught early in the school day because it is thought that students are then at their most alert. It, therefore, does no service to the arts to be relegated to late in the day, while few educationists consider these subjects to be equally important as English or Mathematics. This is despite widespread calls from industry and business for employees who are capable of thinking creatively.

TEACHERS

Throughout all Schafer's writing, there is an emphasis for teachers to be facilitators rather than transmitters of information. In regard to his own teaching, he states that he has tried to make the enthusiastic discovery of music precede the ability to play an instrument or read notes, suggesting that the time to introduce these skills is when the student asks for them. A sharp observation of the teaching profession is his scathing quote that too often "teaching is answering questions which nobody asks."[28] Noting that in a class programmed for creativity there are no teachers, only a community of learners, Schafer follows this with one of his most profound statements:

> In a class programmed for creativity, the teacher must plan for his [sic] own extinction.[29]

NOTATION

In regard to notation, Schafer believes that there is no need to discuss this when students begin composing. Rather, it is only when pieces become more elaborate that a written score may become necessary, after which Schafer lets the students devise their own in any form they wish. He discusses the work of George Self, the English music educator referred to earlier, whose pioneering work in a London school included a means of notating aleatoric sounds. Schafer suggests that music educators could do well to invent notations that can be mastered quickly so that "the devilment of penmanship exercises may never again be allowed to displace the purr of live music-making."[30] Here is the author at his most eloquent and poetic, one of the great pleasures in reading his books decades after they were written.

THE 1970S AND BEYOND

Support for creativity as an aspect of music learning was boosted by the 1982 report of an inquiry conducted by the Gulbenkian Foundation in the United Kingdom, titled *The Arts in Schools*. In one quotation, it was noted that innovation, initiative, and application in solving problems were essential tools for equipping people for life. Thus, "creative thought and action should be fostered in all areas of education," particularly the Arts where they should be "central."[31]

In Australia, the first signs of change in the school curriculum occurred in the 1980s with an obvious commitment to the notion of creativity. In music, this was manifested in a variety of approaches as outlined in documents from each Australian state, all of which mentioned performance, composition, and listening as a central and integrated aspect of their programs.[32] Impetus for this change was boosted in June 1986 when the Australian Education Council (AEC) resolved to support the concept of a national collaborative effort in curriculum development in Australia.[33] By 1991, the AEC had determined that statements and profiles would be developed for eight broad learning areas, of which the arts was one with five strands, one of which was music. Stating that schools should offer opportunities for students to experience activities that included creating, making, and presenting in all the art forms, the writers noted that within these activities, students should be encouraged to take risks, be imaginative, question prevailing values, and explore alternative solutions.[34]

These statements were "gold" to teachers who had previously endured criticism and occasionally outright opposition to the concept of students creating their own music in a classroom program. While Murray Schafer encouraged teachers to engage students in creative practice in the late 1960s and 1970s, it was the AEC's documents twenty years later that gave teachers the authority to allow their students to discover the pleasure of creative music-making. Clearly, the efforts of Schafer and other pioneers from the 1960s had come home to roost in Australian music education. Indeed, from the 1990s onward, Australian curriculum documents have promoted creating, making, and responding to music as key components of classroom practice from the first to the final years of schooling.[35,36]

A reinforcement of Schafer's comment that teachers of creative programs should plan for their own extinction occurred some years ago when I met an ex-student. By then in her late twenties, she was delighted to tell me that she had never forgotten a Year Seven class music lesson based on haiku as suggested in *When Words Sing*. Telling me that it was a class taught by a colleague, the ex-student described her experience as a member of a trio performing a haiku it had written and that read:

Have you ever heard
An eagle on the edge of
Sunrise yelling "Irk!"

My storyteller described how she had stood at the top of stairs in the classroom and in best-eagle tradition had shouted "Irk!" as dramatically as she could. The class, not unexpectedly, responded with enthusiastic applause, much to the delight of the trio. What delighted me, however, was that the class was not taught by my colleague but by me; thus, to echo Schafer, I was "extinct" in my student's recounting.

Writing haiku and performing them with original music became a popular activity in my Year Seven classes, the process of writing poems with seventeen syllables keenly focusing the minds of the young poets. Beginning with a free choice of topic each student invented her own, but when these were read aloud a theme would often emerge. The haiku above was one of a dozen that formed a "Crazy Animals" theme with the students accompanying their words with percussion instruments, voices, and classroom sounds, such as tapping on windows.

One year a Year Seven class used haiku to describe the world immediately following a nuclear disaster when all life was eliminated. This followed the telecast the previous evening of the controversial American film *The Day After* which had been widely publicized before its telecast on Australian television. As most of the class had seen the film and were clearly emotional about its impact, I suggested that everyone write a haiku based on their feelings.

The result was twenty-five reflections on a devastated world, so working in small groups each selected one haiku to create a composition. Some of the poems were dramatic, others clichéd, but the result was a profoundly moving experience, enabling the class to express its feelings through their creativity.

Undoubtedly, one of the most worthwhile outcomes for student composers is the possibility that their creative experiences in school might influence their future careers. While this is unlikely to occur frequently, the Australian and now international composer Liza Lim discovered her gift for creating new sounds in one of my Year Seven classes. By Year Ten, she was writing for the senior orchestra, continuing to write for school ensembles until she left school.

If creative music programs are to be fostered, it is obvious that the training of tomorrow's music teachers must occur with enlightened tertiary lecturers inspiring their students to regard creativity as an essential aspect of classroom programs. That these future teachers need to "plan for their own extinction" may cause some qualms, but it is clear that when they begin teaching, their students should be given every opportunity to realize their own expressive potential. That these experiences may be carried as memories into adulthood, as did the "eagle" who cried "Irk!," should be the desire of all teachers.

Murray Schafer's death occurred as this chapter was being written. Tributes abounded, including one from a former Canadian Broadcasting Corporation music producer who described Schafer's death as "the loss of our greatest composer, one whose creative spirit knew no bounds."[37] In nearly all tributes, Schafer is described as a composer, writer and environmentalist, the last for his compositions involving the sounds of nature. Few referred to him as a music educator, yet it is arguable that his work in this field has had the greatest impact. Indeed, his hope that his thoughts might stimulate music educators has been more than realized since Bartle's 1967 lament on the dearth of creative practice in school music. For this, Australian music education owes Schafer a profound debt.

As one who began school-teaching with a classical music degree but had no idea what to teach, my world changed on reading this Schafer quotation:

> It is my feeling that one learns practically nothing about the actual functioning of music by sitting in mute surrender before it. As a practising musician I have come to realise that one learns about sound only by making sound, about music only by making music .... The sounds produced may be crude; they may lack form and grace but they are *ours*.[38] (Emphasis mine)

Vale Murray Schafer. You taught us all to open our ears.

NOTES

1. Rob Johnson, *The Golden Age of the Argonauts: A Celebration of Australia's Best-Loved Radio Program for Children* (New South Wales: Hodder and Stoughton, 1997).

2. Lindley Evans, *Hello Mr Melody Man: Lindley Evans remembers* (Sydney: Angus & Robertson, 1983).

3. Australian Music Examinations Board (AMEB), *Manual of Syllabuses: Music Syllabuses* (Melbourne: AMEB Ltd., 2020): 37

4. AMEB, *Manual of Syllabuses*, 39.

5. Doreen Bridges, "Music in Australian Public Examinations," *Australian Journal of Music Education*, no. 2 (April 1968): 23.

6. Graham Bartle, "Aspects of Australian Music Education (iii): The Secondary Schools," *Australian Journal of Music Education*, no. 1 (October 1967): 17.

7. Greg Mason 2020, Personal communication, August 3, 2020.

8. Doreen Bridges, "Why Research in Music Education?," *Australian Journal of Music Education* 7 (October 1970): 25.

9. Peter Maxwell- Davies, "School music and the contemporary composer." Paper presented at the Australian UNESCO Seminar on School Music, Sydney Teachers' College and University of Sydney (20–29 May, 1965), 138–145.

10. Herbert Chappell. *The Daniel Jazz* (London: Novello, 1963).

11. Michael Hurd. *Jonah-man Jazz* (London: Novello, 1966).

12. R. Murray Schafer, *The Thinking Ear* (Toronto, Canada: Arcana Editions, 1986), ix.

13. Schafer, *Thinking Ear*, 40.

14. Schafer, *Thinking Ear*, 18.

15. Brian Dennis, *Experimental Music in Schools: Towards a New World of Sound* (Oxford University Press, 1970).

16. George Self, *New Sounds in Class: A Contemporary Approach to Music* (London, Universal Edition,1967).

17. Schafer, *Thinking Ear*, 39.

18. Schafer, *Thinking Ear*, 46.

19. Schafer, *Thinking Ear*, 48.

20. Schafer, *Thinking Ear*, 53.

21. Schafer, *Thinking Ear*, 68.

22. Schafer, *Thinking Ear*, 170.

23. Schafer, *Thinking Ear*, 170–171.

24. James Joyce, *Finnegan's Wake* (London: Faber & Faber, 1939).

25. Schafer, *Thinking Ear*, 182.

26. Schafer, *Thinking Ear*, 221.

27. Schafer, *Thinking Ear*, 248.

28. Schafer, *Thinking Ear*, 241.

29. Schafer, *Thinking Ear*, 245.

30. Schafer, *Thinking Ear*, 266.

31. Fundacão Calouste Gulbenkian, *The Arts in Schools: Principles, Practice and Provision*, ed. Ken Robinson (United Kingdom: Calouste Gulbenkian Foundation, 1982.)

32. Anne Carroll, "Secondary School Music Education in Australia: The Current Picture," *Australian Journal of Music Education*, no. 1 (1988): 92–101.

33. Curriculum Corporation. *A Statement on the Arts for Australian Schools* (Carlton, Victoria, 1994), 58.

34. Curriculum Corporation, *Statement*, 12.

35. Curriculum Corporation, *The Arts—A Curriculum Profile for Australian Schools* (Carlton, Victoria, 1994).

36. Australian Curriculum, *Assessment and Reporting Authority (ACARA), Australian Curriculum* (ACARA, Sydney, 2015).

37. David Jaeger, "R. Murray Schafer, composer, writer and acoustic ecologist, has died at 88." Canadian Broadcasting Corporation (August 14, 2021). https://www.cbc.ca/music/r-murray-schafer-composer-writer-and-acoustic-ecologist-has-died-at-88-1.5404868

38. Schafer, *Thinking Ear*, 46–47.

BIBLIOGRAPHY

Australian Music Examinations Board. *Manual of Syllabuses*. Melbourne, Victoria, 2020.

Bartle, Graham. "Aspects of Australian Music Education (iii): The Secondary Schools." *Australian Journal of Music Education* 1 (October 1967): 16–18.

Bridges, Doreen. "Music in Australian Public Examinations." *Australian Journal of Music Education* 2 (April 1968): 21–23.

Bridges, Doreen. "Why Research in Music Education?" *Australian Journal of Music Education* 7 (October 1970): 25–26.

Carroll, Anne. "Secondary School Music Education in Australia: The Current Picture." *Australian Journal of Music Education* no. 1 (1988): 92–101.

Chappell, Herbert. *The Daniel Jazz*. Novello, London, 1963.

Curriculum Corporation. *A Curriculum Guide for Australian Schools*. Carlton, Victoria, 1994.

Curriculum Corporation. *A Statement on the Arts for Australian Schools*. Carlton, Victoria, 1994.

Dennis, Brian. *Experimental Music in Schools: Towards a New World of Sound*. Oxford University Press, 1970.

Gulbenkian, Fundacāo Calouste. *The Arts in Schools: Principles, Practice and Provision*, ed. Ken Robinson. Calouste Gulbenkian Foundation, United Kingdom, 1982.

Hurd, Michael. *Jonah-man Jazz*. Novello, London, 1966.

Jaeger, David. "R. Murray Schafer, composer, writer and acoustic ecologist, has died at 88." https://www.cbc.ca/music/r-murray-schafer-composer-writer-and-acoustic-ecologist-has-died-at-88-1.5404868

Johnson, Rob. *The Golden Age of the Argonauts: a Celebration of Australia's Best-Loved Radio Program for Children*. Hodder and Stoughton, New South Wales, 1997.

Maxwell- Davies, Peter. "School Music and the Contemporary Composer." Paper presented at the Australian UNESCO Seminar on School Music, Sydney Teachers' College and University of Sydney, 20–29 May, 1965, 138–145.

Schafer, R Murray. *The Thinking Ear*. Arcana Editions. Toronto, Canada, 1986.

Self, George. *New Sounds in Class: A Contemporary Approach to Music*. Universal Edition, London, 1967.

Chapter 13

The Evolution of Music Notation Software

Patrick Horton

Sound and notation have a complex relationship. Representing music in a singular way that captures the mathematical relationships of rhythm and harmony, the nuances of tension, expectancy, and emotion, while highlighting existing low- and high-level associations between pitch, time, timbre, structure, and style, presents an array of challenges.[1] Because of this complexity, hundreds, if not thousands, of musical notations have evolved globally. Each of these musical representations are codes that have their own unique affordances and challenges.

The most common form of musical representation in music education scholarship is likely Western Standard Music Notation (WSMN), yet there have been many others aimed at serving specific musical styles and individuals. An early instrument-specific tablature notation emerged during the Shang dynasty (sixteenth century BCE) called *wenzipu* and provides precise directions for playing techniques needed for the Chinese *qin*.[2] *Klavarskribo* is another instrument-specific tablature developed in Holland in the 1930s as a unique piano notation that is read top to bottom.[3] The Nashville number system was developed in the recording studios of Nashville, Tennessee, United States, in the 1950s to provide musicians with a simple system that highlighted harmonic structures using transposable Arabic numbers rather than more visually awkward Roman numerals.[4] Avant-garde composers John Cage and Pierre Boulez helped to develop several graphic notations in the twentieth century that were aimed at liberating musicians from WSMN.[5] Inspired by a vibrant lineage of musical representation, the Music Notation Project (initially the Music Notation Modernization Association) was founded in 1985 as an organization that sought to "raise awareness of the disadvantages of traditional music notation, to explore alternative music notation systems, and to provide resources for the wider consideration and use of these alternatives."[6]

With notation being so vast and diverse, it is unsurprising that the musical representations are intricately related to music teaching and learning. While Kang and Yoo[7] concluded that student compositions created with notation-based software (as compared to pencil and paper) may be perceived as more creative by music teachers, Stauffer[8] noted the power of "non-notational and intuitive" software to impact learners by expanding their compositional fluency. Additionally, regardless of the software platform, a music teacher's attitudes toward music notation can support or obstruct a student's development.[9] With these complexities in mind, in this chapter, I trace the history of music notation software, examine the biases of each, and explore the implications for music education.

DEFINING MUSIC NOTATION

Music notation is a visual representation of musical sound, either as a record or a set of instructions for performers.[10] Music notation can be viewed as a technological tool that may allow individuals to preserve their musical ideas while also giving performers a way to realize the musical ideas of others. Wiggins and colleagues[11] suggest two additional functions of music notation: analysis and creative generation. With these functions, music notation serves as a code or a system of communication that is used to convert information from one form, such as ideas, objects, or actions, to another. Musical codes such as solfege are common in music pedagogy and highlight teaching and learning as significant features of music notation.[12] An early form of tablature for the Chinese qin relies on master-pupil transmission for accurate interpretation.[13] Similarly, while the Guidonian Hand created by Guido D'Arrezo (c. 991–992—after 1033) may be a common image in music history texts, it was his placement of staff lines to indicate intervals of thirds in the eleventh century that became a significant tool in music education.[14]

With so many functions, music notation provides users with any number of affordances and challenges. American historian Melvin Kranzberg began to acknowledge the complicated impact technology can have when he created his first law of technology stating, "Technology is neither good nor bad; nor is it neutral."[15] A technological tool always has environmental, social, and human impacts that go beyond its immediate purposes. For example, WSMN is a technological tool and musical code that privileges specific ideas such as Western notions of meter and rhythm based on equal divisions of the beat. While some mathematical relationships may be more easily represented with

WSMN, these same rhythmic patterns allow for little nuance without the addition of descriptors such as *rubato* or *swing*.

WSMN also privileges the twelve-tone equal temperament system, a significant technological achievement that has connected musicians all over the globe while also reducing the nuanced range of sonic frequencies to a select few. Similarly, while humans perceive musical units such as melodies and grooves regardless of musical training,[16] notating these using WSMN requires individuals to have a strong understanding of the low-level syntax of pitches, intervals, and durations, musical information that only trained musicians typically distinguish by ear. Thus, we can begin to understand how WSMN holds significant implications for teachers and learners around the world.

At its core, music notation is a coded language that symbolizes musical ideas most often in a visual format. It can be used to communicate musical ideas for preservation, analysis, creation, and transmission. The use of machines, computers, and other devices to communicate musical ideas has opened the fields of music and music education to include new modes and methods, expanding the possibilities for artists, teachers, and learners.

MUSIC NOTATION AND MACHINES

Music notation has had a long history with machines. As early as the 1700s, there were mechanical devices that reproduced music and music coding systems including music boxes, calliopes, and player pianos. These machines used metal drums with pins and holes punched into a paper roll as a type of music notation.[17] The first commercially distributed device called the *Tachigrafo Musicale* was introduced in 1887 and allowed individuals to print music notation with a typewriter-like interface.[18] In 1896, the Telharmonium was the first musical instrument that could produce sound from electrical signals.[19] Developed in 1929, Givelet and Coupleux's programmable organ was the first polyphonic instrument based on electronic oscillators and was considered the first programmable synthesizer.[20] It was not until the 1960s that electric synthesizers were released by Robert Moog and Don Buchla, signally the emergence of electronic instruments for the average consumer.[21]

In the 1950s, early computer software was created on general-purpose computers using native machine languages, expanding the connection between music and machines.[22] In 1957, Max Mathews developed a music-input language at Bell Labs called MUSIC I that allowed computers to precisely reproduce music despite its tedious text-intensive input process.[23] MUSIC V and other developments such as Digital Alternate Representation of Music Scores (DARMS) were developed in the 1960s as improvements on previous text-based music writing software.[24]

Despite the many advancements in musical machines and notation, some had limited impact on music teachers and students. Mainframe computers located primarily on college campuses facilitated computer-aided instruction using software such as PLATO (a library of music teaching materials);[25] however, these room-sized machines were complex and difficult to access. Further technological advances have had more direct impacts on music educators and their use of notation software.

DESKTOP PUBLISHING

It was not until the convergence of three crucial factors that music notation software began to empower teachers and students more significantly. In the late 1970s and early 1980s, the development of personal computers accelerated. The Apple II, TRS-80, and Atari ST all included improved graphics features, quicker processors, and enhanced sound capabilities.[26] Up until then music coding with graphic displays on computers required large mainframe computers. While some music software still required command-line (or text-based) note entry such as the MMI Music Composer, these platforms also featured graphic representations of notes that scrolled across the screen during playback. With these advancements in personal computing, barriers to authoring music were reduced because more people could access WSMN-based music making technologies at home.

WYSIWYG stands for "what you see is what you get" and refers to computer user interfaces that allow content editing in the same format in which it would be printed or displayed. WYS can be impacted by the contrasting visual resolution levels of printers and screens, while, in musical applications, the sonic output increases the complexity of these interfaces because WYG is impacted by computer processors, audio output devices, and human performers. The graphical display was the key piece needed to provide visual feedback to individuals as they used music software.[27] The Mockingbird computer notation system emanating from the Xerox PARC research lab in the early 1980s became an industry standard because of the way musical information was so well described. This software utilized logical (pitch and rhythmic duration), performance (computer playback), and graphical (display in the screen) domains.[28]

Lastly, HP and Apple desktop laser printer technology provided an output resolution high enough that WSMN could be printed and read with accuracy. Simultaneously, the first Postscript music font, Sonata, was developed for this new laser printer technology. Low-cost printing was now accessible at home and in schools.[29] Professional Composer by Mark of the Unicorn was one platform that took advantage of this printing advancement as it became available on the Macintosh platform in the mid-1980s.[30] High-resolution printing provided musicians, teachers, and learners with a way to print notation that could better serve their individual needs.

The combination of home computers, graphical user interface, and laser printer technology converged to make home publishing a possibility. The addition of a computer mouse and music keyboard made this setup a completely interactive environment paving the way for the democratization of music notation. Because text-based code entry was no longer required, music data structures became backgrounded simplifying the editing process. Users could compose for computers with Musical Instrument Digital Interface (MIDI) sounds by inputting WSMN, and they could print their creations at home which supported individual creativity for those without access to publishing equipment.

Two pieces of software, Finale and Sibelius, quickly took hold of the market. Finale featured transposition, error check for meter, and intelligent note placement.[31] Sibelius gained additional support in the educational market because it allowed its eager user base to suggest and, in some cases, design plug-ins or extensions.[32] These programs were soon augmented by MIDI providing immediate sonic feedback to users. MIDI is a code that captures the key being pressed (through a predefined MIDI number, 0-127), on and off times (duration), as well as its velocity (speed at which a key is struck which is mapped to output volume, 0-127).[33] In this sense, MIDI is a musical representation in itself, one that functions not only as a bridge between devices but also as a way for computers and humans to communicate musical ideas with each other. Users receive sonic and visual feedback through computer-to-human interfaces that include audio playback and visual representations, such as WSMN or the MIDI piano roll, and can also input music by using human-to-computer interfaces such as MIDI-enabled controllers and instruments. While MIDI is most commonly visualized in a piano roll interface, it clearly works to communicate musical ideas for preservation, analysis, creation, and transmission—much like other forms of music notation.

While the barrier to music creation began to be lowered with these many advances, it is important to acknowledge the disadvantages built into these technologies. Even with the improved graphical user interface that provided visual feedback and the additional sonic feedback provided by MIDI, there is still a requirement for users to have a basic understanding of WSMN to make sense of a notation-based platform like Finale or Sibelius. The reliance on graphical input for editing remained a significant issue for creators with vision impairment. Despite the advent of Braille music notators, this population remains limited in their use of music software that features WSMN further excluding this population from music making with notation.[34]

Finally, increased abundance does not always result in increased access. While more devices have become available on the market, the combined costs of the hardware and the software can still be too great for many schools. Today, even though devices are more ubiquitous and low-cost or free software platforms such as Noteflight[35] are available, access to technology remains a barrier due to the collective burdensome costs of hardware, software, and Internet access.

LOOP-BASED COMPOSITION

During the early 1990s interest in formulaic computer-based instruction seemed to decrease, while constructivist approaches that focused on exploration and creativity began to take hold.[36] At the same time, more sophisticated software for music notation, production, and creativity began to be used within the curriculum. Another impactful convergence was taking shape.

In the late 1980s, Cubase created the first graphical display for MIDI sequencing that was copied by most of the then software platforms.[37] This graphical interface was built on a timeline that scrolled left to right, removing the need to program MIDI performance data with text-based codes or through a WSMN graphical editor (an unnecessary intermediary). Initially, software such as this was written for specific hardware (in this case, the Atari platform) which limited access. Soon after this, a company called Digidesign released an audio-editing software called Sound Designer which used waveform representations[38] previously only available on specialized hardware.[39] Sound Designer introduced nondestructive editing, giving creators more power to manipulate the visual sonic representation on the screen without losing older data. Previously, editing involved physically cutting and splicing analog tape.[40]

Cubase quickly added a digital audio component to their MIDI sequencer which combined two powerful musical representations into one platform: the graphical MIDI sequencer and the digital audio waveform editor. This began a long lineage of software such as Apple's Logic Pro and MOTU's Digital Performer which all took on the label of Digital Audio Workstation (DAW). Previously, editing MIDI data and digital audio required specialized hardware or workstations; however, at this time both musical representations could be manipulated through a single software platform available on many home computers. These software-based DAWs all featured similar functions including the ability to edit, mix a recording with tools for audio and MIDI tracks, and incorporate different sequencers, drum machines, filters, and plug-ins to create a polished musical production. Concurrently, piano roll notation became a more standard way of interacting with MIDI data reducing additional barriers to music creation by removing the need for users to know how to manipulate text-based MIDI data.

The benefits of multiple representations in the same platform are many. MIDI piano roll sequencers clearly represent the intervallic relationships between notes in harmonic and melodic progressions, while rhythmic values and durations can be compared at a glance. These note-level pieces of musical information are foregrounded. Scholars suggest rethinking the purpose and scope of music notation by elevating the piano roll notation as graphical representation that might provide a more accurate representation of twelve-tone equal temperament tonality and rhythmic onset and duration information.[41] Conversely, waveform representations offer clearer comparisons of amplitude over time including amplitude envelopes such as attack, decay, sustain, and release. Combining these two musical representations in a single platform empowers creators because more information is available throughout the music making process.

Composing, sequencing, and producing music with DAWs remained a specialized task until precomposed loop libraries began to be available. In the early 2000s, ACID Music Studio[42] for Windows followed by Apple's GarageBand[43] represented loop-based sequencers that featured a library of MIDI and digital audio loops. With this software, users could freely move and edit these prerecorded (or sequenced) loops through a simple click-and-drag graphical user interface. In addition to removing the need for users to know how to manipulate text-based MIDI data and WSMN, the included libraries of precomposed musical ideas removed the need for users to know how to generate musical ideas at the note-level, whether through MIDI or WSMN. This allowed users to explore within a musical collage, cutting and pasting musical ideas while they could let their ears be their guide—or a "what you hear is what you get" interface.[44]

At the same time, faster computer processors, expanded storage capabilities, and advanced digital audio compression techniques converged to allow the DAW to be more widely available on desktop and mobile devices. When combined with WYHIWYG software and a simple click-and-drag interface, this convergence further bolstered the democratization of musical creativity. Sonic and visual feedback remained a constant feature, while the resolution of each increased with every software update. The need for formal training in WSMN, piano keyboard skills, or music theory was also reduced, allowing more individuals the ability to create music. Additionally, composers began to sample recordings of sounds they liked removing the need to communicate their ideas through notation. When combined with digital audio waveforms, musical representations available in DAWs are quite flexible allowing teachers and students to select the musical representation that is best for their task, increasing engagement and empowering them to be more creative.

Just as we examined the challenges of WSMN-based software, so must we examine the challenges DAWs present. While WSMN is not typically a part of these standard digital audio and MIDI platforms, Western musical ideas are nevertheless privileged.[45] Western rhythmic relationship such as a 4/4-time signature is regularly the default framework, while achieving other metric structures frequently requires additional obscure steps. In this way, DAW's privilege groove- and loop-based compositions because repetition is something computers do well. Twelve-tone equal temperament is also a default with other divisions of the octave frequently being unachievable without supplemental software. Additionally, the piano keyboard is typically the default interface, further centering a Western way of interacting with music.

The gender of DAW users is another significant issue as nonmale identifying creators have been excluded to a significant degree.[46] Male preservice music teachers report greater computer self-efficacy, or beliefs about their capacity for technology use, than female preservice music teachers.[47] In the music technology classroom, Armstrong found that males were routinely positioned as more "expert" users than females.[48] These gender differences in addition to biases toward other Western musical structures highlight that music software has a complex relationship with its users. While overcoming all these biases is impossible, stretching their boundaries can be significant.

MUSIC NOTATION SOFTWARE IN MUSIC EDUCATION

Just as the use of WSMN software, desktop publishing, MIDI devices, and various DAW platforms have advanced the practice of music making, the inclusion of technology in music classrooms has not always been well accepted.[49] Despite a perceived reluctance, music teacher attitudes and priorities were not found to be predictors of successful music technology integration.[50] This implies that there are other forces working against technology integration for music educators. In fact, teachers in all disciplines have often been challenged to integrate technology into their classrooms, citing barriers such as a lack of computers, inadequate technical support, and insufficient technical training.[51] Regardless of these difficulties, the use of WSMN software, MIDI devices, and DAWs in music education has expanded globally.

In the late 1990s, the presence of music software in Korean music classrooms was increased, supporting musical creativity as students used MIDI and other platforms to create their own music.[52] Beginning in 2001, the Chinese New Curriculum Reform as well as the rapid economic development in Beijing combined to improve school infrastructure in China. This provided greater access to technology for music teachers, including music composing and editing software.[53]

In the UK, Information Communications Technologies (ICT) began to appear in the National Curriculum in the late 1990s. Although it was not mentioned in Key Stage 1, ICT is suggested to be a mode of teaching knowledge, skills, and understanding in Key Stage 2,[54] while pupils in Key Stage 3 are notably required to use ICT to create and manipulate sounds.[55] The most recent Model Music Curriculum by the Department for Education[56] places an emphasis on the inclusion of multiple forms of music notation, with specific mentions of graphic, dot, stick, and staff notations. Though notation software is not specifically indicated, the prevalence and popularity of cloud-based DAWs are acknowledged as potentially significant in schools.

The 1994 U.S. National Standards for Music Education did not directly mention music notation software; however, the authors note in the introduction that music curricula "should utilize current technology to individualize and expand music learning."[57] The National Association for Music Education (then MENC) makes this point clearer in their Opportunity to Learn Standards for Music Instruction[58] where they state that every school should have "appropriate music software, including notation and sequencing software" in addition to printers and sufficient MIDI equipment. The 2014 U.S. National Core Arts Standards for Music also do not specifically mention notation software, yet the Music Technology Strand promotes the utilization of digital tools while the composition and theory strand indicates students should share music by using notation, performance, or technology.[59]

Across Europe, music technology is reported as having many different purposes, such as the support of singing. Sammer, Gall, and Breeze[60] noted that composing and arranging were most frequently cited as skills developed through technology suggesting many European countries integrate music notation software to some degree. While African countries have seen varying music technology integration for several reasons, including inconsistent governmental support and overall cost, the integration of music notation software has been viewed to enhance student creativity.[61] In Singapore, technology is becoming increasingly prominent in music classrooms with the inclusion of midi and keyboard labs.[62]

With this changing technological landscape new challenges and new opportunities have emerged. For students, the challenge of finding tools that best fit their individual musical goals is magnified as technological choices increase and the time needed to learn new platforms can be onerous. Conversely, the ability to use a DAW to create music, layer-by-layer, with premade musical samples means students can compose without advanced knowledge of WSMN, traditionally a prerequisite to music composition. Similarly, the sonic feedback provided by playback features in most WSMN software and

DAWs suggests students are no longer bound by their own performance skills and can compose music they physically cannot perform themselves.

For teachers, the burdens of determining which technologies to include and making time to learn them are increased by the ubiquity and variety of available technologies. With computer labs and smaller devices, many teachers have needed to shift from large-group instruction to helping students work individually or in small groups. While this is challenging, the opportunities for individual assessment and creativity have prompted teachers to use a vastly different collection of strategies in their classrooms.[63] As notation software evolves to include new possibilities, learning spaces transform to meet the needs of students, and access to notation platforms continues to grow, it is important that music educators and scholars continue to explore the many ways changing technologies can be integrated into music classrooms in meaningful and relevant ways.

REDEFINING MUSIC NOTATION

Notation software is one of many technologies that have impacted the way we, as humans, engage with music. Not only are multiple visual representations available to teachers and learners, but they are infinitely editable, providing a collaborative feature that creates a two-way interaction between the music and the human. Similarly, the instant sonic and aural feedback provided by the many different types of software allow for multimodal connections to be made. These multiple representations serve to redefine musical interactions while expanding access to music creation activities.

These new technologies afford us an increasing number of opportunities to utilize alternative notations and alternative pedagogies. Notation in music education should serve the music while providing additional avenues for approaching musical concepts.[64] The Internet has been a more recent support for music learning with free and low-cost platforms such as WSMN-based Noteflight[65] and DAW-based Soundtrap.[66] I will survey a few music notation platforms that are redefining music representation.

While there are many software platforms for developing aural skills as they relate to WSMN, others use music sequencers. Because the piano roll interface offers clear intervallic and metric representations, it can be ideal for learning music theory concepts. Hook theory features a sequencer interface that allows users to create and display analyses of popular music melodies and harmonies in a uniquely colorful way foregrounding note-level information and reshaping how music theory concepts are represented.[67]

Online platform Soundslice allows users to augment audio and video recordings of musical performances with synchronized scrolling WSMN and/or instrument-specific tablature.[68] While this feature is found in professional software platforms, the ability for users to do this without specialized knowledge of video production software is significant. Impromptu is another software platform stemming from the work of Jean Bamberger and utilizes tuneblocks or blocks that background the lower-level musical features of pitches, intervals, and rhythms.[69] These uniquely decorated blocks on the screen foreground higher-level musical ideas like melodies and phrases, concepts learners can perceive with little musical training.[70] This software sought to allow users to create music in a way that focused on their own musical intuitions and provided new ways for musical structures to be introduced.

With an emphasis on unique graphical musical representations, other platforms are redefining the look of music notation. Hyperscribe is a graphical composition environment developed in the MIT Media Lab that interprets user-drawn shapes and then maps them to musical structures,[71] allowing users to compose with little musical training. The Google Chrome Music Lab experiment Kandinsky provides a similar graphical interface.[72]

The interdisciplinary connections between computer technology and music notation are well-developed, and there is a vast array of platforms that are redefining musical representation. Audio programming languages like Max/MSP[73] and Supercollider,[74] live coding platforms like Sonic Pi,[75] and web-based interfaces that bridge text-based code with digital audio sequencers like Tunepad[76] all expand how music is created, learned, analyzed, and recorded.

Leimma is an online platform that allows users to explore and create their own microtonal tuning systems.[77] This software was created to reduce the dominance of Western musical ideas in electronic production. Users can select existing tuning systems from other cultures or divide the octave in any way they choose, shifting the focus away from Western twelve-tone equal temperament. With so many technologies to choose from, selecting the best platform for the musical task at hand is important. Computer technology is clearly influencing how teachers, learners, and creators interact with music and notation.

CONCLUSION

In this chapter, I have highlighted two technological convergences that have impacted how music educators have engaged with music notation software with their students. First, the advent of desktop publishing was brought on by faster desktop computers, graphical user interfaces, and desktop laser printers. These advances combine to create a space where teachers and students could more simply print WSMN that they wrote or arranged. While this moved toward democratizing music printing, barriers for teachers and students remained such as the need for advanced training as well as access to the requisite devices. Second, faster processors, increased storage capabilities, and advanced signal processing techniques along with the advent of DAW's that featured precomposed loops increased access to music making, further democratizing musical creativity. Additionally, the simple click-and-drag interface and the reduced need for advanced musical training supported the success of these new music creation platforms. However, the privileging of Western musical structures and visual information still excludes some users.

For many, but clearly not all, lack of access to software is a barrier to music creation. While access to devices and the Internet is still critical, free and low-cost softwares such as Soundtrap and Noteflight are available on most contemporary devices. While the work is not done, musicians, technologies, students, and—most importantly—teachers all continue to embrace expanded views of notation that allow more people to overcome barriers and gain access to creative music making and learning. While the search for the perfect notational system will likely remain fruitless, the multitude of notational systems designed with and augmented by technology has not only reshaped who is able to create music but also the many ways humans can be musical. Music educators can continue to expand their skills and understanding of various forms of music notation software to provide learners with additional relevant music notation technologies. By allowing learners to select the notation technology that best suits their goals, more paths to success may be opened. Technology can continue to provide new notational tools that are inclusive, collaborative, and truly global.

NOTES

1. Roger B. Dannenberg, "Music Representation Issues, Techniques, and Systems." *Computer Music Journal* 17, no. 3 (1993): 20–30.

2. Ming-Yueh Liang, "The Art of Yin-Jou Techniques for the Seven-Stringed Zither." (PhD Diss., University of California, 1973).

3. Mark Gaare, "Alternatives to Traditional Notation." *Music Educators Journal* 83, no. 5 (March 1997): 17–23.

4. Trevor De Clercq, "The Nashville Number System: A Framework for Teaching Harmony in Popular Music." *Journal of Music Theory Pedagogy* 33, no. 4 (2019): 3–28.

5. Griffiths, *Modern Music: The Avant Garde since 1945* (London: Braziller, 1981).

6. The Music Notation Project, "The Music Notation Project - Alternative Music Notation Systems," Accessed September 13, 2021. https://musicnotation.org/.

7. Sangmi Kang and Hyesoo Yoo, "Elementary Students' Music Compositions with Notation-Based Software and Handwritten Notation Assisted by Classroom Instruments," *Bulletin of the Council for Research in Music Education*, no. 227 (2021): 29. doi: 10.5406/bulcouresmusedu.227.0029.

8. Sandra L. Stauffer, "Composing with Computers: Meg Makes Music," *Research in Music Education* 150, no. Fall (2001): 1–20.

9. Cecilia Hultberg, "Approaches to Music Notation," *Music Education Research* 4, no. 2 (September 2002): 185–97. doi: 10.1080/1461380022000011902.

10. Ian D. Bent et al., "Notation." In *Grove Music Online*. Oxford University Press, 2001. http://www.oxfordmusiconline.com/grovemusic/documentID/omo-9781561592630-e-0000020114

11. Geraint Wiggins et al., "Surveying Musical Representations Systems: A Framework for Evaluation," *Computer Music Journal* 26, no. 4 (2002): 61–68.

12. Eleanor Selfridge-Field, ed., "Introduction: Describing Musical Information," in *Beyond MIDI: The Handbook of Musical Codes*, 163–74 (Cambridge, MA: MIT Press, 1997).

13. Ming-Yueh Liang, and Joseph S.C. Lam, "Qin" in *Grove Music Online*. Vol. 1. Oxford University Press, 2001. doi: 10.1093/gmo/9781561592630.article.47071.

14. Samuel Miller, "Guido D'Arezzo," *Journal of Research in Music Education* 21, no. 3 (October 1973): 239–45. doi: 10.2307/3345093.

15. Melvin Kranzberg, "Technology and History: 'Kranzberg's Laws'", *Technology and Culture* 27, no. 3 (1986): 544–60.

16. Jeanne Bamberger, *The Mind Behind the Musical Ear* (Cambridge, MA: Harvard University Press, 1991), 7–16.

17. David Brian Williams and Peter Richard Webster, *Experiencing Music Technology* (Boston: Schirmer Cengage Learning, 2006), 4–5.

18. Stanley Boorman, Eleanor Selfridge-Field, and Donald W. Krummel, "Printing and Publishing of Music," in *Grove Music Online*. Vol. 1 (Oxford: Oxford University Press, 2001). doi: 10.1093/gmo/9781561592630.article.40101.

19. Reynold Henry Weidenaar, "The Telharmonium," (Ph.D diss., New York University, 1989). http://search.proquest.com/pqdtglobal/docview/303799964/abstract/F781D08AB12E4978PQ/1.

20. Hugh Davies, *Coupleux-Givelet Organ*. Vol. 1 (Oxford: Oxford University Press, 2016). doi: 10.1093/gmo/9781561592630.article.L2290786.

21. Peter Webster, "Historical Perspectives on Technology and Music," *Music Educators Journal* 89, no. 1 (September 2002): 38–43. doi: 10.2307/3399883.

22. Williams and Webster, *Experiencing Music Technology*, 341.

23. Edmund Correia Jr., Eleanor Selfridge-Field, and et al., "Glossary," in *Beyond MIDI: The Handbook of Musical Codes*, ed. Eleanor Selfridge-Field (Cambridge, MA: MIT Press, 1997), 581–610.

24. Eleanor Selfridge-Field, "DARMS, Its Dialects, and Its Uses," in *Beyond MIDI: The Handbook of Musical Codes*, ed. Eleanor Selfridge-Field (Cambridge, MA: MIT Press, 1997), 163–74.

25. Gary Wittlich, "Computer Applications: Pedagogy," *Music Theory Spectrum* 11, no. 1 (1989): 60–65.

26. Williams and Webster, *Experiencing Technology*, 345–46.

27. Boorman, Selfridge-Field, and Krummel, "Printing and Publishing of Music," doi: 10.1093/gmo/9781561592630.article.40101.

28. John Turner Maxwell, "Mockingbird: An Interactive Composer's Aid." PhD diss. (Massachusetts Institute of Technology, 1981), 93–114.

29. Boorman, Selfridge-Field, and Krummel, "Printing and Publishing of Music," doi: 10.1093/gmo/9781561592630.article.40101.

30. Peter R. Webster and David Brian Williams, "Technology's Role for Achieving Creativity, Diversity and Integration in the American Undergraduate Music Curriculum: Some Theoretical, Historical and Practical Perspectives," *Journal of Music, Technology & Education* 11, no. 1 (August 2018): 5–36. doi: 10.1386/jmte.11.1.5_1.

31. Williams and Webster, *Experiencing Music Technology*, 357–96.

32. Flowers and Voss, "User Innovation in the Music Software Industry," 320–25.

33. Hewlett and Selfridge-Field, "MIDI," 41–72.

34. William Christopher Payne et al., "How Blind and Visually Impaired Composers, Producers, and Songwriters Leverage and Adapt Music Technology," in *The 22nd International ACM SIGACCESS Conference on Computers and Accessibility* (Virtual Event Greece: ACM, 2020), 1–12. doi: 10.1145/3373625.3417002.

35. Noteflight, "Noteflight - Online Music Notation Software." Accessed September 12, 2021. https://www.noteflight.com/.

36. Webster and Williams, "Technology's Role," 5–36.

37. Paul White, "Karl Steinberg: Cubase & Computers," *Sound on Sound*, January 1995. https://www.soundonsound.com/people/karl-steinberg-cubase-computers.

38. A waveform is a visual representation of a digital audio signal and generally represents changes in amplitude over time. For more information see Andrew R. Brown, "Presentation Platforms," in *Music Technology and Education: Amplifying Musicality*, 2nd edition (New York: Routledge, 2015), 107–22.

39. Mixdown Staff, "Musicology: A Brief History of the Digital Audio Workstation (DAW)." *Mixdown Magazine* (blog), July 27, 2021. https://mixdownmag.com.au/features/musicology-a-brief-history-of-the-digital-audio-workstation/.

40. Mike Levine, "Recording Basics: The History of the DAW." *Yamaha Music* (blog), May 1, 2019. https://hub.yamaha.com/proaudio/pa-history/the-history-of-the-daw/.

41. Barbara Freedman, *Teaching Music Through Composition* (Oxford, New York: Oxford University Press, 2013).

42. "ACID Music Studio," Accessed September 13, 2021. https://www.magix.com/index.php?id=25295&L=52&_oB=acid-music-studio&AffiliateID=146&phash=e8Zp8lTUPcNlzrGv&gclid=CjwKCAjw7fuJBhBdEiwA2lLMYSPD_pjcTgBmho-t8yn-wIUxYuOJapaO5ws17a_sdpFCD_CLPTJ9cuhoCxdQQAvD_BwE.

43. Apple Inc., *GarageBand for Mac*. Accessed September 13, 2021. https://www.apple.com/mac/garageband/.

44. David Brian Williams, "The Non-Traditional Music Student in Secondary Schools of the United States: Engaging Non-Participant Students in Creative Music Activities through Technology." *Journal of Music, Technology and Education* 4, no. 2 (February 16, 2012): 131–47. doi: 10.1386/jmte.4.2-3.131_1.

45. Tom Faber, "Decolonizing Electronic Music Starts With Its Software | Pitchfork," *Pitchfork*, February 25, 2021. https://pitchfork.com/thepitch/decolonizing-electronic-music-starts-with-its-software/.

46. Adam Patrick Bell, "DAW Democracy? The Dearth of Diversity in 'Playing the Studio,'" *Journal of Music, Technology & Education* 8, no. 2 (July 2015): 129–46. doi: 10.1386/jmte.8.2.129_1.

47. William I. Bauer, "Gender Differences and the Computer Self-Efficacy of Preservice Music Teachers," *Journal of Technology in Music Learning* 2, no. 1 (2003): 9–15.

48. Victoria Armstrong, *Technology and the Gendering of Music Education* (New York: Routledge, 2016).

49. Brian Moore, "Music, Technology, and an Evolving Curriculum," *ASSP Bulletin* 76, no. 544 (May 1992): 42–46: 43. doi: 10.1177/019263659207654409.

50. Jay Dorfman and Rick Dammers, "Predictors of Successful Integration of Technology into Music Teaching," *Journal of Technology in Music Learning* 5, no. 2 (2015): 46–59.

51. National Education Association, *Access, Adequacy, and Equity in Education Technology*. Washington, DC: National Education Association, 2008.

52. Mi-Young Choi, "The History of Korean School Music Education," *International Journal of Music Education* 25, no. 2 (August 2007): 137–49. doi: 10.1177/0255761407079952.

53. Linyuan Guo, "New Curriculum Reform in China and Its Impact on Teachers," *Canadian and International Education/Education Canadiennne et Internationale* 41, no. 2 (2012): 87–105.

54. Department for Education and Employment Qualifications and Curriculum Authority, *The National Curriculum: Handbook for Primary Teachers in England – Key Stages 1 and 2*, 2021. https://assets.publishing.service.gov.uk/government/uploads/system/uploads/attachment_data/file/974366/Model_Music_Curriculum_Full.pdf.

55. Department for Education and Employment Qualifications and Curriculum Authority, *The National Curriculum: Handbook for Secondary Teachers in England – Key Stages 3 and 4*.

56. Department for Education, "Model Music Curriculum: Key Stages 1 to 3," London: HMSO, 1999.

57. MENC Task Force for National Standards in the Arts, *The School Music Program: A New Vision: The K-12 National Standards, PreK Standards, and What They Mean to Music Educators*. Reston, VA: Music Educators National Conference, 1994.

58. MENC National Executive Board, "Opportunity-to-Learn Standards for Music Instruction," Ed. Paul R. Lehman. Music Educators National Conference, 1994. https://nafme.org/opportunity-to-learn-standards-for-music-instruction-grades-prek-12/.

59. State Education Agency Directors of Arts Education, "National Core Arts Standards," 2014. https://www.nationalartsstandards.org/.

60. Gerhard Sammer, Marina Gall, and Nick Breeze, "Using Music Software at School: The European Framework," in *NET MUSIC Project 01: New Technology in the Field of Education (Nuove Tecnologie in Campo Educativo Musicale)*, eds.

Gemma Fiocchetta and Federico Ballanti, 155–77. Anicia srl, 2009. http://www.netmusicproject.org.

61. Benon Kigozi, "Critical Perspectives from Africa," in *The Oxford Handbook of Technology and Music Education*, eds. Alex Ruthmann and Roger Mantie, 2017, 175–89. Oxford University Press, 2017. http://www.oxfordhandbooks.com/view/10.1093/oxfordhb/9780199372133.001.0001/oxfordhb-9780199372133-e-44.

62. Chee-Hoo Lum and Eugene Dairianathan, "Mapping Musical Learning," *International Journal of Music Education* 32, no. 3 (August 2014): 278–95. doi:10.1177/0255761413491206.

63. Janet Mills and Andy Murray, "Music Technology Inspected: Good Teaching in Key Stage 3." *British Journal of Music Education* 17, no. 2 (July 2000): 129–56. doi: 10.1017/S026505170000022X.

64. Bamberger, "The Mind Behind," 269–83.

65. Noteflight, "Noteflight - Online Music Notation Software." Accessed September 12, 2021. https://www.noteflight.com/.

66. "Soundtrap—Make Music Online," Accessed September 13, 2021. https://www.soundtrap.com/.

67. "Hooktheory: Create Amazing Music," Accessed September 13, 2021. https://www.hooktheory.com/.

68. "Soundslice | Create Living Sheet Music," Accessed September 13, 2021. https://www.soundslice.com/.

69. Jeanne Bamberger and Armando Hernandez, *Impromptu [Computer Software]*, 2000. http://www.tuneblocks.com/index.jsp.

70. Jeanne Bamberger, *Discovering the Musical Mind* (Oxford, UK: Oxford University Press, 2013), 269–94.

71. MIT Media Lab, "Project Overview ‹ Hyperscore." Accessed September 12, 2021. https://www.media.mit.edu/projects/hyperscore/overview/.

72. "Chrome Music Lab," Accessed September 13, 2021. https://musiclab.chromeexperiments.com.

73. Cycling '74, *Max/MSP/Jitter* (version 8.1.1), 2020. https://cycling74.com/.

74. *SuperCollider » SuperCollider*, Accessed September 13, 2021. https://supercollider.github.io/.

75. *Sonic Pi—The Live Coding Music Synth for Everyone*. Accessed September 13, 2021. https://sonic-pi.net/.

76. "TunePad." Accessed September 13, 2021. https://tunepad.club/.

77. Khyam Allami and Counterpoint, *Leimma*, 2021. Accessed December 17, 2021. https://isartum.net/leimma/.

BIBLIOGRAPHY

ACID Music Studio. Accessed September 13, 2021. https://www.magix.com/index.php?id=25295&L=52&_oB=acid-music-studio&AffiliateID=146&phash=e8Zp8lTUPcNlzrGv&gclid=CjwKCAjw7fuJBhBdEiwA2lLMYSPD_pjcTgBm-hot8yn-wIUxYuOJapaO5ws17a_sdpFCD_CLPTJ9cuhoCxdQQAvD_BwE.

Allami, Khyam, and Counterpoint. *Leimma*, 2021. Accessed December 17, 2021. https://isartum.net/leimma/.
Apple. "Logic Pro." Accessed September 13, 2021. https://www.apple.com/logic-pro/.
Apple Inc. *GarageBand for Mac*. Accessed September 13, 2021. https://www.apple.com/mac/garageband/.
Armstrong, Victoria. *Technology and the Gendering of Music Education*. New York: Routledge, 2016.
Bamberger, Jeanne. *The Mind Behind the Musical Ear*. Cambridge, MA: Harvard University Press, 1991.
Bamberger, Jeanne. *Discovering the Musical Mind*. Oxford, UK: Oxford University Press, 2013.
Bamberger, Jeanne, and Armando Hernandez. *Impromptu [Computer Software]*, 2000. http://www.tuneblocks.com/index.jsp.
Bauer, William I. Gender Differences and the Computer Self-Efficacy of Preservice Music Teachers. *Journal of Technology in Music Learning* 2, no. 1 (2003): 9–15.
Bell, Adam Patrick. "DAW Democracy? The Dearth of Diversity in 'Playing the Studio.'" *Journal of Music, Technology & Education* 8, no. 2 (July 2015): 129–46. doi: 10.1386/jmte.8.2.129_1.
Bent, Ian D., David W. Hughes, Robert C. Provine, Richard Rastall, Anne Kilmer, David Hiley, Janka Szendrei, Thomas B. Payne, Margaret Bent, and Geoffrey Chew. "Notation." In *Grove Music Online*. Oxford University Press, 2001. doi: 10.1093/gmo/9781561592630.article.20114.
Boorman, Stanley, Eleanor Selfridge-Field, and Donald W. Krummel. "Printing and Publishing of Music." In *Grove Music Online*. Vol. 1. Oxford University Press, 2001. doi: 10.1093/gmo/9781561592630.article.40101.
Brown, Andrew R. "Presentation Platforms." In *Music Technology and Education: Amplifying Musicality*, 2nd edition., 107–22. New York: Routledge, 2015.
Choi, Mi-Young. "The History of Korean School Music Education." *International Journal of Music Education* 25, no. 2 (August 2007): 137–49. doi: 10.1177/0255761407079952.
"Chrome Music Lab." Accessed September 13, 2021. https://musiclab.chromeexperiments.com.
Correia Jr., Edmund, Eleanor Selfridge-Field, and et al. "Glossary." In *Beyond MIDI: The Handbook of Musical Codes*, edited by Eleanor Selfridge-Field, 581–610. Cambridge, MA: MIT Press, 1997.
Cycling '74. *Max/MSP/Jitter* (version 8.1.1), 2020. https://cycling74.com/.
Dannenberg, Roger B. "Music Representation Issues, Techniques, and Systems." *Computer Music Journal* 17, no. 3 (1993): 20. doi: 10.2307/3680940.
Davies, Hugh. *Coupleux-Givelet Organ*. Vol. 1. Oxford University Press, 2016. doi: 10.1093/gmo/9781561592630.article.L2290786.
De Clercq, Trevor. "The Nashville Number System: A Framework for Teaching Harmony in Popular Music." *Journal of Music Theory Pedagogy* 33, no. 4 (2019): 3–28.
Department for Education. "Model Music Curriculum: Key Stages 1 to 3," 2021. https://assets.publishing.service.gov.uk/government/uploads/system/uploads/attachment_data/file/974366/Model_Music_Curriculum_Full.pdf.

Department for Education and Employment Qualifications and Curriculum Authority. *The National Curriculum: Handbook for Primary Teachers in England – Key Stages 1 and 2*. London: HMSO, 1999.

Department for Education and Employment Qualifications and Curriculum Authority. *The National Curriculum: Handbook for Secondary Teachers in England – Key Stages 3 and 4*. London: HMSO, 1999.

Dorfman, Jay, and Rick Dammers. "Predictors of Successful Integration of Technology into Music Teaching." *Journal of Technology in Music Learning* 5, no. 2 (2015): 46–59.

Faber, Tom. "Decolonizing Electronic Music Starts With Its Software|Pitchfork." *Pitchfork*, February 25, 2021. https://pitchfork.com/thepitch/decolonizing-electronic-music-starts-with-its-software/.

Flowers, Steven, and Georgina Voss. "User Innovation in the Music Software Industry." In *The Oxford Handbook of Creative Industries*, edited by Candance Jones, Mark Lorenzen, and Jonathan Sapsed, 320–26, 2015. doi: 10.1093/oxfordhb/9780199603510.013.004.

Freedman, Barbara. *Teaching Music Through Composition: A Curriculum Using Technology*. Oxford, New York: Oxford University Press, 2013.

Gaare, Mark. "Alternatives to Traditional Notation." *Music Educators Journal* 83, no. 5 (March 1997): 17–23. doi: 10.2307/3399003.

Griffiths, Paul. *Modern Music: The Avant Garde since 1945*. London: Braziller, 1981.

Guo, Linyuan. "New Curriculum Reform in China and Its Impact on Teachers." *Canadian and International Education/Education Canadiennne et Internationale* 41, no. 2 (2012): 87–105.

Hewlett, Walter B., and Eleanor Selfridge-Field. "MIDI." In *Beyond MIDI: The Handbook of Musical Codes*, edited by Eleanor Selfridge-Field, 41–72. Cambridge, MA: MIT Press, 1997.

"Home|MOTU.Com." Accessed September 13, 2021. https://motu.com/en-us/.

"Hooktheory: Create Amazing Music." Accessed September 13, 2021. https://www.hooktheory.com/.

Hultberg, Cecilia. "Approaches to Music Notation: The Printed Score as a Mediator of Meaning in Western Tonal Tradition." *Music Education Research* 4, no. 2 (September 2002): 185–97. doi: 10.1080/1461380022000011902.

Kang, Samgmi, and Hyesoo Yoo. "Elementary Students' Music Compositions with Notation-Based Software and Handwritten Notation Assisted by Classroom Instruments." *Bulletin of the Council for Research in Music Education*, no. 227 (2021): 29. doi: 10.5406/bulcouresmusedu.227.0029.

Kigozi, Benon. "Critical Perspectives from Africa." In *The Oxford Handbook of Technology and Music Education*, edited by Alex Ruthmann and Roger Mantie, 175–89. Oxford University Press, 2017. http://www.oxfordhandbooks.com/view/10.1093/oxfordhb/9780199372133.001.0001/oxfordhb-9780199372133-e-44.

Kranzberg, Melvin. "Technology and History: 'Kranzberg's Laws.'" *Technology and Culture* 27, no. 3 (1986): 544–60.

Levine, Mike. "Recording Basics: The History of the DAW." *Yamaha Music* (blog), May 1, 2019. https://hub.yamaha.com/proaudio/pa-history/the-history-of-the-daw/.

Liang, Ming-Yueh. "The Art of Yin-Jou Techniques for the Seven-Stringed Zither." PhD Diss., University of California, Los Angeles, 1973.

Liang, Ming-Yueh, and Joseph S.C. Lam. "Qin." In *Grove Music Online*. Vol. 1. Oxford University Press, 2001. doi: 10.1093/gmo/9781561592630.article.47071.

Lum, Chee-Hoo, and Eugene Dairianathan. "Mapping Musical Learning: An Evaluation of Research in Music Education in Singapore." *International Journal of Music Education* 32, no. 3 (August 2014): 278–95. doi: 10.1177/0255761413491206.

Maxwell, John Turner. "Mockingbird: An Interactive Composer's Aid." PhD diss., Massachusetts Institute of Technology, 1981. https://dspace.mit.edu/bitstream/handle/1721.1/15893/08276879-MIT.pdf?sequence=2.

MENC National Executive Board. "Opportunity-to-Learn Standards for Music Instruction." Edited by Paul R. Lehman. Music Educators National Conference, 1994. https://nafme.org/opportunity-to-learn-standards-for-music-instruction-grades-prek-12/.

MENC Task Force for National Standards in the Arts. *The School Music Program: A New Vision: The K-12 National Standards, PreK Standards, and What They Mean to Music Educators*. Reston, VA: Music Educators National Conference, 1994.

Miller, Samuel D. "Guido D'Arezzo: Medieval Musician and Educator." *Journal of Research in Music Education* 21, no. 3 (October 1973): 239–45. doi: 10.2307/3345093.

Mills, Janet, and Andy Murray. "Music Technology Inspected: Good Teaching in Key Stage 3." *British Journal of Music Education* 17, no. 2 (July 2000): 129–56. doi: 10.1017/S026505170000022X.

MIT Media Lab. "Project Overview ‹ Hyperscore." Accessed September 12, 2021. https://www.media.mit.edu/projects/hyperscore/overview/.

Mixdown Staff. "Musicology: A Brief History of the Digital Audio Workstation (DAW)." *Mixdown Magazine* (blog), July 27, 2021. https://mixdownmag.com.au/features/musicology-a-brief-history-of-the-digital-audio-workstation/.

Moore, Brian. "Music, Technology, and an Evolving Curriculum." *NASSP Bulletin* 76, no. 544 (May 1992): 42–46. doi: 10.1177/019263659207654409.

National Education Association. *Access, Adequacy, and Equity in Educaiton Technology*. Washington, DC: National Education Association, 2008.

Noteflight. "Noteflight - Online Music Notation Software." Accessed September 13, 2021. https://www.noteflight.com/.

Payne, William Christopher, Alex Yixuan Xu, Fabiha Ahmed, Lisa Ye, and Amy Hurst. "How Blind and Visually Impaired Composers, Producers, and Songwriters Leverage and Adapt Music Technology." In *The 22nd International ACM SIGACCESS Conference on Computers and Accessibility*, 1–12. Virtual Event Greece: ACM, 2020. doi: 10.1145/3373625.3417002.

Sammer, Gerhard, Marina Gall, and Nick Breeze. "Using Music Software at School: The European Framework." In *NET MUSIC Project 01: New Technology in the Field of Education (Nuove Tecnologie in Campo Educativo Musicale)*, edited by G. Fiocchetta and F. Ballanti, 155–77. Anicia srl, 2009. http://www.netmusicproject.org.

Selfridge-Field, Eleanor. "DARMS, Its Dialects, and Its Uses." In *Beyond MIDI: The Handbook of Musical Codes*, edited by Eleanor Selfridge-Field, 163–74. Cambridge, MA: MIT Press, 1997.

Selfridge-Field, Eleanor. "Introduction: Describing Musical Information." In *Beyond MIDI: The Handbook of Musical Codes*, edited by Eleanor Selfridge-Field, 3–38. Cambridge, MA: MIT Press, 1997.

Sonic Pi - The Live Coding Music Synth for Everyone. Accessed September 13, 2021. https://sonic-pi.net/.

Soundslice. "Soundslice | Create Living Sheet Music." Accessed September 13, 2021. https://www.soundslice.com/.

Soundtrap. "Soundtrap - Make Music Online." Accessed September 13, 2021. https://www.soundtrap.com/.

State Education Agency Directors of Arts Education. "National Core Arts Standards," 2014. https://www.nationalartsstandards.org/.

Stauffer, Sandra L. "Composing with Computers: Meg Makes Music." *Bulletin of the Council for Research in Music Education* 150, no. Fall (2001): 1–20.

SuperCollider » SuperCollider. Accessed September 13, 2021. https://supercollider.github.io/.

The Music Notation Project. "The Music Notation Project - Alternative Music Notation Systems." Accessed September 13, 2021. https://musicnotation.org/.

"TunePad." Accessed September 13, 2021. https://tunepad.club/.

Webster, Peter. "Historical Perspectives on Technology and Music." *Music Educators Journal* 89, no. 1 (September 2002): 38–43. doi: 10.2307/3399883.

Webster, Peter R., and David Brian Williams. "Technology's Role for Achieving Creativity, Diversity and Integration in the American Undergraduate Music Curriculum: Some Theoretical, Historical and Practical Perspectives." *Journal of Music, Technology & Education* 11, no. 1 (August 2018): 5–36. doi: 10.1386/jmte.11.1.5_1.

Weidenaar, Reynold Henry. "The Telharmonium: A History of the First Music Synthesizer, 1893–1918." Ph.D., New York University, 1989. http://search.proquest.com/pqdtglobal/docview/303799964/abstract/F781D08AB12E4978PQ/1.

White, Paul. "Karl Steinberg: Cubase & Computers." *Sound on Sound*, January 1995. https://www.soundonsound.com/people/karl-steinberg-cubase-computers.

Wiggins, Geraint, Eduardo Reck Miranda, Alan Smaill, and Mitch Harris. "Surveying Musical Representations Systems: A Framework for Evaluation." *Computer Music Journal* 26, no. 4 (2002): 61–68.

Williams, David Brian. "The Non-Traditional Music Student in Secondary Schools of the United States: Engaging Non-Participant Students in Creative Music Activities through Technology." *Journal of Music, Technology and Education* 4, no. 2 (February 16, 2012): 131–47. doi: 10.1386/jmte.4.2-3.131_1.

Williams, David Brian, and Peter Richard Webster. *Experiencing Music Technology*. Boston: Schirmer Cengage Learning, 2006.

Wittlich, Gary. "Computer Applications: Pedagogy." *Music Theory Spectrum* 11, no. 1 (1989): 60–65. doi: 10.2307/745950.

Chapter 14

Musical Futures

Developing an Informal Learning Model for Mainstream Music Education since 2003

Hilary McQueen

This chapter examines the historical circumstances leading to the implementation of an idea for music teaching and learning that evolved into Musical Futures (MF). From its inception in a small group of schools in England in 2002, the approach has taken root and branched out into an international context. Fundamental to the approach is informal learning, which Professor Lucy Green set out in her book *How Popular Musicians Learn*.[1] The seed had been sown for a new music pedagogy, at least new to most of those teaching class music in schools and to those schools adopting the approach. In spite of some excellent examples of innovative practice, in the UK there remain a number of challenges for school music in terms of the curriculum offered.[2]

MUSIC CURRICULAR AND PEDAGOGICAL ISSUES IN THE TWENTIETH CENTURY IN ENGLAND AND WALES

Music education was a source of much debate in the twentieth century. Gordon Cox has written extensively about the history of debates in music education in England and Wales in particular. One question has been whether to include music in a school curriculum at all, part of a broader debate about the purpose of education (see, for example, Biesta 2015).[3] At present, most schools are required to offer music education in the United Kingdom. Its many benefits have been researched and promoted (see, for example, Hallam 2010), although what is or has been offered varies considerably, both in terms of the curriculum and how music is taught.[4]

Cox's overview of the development of school music education in England and Wales traces its rise in the nineteenth century in elementary schools for children aged approximately five to twelve, after which children could leave school. School music consisted of singing, often by ear but later using notation, encouraged by receiving a higher sum of grant money if children were taught to read notation.[5] The 1920s heralded important changes. One such change was using the word "music" instead of singing, and another was the inclusion of basic composition (melody training) and music appreciation. It is notable that recorded music on gramophone records and lessons on the wireless, as they were referred to at that time, had become available and could be used for teaching music.

In the 1940s, secondary school music offered a range of group music-making activities, such as choirs and orchestras. By the 1960s, there had been a shift to a more learner-centered approach, one in which children created and performed music, and to the inclusion of more contemporary music.[6] Both the curriculum and the way it was taught had developed considerably, although this was not the case in all schools. The Newsom Report (Central Advisory Council for Education (England) 1963) comments on the contrast between enthusiasm for music out of school and the lack of interest in the "narrow conception" offered in school music lessons. "Out of school, adolescents are enthusiastically engaged in musical self-education. They crowd the record shops at weekends, listening and buying, and within the range of their preferences they are often knowledgeable and highly critical of performance. . . . Some teach themselves or each other to play an instrument."[7]

The more learner-centered approaches that were developing are evident in Paynter and Aston's book on music education, Sound and Silence. Their book is aimed at generalist music teaching in a bid to encourage greater involvement in school music lessons. They state,

> If any one aspect of education today is characteristic of the whole, it is probably the change of emphasis from children being instructed to children being placed in situations where they can learn for themselves . . . we must face the limitations which an instrument or method of sound organisation presents. We must learn how to discover what the materials can do. This cannot be learned from a text-book. It is knowledge which can only be gained by practical experience. There is much more value in ten minutes spent doodling at the keyboard than in ten weeks reproducing rigid and unimaginative exercises.[8]

Although there was no set curriculum at this time, the authors imply that certain practices were normative. As Kaschub and Smith say, "school music has tended to adopt the pervasive 'one size fits all, everybody needs to know' model, despite the fact that 'one size' rarely 'fits all.'"[9]

One difficulty in music education has been a schism in its purpose, as either a creative subject or one which aims to develop "skills, literacy and the Western musical tradition."[10] To some extent these aims were brought together in the National Curriculum for England and Wales. One of the aims of the National Curriculum was a more equal opportunity for pupils in publicly funded schools. All pupils would be taught core subjects (mathematics, English, and science) and foundation subjects, including music, which were tied to "assessment arrangements," such as setting attainment targets and assessing pupils in relation to those targets at "key stages."[11] Although there was no requirement to teach music in a specific way, the curriculum had to cater for general music education as well as for those wishing to take the qualification that was introduced at the same time for all, the General Certificate of Secondary Education (GCSE), which replaced the bipartite qualifications, O-levels and CSEs, with a more or less academic focus, respectively. A revised version of the curriculum was published in 1995, making better allowance for those with special educational needs.[12] In 1999, another version was produced for Key Stages 1 and 2 with a number of headings. These were controlling sounds (performing); creating and developing musical ideas (composing); responding and reviewing (appraising); and listening and applying knowledge and understanding.[13] These were the curricula in place when Lucy Green wrote her influential book *How Popular Musicians Learn*, which provided the foundation for MF.

Historically, music education had secured a place in the curriculum as a foundation subject up to Key Stage 3 (approximately the age of 14). In addition, the National Curriculum had indicated the opportunities that should be offered to every pupil at all key stages based on paired elements: performing and composing and listening and appraising.[14] Grants were available to resource the new curriculum. How music would be taught to accommodate the curriculum was left to teachers to work out, although the curriculum did refer to "vital ground rules" (section 1.5), such as a balanced program, individual, group, and whole-class work, using information technology and musical repertoire. The recommendation was to draw on a range of music, but the choices should include examples from "the European 'classical' tradition, from its earliest roots to the present day; folk and popular music; music of the countries and regions of the British Isles; a variety of cultures, Western and non-Western" (section 2.4).

Paynter and Aston's hope that learning could be a result of children learning through activities rather than instruction was in danger of being crushed under the weight of such a crowded curriculum. Furthermore, Biesta questions the "learnification" of education, by which he means turning away from the centrality of teachers and the curriculum by shifting the focus to learners and learning. His concern is a lack of clarity about "educational content, purpose, and relationships."[15]

VALUES, IRRELEVANCE, AND ALIENATION: OUTSIDE THE "MAGIC CIRCLE"

Music teachers can be assumed to enjoy music themselves and to play at least one instrument or sing, particularly those teaching in secondary schools (ages eleven—sixteen). Classical music and associated instruments have dominated. These assumptions are supported by the Teacher Identities in Music Education project.[16] Prior to writing How Informal Musicians Learn, Lucy Green had argued strongly against the values inherent in music education that placed classical music and study methods associated with it in a superior position.

> Every way the music teacher turns, towards or against classical music alike, it has traditionally hoisted up the victory flag . . . classical music has achieved this partly through its distinction from its major opponent, pop; and it has defined itself as what counts by virtue of its differentiation from that which does not count . . . it has also been made to count by virtue of its approved and established mode of study. . . . From the inside, it has ensured the continued allegiance of those children who enter its magic circle, to the same old established values.[17]

In spite of valiant efforts by teachers to draw young people into music education, fostering interest in school music lessons remained a challenge. In relation to the rest of the curriculum offered in schools, Paynter noted that "oddly, music seems to have suffered more than most curriculum subjects from the problems of ensuring adequate preparation for the specialists while not losing sight of an obligation to others."[18] One reason could be that far more is learned outside the classroom than is the case for other subjects because of instrumental tuition. In the early 1990s, Cox and Hennessy refer to "disappointing accounts of music in schools from the pupils' point of view."[19] Lucy Green pointed out that the irrelevance of and unfamiliarity with the type of music on offer for the majority of young people led to alienation from the subject. Even if young people brought "their" music into school, the question was what to do with it and how to get around the fact that young people had no desire to study in the classroom the music they listened to out of school (Green 1988; Green 2005). The dilemma persisted; how could learning music in a formal setting be made more relevant to young people who were not part of the "magic circle," or "subculture," as Swanwick called it, that bore little resemblance to subjective experience?[20] Changing the curriculum had proved insufficient. A change in pedagogy was a more fruitful possibility.

NONFORMAL TEACHING AND INFORMAL LEARNING

Lucy Green's book, *How Popular Musicians Learn*, was first published in 2001. As she says in her book, it is not a case of learning either formally or informally but a continuum from very formal at one end to very informal at the other. The focus of the book is on the aural learning practices of popular musicians gleaned from the interviews she carried out with fourteen popular musicians aged between fifteen and fifty with an emphasis on "guitar-based popular and rock music."[21] She defines informal music learning as the acquisition of musical skills and knowledge beyond a formal educational setting and the approach as practices rather than methods, the latter implying more regularized learning than is usually the case. Green states,

> Informal music learning practices may be both conscious and unconscious. They include encountering unsought learning experiences through enculturation in the music environment, learning through interaction with others such as peers, family members or other musicians who are acting as teachers in formal capacities, and developing independent learning methods through self-teaching techniques.[22]

Autodidacticism or self-teaching is associated with the intrinsic motivation to learn and develop assumed by humanistic theory; it is self-directed but not necessarily solitary.[23] A key component in the self-teaching of music is listening. Green draws a distinction between purposive listening (the listening required when copying a piece of music or song, for instance), attentive listening (which is careful listening but with a less-defined purpose), and distracted listening or simply hearing music. For popular musicians, notation, including drum and chord symbols, might be used to capture ideas, but it is not the primary source of learning, unlike for most of those who learn classical instruments. Covers of songs (a reproduction of a piece by a different artist or group) often, but not always, require improvisation or a slightly different version rather than exact copying. This contrasts with learning an instrument formally where the aim is to reproduce a written piece as accurately and proficiently as possible. There is also a predetermined progression from beginner to advanced, reinforced when instrumental students follow the graded exam system.

In addition to learning by listening, the participants in Green's research learned from books and teachers as well as from peers. The consequences of the difference between peer interaction and peer collaboration will be returned to later in this chapter. Peer and group learning are likely to be prompted through working in "bands." In some cases, working with others prompted the desire to learn more theoretical aspects. However, Green reminds the reader that "the written is always secondary to the aural."[24]

Green described five principles that she drew from her research which became the basis for MF. These were the following:

- Pupils choose their own music
- They learn by ear
- Pupils work on their own and with friends who share similar musical tastes
- Learning is more haphazard than in a formal approach and often without expert help
- Activities include listening, composing, performing, and improvising.[25]

In chapter 5 of *How Popular Musicians Learn*, there is a section discussing classroom music education, which outlines the experiences of the majority of students in contrast to the minority who learn an instrument formally, either in groups or individually. The experience of the participants recounted in the book demonstrates a difficulty with general music lessons. The generality meant that those who had had some instrumental teaching found the work too easy. Some even avoided the lessons by "bunking off," "hiding in the toilet," or "mucking around." Others paid little attention. In spite of the interviewees later becoming musicians, there was little interest in what was being taught at school. Their musical skills were used for extra-curricular performances rather than being drawn on in lessons, further marginalizing their skills and interests. A disheartening picture is painted: on the one hand, teachers trying their best to teach music according to what they knew or believed to be appropriate as well as dealing with off-task, difficult behavior, which had been noted by Ofsted school inspectors as a particular problem in Key Stage 3 (eleven- to fourteen-year-olds); on the other hand, a selection of young people interested in popular music but alienated by the formal curriculum, and how it was taught. Green commented on the uncomfortable division between music founded in informal practices and formal ways to learn.[26]

> Whilst formal music education has welcomed popular *music* into its ranks, this is by no means the same thing as welcoming or even recognizing *informal learning practices* related to the acquisition of the relevant musical skills and knowledge. Rather, the inclusion of popular, as well as jazz and other world musics in both instrumental tuition and school curricula represents the addition of new educational content, but has not necessarily been accompanied by any corresponding changes in teaching strategy.[27]

MUSICAL FUTURES: BRINGING AN OUTSIDE, INFORMAL PEDAGOGY INSIDE THE CLASSROOM

In "Music, Informal Learning and the School: A New Classroom Pedagogy," Green explains how her work on the ways that popular musicians learn evolved into what became an internationally recognized pedagogical approach known as Musical Futures. A full description of her research can be found in the book, but some details are included here. From 2002 to 2006, data were collected from twenty-one secondary schools, with a more detailed focus on one class of thirteen- to fourteen-year-olds in seven schools, three in London and four in a county to the north of London, Hertfordshire.[28] The age of the young people is important because it is the end of Key Stage 3 in the UK after which only a selection of subjects is studied for exams such as GCSE.[29]

Green began the research alone, but others joined from the Paul Hamlyn Foundation (PHF), a not-for-profit organization seeking to open the arts and education to everyone.[30] The initial research became part of the PHF's Musical Futures Special Initiative (2003), itself influenced by Green's work. Organizations were invited to explore ways to engage young people "in meaningful and sustainable music activities."[31] The sites chosen for the pathfinder projects were in Hertfordshire, Leeds and Nottingham in England. The action research projects included observations, interviews, and questionnaires for teachers and pupils yielding plentiful, rich data. The project that Lucy Green wrote about consisted of seven stages based on the five principles set out above. Each stage was intended to run for four to six weeks with the recommendation of more formal lessons between the informal ones. Of these stages, the first established the principles for informal learning practices. The teachers were a resource, supporting the targets that pupils had set themselves.

Stage one, "In at the Deep End," consisted of pupils bringing music they liked to the classroom, which they then listened to and tried to copy. The second stage was more guided, a piece chosen by the teacher but learned aurally and with minimal intervention from the teacher. Stage three was the deep end revisited, which could be introduced at a different point in the project rather than after the second stage but with the aim of building on the first stage. Stage four gave the opportunity to compose, just as popular musicians often begin by copying, then move on to improvising and composing. Stage five was modeling composition learning from more expert musicians whether from outside the school or peers. The sixth and seventh stages applied informal learning to classical music.

The departure from a more controlled approach to teaching was challenging. The teachers and Green herself were tempted to step in rather than stand back "when, for example, a pupil might be holding a guitar upside down or across their knees."[32] An interesting phenomenon was that there was a tendency for things to get worse before they got better after initial progress. With an emphasis on lesson objectives, outcomes, measuring learning, and so forth, there was a concern that the approach was not working and more teacher help was needed. However, it transpired that the pupils found a way to work out their difficulties, although help was always available if the young people requested it. Green noted that "a little help without seeking perfection gave a lease for further development by the pupils themselves, and enabled pupils to retain ownership over their musical products and strategies."[33] The teacher's role shifted from transmitting knowledge and seeking "right" answers to observing, diagnosing, and modeling with some additional help needed in later stages. What surprised the teachers were the capabilities of the learners, an indication that their expectations had been too low.

Because the music that the young people brought in was music in the pop charts, some additional resources were needed to reproduce the music, such as electric guitars and drums kits/pads. Not all schools were able to provide these, and the Hertfordshire schools only received the extra resources just as the project started. Although compromise is inevitable, given financial limits, using more authentic instruments avoids being "wrong-footed from the start."[34] This is an important consideration since one of the key outcomes from Stage One of the project for the learners was that they said they had learned how to play instruments. It is noteworthy because they would have played school instruments previously yet apparently did not recognize that experience as learning to play them.

THE PRESENT-DAY AND FUTURE DEVELOPMENTS

MF's website is a good source with a wealth of information and open access materials.[35] Although originally intended for learners in Key Stage 3 and trialed in England, the approach has been adopted by both primary and secondary schools and is now an international venture. However, the precise number of schools adopting the informal learning approach is unknown.

There are core values at the heart of MF which echo the principles that Green set out. The aim is for learning to be

Inclusive—everyone takes part at their own level
Absorbing—learning is practical and hands-on
Relevant—starts with music that learners engage and identify with
Sociable—it is collaborative and with friends
Informal—led by learners with teachers/leaders modeling, guiding, supporting
Varied—learners perform, listen, compose, improvise, work on a range of instruments and voices, use technology, explore a range of genres, and styles
Progressive—music learning experiences are high-quality, authentic where possible, and with clear progression routes
Respectful—all learners, no matter what their ability or experience, are treated as musicians and are supported to learn and develop.[36]

These aims continue to underpin an MF approach. It is a case of "a" rather than "the" MF approach because one of the outcomes of the action research project was the importance of teachers being able to adapt informal learning to the context of the institution, informed by the values listed above.

A number of Champion Schools were identified. These schools were, and still are, committed to the aims of MF, sharing what they do and offering training events. The Champion Schools program was launched in 2008 with Roland, a Japanese company producing electronic instruments and software, providing resources.[37] There are now Champion Teachers, too, who have adopted an MF approach and are keen to share their enthusiasm. At the time of writing, Champions used descriptors such as exciting, inclusive, musically engaging, and student-led to sum up what MF offers.[38]

From its research-informed beginnings in a number of regions in England, MF has expanded to many other countries. There is a dedicated webspace offering training and support for those working in other countries.[39] The countries referred to on the website and in conference programs are Dubai, Ireland, Italy, Germany, Switzerland, Australia, New Zealand, China, Thailand, Malaysia, Singapore, and Brazil. Ruth Wright took the idea of MF to Canada and reported on a pilot project in two schools in Ontario. The outcomes are very similar to other research findings, such as those reported below, with the conclusion that "There appears to be less of a disconnect between the student and the teacher or the student and the curriculum."[40]

RESEARCHING MUSICAL FUTURES

Recent history has demonstrated the impact of MF. There have been a number of research projects, including those commissioned by the PHF, to investigate and evaluate ways in which MF has been incorporated into school music lessons. I had the privilege of being a researcher for one of these projects, speaking to staff and young people as well as observing music lessons in a number of secondary schools. The findings from these studies are included below. They articulate the strength of MF and its openness to evaluation and adaptation.

The PHF asked the Office for Standards in Education to evaluate MF in a sample of schools in Hertfordshire and Nottingham in England.[41] The evaluation focused on Year-Nine students. Ofsted reported the invigoration of teachers, an increase in student motivation with a knock-on, positive effect on the whole school, and more inclusion. The positive comments were tempered with caveats that the sample was small, the long-term impact was yet to be known, and more resources were needed. Inevitably, there were some difficulties arising from the move to a more student-focused approach. For the Nottingham schools, it was moving pupils "beyond their comfort zone," and, for Hertfordshire, it was encouraging students to manage their time and organize resources to avoid time being wasted on setting up instruments.[42] The networks of teachers recommended by Ofsted became a feature of MF, increasing the support available.

In 2008, Professor Susan Hallam and colleagues were commissioned by the PHF to investigate the implementation and impact of MF in English secondary schools.[43] Questionnaires were designed for teachers already using MF, those planning to and for their pupils. There were 1,575 teachers on the MF database who were asked to complete a questionnaire with a response rate of 66 percent. The pupils of thirty teachers received questionnaires. A total of 1,079 young people completed one. In total, 691 teachers were using or planned to use MF. Over half the teachers had implemented informal learning at key stage 3 and most often in year nine (thirteen- to fourteen-year-olds). Teachers reported a positive impact on feeling effective as a teacher, teacher development, and enjoyment of teaching. The approach represented a change that was seen as sustainable. There was also a positive effect on pupil engagement with young people feeling more confident and motivated. There was a call for more support for teachers. This was the year that the teacher resource pack was written, demonstrating MF's responsiveness.

In 2011, a second report was produced, again commissioned by the PHF.[44] The longitudinal study over three years combined survey, interview, and observational data from six case study sites. As one of the researchers, I had the opportunity to observe MF in different contexts and to gain insight into the various approaches taken. Many benefits were reported and observed, similar to those found in the 2008 report but with additional advantages, such as helping with assessment of individuals and developing interest in different kinds of music. Furthermore, the enhanced study skills, such as working as a group and helping others, were beneficial in other subjects. There were some challenges relating to certain groups of students and to the understanding of MF. For instance, Asian students were more likely to say they needed help compared to other ethnicities, and there was a tendency to use the term "band work" as a convenient but inaccurate synonym for MF. Of the seven stages, the last two, applying MF to classical music, were either not reached or deliberately left out. There were various reasons given. One was that it would be a retrograde step because classical music had been introduced in years seven and eight (ages eleven to thirteen). Another was that having instigated the informal learning model in year nine, there was not enough time to include the final stages. The young people's knowledge of classical music, unless learning a classical instrument, was somewhat restricted, with notable exceptions in schools where there were highly skilled teachers taking a positive, eclectic approach to all music. In general, classical music was associated with relaxation for older people. Research has indicated the importance of music to amplify or alter adolescents' moods (Baltazar 2019).[45] This affective aspect is an additional layer that is likely to color experiences of classroom music more than other subjects.

At the end of the 2011 report, some issues arising from the three-year study were set out. There were some concerns about the amount of energy and enthusiasm to manage a more informal approach. Furthermore, teachers with a classical music training might find informal learning challenging having learned more formally themselves. Some of the schools had brought in a wide range of musicians who were more comfortable with informal learning. Finally, encouraging students to study music as an option beyond year nine (year eight in some schools) has implications for the qualification to be taken and the skills needed for that qualification. GCSE and A-level exams have strong associations with the kind of knowledge gained from classical music training. Although an important consideration, my observation of MF indicated that some teachers were able to incorporate wider knowledge through skillful teaching.

There is food for thought in Mariguddi's (2019) thesis on MF based on four English secondary schools.[46] The two schools which had been using an MF approach for longer wondered if there had been a peak of success, and the novelty was wearing off. Perhaps the approach can conflict with other initiatives or policies that take precedence. There could be problems with keeping resources such as instruments and computers up to date and in good condition. Some teachers might be "revolutionaries" and thus looking for new challenges to follow on from MF. MF has only been established relatively recently, so only time will tell what the long-term outcome of the initiative is and how it might evolve.

FINAL CONSIDERATIONS

At the end of her book on a new classroom pedagogy (2008), Lucy Green writes an Afterword, reflecting on the benefits of an informal learning model; "if school pupils were to follow the project and nothing else, they would be likely to miss out on what most people would agree are some essential aspects of the music curriculum. These would include theoretical knowledge of harmony, scales and other pitch relations, rhythm, metre, technical vocabulary, and skills in reading and writing notation."[47] She advocates finding a way to integrate formal and informal learning, examples of which were found in the evaluation described above.

Green considers whether informal learning practices will help to prepare young people for further music study beyond school, including higher education, or the music industry. I was commissioned by the Society for Music Analysis to investigate concerns about a decline in music literacy with a need to fill gaps in knowledge and to alter entry requirements to cater for applicants to higher education music courses who have limited knowledge of music theory.[48] There was general agreement that some knowledge and skills have declined, although music literacy could be defined in different ways. Not all applicants will have experienced MF; therefore, there is a question about music pedagogy more widely and how to balance the needs and preferences of different learners.

Another question concerns the extent to which working with peers can offer the same learning opportunities as working with friends, favored in general and particularly by girls in Hallam et al.'s research.[49] One of MF's core values is working collaboratively with friends. Research has shown that who works with whom can influence outcomes both positively and detrimentally, including regression for girls working together but not for boys.[50] There are complex individual and interpersonal factors to take into account by the teacher and indeed the learners, if applying a more informal pedagogy.

CONCLUSION

The purpose of the chapter was to consider MF in a historical context, reviewing research into its implementation that has informed, and continues to inform, the informal learning approach. However, as Grunzke points out, "informal education significantly predates formal education."[51] It would be erroneous to say that informal learning is not part of a formal education system. Nonetheless, there is reliable evidence that informal learning has revitalized many classrooms. One of the strengths of MF is its adaptability to different contexts. The idea of an informal pedagogy encouraged by MF is important in developing a robust and meaningful learning experience for students. It is yet to be seen if and when the formal system surrounding any subject, including exam curricula and assessments, will adapt to such a pedagogy or if informal learning will conflict with competing demands in formal education.

NOTES

1. Lucy Green, *How Popular Musicians Learn: A Way Ahead for Music Education* (Abingdon: Routledge, 2016).

2. Youth Music and Ipsos MORI, "The Sound of the Next Generation." (2019), accessed December 31, 2021, https://youthmusic.org.uk/sites/default/files/2020-06/The Sound of the Next Generation.pdf.

3. Gert Biesta, "What Is Education For? On Good Education, Teacher Judgement, and Educational Professionalism." *European Journal of Education* (2015) 50, no. 1.

4. Susan Hallam, "The Power of Music: Its Impact on the Intellectual, Personal and Social development of Children and Young People," in *Music Education in the 21st Century in the United Kingdom: Achievements, Analysis and Aspirations*, eds Susan Hallam and Andrea Creech (London: Institute of Education, 2010).

5. Gordon Cox, "Britain: Opportunities and Threats Equally Balanced," in *The Origins and Foundations of Music Education: International Perspectives*, eds Gordon Cox and Robin Stevens (London, Bloomsbury Academic, 2017).

6. Cox, "Britain: Opportunities and Threats."

7. Central Advisory Council for Education (England), "The Newsom Report: Half Our Future." (London, Her Majesty's Stationery Office, 1963) 139.

8. John Paynter and Peter Aston. *Sound and Silence: Classroom Projects in Creative Music* (Cambridge: Cambridge University Press, 1970), 5–7.

9. Michele Kaschub and Janice Smith. "Music Teacher Education in Transition," in *Promising Practices in 21st Century Music Teacher Education*, eds Michele Kaschub and Janice Smith (Oxford: Oxford University Press, 2014), 7.

10. Gordon Cox, "Britain: Opportunities and Threats Equally Balanced," in *The Origins and Foundations of Music Education: International Perspectives*, eds Gordon Cox and Robin Stevens (London, Bloomsbury Academic, 2017), 16.

11. Her Majesty's Stationery Office. "Education Reform Act. England and Wales," accessed December 31, 2021, https://www.legislation.gov.uk/ukpga/1988/40/pdfs/ukpga_19880040_en.pdf, 2

12. Department for Education. 1995. "Music in the National Curriculum", accessed December 31, 2021, https://www.ism.org/images/files/Music-in-the-NC-1995.pdf

13. Department for Education and Employment; Qualifications and Curriculum Authority, 1999. "The National Curriculum: Handbook for Primary Teachers in England. Key Stages 1 and 2," accessed December 31, 2021, https://dera.ioe.ac.uk/18150/7/QCA-99-457_Redacted.pdf

14. Department of Education and Science. 1992. "Music in the National Curriculum (England)." London. https://dera.ioe.ac.uk/17394/2/Music NC 1992_Redacted.pdf

15. Gert Biesta, "Risking Ourselves in Education: Qualification, Socialization and Subjectification Revisited," Educational Theory (2020) 70 no. 1, 91, accessed December 31, 2021, https://doi.org/https://doi.org/10.1111/edth.12411

16. Graham F. Welch, Ross Purves, David J. Hargreaves, and Nigel A. Marshall, "Reflections on the 'Teacher Identities in Music Education' [TIME] Project," *Action, Criticism, and Theory for Music Education* 9, no. 2 (2010): 11–32.

17. Lucy Green, *Music on Deaf Ears: Musical Meaning, Ideology, Education* (Manchester: Manchester University Press, 1988), 68.

18. John Paynter, *Music in the Secondary School Curriculum* (Cambridge: Cambridge University Press, 1982), 8.

19. Graham F. Welch, Susan Hallam, Alexandra Lamont, Keith Swanwick, Lucy Green, Sarah Hennessy, Gordon Cox, Susan O'Neill, and Gerry Farrell, "Mapping Music Education Research in the UK," *Psychology of Music* 32, no. 3 (2004): 264.

20. Welch, et al., "Mapping Music Education Research," 242.
21. Green, "How Popular Musicians Learn," 9.
22. Green, "How Popular Musicians Learn."
23. Rosemary S. Caffarella, "Self-Directed Learning," *New Directions for Adult and Continuing Education.* 57, 27–28.
24. Lucy Green, "How Popular Musicians Learn," 96.
25. Lucy Green, "What Can Teachers Learn from Popular Musicians?" (Institute of Education, London, 2011), accessed January 23, 2022, https://www.youtube.com/watch?v=4r8zoHT4ExY
26. Ofsted, "The Annual Report of Her Majesty's Chief Inspector of Schools 2003/04," (2005), accessed December 31, 2021, https://assets.publishing.service.gov.uk/government/uploads/system/uploads/attachment_data/file/235467/0195.pdf
27. Green, "How Popular Musicians Learn," 184.
28. Lucy Green, *Music, Informal Learning and the School: A New Classroom Pedagogy* (London: Routledge, 2008).
29. Gov.uk. 2021. "The National Curriculum," (2021), accessed December 31, 2021. https://www.gov.uk/national-curriculum.
30. Musical Futures, "Who We Are and What We Do," (2021), accessed 31 December 2021, https://www.musicalfutures.org/who-we-are
31. Musical Futures, "How Musical Futures Began," (2021), accessed December 31, 2021, http://www.musicalfuturesinternational.org/background-and-history.html
32. Green, "Music, Informal Learning," 31.
33. Green, "Music, Informal Learning," 38.
34. Green, "Music, Informal Learning," 48.
35. Musical Futures (2021), accessed 31 December 2021, https://www.musicalfutures.org/
36. "Who We Are and What We Do," (2021), accessed December 31, 2021, https://www.musicalfutures.org/who-we-are
37. Abigail D'Amore, "Musical Futures: An Approach to Teaching and Learning. Resource Pack: 2nd Edition," (2008), accessed December 31, 2021, https://www.musicalfutures.org/wp-content/uploads/2013/01/musicalfutures2ndeditionteacherresourcepacklowres.pdf
38. "Meet Our MF Champions," (2021), accessed December 31, 2021, https://www.musicalfutures.org/who-we-are/the-team
39. "Musical Futures International," (2021), accessed December 31, 2021, http://www.musicalfuturesinternational.org/
40. Ruth Wright, Betty Anne Younker, Carol Beynon, Jennifer Hutchinson, Leslie Linto et al., "Tuning into the Future: Sharing Initial Insights about the 2012 Musical Futures Pilot Project in Ontario," *The Canadian Music Educator* 53, no. 4 (2012): 14.
41. Ofsted, "An Evaluation of the Paul Hamlyn Foundation's Musical Futures Project," (2006), accessed December 31, 2021, http://www.musicalfuturesaustralia.org/uploads/1/2/0/1/12012511/evaluation_of_musical_futures.pdf
42. Ofsted, "An Evaluation of the Paul Hamlyn Foundation's Musical Futures Project," (2006), accessed December 31, 2021, 4, http://www.musicalfuturesaustralia.org/uploads/1/2/0/1/12012511/evaluation_of_musical_futures.pdf

43. Susan Hallam, Andrea Creech, Clare Sandford, Tilja Rinta, and Katherine Shave, "Survey of Musical Futures" (London, Institute of Education, 2008).

44. Susan Hallam, Andrea Creech and Hilary McQueen, "Musical Futures: A Case Study Investigation" (London: Institute of Education, 2011).

45. Margarida Baltazar, "Musical Affect Regulation in Adolescents: A Conceptual Model," in *Handbook of Music, Adolescents, and Wellbeing*, eds., Katrina McFerran, Philippa Derrington, and Suvi Saarikallio (Oxford: Oxford University Press, 2019).

46. Anna Mariguddi, "Perceptions of the Informal Learning Branch of Musical Futures," (2019), accessed December 31, 2021, https://research.edgehill.ac.uk/ws/portalfiles/portal/21110233/Mariguddi_Anna_Final_Viva_PhD_thesis_for_archiving_2019.08.05.pdf

47. Green, "Music, Informal Learning," 181.

48. Hilary McQueen, "Questioning the Gap in Music Literacy in England: Defining a Role for the Society for Music Analysis in Preparing Students for Music Degrees in Higher Education Today," (2021), accessed December 31, 2021, https://www.sma.ac.uk/questioning-the-gap-in-music-literacy-in-england/?doing_wp_cron=1629117837.5207719802856445312500

49. Hallam, et al., "Musical Futures: A Case Study."

50. Diane, M. Hogan and Jonathan R.H. Tudge, "Implication of Vygotsky's Theory for Peer Learning," in *Cognitive Perspectives on Peer Learning*, eds., Angela O'Donnell, and Alison King (Mahwah, NJ: Lawrence Erlbaum Associates, 1999).

51. Andrew Grunzke, "The History of Nonformal and Informal Education," in *The Oxford Handbook of the History of Education*, eds., John L. Rury, and Eileen Tamura (New York: Oxford University Press, 2019), 540.

BIBLIOGRAPHY

Baltazar, Margarida. 2019. "Musical Affect Regulation in Adolescents: A Conceptual Model." In *Handbook of Music, Adolescents, and Well-being.*, edited by Katrina McFerran, Phillipa Derrington and Suvi Saarikallio, 65–74. Oxford: Oxford University Press.

Biesta, Gert, "What Is Education For? On Good Education, Teacher Judgement, and Educational Professionalism," *European Journal of Education* 50, no. 1 (2015): 75–87.

Biesta, Gert, "Risking Ourselves in Education: Qualification, Socialization and Subjectification Revisited," *Educational Theory* 70, no. 1 (2020): 89–104. https://doi.org/https://doi.org/10.1111/edth.12411.

Caffarella, Rosemary S. "Self-Directed Learning," *New Directions for Adult and Continuing Education* 57 (1993): 22–35.

Central Advisory Council for Education (England). "The Newsom Report: Half Our Future." London: Her Majesty's Stationery Office. 1963.

Cox, Gordon. "Britain: Opportunities and Threats Equally Balanced." In *The Origins and Foundations of Music Education: International Perspectives*, edited by Gordon Cox and Robin Stevens, 2nd edition, 9–21. London: Bloomsbury Academic, 2017.

D'Amore, Abigail. 2008. *Musical Futures: An Approach to Teaching and Learning. Resource Pack*, 2nd edition. https://www.musicalfutures.org/wpcontent/uploads/2013/01/musicalfutures2ndeditionteacherresourcepacklowres.pdf.
Department for Education. 1995. "Music in the National Curriculum." https://www.ism.org/images/files/Music-in-the-NC-1995.pdf.
Department for Education and Employment; Qualifications and Curriculum Authority. 1999. "The National Curriculum: Handbook for Primary Teachers in England. Key Stages 1 and 2." https://dera.ioe.ac.uk/18150/7/QCA-99-457_Redacted.pdf.
Department of Education and Science. 1992. "Music in the National Curriculum (England)." London. https://dera.ioe.ac.uk/17394/2/Music NC 1992_Redacted.pdf.
Gov.uk. 2021. "The National Curriculum." https://www.gov.uk/national-curriculum.
Green, Lucy. *Music on Deaf Ears: Musical Meaning, Ideology, Education.* Manchester: Manchester University Press. 1988.
Green, Lucy. How Popular Musicians Learn: A Way Ahead for Music Education. Aldershot: Ashgate. 2001.
Green, Lucy. "Meaning, Autonomy and Authenticity in the Music Classroom (Professorial Lecture)." 2005.
Green, Lucy. *Music, Informal Learning and the School: A New Classroom Pedagogy.* 1st ed. London: Routledge. 2008.
Green, Lucy, "What Can Teachers Learn from Popular Musicians?" Institute of Education, London, 2011.
Green, Lucy. *How Popular Musicians Learn: A Way Ahead for Music Education.* Abingdon: Routledge. 2016.
Grunzke, Andrew. "The History of Nonformal and Informal Education." In *The Oxford Handbook of the History of Education*, edited by John L. Rury and Eileen H. Tamura, 538–53. New York: Oxford University Press.
Hallam, Susan. "The Power of Music: Its Impact on the Intellectual, Personal and Social Development of Children and Young People." In Music Education in the 21st Century in the United Kingdom: Achievements, Analysis and Aspirations., edited by Susan Hallam and Andrea Creech, 2–17. London: Institute of Education, 2010.
Hallam, Susan, Andrea Creech, Clare Sandford, Tilja Rinta, and Katherine Shave. "Survey of Musical Futures." London: Institute of Education. 2008.
Hallam, Susan, Andrea Creech, and Hilary McQueen. "Musical Futures: A Case Study Investigation." London. 2011.
Her Majesty's Stationery Office. Education Reform Act. England and Wales. 1988. https://www.legislation.gov.uk/ukpga/1988/40/pdfs/ukpga_19880040_en.pdf.
Hogan, Diane M, and Jonathan R.H. Tudge. "Implication of Vygotsky's Theory for Peer Learning." In *Cognitive Perspectives on Peer Learning*, edited by Angela M. O'Donnell and Alison King, 39–65. Mahwah, NJ: Lawrence Erlbaum Associates, 1999.
Kaschub, Michele and Janice Smith. "Music Teacher Education in Transition." In *Promising Practices in 21st Century Music Teacher Education*, edited by Michele Kaschub and Janice Smith, 3–24. Oxford: Oxford University Press, 2014.

Mariguddi, Anna. 2019. "Perceptions of the Informal Learning Branch of Musical Futures." https://research.edgehill.ac.uk/ws/portalfiles/portal/21110233/Mariguddi _Anna_Final_Viva_PhD_thesis_for_archiving_2019.08.05.pdf.
McQueen, Hilary. "Questioning the Gap in Music Literacy in England: Defining a Role for the Society for Music Analysis in Preparing Students for Music Degrees in Higher Education Today." 2021. https://www.sma.ac.uk/questioning-the-gap -in-music-literacy-in-england/?doing_wp_cron=1629117837.5207719802856445312500.
Musical Futures. "An Evaluation of the Paul Hamlyn Foundation's Musical Futures Project." 2006. http://www.musicalfuturesaustralia.org/uploads/1/2/0/1/12012511/ evaluation_of_musical_futures.pdf.
Musical Futures. "How Musical Futures Began." 2021a. http://www.musicalfuturesi nternational.org/background-and-history.html.
Musical Futures. "Meet Our MF Champions." 2021b. https://www.musicalfutures .org/who-we-are/the-team.
Musical Futures. "Musical Futures." 2021c. https://www.musicalfutures.org/.
Musical Futures. "Musical Futures International." 2021d. http://www.musicalfuturesi nternational.org/.
Musical Futures. "Who We Are and What We Do." 2021e. https://www.musicalfu tures.org/who-we-are.
Ofsted. "The Annual Report of Her Majesty's Chief Inspector of Schools 2003/04." Norwich. 2005. https://assets.publishing.service.gov.uk/government/uploads/system/uploads/attachment_data/file/235467/0195.pdf.
Paynter, John. *Music in the Secondary School Curriculum.* Cambridge: Cambridge University Press. 1982.
Paynter, John, and Peter Aston. 1970. *Sound and Silence: Classroom Projects in Creative Music. Second.* Cambridge: Cambridge University Press.
Welch, Graham F., Ross Purves, David J. Hargreaves, and Nigel A. Marshall. "Reflections on the 'Teacher Identities in Music Education' [TIME] Project." 9, no. 2 (2010): 11–32.
Welch, Graham, Susan Hallam, Alexandra Lamont, Keith Swanwick, Lucy Green, Sarah Hennessy, Gordon Cox, Susan O'Neill, and Gerry Farrell.. "Mapping Music Education Research in the UK." *Psychology of Music* 32, no. 3 (2004): 239–90. https://doi.org/https://doi.org/10.1177%2F0305735604043257.
Wright, Ruth, Betty Anne Younker, Carol Beynon, Jennifer Hutchinson, Leslie Linto et al. "Tuning into the Future: Sharing Initial Insights about the 2012 Musical Futures Pilot Project in Ontario." *The Canadian Music Educator.* 53, no. 4 (2012): 14–18.
Youth Music and Ipsos MORI. "The Sound of the Next Generation." 2019. https:// youthmusic.org.uk/sites/default/files/2020-06/The Sound of the Next Generation .pdf.

Chapter 15

New Interfaces for Musical Expression
Instrument Making as Music Learning
Andrew Brown

The DIY or maker culture is a postdigital movement prominent in the early twenty-first century which has found its way into some music classrooms in the form of instrument making using techniques of electronics, digital fabrication, and coding. Outside the classroom, this movement characterizes itself as the development of new interfaces for musical expression, or NIME for short. However, in the classroom, instrument making as musical expression still faces an uphill battle to find a place in many music curriculums, even though music education has seen significant development from its historically rigid privileging of repertoire-based composing, performing, and listening activities. There has been a noticeable uptake of acoustic instrument making in music education since the 1970s. Now, in a postdigital era, the tools and knowledge resources are available for easy access to electronic instrument making, and a slow revolution continues to be underway to include the design and building of new interfaces for musical expression as an important part of a rich music education.

INSTRUMENT MAKING AS MUSICAL EXPRESSION

A renewed acknowledgment of instrument design and building as an expression of musicianship came about in the second half of the twentieth century as an expanded understanding of music and musicianship was being articled by music educators such as John Paynter,[1] Rena Upitis,[2] and Atarah Ben-Tovim.[3] These developments drew inspiration from constructivist psychology informed by the writings of Jean Piaget,[4] Jerome Bruner,[5] and Lev Vygotsky.[6] The deeper philosophical home of these ideas is in the work of pragmatists such as John Dewey[7] which included an emphasis on acquiring knowledge through multimodal lived experience.

Instrument making activities in the classroom became popular in the 1970s with the design of, and performance with, handmade acoustic sound devices. Typically, these were simple devices crafted from everyday objects and materials. Since the start of this century, electronic and digital instrumental making practices have been introduced to complement acoustic devices.

An important articulation of the trend to expand the horizon of music making through legitimatizing more activities as part of music education was the writing of Christopher Small from the 1970s[8] to 1990s.[9] His introduction of the term "musicking" to include an expansive array of music-related activities that went beyond nineteenth-century Western art music traditions helped to open the imagination of many music educators to the value of music from different cultures and genres. He also emphasized the practical experience of music making over purely abstract knowledge about it, thus facilitating acceptance of practical activities which could include new instrument design as a legitimate form of musical expression.

Despite several decades having passed since Small's expansion of the definition of music making, the division between performing and instrument making seems well entrenched in music curriculums. As Koji Matsunomi lamented, "Perhaps we are in so much of a hurry to make a sound that we don't take the time to make the technology with which to play."[10] He points out that in many non-western cultural traditions the integrated role of maker-player remains but that industrialized manufacturing processes have steadily diminished pluralist aspects of musicianship and reinforced the use of homogenized and standardized media.

While simple handmade acoustic instruments have been the most popular instruments to make in classrooms in previous decades, in the twenty-first century, electronic musical instruments are the new frontier. So, in this chapter, I will provide an overview of the revolution of electronic music technologies and instrument making in Western music education, shine a light on some of the areas, where there are signs that do-it-yourself electronic instrument making in classrooms is taking hold, and point to resources that can assist those interested in embracing electronic instrument making as a part of a more holistic music education.

NEW INTERFACES FOR MUSICAL EXPRESSION

Since the establishment of the New Interfaces for Musical Expression (NIME) conference, as a workshop at the ACM Conference on Human Factors in Computing Systems (CHI) in 2001 in Seattle, Washington, the academic legitimacy of electronic instrument design and making has matured. NIME grew out of studies in human-computer interface research and continues to have a strong orientation toward the usability of digital technologies. Gestural affordances of an instrument's physical construction were also important, and new interfaces in this community are almost always a mixture of software and hardware.

Around the same time, there was a growing backlash in the music community against the association of digital with perfection.[11] The dominance of compact discs as a music format led to a resurgent appreciation for analogue formats such as vinyl and tape. The popularity of these analogue formats decreased steeply in the 2000s with vinyl records reaching a low in production in 2007 after which there was a rapid return to popularity, and midway through the 2010s sales were higher than even previous historical peaks. Experimental musicians were increasingly drawn to "hacking" digital systems and embracing the "glitch" aesthetic, where these systems deliberately "break down" in interesting ways. A renewed interest in older analogue and modular synthesizers also emerged. These trends were described as "postdigital" by Kim Cascone[12] in 2000, the implications of which continue to play out to this day. It is important to note that to limit discussion about a postdigital aesthetic to sound quality is to short-change the concept from its broader notion as a practice that explores the materialism of electronic music systems for music making.

Another significant development in interfaces for musical expression in the early years of this century was the practice of live coding,[13] where computer programming languages were employed performatively. In this practice, software instruments are built on-the-fly, in code, on stage, as part of the performance. The distinction between instrument, composition, and performance is blurred like never before. As with many of these trends, live coding started with musicians who were also expert technologists developing their own coding environments for performance. Over time, these tools became more accessible and easier to use. Now, live coding languages like SonicPi[14] are regularly used in educational settings, the details of which will be further elaborated later in the chapter.

The postdigital revolution in music making that started around the turn of the century took a while, as these things often do, to infiltrate its way into music education. At that time, the music industry was embracing digital means of production and distribution, while those outside it in academia and as music fans were finding new ways to subvert it, either through embracing the glitch as expression or free online sharing of music as MP3 files. Yet music curriculums of the time tended to implement incremental advances from the innovations introduced in the 1970s. For example, the reasonably enlightened New Zealand Arts Curriculum released in 2000 opens the door to electronic instrument experimentation when it suggests that "Students investigate ways of creating sounds, using conventional and unconventional sound sources" and, more explicitly, that "They explore how technologies contribute to performance, and they record their own and others' performances." Yet, when articulating the ways this is expected to be undertaken, instrument making is omitted. It recommends that students undertake "such activities as listening, moving, singing, and playing."[15] Making the leap to include the design and making of new interfaces for music expression as part of a music education, when it does arise, requires a combination of an openness to embrace electronic technologies, including their faults, as an expressive medium along with accessible means of technological production. To be fair to curriculum designers of that time, despite the DIY movement having grown in the latter half of the twentieth century, accessible tools for electronic instrument making were still evolving as part of the Maker movement.

DIY AND MAKER TOOLS

Part of a response to increased commercialization in our society has been the emergence of the Do-It-Yourself (DIY) movement, now more commonly referred to as the Maker movement. It should be noted that the term "DIY" has in recent times found its way into cultural studies and educational circles as a reference to students taking greater agency in their learning, for example, forming their own ensembles and organizing their own concerts. It has also found resonances with educational trends embracing countercultural aspirations of students, especially as a way of motivating otherwise disengaged youth. Often these trends have been described as Punk Pedagogy.[16] Despite some potential overlap with these trends in the use of the term "DIY," in this article, I'll try to distance myself from that usage and will therefore prefer the term "Maker," and its connotations of designing and building, as an indicator of a connecting with the materiality of sound through instrument making and its significance as part of a broad music education. In short, this article will focus more directly on personalized means of sound production than on individual empowerment.

It is a truism that a wider range of tools will result in a wider range of outcomes and experiences. The types of tools typically associated with the Maker movement include battery-powered electronic circuits, programmable microprocessors, and digital fabrication techniques such as laser cutting and 3D printing. The movement embraces an exploration of electronic and digital media alongside craft-based cyberphysical interactions with materials, digital systems, and musicians.

While the starting point for maker projects is often the reproduction of well-known devices and processes, the end points can be quickly personalized, and outcomes become much more divergent as makers explore pathways of affordance and resistance that materials present. Pragmatists, since Dewey,[17] have pointed out that resolving the tensions between human motivations and material possibilities is an important aspect of artistic practice and cultural development.

EDUCATIONAL TRENDS IN DIGITAL TECHNOLOGIES

An acknowledgment that music is a technology or, at least, that musical instruments are technologies is often overlooked by music educators. So immersed in a particular artistic genre, such as orchestral music or rock and pop music, are educators (and musicians more broadly) that the technological underpinnings of those practices can be taken for granted. Instrument making as a part of music education bursts those bubbles and is often deliberately disruptive of established ways of thinking. The intellectual and skill challenges presented by instrument making encourage reflection on established ways of doing music and of being musical which can lead to enriched understanding of established traditions or to the exploration of possible new traditions.

The first step toward an acknowledgment of technological knowledge as part of a developing musicianship was the revolution in music education, already alluded to, from the 1970s to 1990s. This period saw a change in the core focus of music curricula, from music appreciation to music participation. The new priorities were summed up in phases such as Paynter's "Composing, performing and listening" which encouraged a range of participation and creation alongside a different type of listening from traditional appreciation —one based on sonic awareness and deep listening inspired by the work of R. Murray Schafer[18] and others. Alongside this was an expansion of the types of music that were acceptable within a music curriculum, in particular rock and ethnic musical genres.[19] Yet, despite some excursions into the use of handmade percussion instruments, especially for young children, there was limited attention to instrument making.

In the 2000s, some music educators noticed the disparity between developments in music technologies (many mentioned earlier in this article) and absence of digital technologies in music classrooms. Just as the music industry was entering the postdigital phase, there was an awakening about the absence of digital instruments in music education. The relevance of formalized music curricula was being questioned,[20] and the opportunities for technologies to amplify musicality were being articulated.[21] There was an acknowledgment that digital media were dominating the entertainment industry, leading to calls that "A redefinition of musical literacy also should entail the ability to manipulate and navigate technological tools and equipment—primarily keyboards, computers and [sound] recording and playback equipment."[22] However, despite these developments, too often electronic and digital technologies were treated as media for recording and delivery of information rather than as opportunities for new instruments or for creative expression.[23] Nevertheless, pockets of innovation emerged where electronics were treated as opportunities for bespoke sonic experimentation and laptops and mobile phones were beginning to be employed as instruments in Laptop Orchestras.[24]

A key resource developed at this time was Nicholas Collins' book "Handmade Electronic Music: The Art of hardware hacking."[25] On his website Collins recalls how this book arose as part of his teaching of music and sound at the Art Institute of Chicago as a postdigital response to the lack of tactility in his students' digital media production practices. His course, and the book, introduces interactive electronic sound-making projects as alternatives to the use of a computer. The significance and longevity of this resource are evident in the release of a revised third edition in 2020. It is from these roots that more extensive electronic instrument making activities in education have developed, assisted by a maturing digital revolution in other fields of education.

While computing education had been a part of many classrooms since the 1980s, the production of small, battery-powered, low-cost microprocessors in the early part of the twenty-first century accelerated the accessibility of computing, electronics, and robotics for educationalists and hobbyists alike. At this time, computers had become commodities, and they were large, expensive, and self-contained, and not designed for tinkering or user modification. This was a barrier to the kind of exploration and experimentation available to educators with other materials, like wood or cardboard. This was an issue not only for musicians but also for technology educators and designers of electronic media arts. Staff and students at the Interaction Design Institute Ivrea (IDII) in Ivrea, Italy, would propose a solution to their own needs that met the needs of many others as well.

The Arduino[26] family of microprocessor boards was introduced late in the 2000s and others followed a few years later, including the BBC Micro Bit and various Adafruit boards. These devices were compact, low-powered, computers on boards with input-output pins for attaching hardware sensors and output devices such as lights and speakers. Projects and tutorials using these tools were shared online on sites such as Instructables[27] and included projects for making musical devices.

While significant advances regarding the teaching of computer programming (software development) were made in the 1970s, especially relating to the Logo programming language,[28] there was a second wave of coding education around the turn of the century. Initiatives included the Scratch[29] and Processing[30] environments that included rich media capabilities including sound generation which were a large part of the attraction to learners. The Arduino coding environment was derived from processing, although it utilized a different programming language. These, and other platforms, facilitated a rise in coding education driven by the determination that digital literacy would be essential for this century.

More broadly, the drive for computing education became part of a move to promote the value of science and technology education. The term "STEM"—standing for science, technology, engineering, and maths—education was introduced in 2001 and continues to be a driver of curriculum policy. Numerous attempts to include the arts in this movement, by revising the acronym to STEAM, have been pursued.[31]

Almost all knowledge is multidisciplinary, and connecting music or sound making to STEM can make this more apparent to students. The idea for STEAM projects that include the arts is to undertake intentionally multidisciplinary projects or lessons where learning objectives and assessments from at least two disciplines are pursued. Electronic instrument making is an ideal candidate for STEAM projects given that they intrinsically include technology, physics, and maths alongside design, personal expression, and performance. There are many projects that fit this criterion that are available online, some using maker tools such as Arduino and others more commercially packaged such as the LittleBits electronic music inventor kit.[32]

While the STEM trends in technology-based education were largely motivated by the need for engineering skill development to power the tech industry, the tools and platforms that were developed were also useful for enabling new electronic musical instruments. Indeed, the use of music or, more broadly, "multimedia" projects as a motivational driver for the uptake of STEM skill development is common, especially in the United States, where liberal-arts education promotes the mixing of humanities and science subjects within a program of study.[33]

TRANSFORMATION OR REPRODUCTION

A recurring critique of music education has been its alleged orientation toward the reproduction of musical repertoire at the expense of exploration leading to transformational change in the music field.[34] What is true for music repertoire is even more so for musical instruments. Even when, in music classrooms, there is a focus on composition, soundscapes, or improvisation, there too often remains an assumption that existing instruments will be the vehicle for those activities.

Acoustic instrument making projects have been a feature of modern music education since the 1970s. In reflecting on these experiences, Upitis[35] reports using "junk" materials such as bottle tops, cardboard boxes, straws, and cups cobbled together with nails, glue, tape, and rubber bands. She emphasizes the importance of educators making and learning alongside students in these processes and the value of iteration where students take learnings from one instrument into the next making project. The benefits she highlights include increased understanding of the acoustics of sound, being less inhibited about making sounds on their other instruments, and a greater sense of attachment to the instruments they make. Challenges remain, of course, including students not necessarily taking seriously their musical activities on instruments that are not "real" and how to transfer knowledge and skills, such as improvisation, from handmade to manufactured instruments.

A range of more contemporary versions of acoustic Maker projects are described by Matsunobu[36] and include the Homebrew Ukulele Union,[37] shakuhachi practitioners,[38] electromechanically controlled electric guitar,[39] and Cigar-box guitars.[40] From these projects, he draws out the benefits of tailoring the instruments, repertoire, and outcomes to reflect the local environment and culture in which the activity takes place and to suit the individual musical tastes of students and educators involved.

While instrument building of existing instruments and the use of associated pedagogical insights are very valuable, the "new" in NIME should not be overlooked. Making music with technologies runs the same risks of unimaginative reproduction of culture as any other area of curriculum might. A revolution in music education involves more than a shift in medium, or even more than a shift in activity, for example, from performing to composing or from composing to instrument making. Harking back to the insights of the music educationalists from the 1970s referred to earlier, the privileging of creativity, imagination, and expression is also a part of the NIME agenda. The coupling between tool making and musical expression is, or should be, deeply felt by those involved in music education as it is in the music industry. We have seen over and again that function follows form in new instrument design, for example, when limited digital sample memory led to loop-based musical genres such as Hip-Hop. And limitations motivate innovation, like when the desire for rich gestural expression led to the development of the MIDI Polyphonic Expression (MPE) protocol. We should expect similarly substantial changes in educational culture as we've seen in music culture.

As much as it is useful to familiarize students with existing and historical musical genres, so too it is important that they are encouraged to experiment and contribute to the ongoing cultural evolution. Exploring new electronic music instrument design and building can be an ideal vehicle for motivating students' music making and pushing them to imagine what's possible by going beyond existing musical conventions.

Exemplars of Accessible Electronic Instrument Making

In keeping with this chapter's focus on handmade electronic music, four accessible electronic music projects are reviewed below. Pedagogically, these can be approached similarly to the acoustic instrument making projects previously mentioned, using a hands-on model where students build, compose, perform, and document their explorations using self-constructed instruments.

Atari Punk Console

This simple, yet fun, analogue electronics project does not involve a computer, and making it on a breadboard avoids any soldering. So, it's a great introductory audio electronic instrument project. The circuit design was originally published by Radio Shack in the United States in 1980 and gets its name from the lo-fi sound it produces that is reminiscent of early eight-bit computer game consoles. There is an easy-to-follow tutorial on creating the Atari Punk Console on the Instructables site written by user BrownDogGadgets.[41] The circuit modulates two square wave tones producing rich, enharmonic, overtones. The pitch of each wave adjusts the frequency and timbral character of the tone and can be controlled by dials (pots) or a light-sensitive resistor (LDR).

Phase Drone Synth

Drawing on the materials in the Arduino ecosystem, this project published by Daniel Sinderson in 2021 involves making a two-voice drone synthesizer capable of repetitive pulse changes.[42] The instrument is controlled using a handful of dials (potentiometers) and a button that controls pitch, timbre, and rhythmic (LFO) elements. Sinderson provides the software for the project which utilizes the Mozzi audio synthesis library,[43] and a bill of materials and schematic for the hardware connections are provided online. While it is an entry-level project, some prior experience by an instructor would be required, as are soldering facilities. The Phase Drone Synth provides an exploratory platform that does not try to mimic well established musical conventions but opens up unique avenues for interactive sound design.

Sonic Pi

Sonic Pi is a software environment developed in Cambridge, the UK, and released in 2012. It can run on a range of computing platforms but was originally developed for the Raspberry Pi DIY computer, hence its name.[44]

Designed for Live Coding performances, in Sonic Pi, the idea is to build and manipulate software instruments on the fly. The main developer, Sam Aaron, has worked closely with educationalists to provide a rich set of projects and teaching resources for educational settings. Live Coding, like other handmade instrument making, encourages an improvisatory approach to music making. The use of computer code as a notation for well-established musical principles provides a new perspective on these concepts, one that may even be more accessible for many students.

Beat Machine

The Beat Machine is a bespoke rhythmic synthesizer project that comes in kit form.[45] Originally developed in 2019 by John Ferguson and Andrew R. Brown in Brisbane, Australia, it is a small and inexpensive sequencer/synthesizer that can produce music ranging across conventional to experimental electronic genres. Being battery-powered, it lends itself to mobile contexts and flexible classroom organization. Like projects such as the Homebrew Ukulele Union, the Beat Machine provides an inroad to a reasonably well understood electronic musical culture, styles from electronic dance music to ambient soundscapes, and can assist students to gain deeper insights into the mechanics of these kinds of music making. It can also act as a platform for more advanced students to customize its functionality through reprogramming.

These projects are quite diverse, both technically and sonically. They reveal a wide selection of electronic instrument making opportunities for those more comfortable with either hardware or software or who prefer experimental or conventional musical outcomes.

CONCLUSION

The designing and building of new interfaces for musical expression can be seen as the latest of several waves of innovation in music education during the past century, in what I have described, after Matsunobu, as a slow revolution of the continued extension of valid musical activities finding a place in the music curriculum that now includes handmade electronic musical instrument making.

An acknowledgment that instrument making is a legitimate aspect of a well-rounded music education reflects an acceptance that creative relations with the world are not only about the production of an aesthetic product but also about the need to navigate the affordances and possibilities of our contemporary cultural situation. Aligned with the value of creating new works, new interpretations, and finding a personal musical voice, making handmade electronic musical instruments values the development of new sound making possibilities relevant to our time.

The revolution of NIME teaching has developed since the turn of the century. It has mainly had an impact, thus far, in tertiary educational settings worldwide, where lessons about successful pedagogical practices are well articulated.[46] The uptake of electronic musical instrument making in primary and secondary education is more often associated with STEAM-based engineering initiatives driven by music technology enthusiasts outside of the Arts.[47] NIME teaching within school-based music education is still developing. One pathway to designing new instruments is to the use of unconventional instruments such as laptops and iPads for live performance.[48,49] The required tools and platforms for accessible electronics and digital fabrication are now at hand for students to produce handmade electronic instruments thanks to active development within the broader Maker movement. Examples and inspiration for innovative designs are readily available from the academic NIME community and from active online sharing of resources by DIY electronic music enthusiasts. What is required to speed up the revolution is for more music educators to embrace the possibilities.

NOTES

1. John Paynter, *Sound & Structure* (New York: Cambridge University Press, 1992).

2. Rena Upitis, "The Craft of Composition: Helping Children Create Music with Computer Tools," *Psychomusicology* 8, no. 2 (1990): 151–62.

3. Atarah Ben-Tovim, *Children and Music: A Handbook for Parents, Teachers and Others Interested in the Musical Welfare of Children* (London: A & C Black, 1979).

4. Jean Piaget, *Structuralism* (New York: Routledge & Kegan Paul, 1971).

5. Jerome Bruner, *The Process of Education* (Cambridge, Mass: Harvard University Press, 1960).

6. Lev S. Vygotsky, *Mind and Society* (Cambridge, MA: Harvard University Press, 1978).

7. John Dewey, *Art as Experience* (New York: Putmans, 1934).

8. Christopher Small, *Music, Society, Education* (Hanover, NH: Wesleyan University Press, 1977).

9. Christopher Small, *Musicking: The Meanings of Performing and Listening* (Hanover, NH: Wesleyan University Press, 1998).

10. Koji Matsunobu, "Instrument Making as Music Making: A Slow Food Approach to Musicianship," in *Sound Musicianship: Understanding the Crafts of Music*, ed. Andrew R. Brown (Newcastle upon Tyne: Cambridge Scholars Publishing, 2012), 178–88.

11. Andy Hamilton, "The Art of Recording and the Aesthetics of Perfection," *The British Journal of Aesthetics* 43, no. 4 (2003): 345–62.

12. Kim Cascone, "The Aesthetics of Failure: 'Post-Digital' Tendencies in Contemporary Computer Music," *Computer Music Journal* 24, no. 4 (2000): 12–18.

13. Alex McLean, "Hacking Perl in Nightclubs," perl.com, 2004, http://www.perl.com/pub/a/2004/08/31/livecode.html.

14. Samuel Aaron, Alan F. Blackwell, and Pamela Bernard, "The Development of Sonic Pi and Its Use in Educational Partnerships: Co-creating Pedagogies for Learning Computer Programming," *Journal of Music, Technology & Education* 9, no. 1 (2016): 75–94.

15. Ministry of Education, "The Arts in the New Zealand Curriculum" (Learning Media Limited, 2000), 54–55. https://nzcurriculum.tki.org.nz/content/download/74037/581665/file/TheArtsCurriculum.pdf.

16. Peter J Woods, "The Aesthetic Pedagogies of DIY Music," *Review of Education, Pedagogy, and Cultural Studies* 43, no. 4 (2021): 338–57.

17. Dewey, "Art as Experience."

18. Paynter, "Sound & Structure."

19. Graham Vulliamy and Ed Lee, *Pop, Rock and Ethnic Music in School* (Cambridge, England: Cambridge University Press, 1982).

20. Thomas Regelski, "Reconnecting Music Education with Society," *Action, Criticism, and Theory for Music Education* 5, no. 2 (2006): 1–20.

21. Andrew R. Brown, *Computers in Music Education: Amplifying Musicality* (New York: Routledge, 2007).

22. Robert Mawuena Kwami, "Music Education in a New Millennium," *Ict, Pedagogy and the Curriculum: Subject to Change*, 2001, 216–28.

23. Scott D. Lipscomb, "The Role of Technology in Music Education: A Preconference Satellite Symposium for Tanglewood II," *Journal of Technology in Music Learning* 4, no. 1 (2007): 55–69.

24. Ge Wang and Perry R. Cook, "On-the-Fly Programming: Using Code as an Expressive Musical Instrument," in *Proceedings of the Conference on New Interfaces for Musical Expression* (NIME 04, Hamamatsu, Japan: NIME, 2004), 138–43; Ge Wang et al., "The Laptop Orchestra as Classroom," *Computer Music Journal* 32, no. 1 (2008): 26–37.

25. Nicholas Collins, *Handmade Electronic Music: The Art of Hardware Hacking* (New York: Routledge, 2006).

26. "Arduino" accessed December 20, 2021, https://www.arduino.cc/

27. "Instructables," accessed December 20, 2021, https://www.instructables.com/

28. Seymour Papert, *Mindstorms: Children, Computers, and Powerful Ideas* (New York: Basic Books, 1980).

29. "Scratch Programming Environment," accessed December 20, 2021, https://scratch.mit.edu/

30. "Processing Programming Environment" accessed December 20, 2021, https://processing.org/

31. Joan Platz, "How Do You Turn STEM into STEAM? Add the Arts," *Columbus: Ohio Alliance for Arts Education*, 2007, 1–5.

32. "Littlebits kit" accessed December 20, 2021, https://sphero.com/products/littlebits-electronic-music-inventor-kit

33. Mark Guzdial, "A Media Computation Course for Non-Majors," in *Proceedings of the 8th Annual Conference on Innovation and Technology in Computer Science Education*, 2003, 104–108.

34. Regelski, "Reconnecting Music Education with Society."

35. Rena Upitis, *This Too Is Music* (Portsmouth, NH: Heinemann Publishing, 1990).

36. Matsunobu, "Instrument Making as Music Making: A Slow Food Approach to Musicianship."

37. Matthew D. Thibeault and Julianne Evoy, "Building Your Own Musical Community: How YouTube, Miley Cyrus, and the Ukulele Can Create a New Kind of Ensemble," *General Music Today* 24, no. 3 (2011): 44–52.

38. Koji Matsunobu, "Artful Encounters with Nature: Ecological and Spiritual Dimensions of Music Learning" (PhD Diss., University of Illinois at Urbana-Champaign, 2009).

39. Aengus Martin, Sam Ferguson, and Kirsty A. Beilharz, "Mechanisms for Controlling Complex Sound Sources: Applications to Guitar Feedback Control.," in *NIME* (New Interfaces for Musical Expression, Sydney, Australia: University of Technology Sydney, 2010), 364–67.

40. Mark Frauenfelder, "Traditional Cigar Box Guitar," *Make* 21 (2010): 76–85.

41. "Build an Atari Punk Circuit on a Breadboard," Instructable Circuits, accessed, December 20, 2021, https://www.instructables.com/Build-an-Atari-Punk-circuit-on-a-breadboard/

42. Daniel Sinderson, "PhaseMod Drone Synth," *Arduino Project Hub* (blog), 2021, https://create.arduino.cc/projecthub/scraptured/phasemod-drone-synth-w-arduino-nano-mozzi-7ab2ff.

43. Tim Barrass, "Mozzi," 2020, https://sensorium.github.io/Mozzi/.

44. Aaron, Blackwell, and Bernard, "The Development of Sonic Pi," 75–94.

45. Andrew R. Brown and John Ferguson, "Beat Machine: Embracing the Creative Limitations and Opportunities of Low-Cost Computers," *Leonardo Music Journal* 30 (2020): 8–13.

46. Enrique Tomás, "A Playful Approach to Teaching NIME: Pedagogical Methods from a Practice-Based Perspective," in *Proceedings of the International Conference on New Interfaces for Musical Expression* (NIME, Birmingham, UK: NIME, 2020), 143–48.

47. Jiffer Harriman, "Start'em Young: Digital Music Instrument for Education," in *Proceedings of New Interfaces for Musical Expression* (NIME, Baton Rouge, LA: NIME, 2015), 70–73.

48. Andrew R. Brown et al., "Making Meaningful Musical Experiences Accessible Using the IPad," in *Ubiquitous Music*, ed. Victor Lazzarini, Damián Keller, and Marcelo Pimenta, Computational Music Science (Cham, Switzerland: Springer, 2014), 65–82, http://www.springer.com/computer/information+systems+and+applications/book/978-3-319-11151-3.

49. David A. Williams, "Another Perspective: The IPad Is a REAL Musical Instrument," *Music Educators Journal* 101, no. 1 (2014): 93–98.

BIBLIOGRAPHY

Aaron, Samuel, Alan F. Blackwell, and Pamela Bernard. "The Development of Sonic Pi and Its Use in Educational Partnerships: Co-creating Pedagogies for Learning Computer Programming." *Journal of Music, Technology & Education* 9, no. 1 (2016): 75–94.

"Arduino" accessed December 20, 2021, https://www.arduino.cc/

Barrass, Tim. "Mozzi," 2020, https://sensorium.github.io/Mozzi/.

Ben-Tovim, Atarah. *Children and Music: A Handbook for Parents, Teachers and Others Interested in the Musical Welfare of Children.* London: A & C Black, 1979.

Brown, Andrew R. *Computers in Music Education: Amplifying Musicality.* New York: Routledge, 2007.

Brown, Andrew R. and John Ferguson. "Beat Machine: Embracing the Creative Limitations and Opportunities of Low-Cost Computers." *Leonardo Music Journal* 30 (2020): 8–13.

Brown, Andrew R. et al. "Making Meaningful Musical Experiences Accessible Using the IPad." In *Ubiquitous Music*, edited by Victor Lazzarini, Damián Keller, and Marcelo Pimenta, 65–82. Cham, Switzerland: Springer, 2014,

Bruner, Jerome. *The Process of Education.* Cambridge, Mass: Harvard University Press, 1960.

Cascone, Kim. "The Aesthetics of Failure: 'Post-Digital' Tendencies in Contemporary Computer Music." *Computer Music Journal* 24, no. 4 (2000): 12–18.

Collins, Nicholas. *Handmade Electronic Music: The Art of Hardware Hacking.* New York: Routledge, 2006.

Dewey, John. *Art as Experience.* New York: Putmans, 1934.

Frauenfelder, Mark. "Traditional Cigar Box Guitar," *Make* 21 (2010): 76–85. https://www.instructables.com/Build-an-Atari-Punk-circuit-on-a-breadboard/

Guzdial, Mark. "A Media Computation Course for Non-Majors," in *Proceedings of the 8th Annual Conference on Innovation and Technology in Computer Science Education*, 2003, 104–108.

Hamilton, Andy. "The Art of Recording and the Aesthetics of Perfection." *The British Journal of Aesthetics* 43, no. 4 (2003): 345–62.

Harriman, Jiffer. "Start'em Young: Digital Music Instrument for Education." in *Proceedings of New Interfaces for Musical Expression,* 70–73. Baton Rouge, LA: NIME, 2015,

"Instructables" accessed December 20, 2021, https://www.instructables.com/

Kwami, Robert Mawuena. "Music Education in a New Millennium." *In Ict, Pedagogy and the Curriculum: Subject to Change*, edited by Avril Loveless and Viv Ellis, 216–28. Abingdon, Oxon: Routledge, Falmer, 2001.

Lipscomb, Scott D. "The Role of Technology in Music Education: A Preconference Satellite Symposium for Tanglewood II." *Journal of Technology in Music Learning* 4, no. 1 (2007): 55–69.

"Littlebits kit," accessed December 20, 2021, https://sphero.com/products/littlebits-electronic-music-inventor-kit

Matsunobu, Koji. "Instrument Making as Music Making: A Slow Food Approach to Musicianship." In *Sound Musicianship: Understanding the Crafts of Music*, edited by Andrew R. Brown, 178–88. Newcastle upon Tyne: Cambridge Scholars Publishing, 2012.

Martin, Aengus, Sam Ferguson, and Kirsty A Beilharz, "Mechanisms for Controlling Complex Sound Sources: Applications to Guitar Feedback Control." In *NIME* (New Interfaces for Musical Expression), 364–67. Sydney, Australia: University of Technology Sydney, 2010.

Matsunobu, Koji. "Artful Encounters with Nature: Ecological and Spiritual Dimensions of Music Learning." PhD Diss., University of Illinois at Urbana-Champaign, 2009.

McLean, Alex. "Hacking Perl in Nightclubs," perl.com., 2004, http://www.perl.com/pub/a/2004/08/31/livecode.html.

Ministry of Education. "The Arts in the New Zealand Curriculum." Learning Media Limited, 2000, 54–55, https://nzcurriculum.tki.org.nz/content/download/74037/581665/file/TheArtsCurriculum.pdf.

Papert, Seymour. *Mindstorms: Children, Computers, and Powerful Ideas*. New York: Basic Books, 1980.

Paynter, John. *Sound & Structure*. New York: Cambridge University Press, 1992.

Piaget, Jean. *Structuralism*. New York: Routledge & Kegan Paul, 1971.

Platz, Joan. "How Do You Turn STEM into STEAM? Add the Arts" *Columbus: Ohio Alliance for Arts Education*, 2007, 1–5.

"Processing Programming Environment," accessed December 20, 2021, https://processing.org/

Regelski, Thomas. "Reconnecting Music Education with Society." *Action, Criticism, and Theory for Music Education* 5, no. 2 (2006): 1–20.

"Scratch Programming Environment," accessed December 20, 2021, https://scratch.mit.edu/

Sinderson, Daniel. "PhaseMod Drone Synth," *Arduino Project Hub* (blog), 2021, https://create.arduino.cc/projecthub/scraptured/phasemod-drone-synth-w-arduino-nano-mozzi-7ab2ff.

Small, Christopher. *Music, Society, Education*. Hanover, NH: Wesleyan University Press, 1977.

Small, Christopher. *Musicking: The Meanings of Performing and Listening*. Hanover, NH: Wesleyan University Press, 1998.

Thibeault, Matthew D. and Julianne Evoy. "Building Your Own Musical Community: How YouTube, Miley Cyrus, and the Ukulele Can Create a New Kind of Ensemble." *General Music Today* 24, no. 3 (2011): 44–52.

Tomás, Enrique. "A Playful Approach to Teaching NIME: Pedagogical Methods from a Practice-Based Perspective," in *Proceedings of the International Conference on New Interfaces for Musical Expression*, 143–48. NIME, Birmingham, UK: NIME, 2020.

Upitis, Rena. "The Craft of Composition: Helping Children Create Music with Computer Tools." *Psychomusicology* 8, no. 2 (1990): 151–62.

Upitis, Rena. *This Too Is Music*. Portsmouth, NH: Heinemann Publishing, 1990.

Vulliamy, Graham and Ed Lee. *Pop, Rock and Ethnic Music in School.* Cambridge, England: Cambridge University Press, 1982.

Vygotsky, Lev S. *Mind and Society.* Cambridge, MA: Harvard University Press, 1978.

Wang, Ge and Perry R. Cook. "On-the-Fly Programming: Using Code as an Expressive Musical Instrument," in *Proceedings of the Conference on New Interfaces for Musical Expression,* 138–43. Hamamatsu, Japan: NIME, 2004.

Wang, Ge et al., "The Laptop Orchestra as Classroom," *Computer Music Journal* 32, no. 1 (2008): 26–37.

Williams, David A. "Another Perspective: The IPad Is a REAL Musical Instrument." *Music Educators Journal,* 101, no. 1 (2014): 93–98.

Woods, Peter J. "The Aesthetic Pedagogies of DIY Music," *Review of Education, Pedagogy, and Cultural Studies* 43, no. 4 (2021): 338–57.

Chapter 16

The Intimate Relationship between Technology and Music and Its Revolutionary Impact on Music Education

Renée Crawford

PRELUDE

From the invention of Gray's Musical Telegraph in 1874 to the immersive and interactive, augmented, virtual, and mixed-reality platforms of the 2000s, technology and music have always been intimately related. It is timely to discuss the revolutionary impact that technological change and innovation continue to have on music teaching and learning at a time when music education, schooling and learning are being redefined. Remote-learning capabilities have escalated through necessity, providing opportunities for educators, classrooms, and schools to be accessed offsite, in synchronous and asynchronous settings, removing the boundaries of time and space. The demands of society have dictated a valuing of generic skills sets and knowledge such as creative and critical thinking, concept-based curriculum, and innovative models of teaching and learning. At the center of this revolution is technology. Government and educational authorities have come to view technology as a catalyst of change and a driver of pedagogical development and learning enhancement. However, the question of what we teach, how, and why conjures further exploration about whether technological innovation drives pedagogy, societal expectations, and valued knowledge or whether it is, in fact, the other way around.

Long before the advent of digital technology, music has been at the forefront of technological advancement, with music educators harnessing its potential. Despite this, there continues to be disparity between the resources available to music teachers compared to other disciplines, including a misunderstanding of the teaching and learning potential of music. This chapter provides a brief historical context, highlighting revolutionary timepoints that align with specific technological advancements that have impacted music and in turn education. A pivotal timepoint will focus on the advent of the Musical Instrument Digital Interface (MIDI) in 1980–1983 and the resulting key developments. These discussions position music as an important inclusion of a holistic education and contemporary society.

TIMELINE AND INTERSECTIONS

Music, education, and the industries that support both have evolved and re-evolved as a result of intersections with technological innovation. The timeline sequence summarized below provides an international perspective about the pervasive influence of technology and its enduring effect on societal expectations, valued knowledge, and education. The timeline begins with American electrical engineer Elisha Gray's Musical Telegraph in 1874:

Timeline Sequence
   1874 Musical Telegraph—Elisha Gray—One of the earliest electric musical instruments using vibrating electromagnetic circuits that were single-note oscillators operated by a two-octave piano keyboard. Attributed to the origins of the modern music synthesizer.[1]
   1876 Telephone designs—Alexander Graham Bell—Electronic technologies later used in subsequent music technology.
   1877 Phonograph prototype—Thomas Edison and Emile Berliner—Simultaneously invented the prototype for the electric motor driven phonograph (1888) that would later be known as the gramophone.[2]
   1898 Telegraphone—Valdemar Poulsen—Significant contributions to early radio technology with the magnetic wire recorder and the first continuous wave radio transmitter (Poulsen arc transmitter-1903), which was used in some of the first broadcasting stations until the early 1920s.[3]
   1906 Telharmonium—Thaddeus Cahill—Early electrical organ (Dynamophone) considered to be the first electromechanical musical instrument, where the electrical signal was transmitted over wires and heard through horn speakers. Similar to the later Hammond organ, it used tonewheels to generate musical sounds as electrical signals by additive synthesis.[4]
   1912 Regenerative circuit—Edwin F. Armstrong—Making radio reception practical.
   1917 Theremin prototype—Leon Theremin—One of the first electronic musical instruments and the first to be mass produced. It is played without touching it, as it detects the proximity of the hands and was patented in 1928.[5]

1920 First commercial AM radio Broadcast made by KDKA, Pittsburgh, PA. Pittsburgh's Westinghouse Electric and Manufacturing Company transmitted the first scheduled broadcast (Nov. 2) where KDKA's Leo Rosenberg announced live returns of the Presidential election between Warren G. Harding and James Cox. Westinghouse obtained the first U.S. commercial broadcasting station license just one month prior, from the Department of Commerce's Bureau of Navigation.[6]

1924 Sphäraphon—Jörg Mager—The Electrophon (1921) was a simple monophonic instrument based on the same heterodyne principal as the Theremin, however, notes were instead triggered by rotating a metal handle, creating a glissando type effect on a continuous tone. A semicircular plate marked with chromatic scale intervals were located under the handle and changes in timbre could be applied through various filters. Further developments of the Electrophon lead to the Sphärophon named after the Pythagorean legend of the music of the spheres. Sphäraphon line of electronic instruments presented in 1926.[7]

1931 Stereo Sound—Alan Dower Blumlein—Invented at EMI's Central Research Laboratories, the patent for "Improvements in and relating to sound-transmission, sound-recording and sound-reproducing systems" contains 70 individual claims including the positioning of a pair of microphones, processing of sound from the microphones and equipment to record two channels into a single record groove. The beginning of stereo sound and recording, and completely revolutionised the music and audio-visual industries. The invention was so significant that he was awarded a posthumous Grammy by the Recording Academy in 2017 in recognition of his revolutionary work.[8]

1932 Cardioid ribbon microphone—Harry F. Olson—A device that converts sound energy into electrical energy. It forms the first element in a telephone, a broadcast transmitter, and all forms of electrical sound recording, sound reinforcement, and public address systems. Olsen's patents also include sound absorbers, and the first programmable music synthesizer. Responsible for two of the most famous ribbon microphones the RCA 44 and RCA 77.[9]

1933 FM radio—Edwin H. Armstrong—FM radio invented to reduce static and interference. Experimental Station WA2XMN authorized for experimental FM broadcasts in New Jersey.[10]

1934 Switching circuit—Akira Nakishima's—NEC engineer's switching circuit theory is the mathematical study of the properties of networks of idealized switches and laid the foundations for digital circuit design.

1935 Plastic-based magnetic tapes—BASF, Hammond Organ—Laurens Hammond and John Hanert First prepared by BASF. Type of electric organ manufactured by Hammond Organ Co., Chicago.[11]

1936 Hellertion—Bruno Helberger and Peter Lertes—Developed in Frankfurt, this electronic instrument was similar to the theremin, but with a guide keyboard and pedals to regulate volume and tone-quality. Capable of 4-part harmony, able to simulate human voice and some instruments with a range of almost 6 octaves. Played by pressure on 4 leather bands, which sets up a current.[12]

1938 War of the Worlds—Orson Welles, First director to use studio electronics, during his broadcast of War of the Worlds. When it aired on AM radio it caused mass panic when many listeners believed it was real.[13]

1939 Parallel Bandpass Vocoder—Homer W. Dudley—Dudley was a pioneering electronic and acoustic engineer who created the first electronic voice synthesizer for Bell Labs in the 1930s, which led the development of a method of sending secure voice transmissions during World War Two. Dudley invented the Parallel Bandpass Vocoder System for the artificial production of vocal or other sounds.[14]

1940 Voice Synthesizers—Karl Wagner early development of Voice Synthesizers. Homer W. Dudley introduced the Voder Speech Synthesizer. The Hammond Organ Company releases the Solovox.

1944 The Expression of Zaar—Halim El-Dabh, Rhodes Piano prototype—Harold Rhodes, El-Dabh produces the earliest piece of electroacoustic tape music.[15] First prototype, of the electric piano became popular in the 1970s. Generates sound with keys and hammers, that strike thin metal tines, instead of strings, which vibrate between an electromagnetic pickup to an external keyboard amplifier and speaker. The instrument evolved from Rhodes's attempt to manufacture pianos while teaching recovering soldiers during World War II.[16]

1948 Transistor—Bell Laboratories, Vinyl long-playing (LP) record—Columbia Records. First transistor revealed, a semiconductor device used to amplify or switch electronic signals and electrical power, which became the basic building block of modern electronics. Long-playing (LP) "microgroove" records were the same size as 78-rpm discs (12" in diameter), but played for a full 25 minutes a side instead of only four minutes. Many complete compositions could be heard without the irritation of frequently turning over or changing the record; gone too was the unacceptable physical bulk of recordings of longer works.[17]

1951 EQP-1—Pultec—First passive program equalizer introduced.

1952 RCA—Harry F. Olson and Herbert Belar—Invented the RCA Synthesizer.

1954 Pocket transistor radio—Regency—First portable pocket transistor radio powered by battery debuted.[18]

1955 Sel-Sync (Selective Synchronous Recording)—Ampex, Making audio overdubbing practical. Les Paul makes the first 8-track recordings using the "sel-sync" method in 1956.[19]

1957 ANS (Aleksandr Nikolayevich Skryabin) synthesizer—Evgeny Murzin—MUSIC program—Max Mathews—A photoelectronic musical instrument created by Russian engineer from 1938 to 1957. The technological basis of his invention was the method of graphical sound recording used in cinematography (developed concurrently with US), which made it possible to obtain a visible image of a sound wave, as well as to realize the opposite goal, synthesizing a sound from an artificially drawn sound spectrogram. A similar graphical score was used in the legendary UPIC computer system developed by Iannis Xenakis in 1977. A second model of the ANS was built in 1963–5 and used by composers such as Aleksandr Nemtin, Andrey Volkonsky, Alfred Shnitke, Sofia Gubajdulina, Edison Denisov, Eduard Artemyev, and Stanislav Krejchi. It was praised by Shostakovich, renowned for his condemnatory remarks about electronic music. It was popular for film music, notably used in the score for the science fiction film Solaris (1971) by Eduard Artem'yev.[20] One of computer music's greatest pioneers had his earliest achievement writing the MUSIC program (at Bell Labs—US), used to create a 17 second piece performed in New York on an IBM 704 computer.[21]

1958 Stereo disk recordings—Audio Fidelity, Integrated circuit - Jack Kilby—First commercial stereo disk recordings produced by Audio Fidelity.[22] Implementation of a particular electronic-circuit function in which all the individual devices required to realize the function are fabricated on a single chip of semiconductor, usually silicon. The individual devices normally consist of semiconductor diodes, transistors, and resistors.[23]

1959 The Sideman—Wurlitzer, Oramics—Daphne Oram—First commercial electro-mechanical drum machine. Musician Oram develops a programming technique known as Oramics. The Oramics system is a photoelectric digital/analogue composition machine that gives the composer control of subtle nuances in all parameters (amplitude, envelope shaping, rhythm, timbre control, microtonal pitch, and vibrato).[24] Oram converted the Oramics system to RISC computer technology in the 1990s, suitable for composers to use at home.

1960 Univox, Modern electric guitar—A range of tube amplifiers, electric guitars, and keyboards produced initially in New York by Unicord (1960s). Korg produced about 1971 synthesizers and effects boxes added to the Univox line. Early keyboards were manufactured in Italy by Crucianelli. "Manufacture of Univox guitars was moved to the Matsumoko guitar factory in Japan (1975) and introduced the new line Westbury (1978).[25] Many Univox products were copies of other manufacturers' and the brand did not have a reputation for quality or innovation, although their effects pedals were well regarded. Both the Super Fuzz pedal used by Pete Townshend and the Univibe made famous by Jimi Hendrix are now collector's items. Univox also distributed Korg and Marshall products in the US. The line ended when Unicord was purchased by Korg in 1985."[26]

1961 Standard FM stereo broadcasting—The Commission—Standard FM stereo broadcasting method authorized. The transmission of significant broadcasts followed, such as, the march on Washington (August 28, 1963) when Martin Luther King Jr.'s "I Have a Dream" speech was broadcast by hundreds of radio stations, and when Apollo 11 landed on the Moon (July 20 1969), millions of listeners heard Neil Armstrong say "one small step for man, one giant leap for mankind".[27]

1963 DA-20—Keio Electronics, Compact Cassette—Phillips—Keio Electronics (later Korg) produce an early drum machine. Compact Cassette tape format introduced.

1964 SynKet—Paul Ketoff, R-1 Rhythm Ace—Ikutaro Kakehashi, Paul Ketoff, active in film music recording and in contact with composers interested in electronics, designed the portable (John Eaton inspired) synthesizer SynKet. It was tube-based, non-modular, and largely pre-wired. Sound was generated by three square-wave oscillators and a white-noise generator, and external sources could be introduced. Although never factory-produced, Ketoff constructed a few customized exemplars for composers who requested them, among them Walter Branchi, Egisto Macchi, and Ennio Morricone.[28] The first electronic drum machine and later developed FR-1 Rhythm Ace (1967), the first electronic drum machine to enter popular music.

1965 Moog Sythnesizer—Robert Moog—American engineer developed the modular synthesizer, which revolutionized electronic music and computing by speeding up the process, no longer requiring the assembling and splicing small sections of tape.[29] Provided more practical and affordable electronic music equipment, guided by suggestions and requests from composers including Herb Deutsch, Richard Teitelbaum, Vladimir Ussachevsky, and Wendy Carlos. Moog's principal innovation was the voltage-controlled oscillator to control pitch and fundamental synthesizer concepts such as, modularity, and envelope generators. Numerous models of the first commercial synthesizer were produced (1965–1981), credited for the analog synthesizer as it is known today. Carlos' 1969 'Switched-on Bach' recording demonstrated the synthesizer's capacity to perform classical repertoire, developing its reputation as a serious instrument, and its popularity.[30] Most Moog synthesizers were owned by universities or record labels, used to create soundtracks or jingles. Early use in rock music include the Monkees *Pisces, Aquarius, Capricorn & Jones Ltd.*, and the Doors song *Strange Days* in 1967, George Harrison's *Electronic Sound*, and the Beatles *Abbey Road* in 1969. Also adopted by jazz musicians including Herbie Hancock, Jan Hammer, and Sun Ra. In the 1970s, it became ubiquitous as part of progressive rock bands such as Yes, Tangerine Dream, and Emerson, Lake and Palmer. Keith Emerson was the first major rock musician to perform live with the Moog, a trademark of his performances. In later decades, hip-hop groups (e.g., Beastie Boys) and rock bands (e.g., They Might Be Giants and Wilco) revived interest in early Moog synthesizer timbres.[31]

1967 First PCM recorder—NHK—Pulse-code modulation (PCM), a method to digitally represent sampled analog signals. It is the standard form of digital audio in computers, compact discs, digital telephony and other digital audio applications.[32]

1968 Single-chip microprocessor Tadashi Sasaki, Shin-ei's Uni-Vibe—Fumio Mieda, Dub music—Osbourne Ruddock (King Tubby)—Sharp engineer conceives single-chip computer processor. An effects pedal with phase shift and chorus effects. Jamaican sound engineer pioneers early form of popular electronic music that developed from 1960s–1970s Reggae.

1969 Technics SP-10—Shuichi Obata—Matsushita engineer Shuichi Obata invents first direct-drive turntable.

1971 4004—Masatoshi Shima and Federico Faggin—Busicom's Shima and Intel's Faggin complete the first commercial microprocessor.

1973 Wireless telephone call—Motorola, Yamaha GX-1. Motorola made the first public wireless telephone call.[33] Yamaha release the first polyphonic synthesizer.[34]

1974 Digital synthesizer—Yamaha—First synthesizer that uses digital signal processing (DSP) techniques to make musical sounds. Some emulate analog synthesizers and others include sampling capability in addition to digital synthesis.[35]

1976 CE-1 Chorus Ensemble—Boss—Boss, a Roland subsidiary, release the first chorus pedal.

1977 Apple II, Sord M200, Lkit-16—Apple founder Steve Jobs introduces Apple II, an early home computer. Sord Computer Corporation introduces an early home computer. Panafacom releases an early 16-bit microcomputer.

1978 CR-78—Roland—First microprocessor-driven drum machine.

1980 Flash memory—Fujio Masuoka, TR-808—Roland, DCB protocol and DIN interface to use with TR-808 - Roland, GS-1—Yamaha Electronic non-volatile computer memory storage medium that can be electrically erased and reprogrammed invented at Toshiba. Roland releases the most widely used drum machine in popular music. Roland introduces DCB protocol (data interchange interface) and DIN interface (also called Sync24, is a synchronization interface for electronic musical instruments, later superseded by MIDI). First FM (Frequency modular synthesis) digital synthesizer.[36]

1981 VL-1—Casio, TB-303—Roland, Conceives MIDI—Ikutaro Kakehashi, LMD-649—Toshiba, IBM PC—First commercial digital synthesizer.[37] A bass synthesizer that lays the foundations for acid house music. MIDI (Musical Instrument Digital Interface) conceived by Roland founder, is a revolutionary technical standard that entails a communications protocol, digital interface, and electrical connectors that connect a wide variety of electronic musical instruments, computers, and related audio devices for playing, editing, and recording music. First PCM digital sampler introduced by Toshiba. A 16-bit personal computer introduced by IBM.[38]

1982 Compact disc—Sony and Phillips, Jupiter-6 and Prophet 600—Roland, Commodore 64 Launched CD introduced that moves away from vinyl records. First MIDI synthesizers released, Roland Jupiter-6, and Prophet 600.[39] 8-bit home computer introduced by Commodore International.

1983 Introduction of MIDI—MSQ-700—Roland, TR-909—Roland, MC-202—Roland, DX7—Yamaha Unveiled by Roland's Ikutaro Kakehashi and Sequential Circuits' Dave Smith (American engineer and musician). First MIDI sequencer, using a conventional MIDI keyboard to input and anchor notes it works with a computer program and hardware that allows a composer to arrange a sequence or sequences of musical notes as continuous loops or on receipt of a trigger event.[40] First MIDI drum machine, an electronic musical instrument that creates percussion sounds, drum beats, and patterns. First groovebox, a self-contained digital musical instrument for the production of live, loop-based electronic music providing a high degree of user control facilitating improvisation. First commercially successful digital synthesizer.

1984 Macintosh computer—Apple Inc.—Apple markets the Macintosh computer.

1986 Digital consoles—Electronic device used to combine, route, and change the dynamics, equalization and other properties of multiple audio input signals, using digital signal processing rather than analog circuitry. Although its origins can be traced back to the 1970s, the first digital consoles appeared in 1986, which contributed significantly to professional audio.[41]

1989 Sound Tools—Digidesign—Cubase—Steinberg, Digidesign founders Evan Brooks and Peter Gotcher unveiled Sound Tools, Mac-based (SE or Mac II) 2-track digital recording/editing system. Offering outboard converters, Sound Designer II software cost $3,995.[42] Digital audio workstation (DAW) developed for music and MIDI recording, arranging and editing. The first version was a MIDI sequencer for Atari ST computer. Introduced the concept of the 'arrange page' with a vertical list of tracks and horizontal timeline, a design that quickly became the standard interface for all commercially developed sequencers and music software developers.[43]

The use of technology and its applications in the world have evolved considerably since Edison announced to the world his invention for recording and replicating sound. A plethora of inventions have emerged (notably computers and digital circuitry), which have not only revolutionized many people's lives but also had a significant impact on the development of music, performance, composition, and music education (including analogue synthesizer technology, such as the Theremin, the electric guitar, the tape recorder, and the MIDI protocol).[44] Discussion about technology and its impact on education will undoubtedly comprise varying philosophical viewpoints. Using the timeline presented in the Timeline sequence as a foundation, two questions are considered: "How has technological development and innovation impacted music education?" and "Why is the advent of MIDI and the arrival of the computer post-1980 a revolutionary timepoint?"

THE ADVENT OF MIDI AND THE ARRIVAL OF THE COMPUTER, POST 1980

Change dictated by innovation is multifaceted and to some degree business-driven. Despite the storylines that point to technological advancement as an end goal to commercialization or conversely an industry response to efficiency and more cost-effective measures, a broader perspective is required when thinking about its impact on education and music education. The development of MIDI as an industry standard communications protocol for the control of synthesizers and its later connection and application to computers fundamentally changed the working environment for the music industry and commercial sector.[45] This was a technological revolution that also presented encouraging prospects for both teaching and learning. With hindsight, this innovation did change the platform for music making and sharing practices, which continue to evolve. However, they were not intended to replace the expert music teacher or be viewed as a panacea for all pedagogical and curriculum issues.[46] Despite early adoption by some music educators, in Australia, there remained varying degrees of resistance to the use of digital technology in secondary school programs.[47] Similar to other international studies at the time, primary factors relating to technology hesitancy included a fear of being replaced by technology, lack of confidence and technological literacy, minimal opportunities for professional development, and a lack of resources.[48,49] It soon became an expectation that educators would embed technological tools into their learning tasks and classroom activities.

Many teachers began using digital technology modestly and in ways for teaching and learning practices that could occur without the use of technology.[50] Music, teaching, and learning practices were entrenched with music traditions, pedagogies, and knowledge (e.g., Western art music notation), which were valued as core curricula and central to music education. Digital technology was used very simplistically (e.g., utilizing drill-and-practice programs to develop aural skills, to write a score neatly) to enhance traditional pedagogy rather than to explore music-making and creative possibilities. This signified the beginning of the "teacher as a technician" debate, which impacted initial teacher education courses and professional development and learning as emphasis was placed on developing competent technicians, teachers who could use computers and music technology.[51]

Approaches for how to use MIDI and computers in education emerged from becoming more cost-effective and accessible. In the United States, music technology and computers were used frequently in the classroom setting for intensive skill development. Computer-Aided Instruction (CAI) was considered a highly structured learning environment that used simulated and guided instruction.[52] Contrastingly, Computer-Aided Learning (CAL) was used in the classroom setting in the United Kingdom, where creativity and independent learning were valued in the curriculum.[53] This was considered a less skill-intensive approach used for student engagement and interest and suitable for general music classes where problem-solving was encouraged (a critical thinking approach to creativity). The values and expectations driving the principles that underpin these approaches for using technology in music education reflected the ways that different societies engaged with technology. Although there appeared to be a distinct polarity between the two positions in the United States and the United Kingdom, given the inherent interactive nature of technology, some crossover was evident, including its approach in countries such as Australia where educators often used elements of both CAL and CAI.[54] The evolution of these principle ideas has in part developed the confidence of music educators to incorporate technology in music education as a means of making real-life connections and providing authentic learning contexts. To improve student learning outcomes, it is imperative that there is an understanding of authentic learning practice, requiring

> a holistic view of the ways young people interact in their multifaceted or multidimensional everyday lives be introduced in the way teaching and learning is approached. This includes encouraging an interchangeable environment for experiential learning. Creating authentic learning situations for students to gain vocational experience and knowledge . . . to tie school music to professional music practice via technology and music technology.[55]

These ideas are encapsulated within a multidimensional/nonlinear teaching and learning model, which through the lens of constructivism, relies on the critical interrelated links between valued knowledge and societal expectations, authentic and real-life learning contexts, and technology.[56] This model introduced the notion of a holistic perspective and practice of learning and is used widely, particularly in Australia, as the basis for music pedagogy, curriculum, and lesson development (e.g., 2021 Development of Numeracy Across the Curriculum Resources Project, Department of Education and Training).

RECENT DEVELOPMENTS AND PEDAGOGICAL IMPLICATIONS

The use of technology in education has challenged, reshaped and redefined pedagogy and curriculum, including a reconsideration of the principles and purposes of music teaching and learning. Contemporary times have amplified many of these persistent challenges as the necessity for remote synchronous and asynchronous learning has become prevalent. Ensuring that the use of technology in music continues to provide opportunities for authentic learning that explore experiential and creative endeavors has never been more important. In music, what is valued as knowledge and how that is practiced should remain central to the considerations for how technology should be embedded. Some decades ago, Reimer stated the importance of musical performance as a central role in music education.[57] The practical and music-making aspect of the discipline remains as important today as it did when this was first posed. So the question perhaps becomes how can technology be harnessed to enhance these fundamental elements of music teaching and learning, particularly in the current Covid-19 climate. Redefining the nature and value of music in a multidimensional and paraxial frame is a useful starting point.[58,59] This requires a balanced approach to practical and theoretical music knowledge and skill development. It is suggested that this balance and multidimensionality that enhances teaching and learning in music can be achieved with technology.[60] A recent research project provides a successful example of this in practice where authentic music teaching and learning experiences and opportunities were delivered to students in remote and rural Australian schools.[61] In this regard music is a practical subject that was leading the way in technological innovation for education long before remote education became an absolute necessity.

Despite such technological advancement and progressive thinking, practical subjects such as music and the performing arts continue to be placed lower on the curriculum priority list, overlooked by government and educational authorities in favor of Science, technology, Engineering, Mathematics (STEM) and English. This trend predates the "back to basics" neoliberal movement that fuelled the seminal 1983 U.S. Report a Nation at Risk.[62] Even the revolutionary development of MIDI at this time was no match for the rhetoric that continues to haunt music educators around the world. It is clear that in the current climate, societal expectations and valued knowledge drives pedagogy and that technology provides the platform for which to practice teaching and learning. In a different time, this discussion would be very different, and a reciprocal relationship between technology and pedagogy as influenced by societal expectations and valued knowledge would be expected. There is evidence of this in the emergent approaches of CAL and CAI and to some degree in the historical timeline. Although technology is widely accepted as a catalyst of change and a driver of pedagogical development and learning enhancement, for educators, the question of what we teach, how, and why should remain a key focus. This has never been more relevant as the global society embarks on a time when nothing is certain and the unpredictable implications on teaching and learning are ever-present and rapidly evolving. Important aesthetic, cultural, and well-being experiences provided by the intrinsic and extrinsic benefits that music and performing

Table 16.1 Timeline of Key Technological Advancements Impacting Music Performance, Composition, Production, Consumption, and Distribution

Date	Technological innovation	Contribution to Music
1874	Musical Telegraph—Elisha Gray	One of the earliest electric musical instruments using vibrating electromagnetic circuits that were single-note oscillators operated by a two-octave piano keyboard. Attributed to the origins of the modern music synthesizer.[1]
1876	Telephone designs—Alexander Graham Bell	Electronic technologies later used in subsequent music technology.
1877	Phonograph prototype—Thomas Edison and Emile Berliner	Simultaneously invented the prototype for the electric motor-driven phonograph (1888) that would later be known as the gramophone.[2]
1898	Telegraphone—Valdemar Poulsen	Significant contributions to early radio technology (Poulsen arc transmitter—1903), which was used in first continuous wave radio transmitter with the magnetic wire recorder and the some of the first broadcasting stations until the early 1920s.[3]
1906	Telharmonium—Thaddeus Cahill	Early electrical organ (Dynamophone) considered to be the first electromechanical musical instrument, where the electrical signal was transmitted over wires and heard through horn speakers. Similar to the later Hammond organ, it used tonewheels to generate musical sounds as electrical signals by additive synthesis.[4]
1912	Regenerative circuit—Edwin F. Armstrong	Making radio reception practical.
1917	Theremin prototype—Leon Theremin	One of the first electronic musical instruments and the first to be mass produced. It is played without touching it, as it detects the proximity of the hands and was patented in 1928.[5]
1920	First commercial AM radio Broadcast made by KDKA, Pittsburgh, PA.	Pittsburgh's Westinghouse Electric and Manufacturing Company transmitted the first scheduled broadcast (November 2), where KDKA's Leo Rosenberg announced live returns of the presidential election between Warren G. Harding and James Cox. Westinghouse obtained the first U.S. commercial broadcasting station license just one month prior, from the Department of Commerce's Bureau of Navigation.[6]

Year	Innovation	Description
1924	Sphäraphon—Jörg Mager	The Electrophon (1921) was a simple monophonic instrument based on the same heterodyne principal as the Theremin; however, notes were instead triggered by rotating a metal handle, creating a glissando type effect on a continuous tone. A semicircular plate marked with chromatic scale intervals were located under the handle and changes in timbre could be applied through various filters. Further developments of the electrophon lead to the Sphäraphon named after the Pythagorean legend of the music of the spheres. Sphäraphon line of electronic instruments presented in 1926.[7]
1931	Stereo Sound—Alan Dower Blumlein	Invented at EMI's Central Research Laboratories, the patent for "Improvements in and relating to sound-transmission, sound-recording and sound-reproducing systems" contains seventy individual claims including the positioning of a pair of microphones, processing of sound from the microphones, and equipment to record two channels into a single record groove. The beginning of stereo sound and recording, and completely revolutionized the music and audiovisual industries. The invention was so significant that he was awarded a posthumous Grammy by the Recording Academy in 2017 in recognition of his revolutionary work.[8]
1932	Cardioid ribbon microphone—Harry F. Olson	A device that converts sound energy into electrical energy. It forms the first element in a telephone, a broadcast transmitter, and all forms of electrical sound recording, sound reinforcement, and public address systems. Olsen's patents also include sound absorbers, and the first programmable music synthesizer. Responsible for two of the most famous ribbon microphones the RCA 44 and RCA 77.[9]
1933	FM radio - Edwin H. Armstrong	FM radio invented to reduce static and interference. Experimental Station WA2XMN authorized for experimental FM broadcasts in New Jersey.[10]
1934	Switching circuit—Akira Nakishima's	NEC engineer's switching circuit theory is the mathematical study of the properties of networks of idealized switches and laid the foundations for digital circuit design.
1935	Plastic-based magnetic tapes—BASF	First prepared by BASF.
	Hammond Organ—Laurens Hammond and John Hanert	Type of electric organ manufactured by Hammond Organ Co., Chicago.[11]
1936	Hellertion—Bruno Helberger and Peter Lertes.	Developed in Frankfurt, this electronic instrument was similar to the theremin, but with a guide keyboard and pedals to regulate volume and tone-quality. Capable of four-part harmony, able to simulate human voice and some instruments with a range of almost six octaves. Played by pressure on four leather bands, which sets up a current.[12]

(Continued)

Table 16.1 (Continued)

Date	Technological innovation	Contribution to Music
1938	War of the Worlds—Orson Welles,	First director to use studio electronics, during his broadcast of war of the worlds. When it aired on AM radio, it caused mass panic when many listeners believed it was real.[13]
1939	Parallel Bandpass Vocoder—Homer W. Dudley	Dudley was a pioneering electronic and acoustic engineer who created the first electronic voice synthesizer for Bell Labs in the 1930s, which led the development of a method of sending secure voice transmissions during World War II. Dudley invented the Parallel Bandpass Vocoder System for the artificial production of vocal or other sounds.[14]
1940	Voice Synthesizers	Karl Wagner early development of Voice Synthesizers. Homer W. Dudley introduced the Voder Speech Synthesizer. The Hammond Organ Company releases the Solovox.
1944	The Expression of Zaar—Halim El-Dabh, Rhodes Piano prototype—Harold Rhodes	El-Dabh produces the earliest piece of electroacoustic tape music.[15] First prototype, of the electric piano became popular in the 1970s. Generates sound with keys and hammers that strike thin metal tines, instead of strings, which vibrate between an electromagnetic pickup to an external keyboard amplifier and speaker. The instrument evolved from Rhodes's attempt to manufacture pianos while teaching recovering soldiers during World War II.[16]
1948	Transistor—Bell Laboratories Vinyl long-playing (LP) record—Columbia Records	First transistor revealed, a semiconductor device used to amplify, or switch electronic signals and electrical power, which became the basic building block of modern electronics. Long-playing (LP) "microgroove" records were the same size as 78-rpm discs (12" in diameter), but played for a full 25 minutes a side instead of only 4 minutes. Many complete compositions could be heard without the irritation of frequently turning over or changing the record; gone too was the unacceptable physical bulk of recordings of longer works.[17]
1951	EQP-1—Pultec	First passive program equalizer introduced.
1952	RCA—Harry F. Olson and Herbert Belar	Invented the RCA synthesizer.
1954	Pocket transistor radio—Regency	First portable pocket transistor radio powered by battery debuted.[18]
1955	Sel-Sync (Selective Synchronous Recording)—Ampex	Making audio overdubbing practical. Les Paul makes the first 8-track recordings using the "sel-sync" method in 1956.[19]

1957	ANS (Aleksandr Nikolayevich Skryabin) synthesizer—Evgeny Murzin, MUSIC program—Max Mathews	A photoelectronic musical instrument created by Russian engineer from 1938 to 1957. The technological basis of his invention was the method of graphical sound recording used in cinematography (developed concurrently with United States), which made it possible to obtain a visible image of a sound wave, as well as to realize the opposite goal, synthesizing a sound from an artificially drawn sound spectrogram. A similar graphical score was used in the legendary UPIC computer system developed by Iannis Xenakis in 1977. A second model of the ANS was built in 1963–65 and used by composers such as Aleksandr Nemtin, Andrey Volkonsky, Alfred Shnitke, Sofia Gubajdulina, Edison Denisov, Eduard Artemyev, and Stanislav Krejchi. It was praised by Shostakovich, renowned for his condemnatory remarks about electronic music. It was popular for film music, notably used in the score for the science fiction film Solaris (1971) by Eduard Artem'yev.[20] One of computer music's greatest pioneers had his earliest achievement writing the MUSIC program (at Bell Labs–United States), used to create a 17 second piece performed in New York on an IBM 704 computer.[21]
1958	Stereo disk recordings—Audio Fidelity, Integrated circuit—Jack Kilby	First commercial stereo disk recordings produced by Audio Fidelity.[22] Implementation of a particular electronic-circuit function in which all the individual devices required to realize the function are fabricated on a single chip of semiconductor, usually silicon. The individual devices normally consist of semiconductor diodes, transistors, and resistors.[23]
1959	The Sideman—Wurlitzer, Oramics—Daphne Oram	First commercial electro-mechanical drum machine. Musician Oram develops a programming technique known as Oramics. The Oramics system is a photoelectric digital/analogue composition machine that gives the composer control of subtle nuances in all parameters (amplitude, envelope shaping, rhythm, timbre control, microtonal pitch, and vibrato).[24] Oram converted the Oramics system to RISC computer technology in the 1990s, suitable for composers to use at home.

(Continued)

302 Renée Crawford

Table 16.1 (Continued)

Date	Technological innovation	Contribution to Music
1960	Univox, Modern electric guitar	A range of tube amplifiers, electric guitars, and keyboards produced initially in New York by Unicord (1960s). Korg produced about 1971 synthesizers and effects boxes added to the Univox line. Early keyboards were manufactured in Italy by Crucianelli. "Manufacture of Univox guitars was moved to the Matsumoko guitar factory in Japan (1975) and introduced the new line Westbury (1978)."[25] Many Univox products were copies of other manufacturers and the brand did not have a reputation for quality or innovation, although their effects pedals were well regarded. Both the Super Fuzz pedal used by Pete Townshend and the Univibe made famous by Jimi Hendrix are now collector's items. Univox also distributed Korg and Marshall products in the United States. The line ended when Unicord was purchased by Korg in 1985."[26]
1961	Standard FM stereo broadcasting—The Commission	Standard FM stereo broadcasting method authorized. The transmission of significant broadcasts followed, such as the march on Washington (August 28, 1963) when Martin Luther King Jr.'s "I Have a Dream" speech was broadcast by hundreds of radio stations, and when Apollo 11 landed on the Moon (July 20, 1969), millions of listeners heard Neil Armstrong say "one small step for man, one giant leap for mankind."[27]
1963	DA-20—Keio Electronics, Compact Cassette—Phillips	Keio Electronics (later Korg) produce an early drum machine. Compact Cassette tape format introduced.
1964	SynKet—Paul Ketoff, R-1 Rhythm Ace—Ikutaro Kakehashi	Paul Ketoff, active in film music recording and in contact with composers interested in electronics, designed the portable (John Eaton inspired) synthesizer SynKet. It was tube-based, nonmodular, and largely prewired. Sound was generated by three square-wave oscillators and a white-noise generator, and external sources could be introduced. Although never factory-produced, Ketoff constructed a few customized exemplars for composers who requested them, among them Walter Branchi, Egisto Macchi, and Ennio Morricone.[28] The first electronic drum machine and later developed FR-1 Rhythm Ace (1967), the first electronic drum machine to enter popular music.

Year	Innovation	Description
1965	Moog Synthesizer—Robert Moog	American engineer developed the modular synthesizer, which revolutionized electronic music and computing by speeding up the process, no longer requiring the assembling and splicing small sections of tape.[29] Provided more practical and affordable electronic music equipment, guided by suggestions and requests from composers including Herb Deutsch, Richard Teitelbaum, Vladimir Ussachevsky, and Wendy Carlos. Moog's principal innovation was the voltage-controlled oscillator to control pitch and fundamental synthesizer concepts, such as modularity and envelope generators. Numerous models of the first commercial synthesizer were produced (1965–1981), credited for the analog synthesizer as it is known today. Carlos' 1969 "Switched-on Bach" recording demonstrated the synthesizer's capacity to perform classical repertoire, developing its reputation as a serious instrument, and its popularity.[30] Most Moog synthesizers were owned by universities or record labels, used to create soundtracks or jingles. Early use in rock music include the Monkees *Pisces, Aquarius, Capricorn & Jones Ltd.*, and the Doors song *Strange Days* in 1967, George Harrison's *Electronic Sound*, and the Beatles *Abbey Road* in 1969. Also adopted by jazz musicians including Herbie Hancock, Jan Hammer, and Sun Ra. In the 1970s, it became ubiquitous as part of progressive rock bands such as Yes, Tangerine Dream, and Emerson, Lake & Palmer. Keith Emerson was the first major rock musician to perform live with the Moog, a trademark of his performances. In later decades, hip-hop groups (e.g., Beastie Boys) and rock bands (e.g., They Might Be Giants and Wilco) revived interest in early Moog synthesizer timbres.[31]
1967	First PCM recorder—NHK	Pulse-code modulation (PCM), a method to digitally represent sampled analog signals. It is the standard form of digital audio in computers, compact discs, digital telephony, and other digital audio applications.[32]
1968	Single-chip microprocessor Tadashi Sasaki, Shin-ei's Uni-Vibe—Fumio Mieda, Dub music—Osbourne Ruddock (King Tubby)	Sharp engineer conceives single-chip computer processor. An effects pedal with phase shift and chorus effects. Jamaican sound engineer pioneers early form of popular electronic music that developed from 1960s–1970s Reggae.
1969	Technics SP-10—Shuichi Obata	Matsushita engineer Shuichi Obata invents first direct-drive turntable.

(*Continued*)

Table 16.1 (Continued)

Date	Technological innovation	Contribution to Music
1971	4004—Masatoshi Shima and Federico Faggin	Busicom's Shima and Intel's Faggin complete the first commercial microprocessor.
1973	Wireless telephone call—Motorola	Motorola made the first public wireless telephone call.[33]
	Yamaha GX-1	Yamaha release the first polyphonic synthesizer.[34]
1974	Digital synthesizer—Yamaha	First synthesizer that uses digital signal processing (DSP) techniques to make musical sounds. Some emulate analog synthesizers and others include sampling capability in addition to digital synthesis.[35]
1976	CE-1 Chorus Ensemble—Boss	Boss, a Roland subsidiary, release the first chorus pedal.
1977	Apple II,	Apple founder Steve Jobs introduces Apple II, an early home computer.
	Sord M200	Sord Computer Corporation introduces an early home computer.
	Lkit-16	Panafacom releases an early 16-bit microcomputer.
1978	CR-78—Roland	First microprocessor-driven drum machine.
1980	Flash memory—Fujio Masuoka,	Electronic nonvolatile computer memory storage medium that can be electrically erased and reprogrammed invented at Toshiba.
	TR-808—Roland,	Roland releases the most widely used drum machine in popular music.
	DCB protocol and DIN interface to use with TR-808—Roland,	Roland introduces DCB protocol (data interchange interface) and DIN interface (also called Sync24, is a synchronization interface for electronic musical instruments, later superseded by MIDI).
	GS-1—Yamaha	First FM (Frequency modular synthesis) digital synthesizer.[36]
1981	VL-1—Casio,	First commercial digital synthesizer.[37]
	TB-303—Roland,	A bass synthesizer that lays the foundations for acid house music.
	Conceives MIDI—Ikutaro Kakehashi,	MIDI (Musical Instrument Digital Interface) conceived by Roland founder, is a revolutionary technical standard that entails a communications protocol, digital interface, and electrical connectors that connect a wide variety of electronic musical instruments, computers, and related audio devices for playing, editing, and recording music.
	LMD-649—Toshiba,	First PCM digital sampler introduced by Toshiba.
	IBM PC	A 16-bit personal computer introduced by IBM.[38]

Year	Technology	Description
1982	Compact disc—Sony and Phillips, Jupiter-6 and Prophet 600—Roland, Commodore 64 Launched	CD introduced that moves away from vinyl records. First MIDI synthesizers released, Roland Jupiter-6 and Prophet 600.[39] 8-bit home computer introduced by Commodore International.
1983	Introduction of MIDI MSQ-700—Roland, TR-909—Roland, MC-202—Roland, DX7—Yamaha	Unveiled by Roland's Ikutaro Kakehashi and Sequential Circuits' Dave Smith (American engineer and musician). First MIDI sequencer, using a conventional MIDI keyboard to input and anchor notes it works with a computer program and hardware that allows a composer to arrange a sequence or sequences of musical notes as continuous loops or on receipt of a trigger event.[40] First MIDI drum machine, an electronic musical instrument that creates percussion sounds, drumbeats, and patterns. First groovebox, a self-contained digital musical instrument for the production of live, loop-based electronic music providing a high degree of user control facilitating improvisation. First commercially successful digital synthesizer.
1984	Macintosh computer—Apple	Apple markets the Macintosh computer.
1986	Digital consoles	Electronic device used to combine, route, and change the dynamics, equalization and other properties of multiple audio input signals, using digital signal processing rather than analog circuitry. Although its origins can be traced back to the 1970s, the first digital consoles appeared in 1986, which contributed significantly to professional audio.[41]
1989	Sound Tools—Digidesign Cubase—Steinberg	Digidesign founders Evan Brooks and Peter Gotcher unveiled Sound Tools, Mac-based (SE or Mac II) two-track digital recording/editing system. Offering outboard converters, Sound Designer II software cost $3,995.[42] Digital audio workstation (DAW) developed for music and MIDI recording, arranging and editing. The first version was a MIDI sequencer for Atari ST computer. Introduced the concept of the "arrange page" with a vertical list of tracks and horizontal timeline, a design that quickly became the standard interface for all commercially developed sequencers and music software developers.[43]

[1] Thom Holmes, "Early Synthesizers and Experimenters," in *Electronic and Experimental Music* (Routledge, 2008), 159–90.
[2] John Borwick, and Lewis Foreman, "Recording and reproduction," in *The Oxford Companion to Music*, ed. Alison Latham (Oxford University Press, 2011), https://www.oxfordreference.com/view/10.1093/acref/9780199579037.001.0001/acref-9780199579037-e-5534

[3] Thompson, John Michael Tutill, ed. *Visions of the future: physics and electronics*. Cambridge University Press, 2001, 140.
[4] Reynold Weidenaar, "The First Telharmonium and its Origins," in *Magic Music from the Telharmonium* (Scarecrow Press, 1995), 1–49.
[5] Ann Warde, "Theremin: Ether Music and Espionage by Albert Glinsky," *Computer Music Journal* 26, no. 3 (2002): 84–86.
[6] "History of Commercial Radio," Federal Communications Commission, accessed September 8, 2021, https://www.fcc.gov/media/radio/history-of-commercial-radio
[7] Warde, "Theremin: Albert Glinsky," 84–86.
[8] "Inventor of Stereo Sound Alan Dower Blumlein's World-Changing 1931 Patent Celebrated as Part of the UK Government's 'GREAT for Imagination' Campaign," *EMI Archive Trust*, accessed September 8, 2021, https://www.emiarchivetrust.org/inventor-of-stereo-sound-alan-dower-blumleins-world-changing-1931-patent-celebrated-as-part-of-the-uk-governments-great-for-imagination-campaign/
[9] Andrew Butterfield and John Szymanski. "Microphone," in *A Dictionary of Electronics and Electrical Engineering* (Oxford University Press, 2018). https://www.oxfordreference.com/view/10.1093/acref/9780198725725.001.0001/acref-9780198725725-e-2982.
[10] "History of Commercial Radio," Federal Communications Commission.
[11] Alfred Corbin, *The Third Element: A Brief History of Electronics* (AuthorHouse, 2006), 1–252.
[12] "Hellertion," Oxford Reference, accessed September 8, 2021, https://www.oxfordreference.com/view/10.1093/oi/authority.20110803095929452
[13] "History of Commercial Radio," Federal Communications Commission.
[14] Lawrence J. Raphael, Gloria J. Borden, and Katherine S. Harris. *Speech Science Primer: Physiology, Acoustics, And Perception of Speech*, 23 (Lippincott Williams & Wilkins, 2011), 1–416.
[15] Thom Holmes, "Early Synthesizers and Experimenters."
[16] Alan Lenhoff, and David Robertson, *Classic Keys: Keyboard Sounds That Launched Rock Music* (University of North Texas Press, 2019), 1–416.
[17] Borwick, and Foreman, "Recording and reproduction."
[18] "History of Commercial Radio," Federal Communications Commission.
[19] John Borwick, *Sound Recording Practice*. 4th ed. (Oxford University Press, 1996), 1–624.
[20] Hugh Davies and Andrei Smirnov. "ANS," in *The Grove Dictionary of Musical Instruments* (Oxford University Press, 2014), https://www.oxfordreference.com/view/10.1093/acref/9780199743391.001.0001/acref-9780199743391-e-230.
[21] "A brief history of computer music." *Musicradar*, accessed September 10, 2021. https://www.musicradar.com/news/tech/a-brief-history-of-computer-music-177299
[22] Borwick, and Foreman, "Recording and reproduction."
[23] "Integrated circuit," *Oxford Reference*, accessed September 9, 2021, https://www.oxfordreference.com/view/10.1093/oi/authority.20110803100005927
[24] Hugh Davies, and Sophie Fuller, "Oram, Daphne Blake," in *The Grove Dictionary of Musical Instruments* (Oxford University Press, 2014), https://www.oxfordreference.com/view/10.1093/acref/9780199743391.001.0001/acref-9780199743391-e-5575.
[25] Hugh Davies, "Univox," in *The Grove Dictionary of Musical Instruments* (Oxford University Press, 2014) https://www.oxfordreference.com/view/10.1093/acref/9780199743391.001.0001/acref-9780199743391-e-7986
[26] Davies, Hugh, "Univox."
[27] "History of Commercial Radio," Federal Communications Commission.
[28] Maurizio Corbella, "Paolo Ketoff E Le Radici Cinematografiche Della Musica Elettronica Romana," *Acoustical Arts and Artifacts—Technology, Aesthetics, Communication* 6 (2009): 66–75.
[29] "Synthesizer," in *The Oxford Dictionary of Music*, eds. Kennedy, Joyce, Michael Kennedy, and Tim Rutherford-Johnson (Oxford University Press, 2012), https://www.oxfordreference.com/view/10.1093/acref/9780199578108.001.0001/acref-9780199578108-e-8888
[30] "Synthesizer," *Oxford Dictionary of Music*.
[31] Trevor Pinch, and Frank, Trocco. *Analog Days: The Invention and Impact of the Moog Synthesizer* (Harvard University Press, 2004) 1–384.
[32] Thomas Fine, "The Dawn of Commercial Digital Recording," *ARSC Journal* 46, no. 2 (2015): 289–92.
[33] "History of Commercial Radio," Federal Communications Commission.

[34] Peter Manning, *Electronic and Computer Music*. 4th ed. (Oxford University Press, 2013), 264.
[35] Manning, *Electronic and Computer Music*, 265.
[36] Fine, "The Dawn of Commercial Digital Recording," 289–92.
[37] Manning, *Electronic and Computer Music*, 279.
[38] Manning, *Electronic and Computer Music*, 263.
[39] Manning, *Electronic and Computer Music*, 297.
[40] "Sequencer." Oxford Reference, accessed September 9, 2021. https://www.oxfordreference.com/view/10.1093/oi/authority.20110803100455446
[41] Manning, *Electronic and Computer Music*, 391.
[42] "Sound Tools," The History of Pro Tools, accessed September 10, 2021. https://www.pro-tools-expert.com/home-page/2018/3/27/a-brief-history-of-pro-tools
[43] Allan Watson, "Cultural Production in and Beyond the Recording Studio," Vol. 47. *Routledge Studies in Human Geography* (Taylor & Francis Group, 2014), 22.

arts disciplines offer remain critical. This should be balanced with the valuing of generic skill sets and knowledge and other discipline areas. Providing holistic opportunities for authentic learning experiences will ensure that our young are educated in ways that will allow them to contribute positively to society and be able to navigate unknown territory for which technology will continue to play a central role.

NOTES

1. Thom Holmes, "Early Synthesizers and Experimenters," in *Electronic and Experimental Music* (Routledge, 2008), 159–90.

2. John Borwick and Lewis Foreman, "Recording and reproduction," in *The Oxford Companion to Music*, ed. Alison Latham (Oxford University Press, 2011), https://www.oxfordreference.com/view/10.1093/acref/9780199579037.001.0001/acref-9780199579037-e-5534

3. Thompson, John Michael Tutill, ed. *Visions of the future: physics and electronics*. Cambridge University Press, 2001, 140.

4. Reynold Weidenaar, "The First Telharmonium and its Origins," in *Magic Music from the Telharmonium* (Scarecrow Press, 1995), 1–49.

5. Ann Warde, "Theremin: Ether Music and Espionage by Albert Glinsky," *Computer Music Journal* 26, no. 3 (2002): 84–86.

6. "History of Commercial Radio," Federal Communications Commission, accessed September 8, 2021, https://www.fcc.gov/media/radio/history-of-commercial-radio

7. Warde, "Theremin: Albert Glinsky," 84–86.

8. "Inventor of Stereo Sound Alan Dower Blumlein's World-Changing 1931 Patent Celebrated as Part of the U.K. Government's 'GREAT for Imagination' Campaign," *EMI Archive Trust*, accessed September 8, 2021, https://www.emiarchivetrust.org/inventor-of-stereo-sound-alan-dower-blumleins-world-changing-1931-patent-celebrated-as-part-of-the-uk-governments-great-for-imagination-campaign/

9. Andrew Butterfield and John Szymanski. "Microphone," in *A Dictionary of Electronics and Electrical Engineering* (Oxford University Press, 2018), https://www.oxfordreference.com/view/10.1093/acref/9780198725725.001.0001/acref-9780198725725-e-2982.

10. "History of Commercial Radio," Federal Communications Commission.

11. Alfred Corbin, *The Third Element: A Brief History of Electronics* (AuthorHouse, 2006), 1–252.

12. "Hellertion," Oxford Reference, accessed September 8, 2021, https://www.oxfordreference.com/view/10.1093/oi/authority.20110803095929452

13. "History of Commercial Radio," Federal Communications Commission.

14. Lawrence J. Raphael, Gloria J. Borden, and Katherine S. Harris. *Speech Science Primer: Physiology, Acoustics, and Perception of Speech*, 23 (Lippincott Williams & Wilkins, 2011), 1–416.

15. Thom Holmes, "Early Synthesizers and Experimenters."
16. Alan Lenhoff, and David Robertson, *Classic Keys: Keyboard Sounds That Launched Rock Music* (University of North Texas Press, 2019), 1–416.
17. Borwick, and Foreman, "Recording and reproduction."
18. "History of Commercial Radio," Federal Communications Commission.
19. John Borwick, *Sound Recording Practice*. 4th ed. (Oxford University Press, 1996), 1–624.
20. Hugh Davies and Andrei Smirnov. "ANS," in *The Grove Dictionary of Musical Instruments* (Oxford University Press, 2014), https://www.oxfordreference.com/view/10.1093/acref/9780199743391.001.0001/acref-9780199743391-e-230.
21. "A brief history of computer music." *Musicradar*, accessed September 10, 2021. https://www.musicradar.com/news/tech/a-brief-history-of-computer-music-177299
22. Borwick, and Foreman, "Recording and reproduction."
23. "Integrated circuit." *Oxford Reference*, accessed September 9, 2021, https://www.oxfordreference.com/view/10.1093/oi/authority.20110803100005927
24. Hugh Davies, and Sophie Fuller, "Oram, Daphne Blake," in *The Grove Dictionary of Musical Instruments* (Oxford University Press, 2014) https://www.oxfordreference.com/view/10.1093/acref/9780199743391.001.0001/acref-9780199743391-e-5575.
25. Hugh Davies, "Univox," in *The Grove Dictionary of Musical Instruments* (Oxford University Press, 2014) https://www.oxfordreference.com/view/10.1093/acref/9780199743391.001.0001/acref-9780199743391-e-7986
26. Davies, Hugh, "Univox."
27. "History of Commercial Radio," Federal Communications Commission.
28. Maurizio Corbella, "Paolo Ketoff E Le Radici Cinematografiche Della Musica Elettronica Romana," *Acoustical Arts and Artifacts—Technology, Aesthetics, Communication* 6 (2009): 66–75.
29. "Synthesizer," in *The Oxford Dictionary of Music*, eds. Kennedy, Joyce, Michael Kennedy, and Tim Rutherford-Johnson (Oxford University Press, 2012), https://www.oxfordreference.com/view/10.1093/acref/9780199578108.001.0001/acref-9780199578108-e-8888
30. "Synthesizer," *Oxford Dictionary of Music*.
31. Trevor Pinch, and Frank, Trocco. *Analog Days: The Invention and Impact of the Moog Synthesizer* (Harvard University Press, 2004), 1–384.
32. Thomas Fine, "The Dawn of Commercial Digital Recording," *ARSC Journal* 46, no. 2 (2015): 289–92.
33. "History of Commercial Radio," Federal Communications Commission.
34. Peter Manning, *Electronic and Computer Music*. 4th ed. (Oxford University Press, 2013), 264.
35. Manning, *Electronic and Computer Music*, 265.
36. Fine, "The Dawn of Commercial Digital Recording," 289–92.
37. Manning, *Electronic and Computer Music*, 279.
38. Manning, *Electronic and Computer Music*, 263.
39. Manning, *Electronic and Computer Music*, 297.

40. "Sequencer." *Oxford Reference*, accessed September 9, 2021. https://www.oxfordreference.com/view/10.1093/oi/authority.20110803100455446

41. Manning, *Electronic and Computer Music*, 391.

42. "Sound Tools," *The History of Pro Tools*, accessed September 10, 2021. https://www.pro-tools-expert.com/home-page/2018/3/27/a-brief-history-of-pro-tools

43. Allan Watson, "Cultural Production in and Beyond the Recording Studio," Vol. 47. *Routledge Studies in Human Geography* (Taylor & Francis Group, 2014), 22.

44. Evangelos Himonides, "The Misunderstanding of Music-Technology-Education: A Meta Perspective," ed. Gary E. McPherson and Graham F. Welch. *The Oxford Handbook of Music Education*, 2 (2012): 433–34.

45. Manning, *Electronic and Computer Music*, 263.

46. Renée Crawford, "A Multidimensional/non-linear Teaching and Learning Model: Teaching and Learning Music in an Authentic and Holistic Context." *Music Education Research* 16, no. 1 (2014): 50.

47. Renée Crawford, "Are Resources Solely to Be Blamed? The Current Situation on Music."Education Facilities, Computer and Music Technology Resources in Victoria." *Australian.Journal of Music Education* (2008): 44–55.

48. Crawford, "Are Resources Solely to Be Blamed?", 44–55.

49. Bridget Somekh, "Factors Affecting Teachers' Pedagogical Adoption of ICT," in *International Handbook of Information Technology in Primary and Secondary Education*, eds. Joke Voogt and Gerald Knezek (Springer, 2008), 449–60.

50. Renée Crawford, "An Australian Perspective: Technology in Secondary School Music." *Journal of Historical Research in Music Education* 30, no. 2 (2009): 152.

51. Crawford, "An Australian Perspective," 152–53.

52. Renée Crawford, "The Evolution of Technology: Landmarking Australian Secondary School Music." *Australian Journal of Music Education*, no. 2 (2014): 82.

53. Crawford, "The Evolution of Technology," 82.

54. Crawford, "The Evolution of Technology," 82.

55. Crawford, "The Evolution of Technology," 91.

56. Crawford, "A Multidimensional/non-linear Teaching and Learning Model," 50–51.

57. Bennett Reimer, "Is Musical Performance Worth Saving?" *Arts Education Policy Review* 95, no. 3 (1994): 2

58. Crawford, "A Multidimensional/non-linear Teaching and Learning Model," 50–69.

59. David J. Elliott, *Music Matters: A New Philosophy of Music Education* (Oxford University Press, 1995) 1–380.

60. Crawford, "A Multidimensional/non-linear Teaching and Learning Model," 50–69.

61. Renée Crawford, "Rethinking Teaching and Learning Pedagogy for Education in the Twenty-first Century: Blended Learning in Music Education," *Music Education Research* 19, no. 2 (2017): 195–213.

62. National Commission on Excellence in Education. *A Nation at Risk: The Imperative for Educational Reform* (1983), accessed September 18, 2021. https://edreform.com/wp-content/uploads/2013/02/A_Nation_At_Risk_1983.pdf

BIBLIOGRAPHY

Borwick. John. *Sound Recording Practice.* 4th ed., 1–624. Oxford University Press, 1996.

Borwick, John, and Lewis Foreman. "Recording and reproduction." In *The Oxford Companion to Music*, edited by Alison Latham, Oxford University Press, 2011. https://www.oxfordreference.com/view/10.1093/acref/9780199579037.001.0001/acref-9780199579037-e-5534

Butterfield, Andrew, and John Szymanski, eds. "Microphone." In *A Dictionary of Electronics and Electrical Engineering.*, Oxford University Press, 2018. https://www.oxfordreference.com/view/10.1093/acref/9780198725725.001.0001/acref-9780198725725-e-2982

Corbella, Maurizio. "Paolo Ketoff E Le Radici Cinematografiche Della Musica Elettronica Romana." *Acoustical Arts and Artifacts-Technology, Aesthetics, Communication* 6 (2009): 66–75.

Corbin, Alfred. *The Third Element: A Brief History of Electronics*, 1–252. AuthorHouse, 2006.

Crawford, Renée. "Are Resources Solely to Be Blamed? The Current Situation on Music Education Facilities, Computer and Music Technology Resources in Victoria." *Australian Journal of Music Education* (2008): 44–55.

Crawford, Renée. "An Australian Perspective: Technology in Secondary School Music." *Journal of Historical Research in Music Education* 30, no. 2 (2009): 147–67.

Crawford, Renée. "The Evolution of Technology: Landmarking Australian Secondary School Music." *Australian Journal of Music Education*, no. 2 (2014): 77–92.

Crawford, Renée. "A Multidimensional/Nonlinear Teaching and Learning Model: Teaching and Learning Music in an Authentic and Holistic Context." *Music Education Research* 16, no. 1 (2014): 50–69.

Crawford, Renée. "Rethinking Teaching and Learning Pedagogy for Education in the Twenty-first Century: Blended Learning in Music Education." *Music Education Research* 19, no. 2 (2017): 195–213.

Davies, Hugh. "Univox." In *The Grove Dictionary of Musical Instruments*, Oxford University Press, 2014. https://www.oxfordreference.com/view/10.1093/acref/9780199743391.001.0001/acref-9780199743391-e-7986

Davies, Hugh, and Andrei Smirnov. "ANS." In *The Grove Dictionary of Musical Instruments*, Oxford University Press, 2014. https://www.oxfordreference.com/view/10.1093/acref/9780199743391.001.0001/acref-9780199743391-e-230.

Davies, Hugh, and Sophie Fuller. "Oram, Daphne Blake." In *The Grove Dictionary of Musical Instruments*, Oxford University Press, 2014. https://www.oxfordreference.com/view/10.1093/acref/9780199743391.001.0001/acref-9780199743391-e-5575.

Elliott, David J. *Music Matters: A New Philosophy of Music Education.* Oxford University Press, 1995.

EMI Archive Trust. "Inventor of Stereo Sound Alan Dower Blumlein's World-Changing 1931 Patent Celebrated as Part of the UK Government's 'GREAT for Imagination' Campaign," accessed September 8, 2021. https://www.emi-archivetrust.org/inventor-of-stereo-sound-alan-dower-blumleins-world-changing-1931-patent-celebrated-as-part-of-the-uk-governments-great-for-imagination-campaign/

Fine, Thomas. "The Dawn of Commercial Digital Recording." *ARSC Journal* 46, no. 2 (2015): 289–92.

Federal Communications Commission. "History of Commercial Radio," accessed September 8, 2021. https://www.fcc.gov/media/radio/history-of-commercial-radio

Himonides, Evangelos. "The Misunderstanding of Music-Technology-Education: A Meta Perspective." In *The Oxford Handbook of Music Education,* edited by Gary E. McPherson and Graham F. Welch., Volume 2, 432–456, Oxford University Press, 2012. doi:10.1093/oxfordhb/9780199928019.013.0029_update_001

Holmes, Thom, ed. "Early Synthesizers and Experimenters." In *Electronic and Experimental Music,* 159–90. Routledge, 2008.

Kennedy, Joyce, Michael Kennedy, and Tim Rutherford-Johnson, eds. "Synthesizer." In The Oxford Dictionary of Music, Oxford University Press, 2012. https://www.oxfordreference.com/view/10.1093/acref/9780199578108.001.0001/acref-9780199578108-e-8888

Lenhoff, Alan, and David Robertson. *Classic Keys: Keyboard Sounds That Launched Rock Music.* University of North Texas Press, 2019.

Manning, Peter. *Electronic and Computer Music.* 4th ed., Oxford University Press, 2013.

National Commission on Excellence in Education. *A Nation at Risk: The Imperative for Educational Reform* (1983), accessed September 18, 2021. https://edreform.com/wp-content/uploads/2013/02/A_Nation_At_Risk_1983.pdf

Oxford Reference. "Hellertion," accessed September 8, 2021. https://www.oxfordreference.com/view/10.1093/oi/authority.20110803095929452

Oxford Reference. "Integrated circuit," accessed September 9, 2021. https://www.oxfordreference.com/view/10.1093/oi/authority.20110803100005927

Oxford Reference. "Sequencer," accessed September 10, 2021. https://www.oxfordreference.com/view/10.1093/oi/authority.20110803100455446

Pinch, Trevor, and Frank, Trocco. *Analog Days: The Invention and Impact of the Moog Synthesizer.* Harvard University Press, 2004.

Raphael, Lawrence J., Gloria J. Borden, and Katherine S. Harris. *Speech Science Primer: Physiology, Acoustics, and Perception of Speech.* Lippincott Williams & Wilkins, 2011.

Reimer, Bennett. "Is Musical Performance Worth Saving?" *Arts Education Policy Review* 95, no. 3 (1994): 2–13.

The History of Pro Tools. "Sound Tools," accessed September 10, 2021. https://www.pro-tools-expert.com/home-page/2018/3/27/a-brief-history-of-pro-tools

Thompson, John Michael Tutill, ed. *Visions of the future: physics and electronics.* Cambridge University Press, 2001.

Warde, Ann. "*Theremin: Ether Music and Espionage* by Albert Glinsky," *Computer Music Journal* 26, no. 3 (2002): 84–86.

Watson, Allan. *Cultural Production in and beyond the Recording Studio*. Routledge, 2014.
Weidenaar, Reynold. *Magic Music from the Telharmonium*. Scarecrow Press, 1995.
Voogt, Joke, and Gerald Knezek, eds, '*International Handbook of Information Technology in Primary and Secondary Education,* Springer, 2008.

Conclusion

For centuries, music educators have sought to innovate, refresh, revive, and improve pedagogical and theoretical practice. The most effective of these changes have been highly influential, spreading beyond their point of origin throughout the world and providing fresh approaches in classrooms, studios, ensemble rehearsal venues, and all other spaces and places where music teaching and learning can occur. There is now an embarrassment of riches, a smorgasbord of pedagogies and approaches through which music teachers formatively begin their music learning experiences, and then as music educators choose depending on capacity, context, aptness, and preference. For many undergraduate music teachers, the range of pedagogical approaches can be overwhelming. Teacher training courses in music frequently offer "taster courses," designed to introduce the many concepts and practices to would-be teachers in order for them to consider which of them to explore more thoroughly during the course of their careers. Given the limits to comprehensive access for initial teacher education, there are simply too many complex pedagogical approaches for a trainee teacher to try and master within the course of a few short years. This collection of education big bangs in music education offers scope for both the breadth and depth in which music educators can engage learners, as well as the capacity for those in the profession to be captivated in the lifelong learning it offers.

Revolutions in Music Education aims to be more than an intriguing delve into a set of historical narratives all centered on the same idea—a revolutionary idea that caught fire and remains a mainstay in current practice. Understanding the historical progress of music education is to consider how ideas and approaches came to be and the relevance they have on changing societies, positioning contemporary teachers in a temporal context with which to make informed decisions for the best outcomes for their students.

Considering the complex timeline of events that have shaped our current practice allows us the opportunity to appreciate the glorious efforts which many of us take for granted in our daily music-teaching and music-making activities. Each of the revolutions shares several common tenets, not least of which is the desire to make the learning experience more dynamic, vibrant, and effective for students and teachers. Every development changes how we enact our craft. Some ideas take time to infuse traditional models of instruction that still pervade many institutions today. Other ideas have been with us for so long that, although revolutionary at inception, they now form the "traditional" which continues to be challenged by the new. Some ideas do not survive their initial moment and reach; others (such as those captured in this collection) have become part of the tapestry of music education ecology.

Underpinning each of the praxial changes in pedagogy is a rich vein of philosophical perspectives that have guided thinking, sometimes subverting and eventually changing our principles of musical engagement. Although we have focused on the tangible, we acknowledge and understand the important role intangible concepts play in developing modes of practice. Contributions from relatively contemporary critical thinkers such as Keith Swanwick, David Elliot, Harold Abeles, Bennett Reimer, Thomas Regelski, and Randall Allsup have each redefined our fundamental approaches to the core tenets of musical development such as listening, performing, and composing. We add the dimension of musicking to this triad, allowing a generous and inclusive praxis that adds rehearsing, practicing, composing, arranging, dancing, mixing, and so forth.

For each of the major music education approaches included in this book to become globally recognized systems, they needed to transcend their initial geographical and cultural boundaries. Many such approaches were philosophically and practically constructed to meet specific cultural tenets but became transformed through cross-cultural adaptation and metamorphosis. Such a leap can only occur if ideas are revolutionary enough to make a discernible impact in the multiplicity of socioeconomic and cultural contexts. These are the seismic changes that have endured and thrived, and it boggles the mind to consider the many worthwhile ideas that did not make it to the status of "revolution." No single country can lay claim to ownership of music education as music education can be traced back to the beginnings of humanity. As soon as a chant or song was created, it was shared—taught by one person to another. As soon as a musical instrument was made, someone played it and taught others.

The ongoing need to continue the important work of music education in transforming the lives of individuals requires a commitment to meaningful advocacy. Until every child is given the opportunity to unlock their creative potential through music, we must continue to retell the rich narrative of music education, its history, purpose, and benefits. At the curriculum level, music continues to attempt to claim the necessary space in which to deliver a consequential and developmentally organized syllabus, while at the school level, music teachers are increasingly required to justify the expense of an activity considered by many governing bodies as a fringe subject. With the advent of STEM, the acronym that promotes a focus on Science, Technology, Engineering, and Mathematics in schools, music experienced a setback, being further marginalized in an approach that devalues the importance of creative thinking replete in music and the arts generally.

The origins of each of our chapter topics represent a truly international contribution, visibly reflected in current international conferences on music education which platform new ways of thinking from individuals throughout the globe. The benefits of music learning in practical, innovative, and creative ways have been the foundation for much impactful research in recent decades. Research into these topics has by no means reached some kind of practical limit, and several of our revolutions such as the work of Suzuki and Orff continue to be critiqued more than attracting empirical scrutiny. No longer does the international music education community consider the role of music instruction to simply inform and then measure students about historical repertoire and theoretical concepts. Thanks to dedicated researchers, we are now exploring music's impact on myriad social and cultural impacts spanning socialization, identities, brain function, well-being, health and therapy, lifespan engagement, communication, and many other domains. We now look beyond the classroom to understand how our practices inform community engagement, lifelong learning, creativity and higher-order thinking, metacognition, and commercial industry.

Just as music permeates both mind and body, it continues to transmit an ineffable quality that touches humanity. Despite music now being the most oft used and ubiquitous art form, it still maintains the power to move and change us in an instant. The exciting thing about this is that even amid the technological and social change of the past 30 years, music and music education will continue to evolve, adapt, and innovate. When commentators suggest music can change the world, it already has many times over, and in the skills and actions of music educators it will continue to do so now and into the future.

Index

Page numbers followed with "n" refer to endnotes, and italic page numbers refer to figures and tables.

Abreu, José Antonio, 9, 121, 125–28, 130
ACID Music Studio, 239
acoustic instrument making projects, 278
Adorno, Theodor, 159
Aebersold, Jamey, 104, 107
AEC. *See* Australian Education Council (AEC)
Ahumada, Clarina, 126
Ake, David, 107
Alibhai-Brown, Yasmin, 184
Alice Colvin survey, 205–6
Alma Llanera, 129–30
Ambrosian chant, 37
American Music Educators National Conference (MENC), 56, 70, 99, 157, 186, 241
American Orff-Schulwerk Association (AOSA), 56
anacrusis, 93n18
analogue formats, 273
AOSA. *See* American Orff-Schulwerk Association (AOSA)
Appia, Adolphe, 82, 86
Arduino coding, 276, 277
Armstrong, Louis, 101

Armstrong, Victoria, 240
Aston, Peter, 254, 255
Atari Punk Console, 279
aural training, 85, 90, 91, 218
Aurelian of Réôme, 36
Australia: multicultural music education, 183; popular music education, 158
Australian Education Council (AEC), 227
Australian music education (1945–1965), 217–19
Australian Music Examinations' Board (AMEB) syllabus, 218
authentic learning, 296, 297
autodidacticism, 257

Bach, J. S., 3, 124
badge identity, 163
Ball, Stephen, 157
Bartle, Graham, 218
Beatles, 5
Beat Machine, 280
Bechet, Sidney, 101
Becker, Klaus, 53
Bernstein, Basil, 165
Bernstein, Leonard, 9, 147
Biesta, Gert, 255

big band, 103–4, 106–8
big bang, ix, 7, 315
Big Bangs (Goodall), xi
Blanche E. K. Evans of Cincinnati, 203
Boal-Palheiros, Graca, 160
bodily movement, 83–84, 86
Boethius, ix, x, 38
Boulton, Harold, 182
Bourdieu, Pierre, 110
Breeze, Nick, 241
Bresler, Liora, 161
Breuer, János, 24
Bridges, Doreen, 25, 219
Britten, Benjamin, 146
broadcasts of music lessons, 141–42
broadcast television, 141, 142
Buck, Pearl S., 181
Burney, Charles, 17–18
The Burrowes' Piano Primer, 203
Burtness, Rhoda, 207

Cady, Calvin Bernard, 201–2
CAI. *See* Computer-Aided Instruction (CAI)
CAL. *See* Computer-Aided Learning (CAL)
Campbell, Patricia Shehan, 158–60, 163
Canada: multicultural music education, 183
Carolingian education reforms, 38, 41
Carpenter, Thomas, 140, 141, 143–45
Casa de la Cultura, 124, 125
Cascone, Kim, 273
Challis, Ben, 166
Champion Schools program, 261
Chappell, Herbert, 219
The Children's Hour, 217
Children's orchestras, 122, 124–25, 127
"chiroplast", 200
Ciftcibasi, M. Can, 161
"Circle of Fifths", 21
classical music, 160, 162, 163, 218, 256; and Musical Futures (MF), 262–63; popular and, 155, 156, 159, 164–65

class piano: Alice Colvin survey of classes, 205–6; challenges of, 203, 207–10; decline, 209; instruction, 207–9; issue of access, 209; lack of curricular materials, 203; lack of training/pedagogical knowledge of teachers, 207–8, 293; NBAM survey of classes, 204–5; pedagogy at colleges, 208; pioneers of, 200–202; in public school classrooms, 202–4
Class Piano Readers (Giddings), 206
Cloonan, Martin, 162
closed-circuit television, 141, 142, 149n3
Coker, Jerry, 104
Coleman, Ornette, 105
Collins, Nicholas, 276
colonialization, 184
Colquhoun, Shane, 164
compact discs, 273
Computer-Aided Instruction (CAI), 295–97
Computer-Aided Learning (CAL), 295–97
computer programming, 276–77
computers, 295–96
computing education, 276
Contemporary Group Piano, 206
convergent thinking, 163
Cook, Clifford, 65, 69–72
Corea, Chick, 7
Council of Laodicea, 8, 13, 31, 41; canons of, 31–32
Cox, Gordon, 253–54, 256
creativity, 1, 2, 10, 58, 59, 80, 108, 109, 164, 218, 220, 227–29, 238–42, 244, 296
Cristofori, Bartolomeo, 202
Cubase, 238
cultural authenticity, 187–88
cultural awareness, 185–87
Curwen, John, 15, 24–26; developments of, 21–24; modulators, 22, *23*; Tonic Sol-fa System, 22, *22*, 27
Cutietta, Robert, 158

Dalcroze Eurhythmics (DE), 8, 80, 83–85; disseminating the practice, 89–91; process, 85–89; training, 90–91
DARMS. *See* Digital Alternate Representation of Music Scores (DARMS)
Davies, Peter Maxwell, 219
Davis, Miles, 7
DAW. *See* Digital Audio Workstation (DAW)
DE. *See* Dalcroze Eurhythmics (DE)
De institutione musica (Boethius), ix
De musica (Guido), 40
Department for Education of UK (DFE), 187
de Sigren, Cora Bindhoff, 122
desktop publishing, 236–38
deviant music, 163
Dewey, John, 275
Díaz, Alirio, 124
Diehl, Lily P, 207
Digital Alternate Representation of Music Scores (DARMS), 235
Digital Audio Workstation (DAW), 238–42, 244, 294
Digital Performer, 238
digital technologies, 165, 196, 273, 295; educational trends in, 275–77
dissemination: Dalcroze Eurhythmics (DE), 14, 89–91; Orff's Schulwerk, 14, 54–58
distance learning, 144, 150n24
diverse cultures, 188
DIY movement. *See* Do-It-Yourself (DIY) movement
do (*doh*), 15, 18, 22, 25; impact of solmization and, 26–27
Do-It-Yourself (DIY) movement, 274–75
D'Ombrain, Geoffrey, 26
Dominguez, Hugo, 123, 126
Doni, Giovanni Battista, 18
Downey, Jean, 159
dummy keyboards, 209
Dunbar-Hall, Peter, 158, 163–65

Ear Cleaning (Schafer), 222–23
Educate America Act, 186
educational television (ETV), 145–46
Einzug und Reigen der Kinder und Mädchen (Orff), 52
electronic instrument making, 10–11, 276, 277, 279–81
electronic keyboards, 10, 210
electronic music instruments, 196–97
electronic pianos, 209
electronic technologies, 274, 276
elemental music, 52
Elementare Musikübung (Elemental Music exercises, Orff, Bergese and Keetman), 52
Ellington band, 108
Elliot, David, 182
El Sistema, 9, 98, 121; globalizing, 128–33, *131–33*
English National Curriculum (ENC), 156, 157, 165
English Tonic Sol-fa method, 24
Epistola ad Michahelem (Guido), 39, 40
Epitaph for Moonlight (Schafer), 224–25
Escuela Experimental de Música de La Serena, 123
Estrada, Eva, 128
ethnic musics, 5, 98
ethnomusicology, 180
ETV. *See* educational television (ETV)
Evans, Lindley, 217
extended modulator, *24*

Faulkner, Anne Shaw, 102
Fenwick, G. Roy, 54
"Festival Bach", 125
Field, Inez, 203
50 Choruses for Cornet (Armstrong), 102
Fillmore, James C., 202
Finale, 237
folk musics, 180, 183
formal music learning, 258, 263. *See also* informal music learning

Fowler, Charles, 157
Frazee, Jane, 57
Frith, Simon, 159
Fukui, Naohiro, 55
Fundación de Orquestas Juveniles (FOJI), 128

Gall, Marina, 165, 241
Gallican chant, 37
Gamut, 16, 18
GarageBand, 239
Garson, Alfred, 73
Geen, William, 58
Gehrkins, Karl, 202
General Certificate of Secondary Education (GCSE), 255, 259, 263
Giddings, Thaddeus P., 203–6
Gilbert, Ashley, 165
Giroux, Henry, 109
Glover, Sarah Anna, ix, 15, 22, 25, 26; innovations of, 18–21; modulators, 22, *23*; Norwich Sol-fa ladder, 19, *20*, 21; sevenfold ladder, *21*; solmization syllables, *20*; "Table of Tune", 21
Graham, George Farquhar, 200
graphical display, 236
graphical user interface, 237
graphic notation, 221
Gray, Elisha: Musical Telegraph, 11, 287, 288
Green, Lucy, 157, 159–62, 164, 183, 185, 255–58, 263
Gregorian chant, 34, 41
group piano, 201–2, 207, 210
Grunzke, Andrew, 264
A Guide for Conducting Piano Classes in the School, 205
Guido d'Arezzo, 6, 8, 13, 15, 16, 22, 26; hexachordal system, 16–17 (of solmization), 39–40, 42; and revolution of music pedagogy, 39–40

Hall, Doreen, 54–55
Hallam, Susan, 262, 264
"Handmade Electronic Music: The Art of hardware hacking" (Collins), 276
Hargreaves, David, 160
Haselbach, Barbara, 55
Hebert, David, 158–60, 163
Hendricks, Karin S., 74
Hennessy, Sarah, 256
hermeneutic listening approach, 164
Hess, Juliet, 183
hexachords/hexachordal system, 16–18, *17*; of solmization, 39–40, 42
Holmes, Patricia L., 57–58
Honda, Masaaki, 68–70
Hook theory, 242
horizontal/vertical discourse model, 165
Housewright Symposium on the Future of Music Education, 186
How Music Works (Goodall), x
How Popular Musicians Learn (Green), 255, 257–58
Hucbald, 38–39
Hurd, Michael, 219
Hutcherson, Rita Johnson, 207
Hyperscribe, 243

Iberorquestas program, 128
ICT. *See* Information Communications Technologies (ICT)
IHSE. *See* In Harmony Sistema England (IHSE)
Impromptu, 243
improvisation, 84, 85, 87; jazz, 101–12
informal music learning, 257–61, 263–64; in popular music, 162
Information Communications Technologies (ICT), 241
In Harmony Sistema England (IHSE), 129
innovation, 1, 2; technological. *See* technological innovation
Instituto Experimental Alirio Díaz, 127
instructional television (ITV). *See* televised music instruction
instrument making, 10–11, 271–72, 275–78, 280–81

International Society for Music Education (ISME), 56, 99, 157, 188
International Suzuki Association, 73–74
Internet, 242, 244
Isidore of Seville, 33
ISME. *See* International Society for Music Education (ISME)

Jaques-Dalcroze, Émile, 14, 79, 81–83; Dalcroze Eurhythmics (DE), 8, 80, 83–85 (disseminating the practice, 89–91; process, 85–89)
Jazz, 5, 8, 101–3; education, 97, 110–12 (big band, 103–4, 106–8; challenge for, 112; critics, 109; high school, 107, 109, 110; history and development in United States, 103–5; improvisation, 101–12; innovation, 112; institutionalization of, 8, 104–7; legitimization of, 107; practices, 108–10; secondary, 107–12); learning of, 104, 111
Jérez, Hernán, 124, 127
Jevons, Reginald, 208
John the Deacon, 34–35

Kallio, Alexis, 163
Kang, Samgmi, 234
Kaschub, Michele, 254
Kassner, Kirk, 165
Keetman, Gunild, 51–57
Kendall, John, 65, 69–70
keyboard technologies, 196
Kikugawa, Yatuka, 130
Kind of Blue (Davis), 7
Kinzer, Charles E., 102
Kodály, Zoltan, 15, 23; English Tonic Sol-fa method, 24–26
Kojima, M., 74
Komlos, Peter, 73
Kranzberg, Melvin, 234
Kratus, John, 163

Lamont, Alexandra, 157, 160
Langer, Suzanne, 146

La Orquesta de Niños, 122–24
laser printer technology, 236–37
Latin American music, 181
learnification of education, 255
learning by listening, 257
Lee, Ed., 156, 159–61, 163
Leimma, 243
Levy, Kenneth, 37
Lewison, E. Mildred, 206
Lim, Liza, 228
liturgy: Romanization of, 37–39, 41
live coding, 273
Logic Pro, 238
Logier, Frederick Augustus, 201
Logier, Johann Bernhard, 200–203, 208, 209
Logo programming language, 276–77
loop-based compositions, 238–40
Los Angeles Philharmonic, 129
Lydian Chromatic Concept of Tonal Organisation (Russell), 104

Madsen, Clifford, 143
Maker movement. *See* Do-It-Yourself (DIY) movement
Mantie, Roger, 158
Mantie, Roger Allan, 109, 110
Manual of Harmonics (Nicomachus), ix
Maori music, 184
Mariguddi, Anna, 263
Mark, Michael, 70, 72
Martin, Frank, 80
Martínez, Juan, 124, 127, 130
Mathews, Max, 235
Matsunomi, Koji, 272
McPhail, Graham, 161, 164–65
McPherson, Gary E., 106
medieval music pedagogy, 35–37
Mehl, Margaret, 74
The Melody Way series, 206
mental effects of tones, 25
MF. *See* Musical Futures (MF)
Micrologus (Guido), 39
MIDI. *See* Musical Instrument Digital Interface (MIDI)

MIDI Polyphonic Expression (MPE) protocol, 278
Miessner, W. Otto, 206, 207
Milla, Guillermo, 126
Mochizuki, Kenji, 69
Mockingbird computer notation system, 236
Model Music Curriculum, 241
modulators, 22–23, *23*, 25–27
Morley, Thomas, 17, 18
Morris, John, 57
motivation for popular music, 160–61
movable do. *See do (doh)*
multiculturalism, 5, 179, 181, 182, 184, 188
multicultural music education, 99, 179–82; Australia, 183; authentic practice, 187–88; Canada, 183; cultural awareness through music curriculum, 185–87; technology and, 185; United Kingdom, 182–83
Murray, Margaret, 55–56
music, x, 1; listening, 163–64; pedagogy (medieval, 35–37; revolution of, 39–40); software, 236, 237, 240–41; technology, 10–11, 165–66, 240–41, 295, 296
"Music, Informal Learning and the School: A New Classroom Pedagogy" (Green), 258–59
musical expression, 196; instrument making as, 271–72; new interfaces for, 272–74
Musical Futures (MF), 10, 196, 253, 255, 258–60, 264; aim of, 260–61; classical music and, 262–63; evaluation, 261; expansion, 261; implementation and impact of, 262; research, 261–62; survey report, 262–63
Musical Futures Special Initiative (2003), 259
Musical Instrument Digital Interface (MIDI), xi, 10, 195, 237–40, 294–95, 297

musical learning, 146, 147, 217
"The Musical Soundscape" (Schafer), 222–23
Musical Telegraph, 11, 287, 288
music curriculum, 185–87, 241; cultural awareness through, 185–87; United Kingdom, 183, 253–55; Wales, 253–55
Music Curriculum for Primary Schools in New South Wales (1963), 26
music making, 272; postdigital revolution in, 273
music notation, xi, 1–2, 41, 196; beginnings of, 32–33; computer technology and, 243; defined, 234–35; and machines, 235–36; software, xi, 10, 196 (in music education, 240–42; platforms, 238–40, 242–43)
Music Technology Strand, 241
Musik für Kinder (Music for Children, Orff and Keetman), 54, 56

NASM. *See* National Association for Schools of Music (NASM)
National Association for Music Education. *See* American Music Educators National Conference (MENC)
National Association for Schools of Music (NASM), 186
National Bureau for the Advancement of Music (NBAM), 204–5
National Curriculum for England and Wales, 255
NBAM. *See* National Bureau for the Advancement of Music (NBAM)
Negus, Keith, 146–47
New Interfaces for Musical Expression (NIME), 272–74, 278, 281
Nicholson, Stuart, 107
Nicomachus, ix
NIME. *See* New Interfaces for Musical Expression (NIME)
non-Western music, 180
Norwich Sol-fa ladder, 19, *20*, 21
Nurtured by Love (Suzuki), 74

Odo of Arezzo, 36–37
open-circuit broadcasting, 149n3
orarion, 32, 42n6
ordo psallendi, 34
Orfeón Lamas, 128
Orff, Carl, 8, 49–59
Orff-Schulwerk, 14, 49, 51–52, 164; in Australia, 57–58; rediscovery and revival, 52–53 (dissemination, 54–58); in United States, 56–57
Orquesta Infantil de Carora, 126, 127
Orquesta Juvenil de Venezuela, 127
Orquesta Nacional Infantil de Venezuela, 127
Orquesta Nacional Juvenil, 126, 127
Orquesta Nacional Juvenil Juan José Landaeta, 125
Orquesta Sinfónica Infantil de Carora, 125
overlapping hexachords, 17, 18
Oxford Piano Course series, 206
Ozdemir, Gokhan, 161

Pace, Robert, 206–7
Panofsky, Erwin, 52
Parasiz, Gokalp, 165
Parker, Charles, 159
Parsons, Graham, 184
participatory culture, 148
Pash, Donald, 146
Passeron, Jean-Claude, 110
Paul Hamlyn Foundation (PHF), 259, 261–62
Paul I, Pope, 38
Paynter, John, 254–56, 275
pedagogical issues, 253–55
Peña, Jorge, 9, 121, 125–28, 130, 133; children's orchestras, 124–25; democratizing access to music education, 121–24; music education for children, 123; Western art music, 122
pentatonic scale (*d-r-m-s-l*), 25
Phase Drone Synth, 279
PHF. *See* Paul Hamlyn Foundation (PHF)
piano, 3, 199

piano roll notation, 238–39
Pippin III, 37, 38
pitch notation, 38–40
Plan de Extensión Docente, 123
Plastique Animée, 83, 85
pop, 5, 275. *See also* Jazz
Pope Gregory I. *See* St. Gregory the Great
popular music, 98–99; and classical music, 155, 156, 159, 164–65; defined, 156, 159; education, 9 (Australia, 158; impediments to, 161; informal learning, 162; legitimacy, 159–60; listening to, 163–64; motivational value of, 160–61; negotiating the pedagogy of, 161–62; pedagogical tensions, 164–65; practical pedagogy, 164; repertoire selection issues, 162–63; social context, 159–66; technology and, 165–66; United Kingdom, 156–57; United States, 157–58); formal and informal learning, 257–58; student-centered learning, 161
post-digital, 273, 275
Powell, Bryan, 158
practical pedagogy, 164
Pratte, Richard, 182
Prologus in Antiphonarium (Guido), 39
Prouty, Kenneth. E., 109
psalmody, 32
pseudo-interactive medium, 150n24
PTV. *See* public television (PTV)
public broadcasting system, 142, 151n46
public television (PTV), 146
Punk Pedagogy, 274

Rainbow, Bernarr, 24
real music *vs.* school music divide, 160
recorded music, 4, 68
Regner, Hermann, 57
Regule rhythmice (Guido), 39
Reimer, Bennett, 297
Rhapsody in Blue (Gershwin), 5

rhythmics, 85; exercises, 85, 87, 88
Rhythmics Gymnastic (RG) ball, 88
Rinsema, Rebecca, 158, 164
rock, 5, 163, 257, 275
Rogers, Fred, 139
Rogoff, Barbara, 110
Rollins, Sonny, 105
Roman chant, 34, 37, 41
Romanization of liturgy, 37–39, 41
Routh, Francis, 159
Russell, George, 104

Sammer, Gerhard, 241
Sancte Iohannes, 17
Sarath, Ed., 106
Savage, Jonathan, 165
Sawyer, Keith R., 101
Schaeffer, Pierre, 4
Schafer, Murray R., 10, 195–96, 217, 219–20, 275; *Ear Cleaning*, 222–23; music education (six sessions of, 220–21; for students, 225–26; for teachers, 226); 1970s and beyond, 227–29; *The Thinking Ear*, 220–22; *When Words Sing*, 223–25, 228
Scheme for Rendering Psalmody Congregational (Glover), 19, 21
Schippers, Huib, 180
schola cantorum, 8, 34–35, 38, 41
Schuller, Gunther, 105
Schulwerk. *See* Orff-Schulwerk
science, technology, engineering, and maths (STEM), 277
Scruton, Roger, 157
secondary school music, 254
Self, George, 221, 225, 226
self-teaching, 257
Shamrock, Mary, 57
Shin'ichi Suzuki, 8, 122–23, 125; concerts in Japan, 68–69; development of his approach, 66–67; Talent Education, 14, 65–68 (international uptake, 73; in United States, 69–72); ten music volumes, 68

Sibelius, 237
Sistema Nacional de Formento Musical, 128
Skornia, Harry, 140
Sloboda, John, 162, 163
Small, Christopher, 106, 272
Smith, Janice, 254
Smith, Keith, 57
Smith, Stuart, 158
sol-fa, ix, 15, 16, 18–23, 22, 25–27; syllables, 15–19, 26–27
solfège, 85, 91n2
solmization, 16–18, 196; hexachordal system of, 39–40, 42; impact of, 26–27; syllables, *20*
Somervell, Arthur, 182
Sonata, 236
Sonic Pi, 279–80
Sound Designer, 238
Soundslice, 242–43
Spitz, Emily, 56
Springer, Gregory D., 164
Spruce, Gary, 159
Stan Kenton Band Clinic, 104
Stauffer, Sandra L., 234
STEM. *See* science, technology, engineering, and maths (STEM)
Sternberg, Constantine, 202
St. Gregory the Great, 33–34, 41; biography of, 34–35; and the *schola cantorum*, 34–35
Stockey, B. Hella Prince, 202
student-centered learning, 158, 161
Suzuki Association of the Americas, 73
Swanwick, Keith, 256
Szönyi, Erzsébet, 24, 25

"Table of Tune", 21
Tachigrafo Musicale, 235
Taichi Akutsu, 74
Talent Education, 65–66; method on music education, 73–75; Shin'ichi Suzuki. *See* Shin'ichi Suzuki; theory of, 67; in United States, 69–72

Tanglewood Declaration of 1967, 157, 186
Tanglewood Symposium, 9, 185–86
Tarrant, Mark, 163
taste cultures, 163
Teacher's Manual (Hall), 55
technical evolution, 3
technological innovation, 6, 295, 297; timeline of, 288–94, *298–305*
technology, xi, 4, 10, 98, 185; and digitization, 6; and music, 197, 287, 294–97; pedagogy and, 11, 296–97; for popular music education, 165–66
teletext, 150n24
televised music instruction, 9, 98, 139–42; Bernstein effect, 147; changing conceptions, 144–47; educational impact, 142–44; research on, 142, 143; YouTube and, 148
televised music lessons, 141, 143
Telharmonium, 235
tetrachords/tetrachordal system, 16, 18
The Thinking Ear (Schafer), 220
Thomas, Werner, 59
Till, Rupert, 162
Tillson, Diana, 72
Tobias, Evan, 164
tokenism, 180, 184, 186, 187
Tonic sol-fa system. *See* sol-fa
Tremaine, C. M., 204, 207
Tucker, Judith, 187

United Kingdom: multicultural music education, 182–83; music curriculum, 183, 253; popular music education, 156–57
United States: history and development of Jazz, 103–5; popular music education, 157–58; Talent Education in, 69–72
Urquieta, José, 126
U.S. National Core Arts Standards for Music, 241

U.S. National Standards for Music Education, 241
Ut queant laxis, 40

Vajda, Cecilia, 24
values, 256
Vargas, Pedro, 124–25, 127
vernacular musicianship, 162
vertical ladders, 15
vital ground rules, 255
Vulliamy, Graham, 156, 159–61, 163

Waddell, George, 165, 166
waiata, 184
Waldron, Janice, 148
Wales: music curriculum, 253–55
Walter, Arnold, 54, 56
Wemyss, Kathryn, 158, 164, 165
Western music, 1–2, 179, 183; history and development of, 3–4
Western Standard Music Notation (WSMN), 233–43
When Words Sing (Schafer), 223–25, 228
Whyton, Tony, 105
Wiggins, Geraint, 234
Wild, Nick, 52
Wilder, H. S., 202–3
Williamon, Aaron, 165, 166
Woody, Robert, 161, 162, 164
world music, 9, 99, 183, 187–88
written notation, 2
WSMN. *See* Western Standard Music Notation (WSMN)
WYHIWYG software, 239
WYSIWYG software, 236

Yoo, Hyesoo, 234
Young People's Concerts (Bernstein), 147
YouTube, 148
Ysaÿe, Eugène, 82

Zimmerman, Alex H., 70

About the Contributors

Andrew Brown is an artist and academic whose work focuses on augmenting our creative intelligence through interactions with digital systems. After a career as a professional musician, Andrew's passions fuelled an academic career in teaching and research. First at the University of Melbourne, then at Queensland University of Technology, the Australasian CRC for Interaction Design, and now as professor of digital arts at Griffith University. He is involved in a range of digital arts and design practices, and his current work focuses on interactive and algorithmic media installation, live coding, interactive electronics, and arts education.

Dr. Leon de Bruin (Coeditor) is lecturer in Music at the University of Melbourne, Conservatorium of Music, and coordinator of the Master of Music Performance Teaching degree (MMPT). He is a staunch advocate for quality instrumental music education and music teacher education in Australia. He is Australian Society for Music Education National President and an executive of the ISME Instrumental and Vocal Teaching Forum, the National Alliance for Arts Education (NAAE) and the Australian Alliance of Associations in Education (AAAE). His research work spans instrumental music teacher pedagogy and practice, creativity, cognition, and community engagement with music and phenomenological methodologies. He has published over fifty articles, book chapters, and edited books, including *Creativities in Arts Education, Research and Practice: International Perspectives for the Future of Learning and Teaching*, and *Creativity in Education in the Oxford Research Encyclopaedia of Education*.

Alexandra Carlson is a high school music teacher and oboist based in Syracuse, New York. Her research on *El Sistema* programs in Venezuela and Chile is published in the *International Journal of Music Education* and the *Journal for Historical Research in Music Education*. She holds a master's in music education from the University of Colorado and bachelor's degrees from Northwestern University in Oboe Performance and History with Honors. She was a Fulbright Scholar in Venezuela in 2009–2010, where she studied and taught with *El Sistema* and a Northwestern Latin American Studies Grantee to Chile in 2007, where she also performed in the Orquesta Sinfónica Nacional Juvenil as a full-time member. Previously, she has taught high school and middle school music in Minnesota and Colorado and for the El Sistema-inspired YOURS program in Chicago. She can be reached at carlson.lexi@gmail.com.

Renée Crawford, associate professor, is a leader in the field of authentic learning contexts and digital technology for music teaching and learning in Australia and internationally. Renée is currently an associate professor and director of Graduate Research in the Faculty of Education at Monash University. Renée's career is driven by a commitment to advance the impact and value of Music (Arts) in education and to investigate, develop, and implement effective pedagogy and curriculum. Renée's research interests are linked by discipline, a teacher-led belief about improving and strengthening educational outcomes, and a commitment to innovative practice in teaching and learning. As a mixed-method researcher, her research focuses on teacher-led research practice and the development of professional learning; blended learning and online education contexts; creative and critical thinking; the development of teaching and learning models; inclusive practice and pedagogy and curriculum development that is informed by both current and historical perspectives.

Karin Greenhead teaches Dalcroze Eurhythmics (DE) at the Royal Northern College of Music (RNCM), Manchester, where she developed Dynamic Rehearsal (DR), an application of Dalcroze principles to the rehearsal and performance of repertoire. Her practice is informed by her training and experience as performing musician on opera and concert stages and many years working with dancers. She maintains a worldwide reputation for original and creative work and, since 1999, for writing, presentation, and research. DR and DE are the focus of her doctoral thesis (2019), a phenomenological investigation into the experiences of participants in her lessons. As director of studies for Dalcroze, the UK, she is responsible for the professional training of Dalcroze teachers. She is a founder-member of the scientific committee of the International Conference of Dalcroze Studies (ICDS), secretary to the Collège of the Institut Jaques-Dalcroze, Geneva, whose Diplôme Supérieur she holds, and chair of its Translation and Publication Committee.

Dr. Timothy J. Groulx is associate professor of Music Education at the University of North Florida. He earned his PhD in music education from the University of South Florida, where he was recipient of the presidential fellowship, and earned his bachelor of music and master of music in teaching from Oberlin Conservatory in 1999. He has published research in the *Journal of Research in Music Education, Journal of Historical Research in Music Education, Journal of Band Research, Journal of Music Teacher Education, Music Education Research International,* and *Update!* and serves on the advisory committee for the *International Journal of Music Education, Music Educators Journal,* and *Research Perspectives in Music Education.* He has presented at research and in-service conferences throughout the United States as well as in the United Kingdom, Australia, and New Zealand. His research interests include the intersections of instrumental music education with history, sociology, and social justice.

Patrick Horton is currently a PhD candidate in music education at Northwestern University (NU). Prior to studying at NU, Patrick taught band and music technology courses at the secondary level, motivating him to explore the ways technology can increase access to creativity and music learning for everyone. He is the current curriculum advisor for the Arts and Music Programs for Education in Detention Centers a NU, a program where university student-mentors engage incarcerated youth in exploring the power of hip-hop music to impact social change. Patrick is an active clinician that shares his experiences learning non-western musical traditions as well as practical insights on how to integrate music and technology into a variety of interdisciplinary learning spaces. Patrick currently teaches classes on music and technology for middle school learners with Northwestern's Center for Talent Development. He holds a BME from Ohio State University and an MM from Ball State University.

Dr. Geoffrey M. Lowe is currently a senior research fellow at Curtin University. Prior to this, he was Music Education course coordinator at Edith Cowan University for seventeen years. A pioneer and advocate of the use of popular music in school programs, he has written six popular music reference texts, one of which won an Australian Education publishing prize as Best Secondary Resource in 2008. In addition, he developed a range of popular music and jazz pedagogy courses at ECU and has undertaken a range of research projects into the motivational potential of popular music among lower secondary students. He is particularly focused on popular music best teaching practice. Dr. Lowe is also the National President of the Australian and New Zealand Association for Research in Music Education (ANZARME) and is a sought-after speaker and clinician.

About the Contributors

Dr. Paul Louth is associate professor of music education at Youngstown State University in Youngstown, Ohio, the United States, where he teaches graduate and undergraduate courses in music education research, methods, and foundations. He completed his PhD degree in music education, as well as a master's degree in the same discipline and undergraduate degrees in music performance and music education, in his home country of Canada. In addition to his scholarly work, he is an active composer, having written commissioned works for various ensembles, and he is also a former professional trombonist, secondary school music teacher, and clinician. Dr. Louth's published research focuses on intersections among critical theory, sociology, economics, and music education, with specific interests in music education technology, critical music pedagogy, and the intersection of formal and informal music learning.

Dr. Ros McMillan, A. M. is an Honorary Senior Fellow in arts education at the University of Melbourne, an appointment that followed her retirement after eleven years as Head of Music Education. During a career of over sixty years, she established the Yamaha Music Courses in Australia, was director of music at PLC, Melbourne, and lectured in the University of Melbourne's Faculty of Music and Institute of Education. Ros has presented papers and workshops at fifty-four national and international conferences and has written seven school music texts and over forty chapters and articles in publications including the *British Journal of Music Education*. Her discography consists of thirty CDs and LPs, twenty-six of those playing keyboards in ensembles with her late husband, Brian Brown OAM. In June 2019, she was appointed a Member of the Order of Australia in the Queen's Birthday Honors for significant service to music education in Victoria.

Hilary McQueen studied for a degree in music at Edinburgh University and a degree in psychology with the Open University. She completed her postgraduate studies at Exeter (PGCE) and King's College, London (PhD). Hilary has carried out a range of research spanning psychology, sociology, philosophy, and music. She investigated social motivation and the transition to higher education for a postdoctoral research post at Brighton University. Working mainly with Susan Hallam and Andrea Creech at the Institute of Education, Hilary contributed to reports on music sessions for those in the third age and Musical Futures. Most recently, she was commissioned by the Society for Music Analysis to research a perceived gap in music literacy in those applying to higher education. Hilary works for UCL Institute of Education and the Open University, teaching a range of undergraduate and postgraduate courses. She has taught the piano, singing, and music theory for many years.

About the Contributors

Dr. Jane Southcott (Coeditor) is a professor in the Faculty of Education, Monash University, Australia. Her main research focus is the history of the music curriculum in Australia, America, and Europe. She is an interpretative narrative historian and much of her research is biographical or institutional. Jane is also a hermeneutic phenomenologist who researches community engagement with music, multicultural music education, and cultural identity with a particular focus on positive aging. Jane has been a long-term member of the international executive of the Australian and New Zealand Association for Research in Music Education, holding different positions and organizing national conferences. Currently, she is the president of the association. She teaches in postgraduate and preservice programs and supervises many postgraduate doctoral research students. Dr. Southcott is the coeditor of the *International Journal of Music Education*.

Dr. Andrew Sutherland (Lead Editor) is from Perth, Western Australia. He completed degrees in music at The University of Western Australia, Edith Cowan University, and Monash University. He has published journal articles on a range of topics relating to music performance, music education, and musicology. Having taught music at all levels in Australia, the UK, and, more recently, Hong Kong, his interest for music performance by young people has consequently guided much of his research. Andrew's most recent monograph, *Children in Opera*, received critical acclaim and is a companion text to his next publication with Lexington, *Queer Opera*. Andrew is currently the director of music at Methodist Ladies College and an adjunct lecturer for the Western Australian Academy of Performing Arts.

Carol Williams is an adjunct research fellow of the Centre for Medieval and Renaissance Studies at Monash University and has an established academic career in both musicology and history. She is one of the collaborating editors and translators of the *Ars Musice* of Johannes de Grocheio (2011) and the *Tractatus de tonis* of Guy of Saint-Denis (2017). Coauthored articles include "Ancients and moderns in medieval music theory: From Guido of Arezzo to Jacobus" in *Intellectual History Review* (2017) with Constant Mews and "New Light on Frater Nicolaus de Aversa: His Plainchant Treatise in LHD 244" in *Musica Disciplina* (2015) with Karen Cook. Her most recent work is a book chapter "The Emotional Landscape of Abelard's Planctus David super Saul et Ionatha" In *The Intellectual Dynamism of the High Middle Ages*, edited by Clare Monagle (2021). Carol is also a performing musician, singing and playing harp, vielle and rebec in the early music ensemble, *Acord*.

www.ingramcontent.com/pod-product-compliance
Lightning Source LLC
Chambersburg PA
CBHW021342300426
44114CB00012B/1045